Twenty-First Century Psycholinguistics: Four Cornerstones

Twenty-First Century Psycholinguistics: Four Cornerstones

Edited by

Anne Cutler
Max Planck Institute for Psycholinguistics,
Nijmegen, The Netherlands

IEA
2005

LAWRENCE ERLBAUM ASSOCIATES, PUBLISHERS
Mahwah, New Jersey   London

Camera ready copy for this book was provided by the author.

Copyright © 2005 by Lawrence Erlbaum Associates, Inc.

Lawrence Erlbaum Associates, Inc., Publishers
10 Industrial Avenue
Mahwah, New Jersey 07430
www.erlbaum.com

Cover design by Kathryn Houghtaling Lacey

Library of Congress Cataloging-in-Publication Data

Twenty-first century psycholinguistics : four cornerstones / edited by Anne Cutler.

    p. cm.

"The papers collected ... arose from a series of four workshops (The four corners of psycholinguistics) held at the Max Planck Institute for Psycholinguistics during 2003"—CIP, preface.
Includes bibliographical references and index.
ISBN 0-8058-5208-5 (alk. paper)
1. Psycholinguistics—History. I. Cutler, Anne.
P37.T9   2005
401'.9—dc22   2005040007
                                          CIP

Printed in the United States of America
10 9 8 7 6 5 4 3 2 1

Contents

Preface

The chapters that compose this volume arose from a series of four workshops (The Four Corners of Psycholinguistics) held at the Max Planck Institute for Psycholinguistics during 2003. The purpose of the workshops was to take stock of the state of the discipline of psycholinguistics at a time when the hosting institute (the world's only research institute exclusively devoted to psycholinguistic science) was about to face a challenge in the form of the retirement of its founding director, Pim Levelt.

Each of the workshops took place over two days and involved six presentations (some with more than one presenter) with ample time for discussion. Besides the authors appearing in this volume, the programme also included presentations by Elke van de Meer, Shari Speer, Lera Boroditsky, and Antje Meyer; discussion sessions were introduced by Pim Levelt, Pienie Zwitserlood, Rob Schreuder, Steve Levinson, Gerard Kempen, Ton Dijkstra, Sotaro Kita, Wolfgang Klein, Peter Indefrey, Wietske Vonk, and Anne Cutler.

Each workshop addressed one of the relationships central to psycholinguistics: psychology and linguistics, biology and behavior, comprehension and production, model and experiment. The same four themes form the four Sections of this book. The structure of the book does not exactly reproduce the structure of the workshops, however; in the interests of thematic unity, some authors have found themselves assigned to a section other than that of the rest of the workshop in which they spoke.

Financial support for the workshops was provided by the Max Planck Gesellschaft zur Förderung der Wissenschaften; the workshops were organized by Kerstin Mauth; camera-ready copy for this volume has been created by Rian Zondervan. To all of these, the editor's most profound thanks.

Anne Cutler
Nijmegen
July 2004

1

The Cornerstones of Twenty-First Century Psycholinguistics

Anne Cutler, Wolfgang Klein, and Stephen C. Levinson
Max Planck Institute for Psycholinguistics, Nijmegen, The Netherlands

The name says it all—psycholinguistics is a discipline which draws on multiple sources. It is simultaneously psychology and linguistics. At the heart of the discipline, therefore, is the relationship between these two fields, each of which can boast centuries of research tradition as a recognizable independent field of study. By contrast, psycholinguistics itself is relatively young. Though research in both its parent fields addressed language processing issues in earlier times, psycholinguistics as we understand it today and as a discipline with its own name has only been in existence since the mid-twentieth century.

What does it mean to be a psycholinguist? One must have interest in how language structure relates to language use. This does not exclude a primary bias to one or other of the two underlying sets of research issues. Thus a psycholinguist can be primarily a psychologist, ultimately concerned to understand and explain the mental structures and processes involved in the use of language. But to be properly a psycholinguist, such a psychologist needs also to be concerned about why language has certain universal characteristics, how it can vary in language-specific ways, and how these aspects of structure impinge upon the way language is processed. Likewise, a psycholinguist can be primarily a linguist, whose ultimate concern is with the patterning of language itself; but such a linguist needs also to be interested in patterns evident in language performance and the reasons for those patterns, and needs to be open to evidence from laboratory studies involving highly controlled processing tasks. Still other sets of research issues may be primary—anthropological, for instance (and now all three authors of this introductory essay are represented). But in any case, a psycholinguist is concerned with the *relationship* between language and its use.

Thus psycholinguistics may itself be defined as the study of a relationship. It is the argument of this volume that doing psycholinguistics means addressing at least four further crucial relationships which underlie research in this field. These are cornerstones of current psycholinguistics, and they form the four sections of this volume. This introductory essay is not intended just as an overview and summary of the contents of these four sections, but more as background, in the form of a general outline of how psycholinguistics works (and it includes at least some attention to areas *not* represented in the volume). One of the conclusions which this introduction will motivate is that the way in which these four relationships are important to psycholinguistics today, in the first decade of the twenty-first century, is not necessarily the way things have always been.

PSYCHOLOGY AND LINGUISTICS

It has always been the case that most individual psycholinguists feel a primary affiliation to one or other of the parent disciplines, and unless universities worldwide see fit to establish undergraduate faculties of psycholinguistics—an unlikely eventuality, we guess—this will continue. Psycholinguists generally come to the field via courses taken either in a psychology department or in a linguistics (or language) department. It is, inevitably, very probable that a psycholinguistics course in a psychology department will convey a different way of looking at the subject matter than an equivalent course in a linguistics department. (An undergraduate textbook in psycholinguistics written by a linguist is likely to divide the subject matter into chapters on the processing of phonological, syntactic, semantic information—see e.g., Prideaux, 1984—while a book with the same title written by a psychologist will include chapters on producing, perceiving, and acquiring language—see e.g., Garnham, 1985.)

Sometimes the difference in approach is so fundamental that it would make sense to speak of different disciplines—say, psychology of language and performance linguistics (see e.g., Cutler, 1992). Differences arise due, as described above, to a primary motivation involving questions which are fundamentally psychological (how do humans process language?) or linguistic in nature (why is language the way it is?). But it is a basic tenet of psycholinguistics that both types of questions can best be answered by drawing simultaneously on knowledge from both parent disciplines.

Notwithstanding this belief, it is very obvious that the balance between the two primary motivations has not always been exactly maintained; indeed, the relation has changed regularly across the years. There is thus no guarantee that the situation that obtains now, at the beginning of the twenty-first century, will hold till the century's end. Nonetheless, this is an exciting time for psycholinguistics.

Psychology, linguistics, and adult language processing

The discipline now known as psycholinguistics is only about half a century old, and the name was assigned when the study of adult language processing attracted growing interest within experimental psychology. It is fair to say that throughout its half century of existence this branch of psycholinguistics has been immensely technology-driven. Procedures for chronometric analysis in experimental psychology were in large part responsible for the expansion of research interest to new topics such as language processing, and hence for psycholinguistics appearing when it did. From the mid-twentieth century, the tape recorder made it possible to undertake research on spoken language while satisfying the demand of experimental psychology for strictly controlled and replicable conditions. Later (from the late 1970s to 1980s), a small revolution in models of adult processing followed from the availability of computer-readable vocabularies and large language corpora. Programming techniques developed in engineering and mathematics strongly influenced the type of modeling undertaken in psychology; in particular, connectionist modeling swept through the field to take an unquestionably dominant position from the 1990s.

It is not always easy to separate the relationship between linguistics and psychology from these other influences. Still, there was a time—four or more decades ago—when linguistics clearly set the tone for adult-language psycholinguistic research. The revolution in linguistics which Chomsky initiated in the 1950s and 1960s produced a line of empirical research devoted to deriving processing predictions from linguistic models, in particular from models of the grammar. The Derivational Theory of Complexity thus proposed that the complexity of grammatical derivations of sentences in transformational grammar could directly predict the processing complexity of the same sentences. Experimental support for this proposal was found (e.g., Miller & McKean, 1964), and psycholinguists of the time also tried to tease out contrasting predictions from rival grammatical theories, and set up experiments to test them against one another (e.g., Clifton & Odom, 1966).

This period ended rather abruptly, however. The linguistic theories changed, but they changed in response to linguistic argumentation and not at all in response to the growing body of processing evidence. This was, understandably, not a little frustrating to those psycholinguists who had spent years gathering the relevant evidence. There then followed a time when psychological studies of language processing tried to maintain independence from linguistic theory. It is too simple to say that psychology was displeased by perceived rejection from linguistics — after all, some linguists have been less than pleased over the years over what they saw as lack of sophistication in psychology's use of linguistic proposals. But it was obvious in the 1970s that most research on language processing was not directly informed by linguistics.

This changed with the growth of research in sentence processing driven by models which were truly psycholinguistic, i.e. they were processing models which were intended as linguistic proposals (e.g., Frazier & Fodor, 1978). This line of research became important from the 1980s, and coincided with new interest in cross-linguistic comparison in adult processing — research which necessarily drew on linguistic knowledge about language-particular structural variation, if not on linguistic explanations of it. At this time there was thus the beginning of a correction of the previous asymmetry; processing evidence was both sought in linguistics and had influence on linguistic modeling. This trend continues today, with the main driving force being, however, again technological. Biological evidence, in particular evidence from brain imaging, is almost as desirable in linguistics as in psychology. The twenty-first century may yet see the first linguistic model fully motivated by processing evidence.

Psychology, linguistics, and first language acquisition

The study of child language acquisition has a longer and richer tradition than the study of adult language processing (perhaps in part because observational techniques have always been with us, and these techniques easily produce vast amounts of wonderfully informative child language data). Before the twentieth-century developments which revolutionized linguistics, the study of language acquisition was primarily the domain of psychologists. These researchers — of whom Tiedemann, Preyer, Stern and Stern, Piaget, Vygotsky are the outstanding early examples — considered language acquisition as a part of the general cognitive and social development of the child. The approach which they pioneered is continued up to present times by exponents such as Bruner, Slobin, Bowerman, and linguists who are close to this idea, for example E. Clark. There are three central characteristics of this research tradition: (a) language is viewed as just part of general development; (b) there is a strong empirical orientation; and (c) no particular linguistic framework is relevant, so that where linguistic definitions are important, essentially categories from traditional school grammar are used.

A second and very different research tradition arose in child language studies in the second half of the twentieth century. Jakobson (1941) was an early herald of the change, though the tradition really became clarified with Chomsky's (1965) proposal of a 'language acquisition device' (LAD) which is innate and universal. In theory, this idea made acquisition a core issue in the study of the human language faculty. Work initiated by this idea created a lively second tradition (often actively hostile to the existing tradition), which in turn was characterized by (a) the idea that there is a single 'language module', innate, universal and independent of other cognitive modules; (b) often poor empirical work; and (c) strong adherence to a particular linguistic framework, namely generative grammar in its various forms.

This tradition was very influential in first language acquisition research for several decades — interestingly, even at a time when, as described above, adult processing researchers had temporarily turned their back on linguistic motivations. It is fair to say that its impact has declined considerably over the past few years. The main reason for the decline is theory-internal developments: The minimalist framework, in particular, does not motivate acquisition research. In addition, there was a diminished role for the idea of 'parameter setting' — the notion that language-specific variation can be described in terms of a universal set of parameters which allow variable values, and that children are born with the set of parameters and infer, from the language input they receive, the values which their native language requires for each parameter. This idea, crucial in this tradition of acquisition research since the early eighties, lost its impact once subsequent theoretical accounts assigned parameters to the lexicon, rather than to a core role in the grammar.

Nonetheless, the question which was the basis of Chomsky's LAD proposal and which motivated the parameter-setting account remains central in psycholinguistics: What is the interplay between language-universal and language-specific features in language development? The long tradition of cross-linguistic acquisition research in fact predates the dominance of the linguistically based tradition (see e.g., Slobin, 1985), and it continues apace, drawing both from the general developmental tradition (examples here range from cross-linguistic studies of the perceptual development of phonemic repertoires — see e.g., Werker, 1995, for an overview — to the acquisition of language-specific semantic categories — e.g., Choi & Bowerman, 1992) and also drawing from linguistic theory (especially in phonology — e.g., Peperkamp & Dupoux, 2002 — and in syntax — e.g., Crain & Pietroski, 2002).

Psychology, linguistics, and second language acquisition

For research on acquisition of a second language rather than the first, a different situation holds. For decades after psycholinguistics had begun as an independent discipline, researchers in second language acquisition did not reckon themselves psycholinguists at all; their field was applied linguistics. This was in large part because their work had a practical focus; its primary motivation was to improve language teaching efficacy.

Second language acquisition is not a homogeneous phenomenon, of course: First, it need not wait until first language acquisition is complete, and second, there are several ways to gain access to a new linguistic system, ranging from metalinguistic description (as in the classroom) to everyday communication (as for many foreign workers). In the history of mankind, explicit teaching of a language is a relatively late phenomenon, and untutored learning was and probably still is the most common case. Nonetheless, second language acquisition in the classroom has been the focus of most research in this area, partly because of its practical import and partly because school situations are relatively accessible to empirical manipulation—at least, more accessible than the untutored situation.

This practical focus proceeds from the twin assumptions that there is a well-defined target of the acquisition process (the language to be learned), and that acquisition can be described in terms of to what degree and in which respects this target is missed. Given this "target deviation" perspective, the learner's performance in production or comprehension is not studied in its own right, as a manifestation of language learning capacity, but in relation to a set norm; not in terms of what the learner does but in terms of what he or she fails to do.

In contrast to the motivation of this type of research in the quest for practical improvements in language teaching, empirical work on second language acquisition outside the classroom has been motivated more by linguistic considerations. Concepts such as 'interlanguage', 'learner variety', 'approximate systems' or the like (see von Stutterheim, 1986; Perdue, 1993; Dietrich, Klein, & Noyau, 1995) are typical of this tradition, in which Klein and Perdue (1997) have identified three key assumptions: (a) The acquisition process produces a series of varieties, in which both the internal organization at a given time as well as the transition from one variety to the next are essentially systematic in nature; (b) A small set of principles is present in all such varieties, and the actual structure of an utterance is determined by interaction of these principles with other factors (e.g., source language, characteristics of the input). Importantly, learning a new feature of the target language means reorganization of the whole variety to incorporate the new feature; the balance of the various components of linguistic knowledge about the target language then successively approaches the balance found in native speakers' usage; (c) Learner varieties are not imperfect imitations of a "real language" (the target language), but systems in their own right. Fully developed languages are but special cases of learner varieties, a relatively stable state where the learner stops learning because there is no apparent difference between the individual variety and the environment variety.

On this view, second language acquisition offers a unique window onto the human faculty for language. In untutored adult acquisition, human beings manage to copy, with varying degrees of success, the ways in which other people speak, and they do it by application of a species-specific mental capacity for language acquisition. All learner varieties are then manifestations of the human language faculty. Many learner varieties do not exploit the full potential of this faculty, for example, in terms of syntactic or morphological structure or of lexical repertoire. But note that even elementary learner varieties of Russian use more of the human language faculty's morphological potential than fully-fledged forms of the language family with the most native speakers on earth, that is, Chinese.

Psychology and Linguistics in Section 1

The chapters in Section 1 provide views on many of the topics just mentioned. **Boland** discusses processing evidence which constrains syntactic theory in respect of the distinction between arguments and adjuncts. **Fikkert** discusses evidence from the acquisition of language-specific phonology in the light of current phonological theory. **Haverkort** contrasts linguistically and psychologically motivated accounts of grammatical impairment in aphasia. **Baayen** shows how large computer-searchable corpora can provide valuable psycholinguistic evidence. **Pickering and Garrod** discuss evidence from speaker and listener behavior in dialogue and its implications for the place of the lexicon in psycholinguistic models. And finally, **Poeppel and Embick** address the issue of how neurobiological evidence might indeed lead to new linguistic models.

BIOLOGY AND BEHAVIOR

Psycholinguistics, as a member of the family of disciplines grouped as cognitive science, is in the twenty-first century definitely also part of that family branch now known as cognitive neuroscience. This has subsumed fields which used to be known as neuropsychology and neurolinguistics, and is faster-growing than any other area of psycholinguistics. Although all aspects of cognitive neuroscience are developing at an accelerated pace, there is in particular more and more interest in how language is processed in the brain. As a result, there is also more and more need for graduating psycholinguists to be familiar with techniques of brain research and the cognitive neuroscience literature. The relation between biology and behavior is thus definitely now a part of psycholinguistics; 40 years ago this may have been far less the case.

There is a sense in which cognitive neuroscience research necessarily addresses the relationship between biology and behavior, in a way that is not true of other areas of psycholinguistics; in effect, this relationship is what the field is all about, in that the principal aim is to understand how the brain operates to control and carry out all aspects of cognition.

However the relationship between biology and behavior as it concerns psycholinguistics embraces many more issues than how language is processed in the brain during comprehension or production. For instance, an important issue is the place of language processing in the functioning of the human organism as a whole. This question is represented in psycholinguistics by a growing body of research on how language interfaces with other cognitive faculties and processes.

We can, for example, talk about what we can see. For this to be possible, visual representations must be converted into linguistic representations. But these two types of representation seem to have very little in common: Visual representations are multidimensional, geometric and determinate, linguistic representations are linear, propositional and necessarily vague or general. It is actually quite unclear how these systems interface.

Visual information ties closely into spatial thinking in general, and the relation between language and spatial cognition has attracted much recent interest (see e.g., Bloom, Peterson, Nadel, & Garrett, 1996; Bowerman & Levinson, 2001; Coventry & Garrod, 2004). Take for example someone describing how to get to the railway station: What kind of coordinate systems do they use, and how does this tie in to the coordinate systems used in spatial behavior or spatial thinking? This 'frame of reference' problem has been at the centre of recent controversies (Li & Gleitman, 2000; Levinson, Kita, Haun, & Rasch, 2002; Levinson, 2003; Majid, Bowerman, Kita, Haun, & Levinson, 2004)—some researchers maintaining that the frames of reference used in language are just those used in spatial cognition, and others that while the frames of reference available to cognition are diverse, a specific language standardizes on just a few, partially constructed specifically for linguistic functions. But the main point is that we remain unclear about the nature of the interface between spatial cognition and language. For example, spatial reference distinctions in cognitive neuroscience do not map happily onto what we know about linguistic codings of space, and considerable work will be required to bring these literatures into alignment.

An interesting way to approach some of these problems is through the study of communication in different modalities. Gestures accompanying speech, when (as often) indicating spatial directions, shapes and motions, are also driven by a frame of reference. These are more clearly dependent upon visual and spatial representations, yet they match the frame of reference used in language (Kita, 2003; Levinson, 2003), and indeed match the kind of packaging of information found in the particular language (Kita & Özyürek, 2003). More far-reaching still are sign languages, which are languages in a spatial modality. One might think that all sorts of advantages might accrue to users of a spatial language talking about space, but in fact there are also additional problems of perspective since the signs themselves are, as it were, spatial objects which can be viewed from different directions (see Emmorey, 2002, and this volume). Emmorey has been able to tie research on sign language to work on visual imagery and the underlying neuroscience (thus, for example, signers can more rapidly perform mental rotation, because their language requires special facility with this procedure).

This last finding is an important demonstration of language use exercising an effect upon cognitive processing (and abilities). It is far from the only such demonstration. For instance, bilingualism has also been shown to have far-reaching implications for cognitive processing beyond the realm of language. In a remarkably simple task from the repertoire of cognitive psychology, known as the Simon task, the subject has two response buttons, and is instructed to press (say) the left button if a red patch appears on the computer screen, the right button if a blue patch appears. Response time is slower when locations of visual stimulus and response are not congruent (e.g., the blue patch appears on the left side of the screen; Simon & Wolf, 1963). The extra cost incurred in the incongruent compared with a congruent or neutral condition is held to represent the time needed to inhibit an inappropriate response (pressing the left button), and this cost tends to increase with age. Bialystok, Craik, Klein, and Viswanathan (2004) discovered, however, that the cost is significantly reduced in bilinguals who have maintained use of more than one language throughout life; they suggested that switching between languages develops facility in inhibition of unwanted responses, such that added, quite general, benefits of cognitive control show up, even in such simple tasks. As with the mental rotation abilities of signers, we here see flow-on from use of a linguistic system—or in this case more than one linguistic system—to nominally unrelated aspects of cognition.

However, beyond effects of language use upon cognition there is a further issue of whether (language-specific) linguistic structure may also have effects upon cognitive processing. A simplified working assumption in much of cognitive science is that semantic representations have an independent existence as conceptual representations built of categories, either innate or learned; language is then, as it were, a mere input/output device for encoding and decoding these representations. In much of psychology, 'semantic' is correspondingly equivalent to 'conceptual'. A problem for this view is that languages differ fundamentally in their semantic categories—the concepts built into their grammars and lexicons. The extent of the difference has been partly masked by the fact that psycholinguists have concentrated so much on related European languages; once one looks further afield, it becomes quite difficult to find any exact cross-linguistic matches between linguistically-coded concepts (see e.g., Levinson & Meira, 2003). Once these differences are appreciated, it becomes obvious that one must either abandon the idea that 'semantics = conceptual structure', or accept that speaking a different language might mean thinking differently, or both. This has raised the whole question of whether having language in general, and having a specific language in particular, might partially restructure human cognition.

On the role of language in general it has been suggested that language might play a crucial role in hooking up specialized mental faculties which in other species play a more modular role: Good cases can be made in both spatial and mathematical cognition for such a thesis (Spelke & Tsivkin, 2001; Spelke, 2003). On the role of particular languages, language-specific grammatical categories such as number and gender have been argued to exercise influence on cognitive processes (Lucy & Gaskins, 2001; Boroditsky, 2001; Boroditsky, Schmidt, & Phillips, 2003). Child language acquisition throws important light on these issues (see e.g., Bowerman & Levinson, 2001), as does, again, work on bilingualism (Gullberg, 2003). Recent work (e.g., Gentner & Goldin-Meadow, 2003) also suggests that language-specific semantic categories can affect thinking; again the spatial domain has played an important role here (see Levinson, 2003, for a review).

Another kind of relation between language and other aspects of cognition comes to the fore in studies of linguistic interaction. One traditional area of psycholinguistic interest has been how contextual information is used to resolve reference and ambiguity, and when and how such broader inference is intercalated with specialized comprehension processes. In linguistics, various theories about pragmatic principles and how they might guide some of these processes have been around for some time (see e.g., Sperber & Wilson, 1986; Levinson, 2000), but it is only recently that these theories are being put to experimental test (see Noveck & Sperber, 2004; Hagoort, Hald, Bastiaansen, & Petersson, 2004). Another area where there is currently active interest is in conversation and dialogue. Clark (1996) proposed interesting psycholinguistic perspectives on the mental processes involved in dialogue, and more recently it has been proposed that psycholinguistic mechanisms are evolved for, and deeply attuned to, the rapid exchange of verbal information in conversational settings (see Pickering & Garrod, this volume). There is also research interest in the pre-verbal foundations for verbal interaction in infancy ('protoconversation'), which promises to illuminate basic principles in this area (Rochat, Querido, & Striano, 1999). Overall, it seems reasonable to assume that there are special cognitive abilities and proclivities that lie behind interactive language use, and which interface in complex ways with the language comprehension and production systems.

Biology and Behavior in Section 2

The chapters in Section 2 reflect the variety of ways in which the relationship between biology and behavior can be relevant in psycholinguistics. **Stromswold** reviews the evidence on genetic factors in language performance. Three chapters deal with how language is processed in the brain: **Scott** treats the perception of speech, **Hagoort** the problem of syntactic unification, and **Thompson-Schill** the necessity for selection as part of linguistic processing. The latter two chapters form an interesting contrast in that both deal with the role of Broca's area, which, however, **Hagoort** approaches from the point of view "How does the brain perform this function?" while **Thompson-Schill**'s point of view is "How can we most accurately characterize what Broca's area does?" Finally, **Morgan** discusses how modality-general versus modality-specific effects offer insight into the relationship of biology and behavior in language use, via evidence from the acquisition of sign language.

COMPREHENSION AND PRODUCTION

For many, in fact most of the years that psycholinguistics has existed, it was almost a truism to bemoan the predominance of research on comprehension over research on production. The reasons for this asymmetry were obvious: In any experimental science, control over the conditions in which an experiment is conducted is paramount, and control over stimuli presented for comprehension is trivially easy to achieve while control over language production seems at first glance nigh on impossible. How can one conduct an experiment on spontaneous speech production and yet constrain the speech that is produced? Speakers cannot be simply instructed what to say, for that would remove the central components of the spontaneous production process (not to mention that it would also involve comprehension of the same linguistic material). For decades, this problem stood in the way of laboratory studies of language production. Despite early ingenious use of sentence completion (Forster, 1966) and picture-naming techniques (Oldfield & Wingfield, 1964), language production research relied to a large extent on an indirect view of the production process: inferring the normal processes of operation from observation of the breakdown of those processes. Thus major milestones in the study of language production include views from slips of the tongue (Fromkin, 1973; Garrett, 1975) and language breakdown in aphasia (Coltheart, Patterson, & Marshall, 1980).

Research on language comprehension, in contrast, streamed ahead; visual word recognition, based mainly on evidence from lexical decision and word naming, became a minor industry in itself (Seidenberg, 1995), as did the study of syntactic processing, which also relied principally on visual presentation and timing of reading, either via tracking of eye movements or other less fine-grained measures (Tanenhaus & Trueswell, 1995). From the 1970s on, spoken language comprehension (made empirically more tractable by the development of computer-based speech analysis, storage and presentation techniques) also gradually grew in importance. Word recognition became almost as well-studied in the auditory as in the visual modality, though in sentence processing research visual presentation still predominated over auditory presentation.

So dominant was comprehension research in psycholinguistics that it was possible for an Annual Review of Psychology overview article on "Experimental Psycholinguistics" to begin: "The fundamental problem in psycholinguistics is simple to formulate: What happens when we understand sentences?" (Johnson-Laird, 1974).

This too has changed. Experimental research on language production, and especially the production of spoken language, has undergone a revolution in the past two decades. Levelt and colleagues pioneered techniques for studying the production words and phrases (Levelt, 1992), Bock and colleagues did the same for sentence production (Bock, 1995) and even more importantly these advances have been embedded within a strong background of theoretical explanation. Active competition between models of speech production (see e.g., Dell, 1986; Dell & O'Seaghdha, 1992; Levelt, 1992; Roelofs, 1992) has prompted a stream of empirical tests of the models' predictions, making research on production at last competitive with research on comprehension.

Thus the relation between comprehension and production research, which was very asymmetric in the earlier years of psycholinguistics, is no longer so. This means that the way is now open to models of both processes together. Clearly comprehension and production are closely connected in the speaker-hearer; a model of language use from both perspectives would seem an obvious next step. Curiously, however, there have been very few initiatives of this sort.

Of course, it may turn out to be the case that there are such fundamental differences between the input and the output side of language processing that it makes no sense to connect the modeling efforts. The speaker's task is after all quite different from the hearer's task. The speaker begins with (supposedly) certainty about a message to be conveyed, and the process of speech production consists in converting that message into an appropriate articulatory form. The hearer begins with uncertainty about the message; the process of speech perception consists of testing hypotheses about the components of the speech signal in order to recover encoded message. These differing tasks may have far-reaching implications for the architecture of the respective processing systems. McQueen, Dahan, and Cutler (2003) have argued, for example, that continuous and graded flow of information (allowing multiple competing hypotheses to be continuously compared, re-weighted or discarded) makes sense in comprehension but has no obvious counterpart in production; in production, instead, the certainty of the initial state seems to motivate a more obvious role for discrete units of encoding. Moreover, these units may be units which simply have no direct relevance in perception. Thus there is evidence that syllables play a role in the production process (Cholin, 2004), which is entirely reasonable because syllables are articulatory units, and the units in terms of which speech timing is described; coordination of timing is the essence of speech production. Reconstruction of that timing does not necessarily benefit the listener, however, and reconstruction of units such as syllables is rendered entirely unnecessary by the continuous use of acoustic-phonetic information which characterizes speech recognition. Where syllables do play a role in perception it is an indirect role, for example, in the postulation of lexical boundaries (Content, Kearns, & Frauenfelder, 2001).

Thus psycholinguistics may never achieve an integrated model of language production and perception, because there may be no such integration — the two-way model may be no advance on separate models of the one-way processes. However, we won't know till we try.

Comprehension and Production in Section 3

In Section 3, the chapters by **Vigliocco and Hartsuiker** and by **McQueen** deal with the architecture of the language processing system, comparing production and comprehension but taking a view primarily from production (**Vigliocco and Hartsuiker**) or primarily from comprehension (**McQueen**). **Schiller** discusses how monitoring one's own speech involves the comprehension system in the production process. **Ferreira and Swets** show how nonstandard syntactic forms arise in production and are dealt with in comprehension, thereby illuminating the relation of the two processes; **Sebastián-Gallés and Baus** show how this relation can be very different in a second language from in a first, and how this has implications for our understanding of second language acquisition; and finally, **Emmorey** discusses how language use in a spatial modality informs the relation between perception and production.

MODEL AND EXPERIMENT

Methodologically, psycholinguistics has been fashioned more by psychology than by linguistics, because it has been since its outset an experimental discipline. Of its two parent fields it was, then, psychology which offered an experimental research tradition to draw on. In any experimental discipline, of course, the relation between theory and experiment must be got right, and this is not as easy as it might seem.

Too much modeling is not theory-driven; the model is built in whatever way can be gotten to work, irrespective of whether the resulting inevitable implications for theory are motivated by experimental evidence. This ultra-pragmatic approach to model construction is, for instance, responsible for the inability of human speech science to reach a rapprochement with speech engineering (in which the aim is development of techniques for automatic speech recognition and speech synthesis), despite at least a quarter of a century of determined attempts to learn from each other. Engineers need to have techniques that work, and at the moment the techniques which work best for computer implementation vary in obvious ways from the processes which speech scientists believe human language users employ. Speech scientists find it difficult to accept that engineers do not wish to implement immediately every advance in knowledge about human processing; engineers wish that speech science would provide knowledge in some form that would prove useful, because advances in computer speech processing have slowed to a frustrating succession of tiny increments; but they are generally unwilling to take the steps necessary to implement insights from human processing, that is, build a different kind of model. This would require starting from a basis of reduced recognition performance, which would run counter to the pragmatic imperative.

Computational models of language processing in psychology have to some extent suffered from the same form of pragmatism. The goal of a working computational model was so seductive that many sacrifices—in the form of compromise implementations of model components in a way that would work though it was demonstrably implausible from a psychological point of view—were made to ensure that this goal was achieved. Nonetheless the contribution of modeling to psycholinguistic research has been profound. In the previous section we pointed out that the motor behind the rapid increase in research on language production in recent years was the existence of strong and testable models of the production process. In the same way, models of comprehension have been responsible for driving empirical expansion. Spoken-word recognition has been a field which was highly model-driven, from the earliest days of non-computational models specific to the processing of spoken words (Marslen-Wilson & Welsh, 1978) through the explosive development of computational models beginning with TRACE (McClelland & Elman, 1986). That this development was scientifically productive is perhaps attested in the remarkable degree of agreement achieved by computational models of spoken-word recognition in the late 1990s, in which all available models agreed on the notions of multiple lexical activation and inter-word competition (the models still disagreed on other issues, of course, notably the incorporation of feedback links from logically later to logically earlier stages of processing; and this period of relative unanimity now appears to be coming to an end). Other areas of comprehension research such as visual word recognition or sentence processing have not experienced such a period of intense research activity leading to rapprochement; but both these subfields have a longer history of active research and have amassed a great variety of modeling initiatives. It is instructive, though, to compare research on the processing of spoken words with research on the processing of spoken sentences; there are as yet no strong models of the latter process, which is perhaps why the dominant research methodology in sentence processing is study of reading rather than of speech.

The greater methodological strength in the psychological side of psycholinguistics has led to the interplay of model and experiment in psycholinguistics involving primarily models from psychology. This is not to say that there have not been models which are truly psycholinguistic, informed simultaneously by both research traditions; such models exist, especially in the area of sentence processing (with the Minimal Attachment model of Frazier & Fodor, 1978, as an outstanding example). Purely linguistic theory, however, has not been directly responsible for empirical surges in psycholinguistics in the way that psychological theory has.

But there are changes in the model-experiment relationship in psycholinguistics and its associated fields, as there are changes in all the relationships we have discussed above. Recent developments have been both retrograde—for example, the adoption of essentially psychological modeling notions in linguistics which in a way parallels the adoption of linguistic notions in psychology some four decades ago—and progressive—for example, the emergence of linguistic traditions in which empirical testing is seen as an essential component of theoretical development.

As an example of the former, consider the remarkable current popularity in linguistics of exemplar-based models of word processing (e.g., Bybee, 2001; Jurafsky, Bell, & Girand, 2002; Pierrehumbert, 2002). Although such models originated in psychology (Nosofsky, 1986), they have not been widely adopted in that field (in which for spoken-word processing Goldinger [1998] remains the single common citation). This situation is reminiscent of 1960s psycholinguistics not in this respect, however, but in the unfortunate fact that the sophistication with which linguists have embraced ideas from psychology is no better than was the case the other way round at that time. In brief, there are phenomena which seem to demand an exemplar-based solution (frequency effects on lexical form, for example), and these phenomena are given wide exposure, while phenomena which speak strongly against exemplar models (generalization of new phonological features across the lexicon, for example) are ignored. Since the two classes of phenomena together cannot be accounted for by a radical exemplar model or by a radical abstractionist model, the time is ripe for a new hybrid model of word processing. We predict that such a model is more likely to be developed from the psychological side of the field.

As an example of the latter, progressive, development, consider laboratory phonology, a fairly recent movement in which the experimental tools of phonetics and to some extent psycholinguistics are brought to bear on questions of phonological theory. These, as Pierrehumbert, Beckman, and Ladd (2000) argue in their account of laboratory phonology's genesis and rationale, may be questions springing from any of a number of current theoretical approaches in phonology. Laboratory phonology is not a theoretical school, but a methodological approach which, they maintain, raises the level of scientific contribution possible in phonology.

Model and Experiment in Section 4

The authors in Section 4 do not share a single disciplinary background (**Roelofs, Norris** and **Pitt and Navarro** are psychologists, **Crocker** a linguist, **Fitch** a biologist) but they do share a commitment to explicit modeling in theory development. **Roelofs** lays out a case for long-term investment in a model which can gradually become better (putatively closer to the true state of affairs) as it is refined by continual testing. **Norris** stresses the interplay that is necessary between theory, model, and empirical research. **Pitt and Navarro** describe techniques for determining how best to test between alternative models of the same processes. **Crocker** argues that the modeling enterprise should be rooted in an initial analysis of the demands of the processing task which is being modeled. **Fitch**, finally, spells out four computational distinctions and their implications for models of psycholinguistic processing.

Obviously, many chapters in Sections 1 through 3 also had much to say about the relationship between models and experimental research. The chapters in Section 4 likewise relate to psychology and linguistics (**Pitt and Navarro; Crocker**), production and comprehension (**Roelofs, Norris**), biology and behavior (**Fitch**). It is perhaps inevitable, given the nature of psycholinguistics, that there are elements of our four cornerstone relationships in all four sections of the book. For now, though, we hand the job of tracking them all down over to the reader.

REFERENCES

Bialystok, E., Craik, F. I. M., Klein, R., & Viswanathan, M. (2004). Bilingualism, aging, and cognitive control: Evidence from the Simon Task. *Psychology and Aging, 19*, 290-303.

Bloom, P., Peterson M. A., Nadel L., & Garrett M. F. (1996). *Language and space.* Cambridge, MA: MIT.

Bock, K. (1995). Sentence production: From mind to mouth. In J. L. Miller & P. D. Eimas (Eds.), *Speech, language, and communication* (pp. 181-216). San Diego: Academic Press.

Boroditsky, L. (2001). Does language shape thought? Mandarin and English speakers' conceptions of time. *Cognitive Psychology, 43*, 1-22.

Boroditsky, L., Schmidt, L. & Phillips, W. (2003). Sex, syntax, and semantics. In D. Gentner & S. Goldin-Meadow (Eds.), Language in mind: Advances in the study of language and cognition (pp. 61-80). Cambridge, MA: MIT Press.

Bowerman, M., & Levinson, S. (Eds.). (2001). *Language acquisition and conceptual development.* Cambridge: Cambridge University Press.

Bybee, J. (2001). Phonology and language use. Cambridge: Cambridge University Press.

Choi, S., & Bowerman, M. (1992). Learning to express motion events in English and Korean: The influence of language-specific lexicalization patterns.

Cognition, 41, 83-121.

Cholin, J. (2004). *Syllables in speech production: Effects of syllable preparation and syllable frequency.* Ph.D. dissertation, University of Nijmegen. MPI Series in Psycholinguistics, 26.

Chomsky, N. (1965). *Aspects of the theory of syntax.* Cambridge, MA: MIT Press.

Clark, H. H. (1996). Communities, commonalities, and communication. In J. J. Gumperz & S. C. Levinson (Eds.), *Rethinking linguistic relativity* (pp. 324-355). Cambridge: Cambridge University Press.

Clifton, C., Jr., & Odom, P. (1966). Similarity relations among certain English sentence constructions. *Psychological Monographs, 80*, No. 5 (Whole No. 613).

Coltheart, M., Patterson, K. E., & Marshall, J. C. (Eds.). (1980). *Deep dyslexia.* London: Routledge & Kegan Paul.

Content, A., Kearns, R., & Frauenfelder, U. H. (2001). Boundaries versus onsets in syllabic segmentation. *Journal of Memory and Language, 45*, 177-199.

Coventry, K. R., & Garrod, S. (2004). *Saying, seeing and acting. The psychological semantics of spatial prepositions.* Hove: Psychology Press.

Crain, S., & Pietroski, P. (2002). Why language acquisition is a snap. *The Linguistic Review, 19*, 163–183.

Cutler, A. (1992). Why not abolish psycholinguistics? In W. U. Dressler, H. C. Luschützky, O. E. Pfeiffer, & J. R. Rennison (Eds.), *Phonologica 1988* (pp. 77-87). Cambridge: Cambridge University Press.

Dell, G. S. (1986). A spreading-activation theory of retrieval in sentence production. *Psychological Review, 93*, 283-321.

Dell, G. S., & O'Seaghdha, P. G. (1992). Stages of lexical access in language production. *Cognition, 42*, 287-314.

Dietrich, R., Klein, W., & Noyau, C. (1995). *The acquisition of temporality in a second language.* Amsterdam/Philadelphia: Benjamins.

Emmorey, K. (2002). *Language, cognition, and the brain: Insights from sign language research.* Mahwah, NJ: Lawrence Erlbaum Associates.

Forster, K. I. (1966). Left-to-right processes in the construction of sentences. *Journal of Verbal Learning & Verbal Behavior, 5*, 285-291.

Frazier, L., & Fodor, J. D. (1978). The sausage machine: A new two-stage parsing model. *Cognition, 6*, 291-325.

Fromkin, V. A. (1973). *Speech errors as linguistic evidence.* The Hague: Mouton.

Garnham, A. (1985). *Psycholinguistics: Central topics.* London: Methuen.

Garrett, M. F. (1975). The analysis of sentence production. In G. H. Bower (Ed.), *The psychology of learning and motivation* (Vol. 9, pp. 133-177). New York: Academic Press.

Gentner, D., & Goldin-Meadow, S. (Eds.) (2003). *Language in mind: Advances in the study of language and cognition.* Cambridge, MA: MIT Press.

Goldinger, S. D. (1998). Echoes of echoes? An episodic theory of lexical access. *Psychological Review, 105*, 251-279.

Gullberg, M. (2003). Gestures, referents and anaphoric linkage in learner varieties. In C. Dimroth & M. Starren (Eds.), *Information structure, linguistic structure and the dynamics of language acquisition* [Studies in Bilingualism] (pp. 311-328). Amsterdam: Benjamins.

Hagoort, P., Hald, L., Bastiaansen, M., & Petersson, K. M. (2004). Integration of word meaning and world knowledge in language comprehension. *Science, 304*, 438-441.

Jakobson, R. (1941). *Kindersprache, Aphasie und allgemeine Lautgesetze.* Uppsala: Almqvist & Wiksell.

Johnson-Laird, P. N. (1974). Experimental psycholinguistics. *Annual Review of Psychology, 25*, 135-160.

Jurafsky, D., Bell, A., & Girand, C. (2002). The role of the lemma in form variation. In C. Gussenhoven & N. Warner (Eds.), *Papers in Laboratory Phonology VII* (pp. 3- 34). Berlin: Mouton.

Kita, S. (Ed.). (2003). *Pointing: Where language, cognition, and culture meet.* Mahwah, NJ: Lawrence Erlbaum Associates.

Kita, S., & Özyürek, A. (2003). What does cross-linguistic variation in semantic coordination of speech and gesture reveal?: Evidence for an interface representation of spatial thinking and speaking. *Journal of Memory and Language, 48*, 16-32.

Klein, W., & Perdue, C. (1997). The basic variety (Or: Couldn't natural languages be much simpler?). *SLR, 13*, 301-347.

Levelt, W. J. M. (1992). Accessing words in speech production: Stages, processes and representations. *Cognition, 42*, 1-22.

Levinson, S. (2000). *Presumptive meanings: The theory of generalized conversational implicature.* Cambridge, MA: MIT Press.

Levinson, S. (2003). *Space in language and cognition: Explorations in cognitive diversity.* Cambridge: Cambridge University Press.

Levinson, S. C., & Meira, S. (2003). 'Natural concepts' in the spatial topological domain – adpositional meanings in cross-linguistic perspective: An exercise in semantic typology. *Language, 79*, 485-516.

Levinson, S., Kita, S., Haun, D., & Rasch, B. (2002). Returning the tables: Language affects spatial reasoning. *Cognition, 84*, 155-188.

Li, P., & Gleitman, L. (2002). Turning the tables: Language and spatial reasoning. *Cognition, 83*, 265-294.

Lucy, J., & Gaskins, S. (2001). Grammatical categories and the development of classification preferences: A comparative approach. In M. Bowerman & S. Levinson (Eds.), *Language acquisition and conceptual development* (pp. 257-283). Cambridge: Cambridge University Press.

Majid, A., Bowerman, M., Kita, S., Haun, D. B. M., & Levinson, S. C. (2004). Can language restructure cognition? The case of space. *Trends in Cognitive Sciences, 8*, 108-114.

Marslen-Wilson, W., & Welsh, A. (1978). Processing interactions and lexical access during word-recognition in continuous speech. *Cognitive Psychology, 10*, 29-63.

McClelland, J. L., & Elman, J. L. (1986). The TRACE model of speech perception. *Cognitive Psychology, 18*, 1-86.

McQueen, J. M., Dahan, D., & Cutler, A. (2003). Continuity and gradedness in speech processing. In N. O. Schiller & A. S. Meyer (Eds.), *Phonetics and phonology in language comprehension and production: Differences and similarities* (pp. 39-78). Berlin: Mouton.

20 CUTLER, KLEIN, AND LEVINSON

Miller, G. A., & McKean, K. A. (1964). A chronometric study of some relations between sentences. *Quarterly Journal of Experimental Psychology, 16,* 297-308.

Nosofsky, R. M. (1986). Attention, similarity, and the identification-categorization relationship. *Journal of Experimental Psychology: General, 115,* 39-57.

Noveck, I., & Sperber, D. (2004). *Experimental pragmatics.* Palgrave: Macmillan.

Oldfield, R. C., & Wingfield, A. (1964). The time it takes to name an object. *Nature, 202,* 1031-1032.

Peperkamp, S., & Dupoux, E. (2002). Coping with phonological variation in early lexical acquisition. In I. Lasser (Ed.), *The process of language acquisition* (pp. 359-385). Frankfurt: Peter Lang.

Perdue, C. (Ed.). (1993). *Adult language acquisition: Cross-linguistic perspectives* (2 vols.). Cambridge: Cambridge University Press.

Pierrehumbert, J. B. (2002). Word-specific phonetics. In C. Gussenhoven & N. Warner (Eds.), *Papers in Laboratory Phonology VII* (pp. 101-140). Berlin: Mouton.

Pierrehumbert, J., Beckman, M. E., & Ladd, D. R. (2000). Conceptual foundations of phonology as a laboratory science, In N. Burton-Roberts, P. Carr, & G. Docherty (Eds.), *Phonological knowledge: Conceptual and emperical issues* (pp. 273-303). Oxford: Oxford University Press.

Prideaux, G. D. (1984). *Psycholinguistics: The experimental study of language.* London: Croom Helm.

Rochat, P., Querido, J., & Striano, T. (1999). Emerging sensitivity to the timing and structure of protoconversation in early infancy. *Developmental Psychology, 35,* 950-957.

Roelofs, A. (1992). A spreading-activation theory of lemma retrieval in speaking. *Cognition, 42,* 107-142.

Seidenberg, M. S. (1995). Visual word recognition: An overview. In J. L. Miller & P. D. Eimas (Eds.), *Speech, language, and communication* (pp. 138-179). San Diego: Academic Press.

Simon, J. R., & Wolf, J. D. (1963). Choice reaction time as a function of angular stimulus–response correspondence and age. *Ergonomics, 6,* 99–105.

Slobin, D. I. (1985). *The crosslinguistic study of language acquisition. Vol. 1: The data. Vol. 2: Theoretical Issues.* Hillsdale, NJ: Lawrence Erlbaum Associates.

Spelke, E. S. (2003). What makes humans smart? In D. Gentner & S. Goldin-Meadow (Eds.), *Advances in the investigation of language and thought* (pp. 277-312). Cambridge, MA: MIT Press.

Spelke, E., & Tsivkin, S. (2001). Initial knowledge and conceptual change: Space and number. In M. Bowerman & S. C. Levinson (Eds.), *Language acquisition and conceptual development.* Cambridge: Cambridge University Press.

Sperber, D., & Wilson, D. (1986). *Relevance.* Oxford: Basil Blackwell.

Stutterheim, C. von (1986). *Temporalität in der Zweitsprache.* Berlin: de Gruyter.

Tanenhaus, M. K., & Trueswell, J. C. (1995). Sentence comprehension. In J. L. Miller & P. D. Eimas (Eds.), *Speech, language, and communication* (pp. 217-262). San Diego: Academic Press.

Werker, J. F. (1995). Age-related changes in cross-language speech perception: Standing at the crossroads. In W. Strange (Ed.), *Speech perception and linguistic experience: Issues in cross-language research* (pp. 155-170). Baltimore: York Press.

Section 1

Psychology and Linguistics

2 Cognitive Mechanisms and Syntactic Theory

Julie E. Boland
University of Michigan, USA

As a psychologist who studies sentence comprehension and holds a joint appointment in the departments of psychology and linguistics, I have frequent opportunities to observe the interaction, or lack thereof, between the two disciplines. Although cognitive psychology and formal linguistic theory share some common history in Chomsky's (1959) pivotal review of Skinner's (1957) book on language behavior, these two disciplines have not continued to influence one another to the degree one might expect. For example, theoretical developments in syntax have rarely if ever been motivated by an experimental finding about sentence comprehension. In fact, there is good reason for this. I argue that most psycholinguistic data is irrelevant to formal linguistic theory. Nonetheless, there may be a subset of psycholinguistic data that formal linguists ought to consider. I attempt to delineate this hypothetical subset, using the argument/ adjunct distinction as an example.

To set the stage, consider the domains of cognitive psychology and formal linguistic theory. Cognitive psychology is the study of mental representations and the mental operations for manipulating (creating, accessing, etc.) these mental representations. The central goal is to describe a processing system. In the context of sentence comprehension, a cognitive psychologist might develop a theory of syntactic parsing that specifies the mental representations that are involved, what aspects of linguistic and non-linguistic knowledge are used to create those mental representations, and so forth.

Formal linguistic theory describes what speakers know about their language. The central goal is not to catalogue facts about languages, but rather to characterize the properties of the human mind that make language possible. The descriptive adequacy of a theory is evaluated via the collection and analysis of linguistic intuitions: A grammar must generate all and only those utterances accepted by native speakers. While this might be considered a type of psychological study, it is quite unlike the typical experiments carried out by a cognitive psychologist.

Formal linguistic theory offers cognitive psychologists a framework for partitioning the subcomponents of language processing (phonetics, phonology, syntax, etc.) and the relevant mental representations (noun phrase, empty category, thematic role, etc.). It also provides theories about how the representations are structured, for example, Head-driven Phrase Structure Grammar (HPSG). In turn, psychology provides linguists with methodologies for investigating the cognitive processes of acquisition, comprehension, and production. Such investigations are clearly of general interest to linguists, but they are unlikely to influence formal linguistic theory for reasons that are discussed next.

At the level of syntax, the distinction between cognitive psychology and formal linguistics is echoed in the constructs of the human parsing system on one hand and the grammar on the other. In human comprehenders, parsers operate incrementally, analyzing structure in real time as each word is heard or read. The operation of the parser is subject to performance constraints such as limitations on working memory. In contrast, grammatical operations do not occur in real time (though they may constitute an ordered sequence of representations) and working memory is irrelevant.

Some confusions arise because psycholinguists and linguists often use similar terminology. For example, a syntactician may assume that a derivation has an input and a sequence of representations leading to an output, but neither the input nor the intermediate representations need align directly with the inputs and intermediate representations within a psycholinguistic theory of sentence comprehension or sentence production. Perhaps the most telling contrast between conceptions of the parser and the grammar is that psycholinguists construct different theories to account for comprehension and production, while such a distinction has no place within formal linguistic theory: The entire derivation is an atemporal representation of linguistic competence. It represents our implicit knowledge about the language without describing the cognitive operations necessary to understand or produce it.

The above description assumes weak type transparency between the grammar and the parser (see Berwick & Weinberg, 1984, and Chomsky,

1968, for definitions of weak and strict type transparency, and reasons to avoid strict transparency). Granted, parsing data is directly relevant to theories of grammar if researchers assume strict transparency in mapping from processing to linguistic theory. Fairly strict transparency was maintained in the Derivational Theory of Complexity (e.g., Miller & Chomsky, 1963), which assumed a one-to-one mapping between the transformations in Transformational Grammar and the mental operations involved in parsing. Many scholars consider the Derivational Theory of Complexity to be a historical illustration of the perils of assuming strict transparency between a psycholinguistic theory and some syntactic theory. Even ignoring questions of psychological plausibility, the danger of constructing a processing theory around a linguistic theory that will soon be out of date is enough to scare many psycholinguists away from the strict transparency approach. Not all have been convinced of the danger, however. As recently as 1996, Colin Phillips proposed that the parser and the grammar are essentially the same system.

More frequently, scholars assume weak type transparency between the grammar and the parser, with some unknown set of linking assumptions mapping between linguistic theory and cognitive processes. The output of the parser and the output of the grammar must be roughly compatible, but the two systems may arrive at their respective outputs in very different ways. I say "roughly compatible" because the class of parseable sentences is not equivalent to the class of grammatical sentences. The odd cases are normally explained by performance factors. For example, working memory constraints might prevent comprehension of a doubly center-embedded, but grammatical, sentence, while the ability to recover from a disfluency could enable comprehension of a superficially ungrammatical sentence.

Even under weak transparency, there is some appeal for linguistic theories that map straightforwardly to processing data. For example, Jackendoff (2002) stated that a more satisfactory union of linguistics and psycholinguistics was one of his goals in developing a new linguistic framework. From the perspective of a psycholinguist, there is a big advantage to linguistic formalisms, such as those in Categorial Grammar (e.g., Steedman, 1996), that can be incorporated into a processing model in a straightforward manner. Yet, even though I am more likely to use formalisms from Categorial Grammar than those from Minimalism (Chomsky, 1995) to describe the syntactic representations that are accessed from the lexicon and used during sentence comprehension, I remain agnostic as to which theory provides a more optimal account of linguistic knowledge. My agnosticism stems from the belief that, while simple linking assumptions between linguistic and psycholinguistic theories would be ideal, the adequacy of a linguistic theory depends upon internal criteria and does not hinge upon the linking assumptions.

In contrast to my view, some researchers find formal linguists' lack of interest in psycholinguistic data quite troubling. For example, Edelman and Christiansen (2003: 60) argued for "the need to demonstrate the psychological (behavioral), and eventually, the neurobiological, reality of theoretical constructs" such as the operations merge and move with the Minimalism Program of syntactic theory. However, unless one assumes strict transparency, experimental psycholinguistic data is not needed to test these theoretical constructs. Phillips and Lasnik (2003) did take the strict transparency view and replied to this criticism by providing a list of experimental papers demonstrating that agreement violations produce a particular kind of electrical brain response, and that readers reactivate *boxer* at the underlined gap location in *The boxer that the journalist questioned __ got angry*. While such results are consistent with particular grammatical formalisms, these data are beside the point. They are not relevant to the theoretical foundations of Minimalism questioned by Edelman and Christiansen, and such experimental data has had no observable impact on the development of syntactic theory. One could take the position that linguistic theory **should** account for the available psycholinguistic data, including performance factors such as working memory constraints and garden path recovery strategies. Jackendoff (2002) is an example of a move in this direction. However, such an obligation would dramatically change the goal of most formal linguists from the description of linguistic knowledge to the description of how linguistic knowledge is implemented within a processing system that operates in real time.

I do not mean to imply that psychological data is completely irrelevant to linguistic theory or that linguistic intuitions have a privileged access to the mental representations postulated by syntactic theories. Psychological data is directly relevant if a linguistic theory predicts that constituents of Type X will be processed differently than constituents of Type Y. All grammatical theories make this type of prediction with regards to grammaticality: The word strings that can be generated by the grammar should be those strings judged to be acceptable. These predictions are usually tested via linguistic intuitions, but they can be tested experimentally by predicting patterns of syntactic anomaly effects in, for example, an event-related potential paradigm. There is little justification for such efforts from the point of view of syntactic theory, because linguistic intuitions can be collected much more quickly, easily, and inexpensively. Although there are numerous concerns about the reliability of linguistic intuitions, similar concerns apply to experimental research. Collecting either linguistic intuitions or experimental data requires considerable expertise.

The important question is: Are there cases in which linguistic theory predicts that different types of constituents will be processed differently *and* linguistic intuitions and formal linguistic methods alone have not provided clear data? Both conjuncts might be true for distinctions in formal linguistic theory that entail a distinction in how linguistic knowledge is stored in long-term memory. One example is the well-known debate about the past tense. The traditional approach assumes that only irregular verbs explicitly encode the past tense within the lexicon (e.g., Pinker & Prince, 1988). For regular verbs, the past tense is formed by applying a rule. The opposing connectionist view is that both regular and irregular past tenses are formed via the same mechanism (based on the properties of all the individual lexical items), without any explicit rules (Rumelhart & McClelland, 1986). However, the connectionist account doesn't threaten the existence of explicit rules **within** linguistic theory if such rules still provide an elegant description of our linguistic knowledge. Under weak transparency, linguists can consider the connectionist account to be one possible implementation of the rules vs. lexical-specification contrast within the formal theory.

The past tense example illustrates the first half of an interesting asymmetry. Psychological evidence that an item-based mechanism can mimic rule-governed behavior is not enough to eliminate rules within linguistic theory. In contrast, psychological evidence that the necessary knowledge is not specified within the lexicon does strongly suggest the use of a general rule. For an example of psychological data of the latter type, consider the linguistic distinction between arguments and adjuncts.

ARGUMENTS VERSUS ADJUNCTS

Most syntactic theories distinguish between arguments and adjuncts in terms of lexical specification. In the sentence, *Chris gave Kim some candy on Tuesday in the park*, the verb *gave* is the lexical head of the verb phrase (VP). As such, it specifies three arguments and assigns a thematic role to each: *Chris* (agent), *Kim* (recipient), and *candy* (theme). In contrast, *Tuesday* and *the park* are adjuncts, getting their thematic roles from the prepositions that head their phrases. Many syntactic theories have a structural distinction as well: Arguments are sisters to the head, while adjuncts are sisters to a phrasal node (e.g., Chomsky, 1995). Processing evidence can't address the structure of the phrase tree as long as we assume weak type transparency, but if arguments and adjuncts are processed differently because arguments are lexically specified and adjuncts are not, processing evidence may be able to distinguish the difficult cases. Critically, we need psychological evidence that adjuncts are **not** lexically specified.

There are many difficult cases in which linguistic intuitions fail to clearly distinguish which phrases are adjuncts and which are arguments. One such example is the underlined prepositional phrase (PP) in *Kim changed the tire with a monkey wrench*. Although numerous tests have been devised for soliciting the critical intuitions, instrument PPs remain difficult to categorize (e.g., Larson, 1988; Schutze & Gibson, 1999). Following linguistic tradition, ungrammatical sentences will be preceded by an asterisk in the following examples. Like typical arguments, instruments can't normally be iterated (*John cut the meat with a knife with the sharp end.*), but they can be extracted from weak islands (*With which key do you deny that the butler could have opened the door?*). However, like typical adjuncts, they allow pro-form replacement (*John will eat the cake with a fork and Mary will do so with a spoon.*). One might conclude that there is no sharp distinction between arguments and adjuncts—such a possibility is discussed below. Whether or not a sharp distinction exists, the argument/adjunct contrast could be a case in which psycholinguistic data is more informative than intuitions. The degree to which the argument/adjunct distinction is unique in this respect will be discussed in the final section of this chapter.

Although the argument/adjunct distinction figures prominently in many linguistic and psycholinguistic theories, there have been attempts to reshape the distinction or to eliminate it entirely. For example, Steedman's (1996: 77) Categorial Grammar assumes that "all PPs, even those that would normally be thought of as modifiers rather than sub-categorized, are in fact arguments." Alternatively, some linguists have argued that the distinction is not binary (e.g., Grimshaw, 1990). Within cognitive psychology, MacDonald, Pearlmutter, and Seidenberg (1994) envisioned an argument/adjunct continuum, with arguments and adjuncts differing only in the frequency of co-occurrence with the lexical head. It's worth noting that the argument/adjunct status of instruments and other phrases may differ from one verb to another.

In summary, there are at least two controversies within formal linguistic theory that psycholinguistic data may speak to. The first is whether there is in fact any distinction between the lexical specification of arguments and adjuncts. Secondly, if such a distinction is to be maintained, psycholinguistic data may help resolve the debate over problematic cases such as instrument PP's.

To address the argument/adjunct distinction from a psycholinguistic perspective, I make the following assumptions. Much of syntactic knowledge is stored lexically and accessed via word recognition. Syntactic structures are built incrementally during sentence comprehension, and new constituents are attached to the developing structure via competition between lexical alternatives. Constraints from any level of representation can influence competition, but the relative frequency of lexical forms is especially powerful: Just as more frequent meanings of semantically ambiguous words, are accessed more easily than less frequent meanings, so more frequent syntactic forms are more easily accessed. Thus, lexically specified structures exhibit lexical frequency effects. Consider the following example. Both *delegate* and *suggest* can head either a dative or a simple transitive structure, but the dative form is relatively more frequent for *delegate*. This is illustrated in Figure 2.1, with the more frequent structure in boldface. Lexicalized versions of both structures are accessed by recognition of either verb, but weighted by frequency. An alternative that is more strongly available is assumed to be easier and/or faster to integrate with the developing structure. Thus, *to the students* would be attached more easily following *delegate* than *suggest*, because the PP is specified by the dominant structure in the former case. The subcategorization preference effects reported by Stowe, Tanenhaus, and Carlson (1991), Trueswell (1996), and others provide evidence for this type of lexical frequency effect.

If argument slots are represented in the lexical entries of their heads, but adjunct slots are not, only arguments could be attached using the tree-adjoining mechanism summarized above and illustrated in Figure 2.2. Given the structures in Figure 2.1, attaching an adjunct such as *during the meeting* would have to be accomplished using some other mechanism such as an attachment rule that is not associated with any particular lexical head. Under this type of a two-mechanism account, lexical

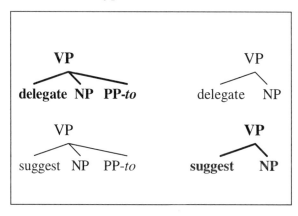

FIG. 2.1. Alternative syntactic forms of *delegate* and *suggest*.

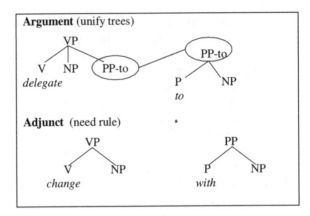

FIG. 2.2. The upper portion of the figure illustrates a lexical unification mechanism for argument attachment. The lower portion of the figure illustrates that same mechanism cannot be used for adjunct attachment if adjunct slots are not lexically specified by the head (i.e., *change*).

frequency effects would be predicted for arguments, but not for adjuncts. This Argument Structure Hypothesis is relevant to linguistic theory because it makes the prediction that argument phrases will be processed differently than adjunct phrases.

Testing the Argument Structure Hypothesis with reading paradigms

In the previous section, I suggested that argument status can be diagnosed by the presence/absence of a certain type of lexical frequency effect. One challenge for testing this Argument Structure Hypothesis is distinguishing lexical frequency effects from plausibility effects and other factors that might influence our dependent measure, such as reading time on the phrase of interest. In the current section, I will illustrate this problem using a finding from Spivey-Knowlton and Sedivy (1995), and suggest the solution offered by Boland, Lewis, and Blodgett (2004).

Some potential counter-evidence to the Argument Structure Hypothesis was reported by Spivey-Knowlton and Sedivy (1995). Using stimuli like those in (1), they found that VP-attached PP adjuncts were read more quickly than noun phrase (NP)-attached adjuncts following an action verb, while the reverse pattern was found for psych/perception verbs. Because action verbs are more likely to be modified by a PP headed by *with* (see Table 2.1), this data pattern might represent a lexical frequency effect, with the co-occurrence frequency between the adjunct and its lexical head influencing the ease of attachment. If so, it demonstrates that PP adjuncts are lexically specified, contrary to the Argument Structure Hypothesis. However, an alternative account is based upon a difference in local plausibility. On reading *The mechanic changed a tire with* ... it might seem more appropriate to say what or who the tire was changed with, rather than to further define the tire as being one with some property. In contrast, for the psych/perception verb example, noticing with someone or something is less plausible than the customer being defined by some property that can be expressed in a *with-PP*. The plausibility account is consistent with the Argument Structure Hypothesis, because both NP-attached and VP-attached adjunct options could be generated by rule rather than lexically specified.

(1) Spivey-Knowlton and Sedivy (1995) stimuli
  Action Verbs
    The mechanic changed a tire...
    ...with a faulty valve (NP-attached, slow)
    ...with a monkey wrench (VP-attached, fast) [Instrument]
  Psych/Perception Verbs
    The salesman noticed a customer...
    ...with ripped jeans (NP-attached, fast)
    ...with a quick glance (VP-attached, slow)

In a recent paper, some colleagues and I tested the lexical frequency hypothesis to determine whether the adjuncts were in fact lexically specified (Boland et al., 2004). Unfortunately, no dependent measure provides a pure index of lexical frequency effects, uncontaminated by other variables. However, it may be possible to distinguish lexical frequency effects from other influences on reading time. In a theoretical approach that I have advocated (Boland, 1997; Boland & Blodgett, 2001), lexical frequency has a privileged status in influencing syntactic analysis: Lexical frequency, but not plausibility, influences the initial generation of syntactic structure(s), while both lexical frequency and plausibility

TABLE 2.1.
Spivey-Knowlton and Sedivy (1995) Normative Data for action verbs and psych/ perception verbs, concerning the VP-attachment bias for PP's headed by *with*

Verb Class	The N V'd the N with... VP-attached Sentence Completions	Brown Corpus: Number VP-attached with-PP's
Action	90%	40
Psych/Percept	24%	4

influence syntactic ambiguity resolution, as shown in Figure 2.3. This approach maintains a distinction between the generation of syntactic structure and selection processes that operate when multiple grammatical structures are possible. The distinction between the generation of syntactic structure and syntactic ambiguity resolution is explicit in some parsing theories (e.g., Altmann & Steedman, 1988; Boland, 1997) and acknowledged as functionally necessary in others (Spivey-Knowlton & Tanenhaus, 1998).

Frequency effects in syntactically unambiguous sentences provide the strongest evidence for the lexicalization of syntactic knowledge, because the effects must arise during lexical access and generation of syntactic structure. To illustrate, compare the noun–verb homographs in (2): *play* occurs most often as a verb, while *duck* occurs most often as a noun. Boland (1997) and Corley (1998) each found that encountering a lexically ambiguous word in its less frequent syntactic form increased reading time compared to encountering its more frequent form. Thus in (2), reading times for *duck* are faster than for *play*, because the syntactic context is consistent with the dominant form of *duck*, but the subordinate form of *play*. Importantly, reading times in syntactically ambiguous sentences (i.e., *She saw her play)* are influenced by high level constraints like discourse congruency, but reading times in unambiguous sentences like (2) are not (Boland, 1997). Boland and Blodgett (2001) found additional evidence that lexical frequency constraints and discourse constraints impact sentence comprehension in different ways. In an eye tracking experiment that used unambiguous

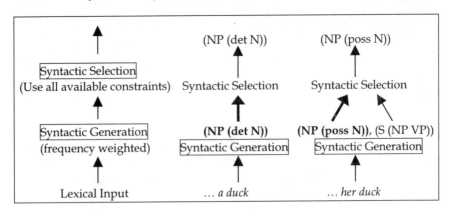

FIG. 2.3. The architecture of the parsing model is given on the left, the representations generated by the model are provided for an unambiguous example (center) and an ambiguous example (right).

target sentences like those in (2), we found lexical frequency effects only in first pass measures of processing difficulty, while discourse congruency effects were limited to second pass measures. In the absence of any alternative structures, discourse congruency had no impact on syntactic analysis. Rather, the second pass effects were presumed to reflect an anomaly within the discourse level representation. Together, these findings suggest that lexical frequency affects lexical access and syntactic generation, but discourse congruency does not. Instead, discourse congruency plays a role in ambiguity resolution (syntactic selection) and relatively late discourse coherence processes.

(2) a. *She saw a play.*
   b. *She saw a duck.*

Under this approach, we can minimize the influence of factors that affect selection processes by using maximally unambiguous contexts, as in (3). Doing so should increase the role of lexical frequency relative to plausibility in syntactic processing. Thus PP adjuncts like those used in Spivey-Knowlton and Sedivy (1995), should no longer be influenced by verb type. In contrast, lexical frequency effects should be found for VP-attached PP arguments, so we added some dative sentences in order to demonstrate a true lexical frequency effect.

(3) Boland et al. (2004) VP-attachment stimuli
   VP Adjuncts
      High Lexical Frequency of VP Attachment
      The tire that the mechanic changed with a monkey wrench ...
      Low Lexical Frequency of VP Attachment
      The customer that the salesman noticed with a quick glance ...
   VP Arguments
      High Lexical Frequency of VP Attachment
      The chores that the parents delegated to their kids ...
      Low Lexical Frequency of VP Attachment
      The chores that the parents suggested to their kids ...

Consider the context *The mechanic changed the tires....* If the next word is *with*, English syntax allows for two possible adjunct attachments of the PP headed by that preposition: modification of the VP or modification of the direct object NP. If these attachment alternatives are both rule-generated and thus equally available, one must use pragmatic knowledge or some other mechanism to select the most likely attachment site. In contrast, pragmatic knowledge and plausibility would play a reduced role if we decreased the availability of NP attachment by fronting the direct object: *The tire that the mechanic changed with* ... In this case, structural factors such as recency and complexity make VP attachment more accessible and would likely swamp the selection process.

Even in such relatively unambiguous structures, if the verb takes an argument PP, we should see effects of lexical frequency. Consider the context *The chores that the parents delegated/suggested* ... A PP like *to the children* should be read more quickly following *delegate* compared to *suggest* because the dative syntactic structure (shown on the left half of Figure 2.1) is more strongly available for *delegate* than for *suggest*. The lexical frequency effect arises because access to the competing argument structures is weighted by relative frequency.

These predictions were tested by Boland et al. (2004) and confirmed using both self-paced, phrase-by-phrase reading and eye-fixation measures. The Spivey-Knowlton and Sedivy (1995) contrast between action verbs and psych/perception verbs was replicated in locally ambiguous structures like those in (1), but was greatly reduced in the maximally unambiguous versions shown in (3). That is, self-paced reading times for the VP-attached PPs were faster in the action verb condition than the psych/perception verb condition in the locally ambiguous structures like those in (1), but not in the versions in (3) that were strongly biased toward VP attachment. Importantly, lexical frequency effects were obtained in the unambiguous structures for dative argument PP's: Self-paced reading times for the PP following a high-frequency dative like *delegate* were faster than after a low-frequency dative like *suggest*. The eye-tracking data were particularly informative because they offered additional details about the relative timing of the argument and adjunct effects. The lexical frequency effects for the dative arguments were apparent in the early eye movement measures such as the first-fixation and the first-pass reading times over the PP. In contrast, the attachment site by verb class interaction, replicating the Spivey-Knowlton and Sedivy (1995) finding on locally ambiguous adjuncts, was found only in the total time on the PP region. There were no first-pass effects during the PP for the adjunct stimuli in either the locally ambiguous condition (1) or the maximally unambiguous condition (3).

In summary, Boland et al. (2004) found lexical frequency effects in argument attachments, but not adjunct attachments. This suggests that arguments are attached using detailed lexical information that is weighted by frequency, while adjuncts are attached using more global syntactic knowledge. In our eye-tracking replication, the adjunct effects analogous to those reported by Spivey-Knowlton and Sedivy (1995) occurred later than the lexical frequency effects and were most likely caused by the influence of pragmatics on syntactic selection. The contrast between the argument and adjunct stimuli observed by Boland et al. suggests that the PP's assumed to be adjuncts, including the instrument PP's, are not lexically specified by the verbal heads. This finding ought to be considered, along with traditional linguistic tests, when evaluating the argument status of instrument PP's.

Implicit arguments in listening paradigms

Frequency effects are one consequence of the lexical specification of arguments. Such effects are an empirical marker of argument status that can be investigated in psycholinguistic experiments. Another consequence of the Argument Structure Hypothesis is that recognition of a lexical head provides access to the thematic roles associated with frequently occurring arguments. This prediction is supported by reading experiments that have demonstrated that verbs implicitly introduce their arguments into the discourse, without the arguments being explicitly mentioned (e.g., Mauner, Tanenhaus, & Carlson, 1995). Converging evidence can be found within a listening paradigm.

We tend to look at things as they are mentioned, if the mentioned items are in the visual environment. This phenomenon extends to items that have not (yet) been explicitly mentioned. For example, Sussman, Campana, Tanenhaus, and Carlson (2002) found that listeners made an eye movement to an appropriate instrument (a pencil) on hearing *Poke the dolphin* but not *Touch the dolphin*. Even though no instrument was mentioned, listeners used their knowledge about the two verbs to decide whether to manipulate the dolphin with their finger or a pencil in a real-world environment. Listeners were also sensitive to contextual factors that altered verb meaning. For example, they looked at a potato peeler when asked to *Peel the potato*, but not when asked to *Peel the banana*.

Sussman et al.'s (2002) directed action task does raise a concern that the eye-movement pattern is caused by guessing strategies. Normal conversation involves a great deal of strategic guessing about the speaker's intent, so this is not a problem if the goal is to study the output of the complete comprehension process. However, if there are some partially or fully automatized aspects of syntactic and semantic processing, the directed action paradigm is not ideal for studying the representations that result from those automatized processes alone. For example, one might question whether the recognition of *poke* **obligatorily** introduces an instrument into the discourse.

Encouragingly, there is converging evidence for the automatic activation of thematic role information from passive listening tasks. In one study, Altmann and Kamide (1999) had people listen to a sentence like *The boy will move/eat the cake* while looking at a semi-realistic scene with a boy, a cake, and some inedible (but moveable) toys. Altmann and Kamide found more and faster looks to the cake following *eat* compared to *move*, beginning prior to the onset of *cake*. Altmann and Kamide concluded that the verb's thematic roles were used to pro-actively restrict the domain of subsequent reference.

Even in a passive listening task, it is difficult to identify the cause of the anticipatory fixations, because both linguistic and general world knowledge could have contributed to the effect. An important question is whether the discourse elements that can be introduced by a verb are limited to members of its thematic grids. In other words, do a verb's arguments hold a privileged status or are all related words and concepts accessed in the same way? If it is solely the verb's argument structure that is driving eye movements, then listeners should not look at a bed upon hearing *The girl slept* because *bed* cannot be an argument of *slept*. Alternatively, listeners might look at a bed because beds are part of a prototypical sleeping event and are thus conceptually related to sleep. Furthermore, discussions about sleep often include mention of a bed, so linguistic co-occurrence frequency is high and the co-occurrence of sleeping and beds in participants' actual experience is likely to be extremely high. One might consider an account of Altmann and Kamide's (1999) effect that is akin to semantic priming—a conceptual, essentially intra-lexical, process. However in more recent work, Kamide, Altmann, and Haywood (2003) found that combinatory semantics rather than simple lexical relationships influenced eye movements. For example, when viewing a carnival scene, listeners looked at a motorcycle upon hearing *The man rode ...* and looked at a merry-go-round upon hearing *The girl rode ...* Thus, knowledge higher-level than simple lexical associations must have influenced gaze. Was it argument structure or real world knowledge, or both?

I investigated this question using a passive listening paradigm (Boland, 2004). Across three experiments, effects of both argument status and real world knowledge were found. The first experiment manipulated both the argument structure of the verb and the typicality/co-occurrence frequency of the target argument/adjunct. Example stimuli are in (5); the typical/atypical target is underlined. The goal was to distinguish between anticipatory looks to target pictures representing potential arguments and anticipatory looks to pictures that were strongly associated with the verb, but did not have the linguistic status of argument. The intransitive-location stimuli provide a clear case of an adjunct target (bed/bus), the dative-recipient stimuli provide a clear case of an argument target (teenager/toddler), and the action-instrument stimuli provide an intermediate case in which the targets are arguably adjuncts (stick/hat). Acceptability ratings insured that sentences with typical targets were judged to be more acceptable than sentences with atypical targets. Furthermore, typical targets were more likely to co-occur with their verbs. Importantly, there was no evidence that typical recipients had a higher co-occurrence frequency than typical locations — if anything, the opposite was true.

(5) Example stimuli from Boland (2004), Experiment 1.
Intransitive-Location.
The girl slept for a while on the bed/bus this afternoon.
(pictures: girl, bed/bus, pillow, toy car)
Action-Instrument.
The donkey would not move, so the farmer beat it vigorously with a stick/hat every day.
(pictures: donkey, farmer, stick/hat, grass)
Dative-Recipient.
The newspaper was difficult to read, but the mother suggested it anyway to her teenager/toddler last week.
(pictures: newspaper, mother, teen/toddler, dictionary)

The primary finding in Experiment 1 was that dative verbs prompted more anticipatory looks to potential recipients than transitive action verbs prompted to potential instruments or intransitive verbs prompted to potential locations. That is, listeners were more likely to fixate the teenager or toddler in the dative example than the bed/bus or stick/hat from the intransitive and action verb examples. The relevant time window for examining these anticipatory looks was from verb onset to the onset of the PP that mentioned the target. The argument status effect began about 500 ms after verb onset, suggesting that it occurred soon after lexical access of the verb. Interestingly, listeners were just as likely to fixate the atypical recipient (toddler) as they were to fixate the typical recipient (teenager). In both the typical and atypical conditions, the potential referent met the lexical constraints on recipients for that particular verb. If verbs specify the syntactic and semantic constraints on their arguments, recognizing a verb would make available knowledge about that verb's arguments, and entities that satisfy the syntactic and semantic constraints could be identified in the current discourse model or the situational context.

In the first experiment, the argument structure of the dative verbs introduced an abstract recipient, but only one potential referent was pictured — the same one that was ultimately mentioned. A second experiment used the same sentences, but presented both typical and atypical targets (the recipients, instruments or locations) on each trial. This experiment produced clear typicality effects, suggesting that when more than one potential referent is pictured, real world knowledge is used to focus attention on the most appropriate referent. This account is consistent with prior evidence that pragmatic constraints influence ambiguity resolution, but not the generation of linguistic structure (Boland, 1997).

The argument status effect was replicated in a third experiment, in which a single animate NP (and the corresponding picture) served as an argument in the dative condition (6a) and as an adjunct in the action verb condition (6b). No instrument was mentioned in the critical trials, though a prototypical instrument for the action verb was always pictured, and in filler trials, pictured instruments were mentioned. There were more looks to the target picture when it was an argument (recipient) than when it was an adjunct (benefactor, instrument) during the interval 500 to 1000 ms after the onset of the verb. There were very few fixations on the pictured instrument during this time-frame, and there was no difference in the probability of a look to a prototypical adjunct (*fix*-tools) and an improbable adjunct (*mention*-tools). Co-occurrence frequency does not provide an alternative explanation. There were no reliable differences in co-occurrence frequency among the dative-recipient, action-benefactor, and action-instrument pairs.

(6) *One window was broken, so the handyman…*
    [pictures: window, handyman, couple, tools]
        a. *mentioned it right away to the owners.* (recipient-Argument)
        b. *fixed it hurriedly for the owners.* (benefactor-Adjunct)

Together, these findings demonstrate that linguistic constraints play a privileged role in guiding visual attention in this passive listening paradigm. Furthermore, these argument status effects suggest an important distinction between adjuncts and arguments in terms of how verbs introduce entities into the discourse. A verb implies its arguments, but not adjuncts, before they are explicitly mentioned. In addition, these results suggest another experimental test of argument status.

CONCLUSIONS

In summary, the results from reading and listening paradigms converge to support the view that arguments and adjuncts have a different status in parsing. In the reading experiments summarized above, there were lexical frequency effects for PP arguments but not PP adjuncts, suggesting that only the arguments were syntactically analyzed via a lexicalized mechanism. In the listening experiments, verbs implicitly introduced their arguments, but not adjuncts, and visual attention was drawn to likely referents of those arguments. This is to be expected if only arguments are represented in the lexical entries of their heads. These findings are relevant to two major issues in parsing theory: How is syntactic knowledge stored and accessed? What are the mechanisms for attaching new constituents to the developing syntactic representation?

Are these results also relevant to formal syntactic theory? The psycholinguistic focus on arguments and adjuncts in the discussion above is obviously motivated by the argument/adjunct distinction in formal linguistic theory. In this case and many others, psychologists who study sentence comprehension rely on linguistic theory for insight into the nature of our mental representations and vocabulary for describing them. However, the insights don't flow as freely in the other direction. Formal linguists don't often try to account for phenomena that psychologists discover about the mental representations involved in language processing. This may be because formal linguistics has little to gain from cognitive psychology under weak transparency assumptions. But what about the exceptional cases?

I have suggested that assertions about lexical specification within syntactic (and morphological) theory are in fact claims about how linguistic knowledge is stored, accessed, or acquired. As such, some of these assertions may be tested more definitively with experimental methods than with linguistic intuitions. If the experimental data are clear, and if linguistic theory makes note of them, the experimental paradigms reviewed above may be able to resolve some of the debates about the distinction between arguments and adjuncts.

In contrast, psycholinguistic research cannot resolve purely structural debates about the geometry of the phrase structure tree or the nature of a derivation within syntactic theory, because these constructs do not generate straightforward predictions about processing. An example is the extensive line of experimental research (e.g., Clahsen & Featherston, 1999) investigating the psychological reality of "traces" left behind by movement in certain theories of syntax. The Trace Reactivation Hypothesis is usually stated as the prediction that an antecedent will be reactivated at its trace site. For example, in the sentence, *In which box did you put the cake__?*, the fronted PP *in which box* is the locative argument of *put*. The PP is said to have moved out of its canonical position, leaving behind a trace, which is represented by the underline. During comprehension of such a sentence, *in which box* would be coindexed with the trace, and as a result, the PP could then be interpreted as the appropriate argument of *put*. The fundamental problem is that recognition and coindexing of the long distance dependency is a complicated **processing** issue that has not been carefully addressed in the trace reactivation literature. Researchers generally assume that coindexing—and therefore reactivation—occurs at the linear position of the trace. In our example, coindexing would take place after the offset of *cake*, so priming of *box* would be predicted at that point in the sentence. Unfortunately, because traces are phonologically null, the listener or reader does not perceive a trace directly. Therefore, recognition and coindexing of the purported trace need not coincide with its linear position in a sentence. If they are psychologically real, traces must be postulated on the basis of cues that may or may not be adjacent to the trace site. For example, recognition of *put* could initiate projection of a VP with slots for a direct object and a locative PP. If so, a trace could immediately be posited and coindexed with *in which box*, leading to priming of *box* at *put*. Depending upon the strategy used by the parser, other alternatives are also possible. In short, a syntactic theory of traces makes no predictions about when or if priming should occur unless it is wedded to well-articulated processing theory that specifies how and when traces are postulated, as well as how previously encountered phrases will persist or decay in working memory. Because these processing questions are themselves controversial, it is difficult to see how psycholinguistic research can resolve syntactic debates over traces.

Even if some psycholinguistic data do influence a few corners of formal linguistic theory, we are not on the brink of a revolution in linguistic methodology. Psycholinguistic data—and data from cognitive neuroscience for that matter—will always play a secondary role in formal linguistic theory, adjudicating between linguistic theories that are equally elegant and account for the traditional data (linguistic intuitions from a variety of languages) equally well. This is as it should be, under the assumptions of weak transparency. Linguistic theory does not attempt to describe neural or behavioral patterns, but rather the knowledge state that gives rise to those neural and behavioral patterns. Linguistic assertions about lexical specification are unusual in that these assertions concern the linking assumptions between formal theories of linguistic knowledge and processing theories of how linguistic knowledge is stored, accessed, and used. For the most part, the linking assumptions among the knowledge state, the behavior, and the neural activity remain underspecified in both linguistic and psycholinguistic theories.

ACKNOWLEDGMENTS

This chapter benefited from numerous conversations with my University of Michigan colleagues prior to the conference. These colleagues include Steve Abney, Sam Epstein, Richard Lewis, Jenny Vannest, and others. I would also like to thank the attendees at the Four Corners workshop on the interface between psychology and linguistics for many fruitful discussions.

REFERENCES

Altmann, G. T. M., & Kamide, Y. (1999). Incremental interpretation at verbs: Restricting the domain of subsequent reference. *Cognition, 73*, 247-264.

Altmann, G. T. M., & Steedman, M. (1988). Interaction with context during human sentence processing. *Cognition, 30*, 191-238.

Berwick, R. C., & Weinberg, A. S. (1984). *The grammatical basis of linguistic performance: Language use and acquisition.* Cambridge, MA: MIT Press.

Boland, J. E. (1997). The relationship between syntactic and semantic processes in sentence comprehension. *Language and Cognitive Processes, 12*, 423-484.

Boland, J. E. (2004). Visual arguments. To appear in *Cognition*, pending revisions.

Boland, J. E., & Blodgett, A. (2001). Understanding the constraints on syntactic generation: Lexical bias and discourse congruency effects on eye movements. *Journal of Memory and Language, 45*, 391-411.

Boland, J. E., Lewis, R., & Blodgett, A. (2004). *Distinguishing generation and selection of modifier attachments: Implications for lexicalist parsing and competition models.* Manuscript submitted for publication.

Chomsky, N. (1959). Review of Skinner's verbal behavior. *Language, 35*, 26-58.

Chomsky, N. (1968). *Language and mind.* New York: Harcourt, Brace, and Jovanovich.

Chomsky, N. (1995). *The minimalist program.* Cambridge, MA: MIT Press.

Clahsen, H., & Featherston, S. (1999). Antecedent priming at trace positions: Evidence from German scrambling. *Journal of Psycholinguistic Research, 28*, 415-437.

Corley, S. (1998). *A statistical model of human lexical category disambiguation.* Doctoral dissertation, University of Edinburgh.

Edelman, S., & Christiansen, M. (2003). How seriously should we take Minimalist syntax? *Trends in Cognitive Sciences, 7*, 61-62.

Grimshaw, J. (1990). *Argument structure.* Cambridge, MA: MIT Press.

Jackendoff, R. (2002). *Foundations of language: Brain, meaning, grammar, evolution.* Oxford: Oxford University Press.

Kamide, Y., Altmann, G. T. M., & Haywood, S. (2003). Prediction and thematic information in incremental sentence processing: Evidence from anticipatory eye-movements. *Journal of Memory and Language, 49*, 133-156.

Larson, R. (1988). On the double object construction. *Linguistic Inquiry, 19*, 335-392.

MacDonald, M. C., Pearlmutter, N. J., & Seidenberg, M. S. (1994). The lexical nature of syntactic ambiguity resolution. *Psychological Review, 101,* 676-703.

Mauner, G., Tanenhaus, M. K., & Carlson, G. N. (1995). Implicit arguments in sentence processing. *Journal of Memory and Language, 34,* 357-382.

Miller, G., & Chomsky, N. (1963). Finitary models of language users. In R. D. Luce, R. R. Bush, & E. Galanter (Eds.), *Handbook of mathematical psychology* (Vol. 2, pp. 419-492). New York: Wiley.

Phillips, C. (1996). *Order and structure.* Doctoral dissertation, Department of Linguistics and Philosophy, MIT, MA.

Phillips, C., & Lasnik, H. (2003). Linguistics and empirical evidence. *Trends in Cognitive Sciences, 7,* 62-63.

Pinker, S., & Prince, A. (1988). On language and connectionism: Analysis of a parallel distributed processing model of language acquisition. *Cognition, 28,* 73-193.

Rumelhart, D. E., & McClelland, J. L. (1986). *Parallel distributed processing: Explorations in the microstructure of cognition. Vol. 1, Foundations.* Cambridge, MA: MIT Press.

Schutze, C., & Gibson, E. (1999). Argumenthood and English prepositional phrase attachment. *Journal of Memory and Language, 40,* 409-431.

Skinner, B. F. (1957). *Verbal behavior.* New York: Appleton-Century-Crofts.

Spivey-Knowlton, M., & Sedivy, J. (1995). Resolving attachment ambiguities with multiple constraints. *Cognition, 55,* 227-267.

Spivey-Knowlton, M., & Tanenhaus, M. K. (1998). Syntactic ambiguity resolution in discourse: Modeling effects of referential context and lexical frequency within an integration-competition network. *Journal of Experimental Psychology: Learning, Memory and Cognition, 24,* 1521-1543.

Steedman, M. (1996). *Surface structure and interpretation.* Cambridge, MA: MIT Press.

Stowe, L., Tanenhaus, M., & Carlson, G. (1991). Filling gaps on-line: Use of lexical and semantic information in sentence processing. *Language and Speech, 34,* 319-340.

Sussman, R. S., Campana, E., Tanenhaus, M. K., & Carlson, G. (2002). *Verb-based access to instrument roles: Evidence from eye movements.* Poster presented at the 8th Annual Architectures and Mechanisms of Language Processing Conference, Tenerife, Canary Islands, Spain.

Trueswell, J. C. (1996). The role of lexical frequency in syntactic ambiguity resolution. *Journal of Memory and Language, 35,* 566-585.

3

Getting Sound Structures in Mind: Acquisition Bridging Linguistics and Psychology?

Paula Fikkert
University of Nijmegen, The Netherlands

Acquisition data have never prominently figured in linguistics despite the fact that the ultimate goal of linguistics is to understand what constitutes knowledge of language and how this knowledge is acquired. In his recent GLOW lecture, Chomsky (2004) stressed that in order to answer these questions it is important to gain insight into how a lexicon is built up during acquisition, and what lexical representations look like. Here, I focus on representations of sound structures in the lexicon.

So far, child data have always been considered as external evidence in linguistics, just like results from psycholinguistics have been (Boland, this volume). Consequently, I know of no linguistic theory that has undergone changes based on new results in research on child phonology. At best, child language data have been used as additional evidence for particular linguistic claims. On the other hand, linguists take learnability very seriously, as any grammar, being it syntactic or phonological, should in principle be learnable on the basis of the primary language data that a child encounters. Although many researchers recognize that child language data would ultimately bear on the issue, the realistic study of child language acquisition has been considered "much too complex to be undertaken in a meaningful way" (Chomsky & Halle, 1968: 331). Since 1968, this view has not changed dramatically, although the rise of Optimality Theory (OT) (Prince & Smolensky, 1993) has instigated a spurt of new research on acquisition of phonology.

Studies in acquisition of phonology have mostly been concerned with why children produce words differently from adults. Most researchers have explained the differences by assuming different phonological

43

systems for children and adults. This is true for early generative studies on phonological acquisition (Smith, 1973), as well as current studies on acquisition in OT (see Kager, Pater, & Zonneveld, 2004). In fact, phonological representations have not been central in generative studies of phonological acquisition, even though they have been so prominent in 'adult' phonology, which aimed at providing the most elegant and economic descriptions of lexical representations, using universal phonological units only. Moreover, information that can be supplied by rules is often assumed to be absent in the representations, leading to abstract underspecified phonological representations (e.g., Chomsky & Halle, 1968; Lahiri & Marslen-Wilson, 1991; Steriade, 1995).

In psychology, infant speech perception studies, have recently given rise to a new view of language acquisition (Kuhl, 2000). In the seventies and eighties researchers argued that children pick up salient parts of the input first (e.g., Ferguson & Garnica, 1975; Waterson, 1981), and have initially global representations of words that only become more detailed under pressure of the increasing lexicon. Changes in the lexical representations served an efficient organization of the lexicon. Today, most psychologists studying language acquisition assume that children have detailed phonetic representations from a very early stage. By simply listening to language infants acquire sophisticated information about what sounds and sound patterns occur in the language, which of those patterns are frequent and which are likely to co-occur. Moreover, they do so long before they utter their first word. If infants already know so much about their language before speaking it, any discrepancies between this knowledge of the sound patterns of words and the actual way in which they produce them must lie in production skills, either due to underdeveloped or untrained articulatory routines or by processing limitations, such as limited memory, weak entrenchment of forms, etc. Although it is often claimed that production plays a role in development, its role in understanding language acquisition is fairly limited in most current views. The usual assumption is that perception precedes production and production hardly influences perception of mental representations.

Thus, both psychologists and linguists are concerned with the manner in which the sound structure of words is represented in the mental lexicon. Psychologists are interested in the units that are used for speech recognition and speech processing. Linguists, in particular phonologists, are concerned with the form of phonological representations, the units of which they are composed and the phonological processes that relate different appearances of words. Linguists aim to discover which structures are universal and how much variation exists among the world's languages. Their ultimate goal is to define linguistic competence. Psycholinguists strive for understanding how knowledge of language is used in perception and production, i.e. linguistic performance.

Yet, a number of great linguists have explicitly assumed that linguistic competence should have psychological reality, meaning that it should be reflected in performance. Halle (2002), for example, states the following: "Speakers find it difficult to memorize the stress contours of each word separately, but find it easy to compute the stress contours by means of rules". Hence, stress need not be part of each individual lexical item, but can be computed by stress rules. Similarly, Kaye (1989) has argued that processing considerations are the ultimate cause of phonological phenomena. Many phonological processes, such as vowel harmony, have a delimitative function and help detecting morpheme boundaries. Lahiri and Reetz (2002) go even further by arguing that speech perception highly benefits from abstract phonological representations in the mental lexicon: The less information is stored in the lexicon the less the change that it mismatches with the incoming acoustic signal or, put differently, the more likely a word is being recognized. However, despite the fact that phonologists have often (mostly implicitly) assumed psychological reality of phonological rules and representations, seldom have they gone out of their way to prove this in a way that has convinced psycholinguists. On the other hand, psychologists have largely ignored results from theoretical linguistics.

With the appearance of Optimality Theory (OT) in the early nineties the focus in generative phonology has been shifted from underlying representations (input) to surface representations (output). In OT phonology is viewed as a set of universal (innate) constraints that link input and output structures. Each language has ordered these constraints in a language particular way. The constraint order evaluates all possible output forms of words and selects one as the most optimal candidate. An important difference with the 'traditional' view of phonology is the focus on output structures. This is also reflected in the principle of 'Richness of the Base', which states that there are no restrictions on input representations. The constraint hierarchy contains different types of constraints. In the simplest model of OT the constraint set is composed of *markedness constraints*, which ban marked structure, previously captured by rules or morpheme structure conditions, and *faithfulness constraints*, which formally link input and output structures and demand that output structures equal input structures. Thus, to evaluate output structures, the input representation still is important, as it determines the satisfaction of faithfulness constraints. However, abstractness of phonological input representations is not an issue that is investigated in OT and in practice, many phonologists working in OT have adopted a much more liberal notion of lexical representation than earlier generative phonologists, often allowing for considerable phonetic details in the lexical representation, such as information about prosodic structure.

In psychology, too, the current view seems to be that representations contain detailed information, based on a growing number of studies showing that both adult and child listeners use detailed and context-sensitive information of spoken words. It has therefore been questioned whether one can hold on to the sharp division between speech processing and phonological representations (Bybee, 2001; Fisher, Church, & Chambers, 2004). However, so far, the existence of abstract phonological representations has not been completely denied, as listeners are able to recognize words despite of considerable variation across speakers and environments. Even though many researchers now favor phonetically detailed stored representations, often they also assume a process of 'normalization', which ensures that only context-independent information is kept in the sound representation (Lively, Pisoni, & Goldinger, 1994; see Fitzpatrick & Wheeldon, 2000 for a good overview).

In this chapter I want to show that children's production forms provide evidence for the claim that children (1) build up abstract phonological representations of words and (2) make generalizations over their own productive lexicon resulting in phonological constraints which are part of children's developing phonological system. This view has serious consequences for OT, at least as a theory of acquisition. On the one hand markedness constraints emerge in the course of development instead of being innately present. On the other hand, representations also develop; hence, the interpretation of faithfulness constraints is not stable either. Moreover, I assume that there is a single abstract phonological representation mediating between word recognition and production. In the second part of the chapter I argue that these claims not only make it possible to understand the production patterns attested in spontaneous child language, but also provide a way of linking results from early word recognition and production studies. I can only provide a sketch of my ideas, as each subpart is in it self very complicated. My view is undoubtedly colored by my own background as a linguist.

EARLY SPEECH PRODUCTION

One of the first acquisition studies, which tried to link formal phonological theory and language acquisition is Jakobson's monumental 'Kindersprache' (1941/1968). Jakobson assumed that "phonology begins with the selection of sounds accompanied by the first meaningful use of remembered sound patterns". In other words, the child does not start to build up a phonological system before he or she has words. Acquisition is seen as the unfolding of a universally determined feature tree. That is, the child sequentially acquires phonological contrasts following general markedness principles. As a consequence, the order of acquisition is fairly fixed, with only a certain number of possible learning paths. The first contrast is between a maximally closed, minimally sonorant consonant (labial stop) and a maximally open, maximally sonorant vowel (low vowel /a/). Within the stop series the next contrast to be acquired is the contrast between a labial and a coronal (/p/-/t/) and within the vowels between high and low vowels (/i/, /u/ versus /a/), etc. Although Jakobson expressed development in terms of features, it is implicit in his approach that the development takes place within lexical representations. Jakobson's theory has been very influential, but as Kiparsky and Menn (1977) convincingly argue, it is very hard to falsify.

In recent work Fikkert and Levelt (2004) have investigated place of articulation (PoA) patterns in early production in great detail to investigate how PoA is represented in early word forms. To this extent they coded spontaneous production data for PoA, while abstracting away from all other phonological features. This has been done with all data of five of the youngest children from the CLPF database. These children varied in age between 1;0 and 1;7 at the start of a one-year period of data collection (Fikkert, 1994; Levelt, 1994). We assumed the main PoA distinctions: Labial, Coronal, and Dorsal, for both consonants and vowels, as given in (1). All consonants in CVC(V) words were coded as Labial (P), Coronal (T), or Dorsal (K). All stressed vowels were coded as Labial/Dorsal (O)[1], Coronal, (I) or Low (A). As low vowels do not have features under the Articulator node, but only under the Tongue Height node I will not discuss low vowels here (but see Fikkert & Levelt, 2004).

(1)   PoA

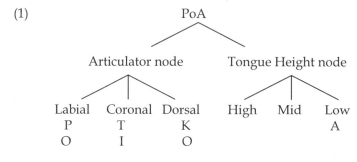

---

[1]All back (Dorsal) vowels are round (Labial). Dutch also has front rounded vowels, which are seldom produced by these children, and are ignored here.

We coded all words that children targeted in the same way. Words with clusters were reduced to the PoA of the first obstruent in obstruent-liquid clusters, and to that of the second obstruent in s-obstruent clusters. Thus, a word like *fles* 'bottle' is coded as PIT, *school* 'school' as KOT. Once all produced forms and targets were reduced to abstract PoA patterns, two striking observations appeared.

First, the shape of words in the children's lexicons only gradually becomes more complex. At the earliest stage (I) all words are 'harmonic', that is, all sounds of the word share PoA features, which seems to be determined by the stressed vowel of the word. Initially, most children only have labial POP and coronal TIT words, although some also have dorsal KOK word forms. The whole word shares just one PoA feature (C1 = C2 = V). The words do not seem to be segmentalized yet. Segmentalization is a gradual process. After a stage with only POP, TIT, and for some children KOK words, PIP, TOT, and KIK words appear. At this stage (II), the vowel may have a different PoA from the consonants, and can in fact be any vowel (symbolized by 'v'), while the consonants still share PoA features (C1 = C2). Thus, the representations are more differentiated than at the previous stage. Still later, the two consonants of the word may also differ in PoA features. Now, the word is fully segmentalized, and starts to resemble the adult representations.

Within the 'full segmentalization stage' there is also a clear ordering. First, children produce PvT words (III). Subsequently, words in which the second consonant is dorsal appear, like PvK and TvK (IV). Coronal seems to be unrestricted and is assumed to be the default PoA in Dutch (Paradis & Prunet, 1991; Levelt, 1994). This means that if a segment has no PoA specification in the lexicon, it will be realized as coronal, as we will see below. Words with labial in final position (V) and dorsal-initial words (VI) are generally acquired very late. This is schematized in (2)

(2)

Stage	Development	Added production patterns
I	$C_1 = C_2 = V$	POP, TIT, KOK
II	$C_1 = C_2$	PIP, TOT, KIK
III	$C_1 = P, C_2 = \emptyset$	PvT
IV	$C_2 = K$	PvK, TvK
V	$C_2 = P$	TvP
VI	$C_1 = K$	KvT, KvP

The second striking observation is that children's early productions are very 'faithful'. That is, children use the same PoA features as required to produce the target words. This implies a selection strategy: Only target words that can be produced correctly are attempted. At a later stage, a particular word pattern that has been produced for some time as a faithful rendition of a form in the child's lexicon will also be used for target words that the child is unable to produce correctly—and was unwilling to attempt before—resulting in unfaithful output patterns. In other words, once a child's production lexicon contains for example a certain number of PvT words, the child appears to generalize over this productive lexicon and derive a rule or constraint stating that labial consonants are at the left edge of the word: Labial Left (e.g., Levelt, 1994).

(3) Labial Left: [LAB
    If the word contains a labial, this labial feature must be realized at the left edge.

As soon as this rule or constraint is introduced into the child's phonology, its presence may be felt in words like *kip* 'chicken' or *slapen* 'sleep', which will be produced, unfaithfully, with an initial labial, by either undergoing Consonant Harmony (4a) or Metathesis (4b), two processes commonly mentioned in the literature on child phonology:

(4) Constraint [LAB at work
    a. Consonant harmony
       sloffen   /slɔfə[n]/   'slippers'   [pɔfə]
       kip   /kɪp/   'chicken'   [pɪp]
    b. Metathesis
       kip   /kɪp/   'chicken'   [pik]
       slapen   /slapə[n]/   'sleep'   [patə]

In other words, the child's generalization over his or her own productive lexicon has resulted in the beginning of an abstract phonological system with high-ranked markedness constraints.

Similarly, once the child's lexicon contains a number of words in which the second consonant is dorsal, this apparently leads to the following generalization about the feature: Dorsal consonants are not realized word-initially; that is, No Dorsal Left:

(5) No Dorsal Left: *[DORS
    Dorsal is not allowed at the left edge of a word.

As the result of the emergence of the constraint *[DORS dorsals are no longer permitted word-initially, not even in 'harmonic' words like *koek* 'cookie' or *kijk* 'look'. This is nicely illustrated in the data from Noortje in (6). While at an early stage KvK words, that is, words with two dorsal consonants between any vowel (V), were correctly produced by Noortje (6a), at a subsequent stage, these words are realized with a word-initial default coronal. This lasts for a period of three months (6b). After this period, dorsal-initial words reappear in Noortje's productive vocabulary (6c), clearly signaling the relaxation of the *[DORS constraint.

(6) Developmental production data of Noortje
  a. Holistic and partial segmentalization stage

koek	/kuk/	'cookie'	[kuk]	(2;3.7)
klok	/klɔk/	'clock'	[kɑk]	(2;5.23)
kijk	/kɛik/	'look'	[kɛik]	(2;5.23)
kikker	/kɪkər/	'frog'	[kɪk]	(2;2.21)

  b. Full segmentalization stage, early

koek	/kuk/	'cookie'	[tuk]	(2;8.17)
klok	/klɔk/	'clock'	[dɔk]	(2;8.17)
kijk	/kɛik/ 'look'	[tɛik]		(2;8.17)
kikker	/kɪkər/	'frog'	[tikɑ]	(2;9.1)

  c. Full segmentalization stage, late (adult-like)

| kruk | /krʉk/ | 'handle' | [kyk] | (2;9.29) |
| kuiken | /kœykə[n]/ | 'chicken' | [kœyk] | |

(2;10.12)

The two observations—gradual segmentalization and specification of lexical representations and initial faithfulness—together have led us to the following interpretations of the facts. At first, children's representations are holistic in the sense that the whole word has one PoA and is largely unanalyzed. Subsequently, children discover that consonants and vowels may have their own specification. This leads to more differentiated representations, in which the consonants of the word still share PoA features. Finally, children can fully segmentalize words.

For reasons of efficiency of parsing children may have generalized over the words in their relatively small productive lexicon: If all segmentalized words are P-initial, this may result in the constraint: [LABIAL. In a similar vain, the constraint *[DORSAL may emerge at a later stage based on the fact that if a word has a dorsal, it always appears in C2 position. Ultimately, the child has to learn that these constraints are only soft constraints in the language, as Dutch does allow words to begin with dorsal obstruents, and does not require labial to be word initial.

Alternative explanations all fare less well. One obvious explanation could be that the developmental order follows from the frequency of the different patterns in the input (e.g., Bybee, 2001). This explanation cannot account for the early stages in which words are completely or partially harmonic. Particularly, PvP and KvK words are of very low frequency in the target language; yet, they are produced early.

Others have argued that early production patterns may be explained in terms of ease of articulation (MacNeilage & Davis, 2000; Davis, MacNeilage, & Matyear, 2002). They have proposed four potentially universal organization patterns for babbling and early speech: the first and most basic pattern of labial consonants with central vowels (PA), subsequently, coronal consonants with front vowels (TI), followed by dorsal consonants with back vowels (KO), and finally words consisting of a labial consonant, a vowel and a coronal consonant (PvT). Although these patterns show similarity to the patterns described above, the model cannot account for the co-occurrence of labial consonants with round vowels, which are frequently attested in Dutch child language, nor for the U-shaped developmental pattern in (6) or the default behavior of coronal.

Optimality Theory does not offer a viable solution either. In this theory it is standardly assumed that representations are fully specified, that all markedness constraints outrank all faithfulness constraints at the initial stage, and that development implies the demotion of markedness constraints. Without going into much detail (see Fikkert & Levelt, 2004), it will immediately be clear that the data in (6) are hard to account for. The words in (6b) are neither more faithful nor more marked than those in (6a), and if anything, the forms in (6b) seem to be less marked than those in (6a), suggesting promotion of markedness constraints, which goes counter the current ideas about developmental reranking. The forms in (6b) cannot be explained as instances of lexical diffusion either, as for a period of three months all dorsal-initial words are affected, old and new.

We argue that an account that assumes both initially underspecified and developing representations and a developing grammar (consisting of emerging constraints) provides an adequate and elegant description of and insight in children's early production data.

INFANT PERCEPTION AND EARLY WORD RECOGNITION

There is an interesting paradox if we consider the results from early perception studies. These studies all show that children have a remarkably good knowledge of the sound structure of their native language even before having a lexicon. Ever since the pioneering research by Eimas and colleagues (1971), we know that newborns are excellent universal listeners who are able to discriminate virtually all possible contrasts employed by human languages. In their influential work Werker and Tees (1984) have shown that the perception of consonants becomes language-specific at about ten months. Apparently, children become more efficient listeners and pay attention to what is of importance to understand their native language. Kuhl, Williams, Lacerda, Stevens, and Lindblom (1992) have shown that vowel contrasts already become language specific at about six months of age. Thus, both in perception and production acquiring vowels precedes the acquisition of consonants. At nine months of age children are sensitive to the difference between phonotactically possible and impossible strings of segments in their native language, to low- and high-frequent phonotactic sequences, to the dominant stress pattern of their language (e.g., Jusczyk, 1998). In other words, all this research shows that children already know quite a bit about their native language before they have uttered their first word.

This knowledge comes in handy. Knowing how possible words of the native language should sound, is very useful in segmenting the acoustic speech stream into words, which is a prerequisite for word learning. Does this knowledge reflect the child's phonological system? And if so, how can it be that children use their phonology for early speech perception, but only later build up a phonology for speech production?

Of particular interest are recent results from early word recognition studies, which to date have delivered contradictory results. Word recognition experiments have shown that 7 1/2 month-old children are able to recognize words (*feet, bike*) in running speech after a brief period of familiarization to those words. However, if the test word is slightly changed after familiarization (to *zeet* or *feek*, or to *gike* or *bipe*) children are no longer able to recognize the words (Jusczyk & Aslin, 1995; Tincoff & Jusczyk, 1996), suggesting that infants must have stored the words with phonetic detail. However, research by Werker and colleagues (1997, 2002) showed that perception is considerably less perfect if the lexicon is involved. They combined word perception with word learning and showed that 14-month-old English children can distinguish between words that sound dissimilar (*neem–lif*) in a word learning task. However, they could not distinguish between words that sound very similar (*bih–dih, bin–din*). In a pure discrimination task, however, they had no problems distinguishing between *bin* and *din*, suggesting that children are still able to perceive phonetic detail. These results indicate that discrimination of the sound patterns of lexical items is not the same as identification of these items in the lexicon. Werker and colleagues suggested two possible explanations: either words are not stored with all phonetic detail, but are more abstract, or the processing load in the word learning task was too high for 14-month-old children. I argue that the two are linked.

UNDERSPECIFICATION ACCOUNTS FOR BOTH
EARLY PERCEPTION AND PRODUCTION

On the basis of production studies, we have argued for un(der)specified phonological representations. Given that the onset of speech more or less coincides with the age of the children in the experiments of Werker and colleagues, it could well be that children at this point in their development do not yet have fully segmentalized phonological representations. As these children have very small vocabularies (well below 25 words), it may be the case that these children still are in the first developmental stage (2), and that they have represented *bi(n)* and *di(n)* as holistic units, in which the vowel determines the PoA specification. In that case, both forms would have the same phonological representation (no specification of PoA features, as in (7ab)) and it is only expected that children do not distinguish the two in a word recognition study: Matching the features of the incoming signal with the stored features results 'no-mismatch' in (7ab). The fact that children can discriminate 'b' and 'd' in a pure discrimination task (features detected in the signal), does not mean that they use those features for specification in the lexicon.

(7)   Word perception based on abstract phonological representations

word learned	lexical feature (stage I)	feature in signal (C)	matching condition
a. bin / din	[Ø]	[lab] (bin)	no-mismatch
b. bin / din	[Ø]	[cor] (din)	no-mismatch
c. bon / don	[lab]	[lab] (bon)	match
d. bon / don	[lab]	[cor] (don)	mismatch

A representational account makes the prediction that there is a difference between *bin-din*, with an underspecified coronal vowel (7ab) and *bon-don*, with a specified vowel (7cd). The prediction is that children are able to distinguish *bon* from *don*, as here *don* mismatches with *bon* (7d), but not *bin* from *din*. This is currently being tested and initial results seem to confirm this prediction (Fikkert, Levelt, & Zamuner, in prep.).

By assuming underspecified lexical representations we can account for the gradual and systematic changes encountered in child production studies. Moreover, we can also provide a straightforward account for the difference between discrimination of sounds, which is based on phonetic detail, and identification of words, which is based on stored phonological features. If it is assumed that lexical phonological representations are phonetically detailed, the difference between perception, recognition, and production remains unaccounted for. Importantly, our account does not exclude the possibility that processing limitations underlie both production and perception in child language. Children can perceive all phonetic details, but only store the most salient phonological features in their mental representations. As children become better word learners, and have set up a phonological system to aid them in word recognition and word processing, they may be able to store more details. Similarly, in demanding perception tasks they may initially recover only the most salient features from the stored representation, while at a later stage when they become better in word learning, they will retrieve more features from the lexicon.

CONCLUSION

Acquisition is an important meeting place where linguistics and psycholinguists can lend each other an ear. We have seen that by using concepts from linguistics, in particular the PoA features in abstract phonological representations, insight can be gained into developmental patterns. These, in turn, can form a testing ground for psycholinguistic experiments. The abstraction over broad primary PoA features cannot be accounted for on purely phonetic grounds, as it is not immediately clear what the phonetic correlates of labial and dorsal consonants and vowels are. Rather, it seems to reflect a principled linguistic organization of sound structures. In turn, these abstract sound patterns can provide clear and testable hypothesis for both psycholinguistic research in general, and language acquisition in particular. Thus, acquisition studies may be a way to bridge the gap between linguistics and psychology.

I have furthermore argued that the set of constraints in child language emerges gradually, and it has to be seen whether ultimately children arrive at the same set of constraints that has currently been used in OT. Here, the detailed study of acquisition could ultimately feed linguistic theory. The study of child language acquisition has clearly shown that the current learnability models are all too simplistic in their assumptions of innate constraints and 'adult-like' representations. So far, constraints have hardly found their way into psycholinguistics experiments (but see Davidson, Jusczyk, & Smolensky, 2004). It is still a long but interesting way to test the psychological reality of linguistics theories.

ACKNOWLEDGMENTS

My thanks to Aditi Lahiri, Claartje Levelt, and Tania Zamuner for valuable comments on this chapter. This research is supported by NWO project 016.024.009.

REFERENCES

Bybee, J. (2001). *Phonology and language use.* Cambridge: Cambridge University Press.

Chomsky, N., & Halle, M. (1968). *The sound pattern of English.* New York: Harper & Row.

Chomksy, N. (2004). Key note lecture, GLOW 2004. Thessaloniki, Greece.

Davidson, L., Jusczyk, P. W., & Smolensky, P. (2004). The initial and final states: Theoretical implications and experimental explorations of Richness of the Base. In Kager et al. (Eds.), *Constraints in phonological acquisition* (pp. 321-368). Cambridge: Cambridge University Press.

Davis, B. L, MacNeilage, P. F., & Matyear, C. L. (2002). Acquisition of serial complexity in speech production: A comparison of phonetic and phonological approaches to first word production. *Phonetica, 59,* 75-109.

Eimas, P. D., Siqueland, E. R., Jusczyk, P. W., & Vigorito, J. (1971). Speech perception in infants. *Science, 171,* 303-306.

Ferguson, C. A., & Garnica, O. K. (1975). Theories of phonological development. In E. H. Lenneberg & E. Lenneberg (Eds.), *Foundations of language development* (Vol. 1, pp. 153-180). New York: Academic Press.

Fikkert, P. (1994). *On the acquisition of prosodic structure.* Doctoral dissertation, University of Leiden, HIL Dissertations 6. The Hague: HAG.

Fikkert, P., & Levelt, C. C., & Zamuner, T. (in prep.). Perception through production? Manuscript. Radboud University Nijmegen & University of Leiden.

Fikkert, P., & Levelt, C. C. (2004). How does place fall into place? The lexicon and emergent constraints in the developing phonological grammar. Manuscript. Radboud University Nijmegen & University of Leiden.

Fischer, C., Church, B. A., & Chambers, K. E. (2004). Learning to identify spoken words. In D. G. Hall & S. R. Waxman (Eds.), *Weaving a lexicon.* (pp. 3-40). Cambridge, MA: MIT Press.

Fitzpatrick, J., & Wheeldon, L. (2000). Phonology and phonetics in psycholinguistc models of speech perception. In N. Burton-Roberts, P. Carr & G. Docherty (Eds.), *Phonological knowledge. Conceptual and empirical issues* (pp. 131-160). Oxford: Oxford University Press.

Halle, M. (2002). *From memory to speech and back. Papers on phonetics and phonology 1954-2002.* Berlin: Mouton.

Jakobson, R. (1941/1968). *Child language, aphasia and phonological universals.* The Hague & Paris: Mouton.

Jusczyk, P. W. (1998). Constraining the search for structure in the input. *Lingua, 106,* 197-218.

Jusczyk, P. W., & Aslin, R. N. (1995). Infants' detection of sound patterns of words in fluent speech. *Cognitive Psychology, 29,* 1-23.

Kager, R., Pater, J., & Zonneveld, W. (2004). *Constraints in phonological acquisition.* Cambridge: Cambridge University Press.

Kaye, J. (1989). *Phonology: A cognitive view.* Hillsdale, NJ: Lawrence Erlbaum Associates.

Kiparsky, P., & Menn, L. (1977). On the acquisition of phonology. In J. MacNamara (Ed.), *Language and thought* (pp. 47–78). New York: Academic Press.

Kuhl, P. K. (2000). A new view of language acquisition. *PNAS* 97, 11850–11857.

Kuhl, P. K., Williams, K. A., Lacerda, F., Stevens, K. N., & Lindblom, B. (1992). Linguistic experience alters phonetic perception in infants by 6 months of age. *Science, 255,* 606–608.

Lahiri, A. & Marslen-Wilson, W. (1991). The mental representation of lexical form: A phonological approach to the recognition lexicon. *Cognition, 38,* 245–294.

Lahiri, A., & Reetz, H. (2002). Underspecified recognition. In C. Gussenhoven & N. Warner (Eds.), *Laboratory Phonology 7* (pp. 637–676). Berlin: Mouton.

Levelt, C. C. (1994). *On the acquisition of place.* Doctoral dissertation University of Leiden, HIL Dissertations 8. The Hague: Holland Academic Graphics.

Lively, S. E., Pisoni, D. B., & Goldinger, S. D. (1994). Spoken word recognition. In M. A. Gernsbacher (Ed.), *Handbook of psycholinguistics* (pp. 265–301). New York: Academic Press.

MacNeilage, P. F., & Davis, B. L. (2000). Origin of the internal structure of word forms. *Science, 288,* 527–531.

Paradis, C., & Prunet, J.-F. (1991). *Phonetics and phonology. Vol. 2. The special status of coronals.* San Diego, CA: Academic Press.

Prince, A., & Smolensky, P. (1993). Optimality Theory: Constraint interaction in generative grammar. Manuscript University of Rutgers & University of Colorado at Boulder.

Smith, N. V. (1973). *Acquisition of phonology.* Cambridge: Cambridge University Press.

Stager, C. L., & Werker, J. F. (1997). Infants listen for more phonetic detail in speech perception than in word learning tasks. *Nature, 388,* 381–382.

Steriade, D. (1995). Underspecification and markedness. In J. A. Goldsmith (Ed.), *The handbook of phonological theory* (pp. 114–174). Cambridge, MA: Blackwell.

Tincoff, R., & Jusczyk, P. (1996). Are word-final consonants perceptually salient for infants? Poster presented at the Fifth Conference on Laboratory Phonology.

Waterson, N. (1981). A tentative developmental model of phonological representation. In T. Myers, J. Laver & J Anderson (Eds.), *The cognitive representation of speech.* Amsterdam: North-Holland.

Werker, J. F., Fennell, C. T., Corcoran, K., & Stager, C. L. (2002). Infants' ability to learn phonetically similar words: Effects of age and vocabulary size. *Infancy, 3,* 1–30.

Werker, J. F., & Tees, R. C. (1984). Cross-language speech perception: Evidence for perceptual reorganization during the first year of life. *Infant Behavior and Development, 7,* 49–63.

4 Linguistic Representation and Language Use in Aphasia

Marco Haverkort
*University of Nijmegen, The Netherlands,
and Boston University, USA*

IMPAIRED LANGUAGE USE IN AGRAMMATISM

This paper argues that a clear distinction should be made between the representation of linguistic knowledge and the use that is made of such a knowledge representation in processes of language comprehension and production. Observations from agrammatic aphasia support such a distinction: Patients still have the grammatical knowledge of their native language available, but cannot make use of it quickly enough in *on-line* processes of language production and comprehension. Instead, patients adapt to these limitations by using syntactic structures that are less complex, for instance, by omitting some functional projections; these simplified structures can be handled by patients, because they impose less burden on working memory. In the second part of the paper, it is shown that choices of the impaired system, more specifically these adaptive simplifications of syntactic structure, are directed by the grammatical representation of the language. They interact with probabilistic information in the form of markedness.

Agrammatism often accompanies Broca's aphasia. Across languages, patients with agrammatism exhibit a number of characteristics. Their speech is slow and disfluent, their phrases are short, and their syntax is simplified: Subordinate clauses are rare, as is modification, and if the latter occurs at all, there is a preference for functor modification (DET-N, NUM-N). Functional morphemes are elements that form a closed class, that are generally phonologically and morphologically dependent, that

57

allow only one complement which is not an argument, and that lack referential content; they include auxiliaries, copular verbs, verbal inflections, prepositions, pronouns, articles, and conjunctions. In agrammatic aphasia, these are omitted or replaced by semantically and morphologically less marked forms (e.g., infinitival verb forms). The richer the inflectional paradigms in a language, the more substitutions are found. Finally, aphasic patients adhere to canonical word order (Menn & Obler, 1989).

In the literature, two types of accounts of agrammatism can be found. According to *grammar-based accounts*, patients have a grammar that differs qualitatively from that of normal, unimpaired language users: For instance, it lacks specific principles or constraints, or is parameterized differently. According to *processing-based accounts*, the phenomena found in the language of these patients can be explained in terms of quantitative restrictions on language processing mechanism, more specifically working memory limitations and timing problems during the process of integrating different types of grammatical information. A number of observations support the thesis that the grammatical representations of these patients are intact, but cannot be used adequately in *on-line* language comprehension and production due to processing limitations.

First, most patients show spontaneous post-onset recovery, during which there are no indications that the language is actually being re-acquired; this recovery—which is a consequence of a physiological 'clean-up' after the stroke—can most straightforwardly be explained by assuming that, while grammatical knowledge is available to the patient, he is not always able to use it adequately, due to processing problems, which in turn are due to physiological changes caused by the brain damage. This processing account can also explain within-patient variation from one moment to the next; here, assuming that the patient re-acquires the language is even less likely, as it concerns a wave-like sequence, where good and bad moments alternate. These fluctuations in behavior can be explained in terms of factors such as concentration, tiredness, distraction, etc. which can all influence fluency of processing.

An explanation along these lines is also supported by the observation that there is task-dependent variation: Whereas patients may perform at chance level with certain types of sentences (passives, object relative clauses, object clefts) in a sentence-picture matching task, they may perform close to ceiling level with these same types of sentences in a grammaticality judgment task, indicative of the availability of the patients' grammatical knowledge. Grammaticality judgment tasks are less taxing than sentence-picture matching, as one only needs to build up a syntactic representation for the incoming string of words: If that representation crashes during the derivation, the sentence is ungrammatical, but otherwise it is grammatical (Chomsky, 1995). In a sentence-picture matching task, however, a semantic representation also must be constructed and mapped onto the syntactic structure, conceptual representations of the pictures need to be built up, and the two must be compared, in order to find the closest match.

Syntactic priming tasks also suggest that grammatical representations are available to patients, but can only be used *on-line* with a delay. The time it takes subjects to make a cross-modal lexical decision on the italicized words in (1), for instance, is significantly less when the word in question fits the preceding syntactic context than when it does not (the latter indicated by *). This can be seen in Figure 4.1, where the vertical axis depicts the difference between the two decisions in milliseconds.

(1) a. we zijn *getest/*gewandeld*
        we are tested/walked
     b. we kunnen *praten/*neus*
        we can talk/nose
     c. op de *tafel/*rood*
        on the table/red   (Haarmann, 1993)

As Figure 4.1 shows, the aphasics show an equally robust priming effect as the normal, unimpaired control subjects—a facilitation of 60 ms in making the lexical decision—but only if the stimulus-onset asynchrony (SOA)—the time between hearing the last word of the syntactic context and being presented with the word for which a lexical decision needs to be made—is increased to 1100 ms. In other words, they need extra time

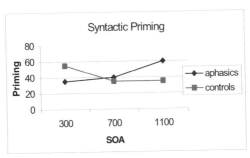

FIG. 4.1. Syntactic priming effects. The horizontal axis shows the SOA, i.e., the delay (in ms) between offset of the syntactic frame and presentation of the string of letters for lexical decision. The vertical axis shows priming, i.e., how much faster a lexical decision is made for words that fit in the syntactic frame than for words that do not.

for a significant effect to show up, that is, to build up the syntactic representation that facilitates the decision, whereas with normal, unimpaired subjects, the priming effect wears off when the SOA is increased. The fact that an effect shows up can only be explained if the relevant lexico-syntactic knowledge is available to the patients.

Similarly, semantic priming effects occur in normal, unimpaired subjects when, as in (2) and (3), at the trace position of a moved constituent a word is presented that is either semantically related or unrelated to the moved constituent. Lexical decision is faster for related words, as the semantic information of the moved constituent is re-activated at the position of the trace (Burkhardt, Pinango, & Wong, 2003).

(2) The kid loved the cheese $which_i$ the brand new microwave melted t_i yesterday afternoon while the whole family was watching TV
(3) *The butter in the small white dish$_i$* melted t_i after the boy turned on the brand new microwave

To obtain a similar priming effect for aphasics, however, the semantically (un)related word must be presented with a 600 ms delay, measured from the trace position. This again is consistent with slower processing. As with syntactic priming, the fact that systematic priming effects are found shows that the relevant syntactic knowledge is available to the patient, and that reactivation of the semantic information of the moved constituent takes place at the trace position, even when this only happens with a delay due to processing limitations.

This discussion shows that a clear distinction should be made between the grammatical representation and the use that is made of that representation in language processing: One can be impaired while the other is not. An account cast in terms of syntactic representations alone cannot explain the relevant data: Processing mechanisms are necessary in order to account for the pathological data in agrammatism.

FUNCTIONAL CATEGORIES IN AGRAMMATISM

Pollock's (1987) split INFL proposal led to a proliferation of functional categories (corresponding to the closed-class functional morphemes discussed in the preceding section) in syntactic theory. The hierarchical position of the different functional elements is a central issue. With just tense (TNS) and agreement (AGR) represented separately, there are two possible structures:

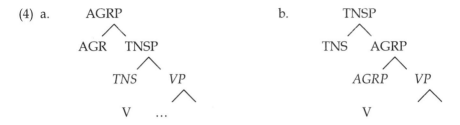

(4) a.   AGRP   b.   TNSP

In pre-minimalist models of syntax, the verb stem was assumed to move up to collect inflectional morphemes; as a consequence, there was an isomorphism between syntax and morphology, in that the structure of complex words that were thus derived reflected the underlying syntactic structure. As the following sets of examples show, the order of tense and agreement morphology in relation to the verb stem differs across languages, even though the linear order of tense and agreement is the same in these languages:

(5) a. parl-er-ai   French
         talk-FUT-1S
     b. legg-eva-no   Italian
         read-IMP-3P
     c. vertel-de-en   Dutch
         tell-PAST-PL
(6) a. ad-y-segh   Arabic
         FUT-3MS[1]-buy
     b. sa-ya-shtarii   Berber
         FUT-3MS-buy

Under pre-minimalist assumptions, this difference reflected a difference in syntactic structure between these languages. In French, Italian, and Dutch, the verb stem first moves up to tense and subsequently the [V-TNS] combination moves up to agreement, resulting in the complex structure [[V-TNS]-AGR]; the underlying structure is thus that in (4a), where AGR dominates TNS. Arabic and Berber differ, not just in that they are prefixing languages, but also in that the order in which tense and agreement morphemes append to the verb stem is the reverse, and hence the syntactic structure underlying these forms is the reverse: TNS is in a hierarchically higher position than AGR, as in (4b), so that it is added to

---

[1]3MS: third person masculine singular.

the verb stem after AGR, and thus occupies a more peripheral position with respect to the verb stem.

In minimalism (Chomsky, 1995), the idea that the verb stem moves up to merge with actual morphemes has been abandoned in favor of a more abstract idea: The verb is inserted in VP fully inflected and moves through the functional heads in its extended projection in order to check abstract features; the features on the verb need to be identical to those in the syntactic context in which it is inserted; if there is a mismatch (leading for instance to a disagreement between person and number features of the subject and the finite verb), the derivation crashes and is ungrammatical. One obvious reason why this more abstract derivation is to be preferred is that it does not run into problems with past tense forms of irregular verbs (*write—wrote*), where there is no morpheme being added to the stem, but the change in tense is represented by a vowel change instead. The more abstract representation of minimalism is thus to be preferred over pre-minimalist representations.

Establishing the hierarchical position of specific functional categories is more problematic under minimalist assumptions, however. In the French paradigm shown in (7), it can no longer be determined where the different functional heads are located with respect to each other; only the surface position of the verb with respect to other constituents can be established and hence the number and location of functional heads. The finite verb needs to precede both the negative particle *pas* and the adverb *souvent*, whereas the infinitival verb can follow both, appear in between them, but can not precede both, as summarized schematically in (8):

(7) a. * Elle ne pas souvent *mange* de chocolat
         she NEG not often eats of chocolat
    b. * Elle ne pas *mange* souvent de chocolat
    c.   Elle ne *mange* pas souvent de chocolat
    d.   Ne pas souvent *manger* de chocolat, c'est triste
           NEG not often eat of chocolat that is sad
    e.   Ne pas *manger* souvent de chocolat, c'est triste
    f. * Ne *manger* pas souvent de chocolat, c'est triste

(8) a. V_{fin} – NEG – Adv
    b.   NEG – V_{inf} – Adv
    c.   NEG – Adv – V_{inf}

Since there are three positions where the verb can surface, there must be minimally two functional heads, one preceding the negative particle and one in between this particle and the adverb position. The counterparts of structures (4a) and (4b), extended in (9) and (10) (see p. 64), could in principle both represent the structure of a French clause; the morphology of the verb no longer provides any information in this respect, and there is nothing in minimalist accounts that forces a specific order of feature checking, unlike in unification-based models of grammar, where the complex feature structures dictate that features be checked from the periphery inward (Pollard & Sag, 1994; Shieber, 1986).

The issue of the relative hierarchical position of tense and agreement can be determined quite straightforwardly on the basis of elicitation data from aphasics, however. Cahana-Amitay (1997) presented Dutch and English aphasics with sentences like those in (11); the patients' task was to complete the sentence by providing an inflected verb and any other material necessary to make it a grammatical sentence.

(11) a.　Vroeger waren ze gauw boos, maar tegenwoordig .....
　　　　　formerly were they quickly angry but nowadays
　　　b.　Tegenwoordig fietst hij naar school, maar vroeger .....
　　　　　nowadays rides he to school but formerly
　　　c.　Yesterday, she was at school, but today .....
　　　d.　This week, he walks to work, but last week .....

As this was a complex task for the patients, that needed to be done under time pressure, a lot of verb forms were used that were not appropriate in the given context. A first, important observation is that the substitutions patients used were all existing forms from the Dutch and English inflectional paradigm, respectively. Second, as Table 4.1 shows, not all logically possible types of substitution errors occurred:[2]

TABLE 4.1.

Error types (%)	English	Dutch
mixed tense/agreement	40.4	82.6
tense	59.6	15.9
agreement	0	1.5

[2]The difference in error rates between the Dutch and English patients can be explained in terms of the severity of the aphasia in the two subject groups: The Dutch patients were more severely affected.

(9)

(10)

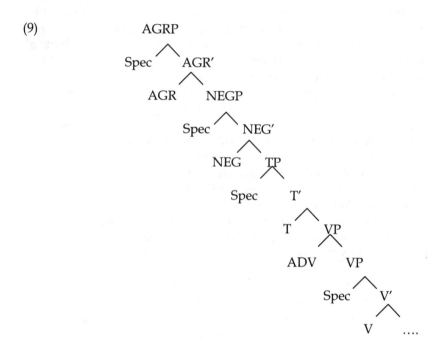

As can be seen from Table 4.1, two types of errors—combined tense and agreement errors (*yesterday I is away*) and pure tense errors (*yesterday I am away*)—occur, but a third, logically possible error type—pure agreement errors (*yesterday I were away*)—does not occur, or only very rarely. What this distribution of errors suggests is that tense dominates agreement:

(12) TP > AGRP > VP

Under this perspective, information can become unavailable from the top down when patients reduce complexity of the syntactic representation they produce, in order to meet processing limitations. Tense can thus become selectively unavailable – either because it is pruned from the tree, or because the verb cannot be moved up that far by the patient due to working memory limitations, and hence the relevant feature cannot be checked, and a mismatch is not registered by the patient. In still worse cases, both tense and agreement can become unavailable. When the verb moves up to tense to check its abstract features, though, it moves through agreement, which explains why pure agreement errors do not occur: Information can only become unavailable from the top down. It is not the case that segments anywhere in the representation become unavailable haphazardly, as that would predict that any logically possible type of substitution error should in fact occur, counter to fact. Under these assumptions, patients adhere to the syntactic constraints, that is, the functional architecture underlying sentence structure in their language, and the distribution of substitution errors is easily accounted for.

Further experiments along these lines by Kolk, Kok, Zevenbergen, and Haverkort (2003) have further shown an asymmetry in substitutions: Past tense verb forms are substituted by present tense forms, but only very rarely the other way around, if at all. The past tense forms in Dutch and English are more marked than their present tense counterparts.

Markedness can be determined along several different dimensions (see Jakobson, 1941/1968, and Croft, 2003 for more discussion):

(13) Markedness
  - Morphological markers: the marked value of a category has at least as many morphemes as the unmarked value
  - Order of acquisition: the unmarked value is acquired before the marked one; the mirror image is found in language loss
  - Language universals: the unmarked value occurs in at least as many languages as the marked value
  - Frequency: the unmarked value occurs at least as often as the marked value in a representative language sample

- Distribution: the unmarked value occurs in at least as many grammatical contexts (constructions) as the marked value
- Semantico-conceptual default: the unmarked interpretation of a form is the one it receives in a neutral context

Past tense in Dutch and English is more marked in terms of morphological structure: The past tense verb forms contain an extra morpheme (-ed in English, -de or -te in Dutch, cf. Booij, 2003), as illustrated by the Dutch paradigm in (14):

(14)   *Dutch*   wandelen 'walk'

		Present	Past
Sg.	1	wandel	wandel-de
	2	wandel-(t)	wandel-de
	3	wandel-t	wandel-de
Pl.	1	wandel-en	wandel-d(e)-en
	2	wandel-en	wandel-d(e)-en
	3	wandel-en	wandel-d(e)-en

A complexity ratio can be calculated by dividing the number of morphemes used in the present tense paradigm by those used in the past tense paradigm. When the ratio is close to 1, there is a pretty close match in complexity between the two paradigms; when it is lower than 1, it means the past tense paradigm is morphologically more complex than the present tense counterpart. For Dutch, the ratio is 0.55, clearly indicating that the past tense paradigm is morphologically more complex than its present tense counterpart.

Besides being morphologically more marked, the past tense is also more marked in terms of its distribution. A simple past tense in Dutch is used only in a restricted number of contexts (after a restricted set of adverbs, such as *vroeger* (formerly) and to indicate that an event occurred habitually); to express a past event, the perfect is used in the unmarked case and the simple past tense is losing ground, as in German.

Based on the dimensions of markedness summarized in (13), the markedness hierarchy for Indo-European tenses is as follows: present < past < future (where X < Y = X is less marked than Y). In a language where the complexity ratio is much closer to 1, such as Modern Hebrew, where it can be as high as 0.94 (see the paradigm for *write* in [15]), patients do not exhibit an asymmetry in their substitutions as the Dutch patients do (Friedmann & Grodzinsky, 1997, 2000; Kolk et al., 2003).

(15)   *Hebrew*   K-T-V   'write'

			Present	Past
Sg.	1	masc	kotev	katavti
		fem	kotevet	katavti
	2	masc	kotev	katavta
		fem	kotevet	katavt
	3	masc	kotev	katav
		fem	kotevet	katva
Pl.	1	masc	kotvim	katavnu
		fem	kotvot	katavnu
	2	masc	kotvim	katavtem
		fem	kotvot	katavten
	3	masc	kotvim	katvu
		fem	kotvot	katvu

CONCLUSION

In conclusion, module-specific, that is, lexico-syntactic information (phrase structure, argument structure) is retained in aphasia, and directs choices of the impaired system in simplifying syntactic structure. Domain-general components (working memory) are impaired; this is supported by data from Positron Emision Tomography (see Stowe, Haverkort, & Zwarts, 2004), and it is in line with the central assumptions of Adaptation Theory (Kolk et al.), in which timing and working memory constraints are the relevant factors. Moreover, probabilistic information, in the form of markedness, directs choices of the impaired system, leading the patient to choose less marked forms in the paradigm and thus leading to a clear asymmetry where markedness distinctions exist.

Assuming abstract linguistic representations allows for a unified account of both linguistic and psycholinguistic phenomena. It has also been shown that psycholinguistic evidence should be taken as serious evidence in deciding between different linguistic representations. There is thus an interdependence between linguistic representations and psycholinguistic processes.

ACKNOWLEDGMENT

The research of Marco Haverkort was supported by a grant from the Royal Netherlands Academy of Sciences (KNAW).

REFERENCES

Booij, G. (2003). *The morphology of Dutch*. Oxford: Oxford University Press.

Burkhardt, P., Pinango, M., & Wong, K. (2003). The role of the anterior left hemisphere in real-time sentence comprehension: Evidence from split intransitivity. *Brain and Language, 86*, 9-23.

Cahana-Amitay, D. (1997). *Syntactic aspects of production of verbal inflection in aphasia*. Doctoral dissertation, Boston University.

Chomsky, N. (1995). *The minimalist program*. Cambridge, MA: MIT Press.

Croft, W. (2003). *Typology and universals*. Cambridge: Cambridge University Press.

Friedmann, N., & Grodzinsky, Y. (1997). Tense and agreement in agrammatic production: Pruning the syntactic tree. *Brain and Language, 56*, 397-425.

Friedmann, N., & Grodzinsky, Y. (2000). Split inflection in neurolinguistics. In M.-A. Friedemann & L. Rizzi (Eds.), *The acquistion of syntax: Studies in comparative developmental linguistics*. London: Longman.

Haarmann, H. (1993). *Agrammatic aphasia as a timing deficit*. Doctoral dissertation, University of Nijmegen.

Jakobson, R. (1941/1968). *Child language, aphasia and phonological universals*. The Hague: Mouton.

Kolk, H., Kok, P., Zevenbergen, F., & Haverkort, M. (2003). Agrammatic sentence production: An experimental analysis. Manuscript University of Nijmegen.

Menn, L., & Obler, L. (1989). *Agrammatic aphasia. A cross-linguistic narrative sourcebook* (3 Vols.). Amsterdam: John Benjamins.

Pollard, C., & Sag, I. (1994). *Head-driven phrase structure grammar*. Chicago: University of Chicago Press.

Pollock, J.-Y. (1987). Verb movement, universal grammar and the structure of IP. *Linguistic Inquiry, 20*, 365-424.

Shieber, S. (1986). *An introduction to unification-based approaches to grammar*. Stanford: CSLI.

Stowe, L., Haverkort, M., & Zwarts, F. (2004). Rethinking the neurological basis of language. Manuscript University of Groningen & University of Nijmegen. To appear in *Lingua*.

5

Data Mining at the Intersection of Psychology and Linguistics

R. Harald Baayen
University of Nijmegen and Max Planck Institute for Psycholinguistics, Nijmegen, The Netherlands

Large data resources play an increasingly important role in both linguistics and psycholinguistics. The first data resources used by both psychologists and linguists alike were word frequency lists such as Thorndike and Lorge (1944) and Kučera and Francis (1967). Although the Brown corpus on which the frequency counts of Kučera and Francis were based was very large for its time, comprising some one million word forms carefully sampled from different registers of English, many common words did not appear in the frequency lists, while others appeared with counterintuitive frequencies of use.

Gernsbacher (1984) addressed this issue, claiming that subjective frequency estimates would be superior to objective frequency counts. Corpus-based frequency counts would be inherently unreliable due to regression towards the mean. In another corpus, higher frequency words would be less frequent, and lower frequency words would be more frequent. These considerations have led many psychologists to turn away from research directly addressing frequency effects in lexical processing. This distrust in psychology of corpus-based frequency data mirrors the rejection of corpora as a valid source of information about grammar in generative linguistics.

Fortunately, more and larger corpora were developed, driven in part by the needs of commercial lexicography, in part by the research interests of corpus linguistics, and in part by the growing needs for reliable data in computational linguistics and linguistic engineering. These developments made the creation possible of the CELEX lexical database, an initiative of the psycholinguist Levelt, which is widely used in both the (computational) linguistic and psycholinguistic research communities. For English, this resource provides the frequencies in the Cobuild corpus at the time that this corpus comprised some 18 million words. The British National Corpus (BNC) currently is the largest available tagged corpus of British English, with 100 million words, of which 10 million transcribed spoken English. Thus, linguistics now has at its disposal large data resources, although much remains to be done with respect to annotation and the sampling of everyday spoken language. The largest unstructured source of examples of language in use is, nowadays, the World Wide Web, which combines the advantage of quantity with the disadvantages of the absence of linguistic annotation and the restriction to written language.

The lexical resources developed specifically within psychology are relatively new, scarce, and small compared to linguistic corpora. Perhaps the most important large data resources are WordNet (Miller, 1990; Fellbaum, 1998), the Florida association norms (Nelson, McEvoy, & Schreiber, 1998), and the databases of visual lexical decision latencies, word naming latencies, and subjective frequency ratings of Balota, Cortese, and Pilotti (1999) and Spieler and Balota (1998). These resources provide psycholinguistics with a wealth of data on the behavioral properties for thousands of words. Although here too much remains to be done, especially from a morphological point of view, these behavioral data resources are a tremendous step forwards compared to the small numbers of items typically studied in factorial psycholinguistic experiments.

The aim of this chapter is to show that, when combined, the linguistic and psychological resources become a particularly rich gold mine for the study of the lexicon and lexical processing. I will illustrate the new methodological possibilities for data mining by examining the databases compiled by Balota and colleagues, in combination with CELEX, the BNC, and WordNet. For 1424 monomorphemic and monosyllabic nouns, and 832 monomorphemic and monosyllabic verbs, we study the predictive potential of a range of variables for three behavioral measures: visual lexical decision latencies and word naming latencies in ms, and subjective familiarity ratings on a 7-point scale.

In what follows, I will show that mining these combined resources yields several new insights. Section 1 examines the correlational structure of the predictors, and sheds new light on the nature of word frequency. Section 2 shows that subjective frequency ratings are an independent variable in their own right, just as response latencies in, for instance, visual lexical decision or word naming. Section 3 illustrates how the information carried by response latencies can be mined by means of lexical covariates, and calls attention to the methodological advantages of regression above factorial designs and the importance of relaxing the linearity assumption.

DATA MINING THE PREDICTORS

Lexical variables that are regularly considered in studies of lexical processing are frequency, length, number of neighbors, and bigram frequency. Frequency of use is well-studied and highly robust predictor. In this study, we will estimate a word's frequency of occurrence by means of the token frequency of its orthographic form in the subcorpus of written English that is part of the BNC, a subcorpus comprising 89.7 million words.

Although this subcorpus has the advantage of being large, it need not be the case that its frequency estimates are the best predictors for lexical processing. Frequency estimates based on spoken language are likely candidates of having superior predictivity, as speech is more fundamental to normal day-to-day communication than writing. Fortunately, the BNC also contains two subcorpora of spoken English. The demographic subcorpus (4.2 million words) provides transcriptions for spontaneous conversations of speakers sampled across England recorded with portable tape recorders. The context-governed subcorpus (6.2 million words) provides transcriptions of oral language in more formal contexts, often requiring preparation, such as speeches, sermons, and lessons. As the three subcorpora of the BNC differ in size, we scale the frequencies to a corpus size of 1 million words.

Word length is a second variable that is often taken into consideration. In what follows, we consider word length measured in letters. A third variable that has received widespread attention (e.g., Andrews, 1989; Grainger & Jacobs, 1996) is the density of a word's orthographic similarity neighborhood. Orthographic (or phonological) similarity is generally quantified in terms the number of words of the same length that are identical to a given target word except for one letter. The neighborhood density can then be estimated in terms of the count of such orthographic neighbors. A fourth variable is a word's mean bigram frequency. In this chapter, the mean bigram frequency is calculated as the mean of the logarithms of the frequencies of the pairwise letter pairs (including the initial and final spaces as letters). As the bigram consisting of the first two (non-space) characters might be predictive for word naming, it is included as well. Note that word length, neighborhood density, bigram frequency, initial bigram frequency, and also frequency of occurrence, are all measures of a word's form.

More recently, various lexical measures for a word's meaning have been explored. Best studied is the morphological family size measure, the number of complex words in which a given word occurs as a constituent (see e.g., Schreuder & Baayen, 1997). Following Moscoso del Prado (2003), we also consider two related measures, the derivational and inflectional entropy. The entropy of a probability distribution is defined as $\Sigma\ p\ \log(1/p)$, and quantifies the amount of information of that distribution. Applied to the probabilities (estimated by relative frequencies) of a word's morphological family members, one obtains the derivational entropy, which can be viewed as a variant of the family size measure in which the family members are weighted for their token frequency. The entropy can also be calculated for a word's inflectional variants, in which case it estimates the information complexity of that word's inflectional paradigm.

Two other semantic measures first explored in Baayen, Feldman, and Schreuder (2004) address a word's number of meanings by means of the synsets listed in the WordNet resource. WordNet (Miller, 1990) is a lexical database in which words are organized in synonym sets, known as synsets. For *hand*, WordNet lists several synsets, for instance, {*hand, manus, hook, mauler, mitt, paw*}, {*handwriting, hand, script*}, {*hand, deal*}, {*'hired hand', hand, 'hired man'*}, {*pass, hand, reach, 'pass on', 'turn over', give*}. By counting the number of different synsets in which a word is listed in WordNet, we can gauge how many different meanings a word has. In what follows, I consider two complementary measures. The first measure counts the number of different synsets in which the word is listed as such. I will refer to this measure as the simple synset count. The second measure counts the number of synsets in which the word is part of a compound or phrasal unit (such as *hired hand* in the *hand* example). I will refer to this count as the complex synset count.

Many of these predictors are known to be intercorrelated. For the system of correlations of frequency, word length, number of meanings, and dispersion (the number of different texts in which a word occurs), the reader is referred to Köhler (1986). The correlational structure of family size, derivational entropy, word frequency, and word length is investigated in Moscoso del Prado (2003). In the following analyses, we logarithmically transformed all measures with skewed distributions (frequency, family size, derivational entropy, and the synset measures) in order to reduce potential atypical effects of high-valued outliers.

Figure 5.1 provides a summary of the correlational structure of the numerical predictors by means of a hierarchical cluster analysis using Spearman's ρ^2 as a nonparametric distance measure. Interestingly, the BNC frequency measures cluster with the WordNet synset measures and also with the paradigmatic morphological measures family size and derivational entropy. The measures of word form, word length, mean bigram frequency, and number of neighbors, appear in a different branch of the dendrogram together with the frequency of the initial bigram. Although all numerical predictors are correlated, word frequency emerges from the distributional statistics of English primarily as a semantic measure, and not as a measure of form-related lexical properties. Baayen et al. (2004) came to similar conclusions using a different technique, principal components orthogonalization. This distributional observation supports the hypothesis of Balota and Chumbley (1984) that the word frequency effect has a strong post-access component, and argues against the idea that frequency effects would arise primarily or exclusively at the access level.

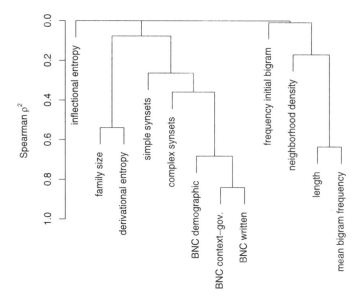

FIG. 5.1. Hierarchical clustering of the predictors for the ratings and response latencies in the Balota database.

Note, finally, that the written frequencies reveal a tighter correlation with the context-governed frequencies than with the demographic frequencies, the frequencies recorded for the spontaneous conversations. This tighter correlation is in line with the more formal character of both the context-governed samples and the written samples in the British National Corpus. In the next sections, we see that this clustering of the frequency measures is reflected in behavioral measures of lexical processing.

DATA MINING FAMILIARITY RATINGS

Are familiarity ratings an alternative, perhaps better frequency measure than corpus-based frequency counts, as suggested by Gernsbacher (1984)? Although this is commonly believed, we can ask ourselves whether ratings measure only frequency of occurrence. Would subjects be able to tap into frequency without being influenced by the many other variables that are known to affect, for instance, lexical decisions?

To address this question, let's fit a multiple regression model to the ratings in the database of Balota and colleagues. Before doing so, two preliminary questions need to be addressed. First, the substantial correlational structure characterizing our set op predictors points to a collinearity problem. When the predictors are highly collinear, as in this data set, it is difficult to tease the effects of the individual predictors apart (see Baayen et al., 2004, for detailed discussion). For the present purpose, it suffices to address the high collinearity of the three frequency measures. It makes no sense to include all three in the same regression model. In what follows, I therefore selected the written frequency as primary frequency measure. In order to study the potential predictivity of the other frequency measures, I constructed two new variables, the standardized differences between the written frequency and the two spoken frequencies. These standardized differences are only mildly correlated with the written frequencies ($r = -0.069$ for the demographic standardized differences, $r = -0.19896$ for the context-governed standardized differences).

Second, it is important not to impose a-priori that a predictor enters into a linear relation with the dependent variable. A flexible way of exploring potential non-linearities is to make use of restricted cubic splines (see e.g., Harrell, 2001: 16-24). In construction, a spline is a flexible strip of metal or piece of rubber that is used for drawing the curved parts of objects. In statistics and physics, a spline is a function for fitting nonlinear curves. This function is itself composed of a series of simple cubic polynomial functions defined over a corresponding series of intervals. These polynomials are constrained to have smooth transitions where they meet, the knots of the spline. The number of intervals is determined by the number of knots. In order to capture more substantial nonlinearities, one will need more knots. In other words, the number of knots is a smoothing parameter. In the following analyses, I have used the minimum number of knots necessary to model non-linearities.

Figure 5.2 shows that subjective familiarity ratings are indeed a dependent variable in their own right. Each panel shows the partial effect of a predictor on the rating scores in the database of Balota and colleagues in the model resulting from a stepwise multiple regression analysis. The first row of panels shows relations that have a significant non-linear component (p < 0.0001 for the nonlinear component of word frequency, p = 0.0002 for the nonlinear component of the frequency difference, and p = 0.0409 for the nonlinear component of family size).

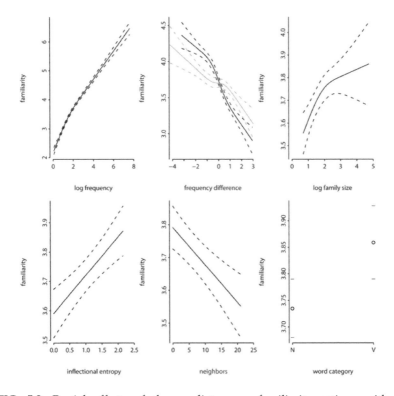

FIG. 5.2. Partial effects of the predictors on familiarity ratings with 95% confidence intervals. Only significant effects (linear and nonlinear) are shown ($\alpha = 0.05$). $R^2 = 0.696$, bootstrap corrected $R^2 = 0.695$.

These non-linear relations were fitted using restricted cubic splines with four, four, and three knots respectively. The second row of panels presents the linear effects of inflectional entropy and neighborhood density, and the factorial effect of word category.

Note, first of all, that there is a strong nearly linear relation between written frequency in the BNC and familiarity ratings, with very narrow 95% confidence intervals. This shows that subjective frequency estimates are good predictors for objective corpus-based (relative) frequencies, as expected.

The second panel in the top row shows that familiarity ratings decrease as the frequency difference increases. The black lines represent the frequency difference with the demographic subcorpus (the spontaneous conversations), the grey lines represent the corresponding difference with the context-governed subcorpus (the more formal oral language). Positive values indicate a word is encountered more in writing than in speech, negative values indicate the word is more typical of speech than of writing. What this panel shows, then, is that words that are typical of speech are rated more highly than words that are predominantly written. Note that this effect is stronger for the demographic subcorpus than for the context-governed subcorpus. This suggests that an optimal frequency measure for predicting ratings should be based on a large corpus of spontaneous conversations. Apparently, subjective frequency estimates tap primarily into frequency of exposure and use in spontaneous everyday spoken discourse.

The remaining panels show that subjective frequency estimates capture more than just frequency of occurrence. Family size predicts the ratings, with higher families leading to higher ratings (cf. Schreuder & Baayen, 1997). The nonlinearity points to a ceiling effect for large families. A large inflectional entropy likewise leads to higher ratings, suggesting that a greater information load of the inflectional paradigm causes a word to be perceived as more familiar. On the other hand, neighborhood density is negatively correlated with the familiarity ratings. Note that even word category differences (Wcat) are reflected in the ratings, with verbs eliciting higher ratings than nouns.

The observation that familiarity ratings are an independent variable in their own right, just as response latencies or eye fixation durations, has important methodological consequences. Ratings should not be used as a substitute for corpus-based frequency counts. Matching for familiarity ratings, for instance, implies at least partial matching for a series of other variables, potentially including variables of interest, and reduces the likelihood of finding significant effects. Likewise, familiarity ratings should not be included along with frequency counts in a regression analysis of, for instance, lexical decision, just as one would not normally include lexical decision latencies as a predictor for, for example, eye fixation durations.

DATA MINING RESPONSE LATENCIES

The databases compiled by Balota and colleagues also make available response latencies for visual lexical decision and word naming. Again, we make use of restricted cubic splines in order to trace potential nonlinearities. In order to reduce the skewness of the distributions of latencies, the latencies in both tasks were logarithmically transformed (using the natural logarithm). Figure 5.3 shows the partial effects of the predictors on word naming, Figure 5.4 is the corresponding plot for visual lexical decision. Only significant predictors are shown, and nonlinearities are shown only when significant.

As in the analysis of the ratings, frequency of use as gauged by the BNC counts of written English is a strong predictor for both tasks. Note that the confidence intervals are quite narrow, and more so for the low frequency words than for the high-frequency words. The wider confidence intervals for the higher frequencies are a consequence of the relative data sparseness in the higher frequency ranges, even after the logarithmic transform. The narrow confidence intervals even for the lowest frequency ranges show that there is no reason to be particularly concerned about the reliability of corpus-based estimates of the frequencies (probabilities) of low-frequency words.

In both lexical decision and word naming, the frequency difference measure comparing the written frequency with the frequency in the spontaneous conversations (the demographic subcorpus) is positively correlated with RT. No such correlation is present for the comparison with the frequencies in the context-governed subcorpus. Whereas the ratings revealed a reduced effect for the context-governed counts, the latency measures restrict the effect to truly spontaneous, unprepared speech. This supports the hypothesis that the word frequency effect is grounded in casual day-to-day verbal interaction.

What is striking is the large number of predictors that enter into nonlinear relations with the response latencies. Some of these non-linearities are readily interpretable. For instance, there seems to be a floor effect for word frequency in both tasks for the higher-frequency words. The U-shaped curves for word length might reflect response optimization for the most frequently occurring word length (the median word length in the data is 4 letters). However, for the U-shaped curves for the family size measure and for the simple synset counts I do not have

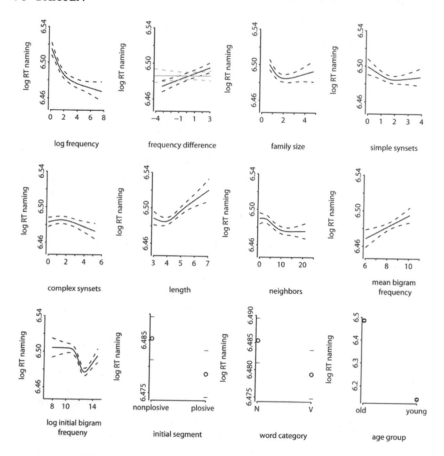

FIG. 5.3. Partial effects of the predictors on word naming latencies with 95% confidence intervals. Only significant effects (linear and nonlinear) are shown (α = 0.05). R2 = 0.942, bootstrap corrected R2 = 0.941.

an explanation. Apparently, the advantage of having, for example, more morphological family members turns into a disadvantage when the family size becomes very large. More research and modeling is required here.

Note that in both tasks, the age group of the participants is a very strong predictor of the response latencies, as illustrated by the relevant panels on the third rows of Figures 5.3 and 5.4. The 95% confidence intervals are so narrow that they are indistinguishable form the circles representing the group means.

There are a number of differences between the two tasks. In visual lexical decision, the effect of word category did not reach significance, in word naming, it did. The log initial bigram frequency, included as a covariate for word naming, turned out to be a significant predictor in both tasks, a simple facilitatory linear predictor in visual lexical decision, and a strangely shaped non-linear predictor in word naming. In the word naming study, the nature of the initial phoneme (plosive vs. non-plosive) was included as a control variable for the voicekey. Plosives elicited shorter latencies than non-plosives: The voice key is especially sensitive to the burst of the plosive.

Another interesting difference between the two tasks concerns the effect of neighborhood density, non-linear but facilitating in word naming, but U-shaped in visual lexical decision. In Figure 5.4, the panel for neighborhood density on the second row, with the scale on the Y-axis fixed to the range of the frequency effect, is repeated on the third row, with the scale on the Y-axis set to the range of the effect of neighborhood density itself. Although the effect of neighborhood density is relatively small, the U-shaped form of the graph in the visual modality is especially interesting, as it suggests an inhibitory component for larger neighborhood sizes, as reported for French (Grainger & Jacobs, 1996) but not for English (Andrews, 1989). An inhibitory effect for neighborhood density in reading was also observed by Baayen et al. (2004) after addressing the problem of collinearity, once the effect of semantic variables has been partialled out.

From a methodological point of view, these nonlinearities bear witness to the importance of exploratory regression analysis without a-priori assumptions about linearity, and to the dangers of factorial designs for the study of numeric variables. Consider again the count of orthographic neighbors in visual lexical decision. A factorial design contrasting high versus low conditions for this variable would fail to observe that it is a relevant predictor. In addition, the arbitrariness of the cutoff points for factorial contrasts increases the risk of inconsistent results across replication studies using different materials. The inconsistent results reported in the literature for neighborhood density might have arisen precisely because of these reasons.

CONCLUDING REMARKS

Data mining the combined large lexical data resources of linguistics and psychology has led to a number of insights. First of all, it suggests that the linguistic variable of 'word frequency' should be rehabilitated in psychology. The present study illustrates the reliability of word frequency as a predictor of behavioral measures, even though Gernsbacher (1984) previously discredited such counts and falsely accused them of regression toward the mean (see Baayen, Moscoso del Prado, Schreuder, & Wurm, 2003, for technical discussion).

In addition, the measure comparing written frequency in the BNC with spoken frequencies revealed that frequency in spontaneous, unprepared speech is the optimal predictor. As pointed out by Gernsbacher (1984), corpus-based frequency counts are sometimes rather counterintuitive, especially when based on written language sampled from more formal registers. This study provides an example of how this issue can be addressed by bringing appropriate covariates for register variation such as the frequency difference measures into the statistical model.

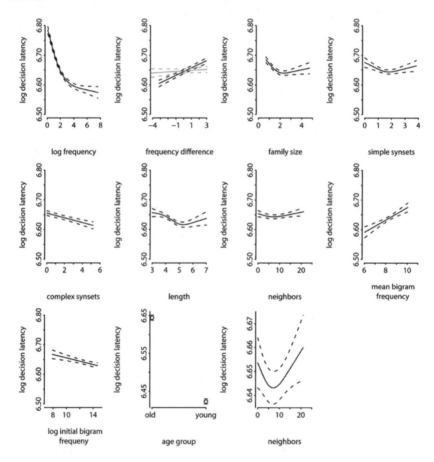

FIG. 5.4. Partial effects of the predictors on visual lexical decision latencies with 95% confidence intervals. Only significant effects (linear and nonlinear) are shown ($\alpha = 0.05$). $R^2 = 0.729$, bootstrap corrected $R^2 = 0.727$.

Second, this exercise in data mining shows that the complexity of subjective frequency ratings has been underestimated. Introspection does not produce pure estimates of frequency of occurrence, but estimates that capture a wide range of other variables in addition to frequency. The methodological consequence of this finding is that matching on familiarity, or including familiarity as a covariate, should be avoided.

Third, this study demonstrates the methodological importance of data mining with tools that are appropriate for detecting the functional relations between predictors and behavioral measures in their full complexity. Current research on lexical processing makes use mostly of factorial designs and occasionally of linear regression. With respect to factorial designs, however, the dichotomization required to transform a numerical variable into a factor brings along a number of disadvantages.

The imposition of factor levels such 'high' and 'low' forces the researcher to impose arbitrary cutoff points, and the gain in power obtained by considering only extreme values is offset by the risk of having studied atypical extremes and comes with the price of having no insight whatsoever into the shape of the regression function, which, as the examples discussed in this study demonstrate, may be highly non-linear. U-shaped curves such as observed for neighborhood density may wreak havoc in a literature based exclusively on factorial experiments. It is important to realize the importance of non-linearity. Straight lines are ubiquitous in man-made environments, but exceptional in the natural world. Note that even the linear relations in Figures 5.3 and 5.4 imply non-linear relations between the untransformed response latencies and the relevant predictors — there is not a single linear predictor for the RTs in milliseconds.

An additional problem with factorial designs is that they require matching on all other potentially relevant variables. For the lexical data such as illustrated in this chapter, we have no less than 9 significant numerical predictors for visual lexical decision as well as for word naming, and more variables are sure to be discovered. It is simply impossible to match a dichotomous contrast in one of these variables on all the others. In other words, even though for many psycholinguists a 'real' experiment is a factorial experiment, this view is misguided for any domain of inquiry in which the dichotomized continuous variable is one of a cluster of correlated variables. In short, only use a factor when no more fine-grained numerical information is available.

Even when the main variable of interest is a true factor (such as word category in the present examples), it is important to include all known potentially relevant covariates in the design, in order to guarantee incrementality in research and to avoid a random walk through the complex multidimensional parameter space that is under investigation in (psycho)linguistics.

A final insight that this study has to offer is that the tighter correlation of the word frequency measure with measures of word meaning compared to measures of word form sheds new light on the (psycho)linguistic interpretation of lexical frequency. Whereas previous research in quantitative linguistics has addressed the mathematical form of the functions relating frequency to other lexical measures (see e.g., Köhler, 1986), the present study addressed the tightness of these relations. This led to the insight that that word frequency is primarily a measure of conceptual familiarity.

In conclusion, the construction of large data resources, both in linguistics and in psychology, although labor intensive and time consuming, is essential for understanding the more subtle details of linguistic structure and its consequences for language processing.

REFERENCES

Andrews, S. (1989). Frequency and neighborhood size effects on lexical access: Activation or search? *Journal of Experimental Psychology: Learning, Memory, and Cognition, 15,* 802-814.

Baayen, R., Feldman, L., & Schreuder, R. (2004). *Collinearity and non-linearity in regression analyses of simple word recognition, word naming, and subjective frequency estimation.* Manuscript submitted for publication.

Baayen, R. H., Moscoso del Prado, F., Schreuder, R., & Wurm, L. (2003). When word frequencies do NOT regress towards the mean. In R. H. Baayen & R. Schreuder (Eds.), *Morphological structure in language processing* (pp. 463-484). Berlin: Mouton de Gruyter.

Balota, D. A., & Chumbley, J. I. (1984). Are lexical decisions a good measure of lexical access? The role of word frequency in the neglected decision stage. *Journal of Experimental Psychology: Human Perception and Performance, 10,* 340-357.

Balota, D., Cortese, M., & Pilotti, M. (1999). *Visual lexical decision latencies for 2906 words.* [http://www.artsci.wustl.edu/~dbalota/lexical_decision.html]

Fellbaum, C. E. (1998). *WordNet: An electronic database.* Cambridge: MIT Press.

Gernsbacher, M. A. (1984). Resolving 20 years of inconsistent interactions between lexical familiarity and orthography, concreteness, and polysemy. *Journal of Experimental Psychology: General, 113,* 256-281.

Grainger, J., & Jacobs, A. M. (1996). Orthographic processing in visual word recognition: A multiple read-out model. *Psychological Review, 103,* 518-565.

Harrell, F. E. (2001). *Regression modeling strategies (Statistics and Computing Series).* New York: Springer.

Köhler, R. (1986). *Zur linguistischen Synergetik: Struktur und Dynamik der Lexik.* Bochum: Brockmeyer.

Kučera, H., & Francis, W. N. (1967). *Computational analysis of Present-Day American English*. Providence, RI: Brown University Press.

Miller, G. A. (1990). Wordnet: An on-line lexical database. *International Journal of Lexicography, 3*, 235-312.

Moscoso del Prado, F. (2003). *Paradigmatic effects in morphological processing: Computational and cross-linguistic experimental studies.* MPI Series in Psycholinguistics, Max Planck Institute for Psycholinguistics, Nijmegen, The Netherlands.

Nelson, D. L., McEvoy, C. L., & Schreiber, T. A. (1998). *The University of South Florida word association, rhyme, and word fragment norms.* http://www.usf.edu/FreeAssociation/.

Schreuder, R., & Baayen, R. H. (1997). How complex simplex words can be. *Journal of Memory and Language, 37*, 118-139.

Spieler, D. H., & Balota, D. A. (1998). *Naming latencies for 2820 words.* [http://www.artsci.wustl.edu/~dbalota/naming.html]

Thorndike, E. L., & Lorge, I. (1944). *A teacher's word book of 30.000 words.* New York: Columbia University Press.

6

Establishing and Using Routines During Dialogue: Implications for Psychology and Linguistics

Martin J. Pickering
Department of Psychology, University of Edinburgh, UK

Simon Garrod
Department of Psychology, University of Glasgow, UK

The study of dialogue provides a radically different conception of psycholinguistics from the traditional study of language comprehension and language production in isolation. In what ways might the study of dialogue prove informative about the relationship between language processing and adjacent areas of enquiry, such as linguistics, language acquisition, and cognitive psychology more generally? One particular topic that appears very different when considered in terms of dialogue processing is the nature of the mental lexicon.

The standard position in language processing is that the mental lexicon is a largely fixed resource, acquired during early development. Although people can of course add new lexical entries during their adult life, this is generally seen as a marginal activity. Studies of processing assume that people already know the language that they use, and that the interesting questions involve how they put that knowledge to use (e.g., selecting between pre-existing meanings for a word). There is a clear demarcation between acquisition and processing. In addition, the lexicon is treated as a store that principally consists of small units (either words or morphemes) and that knowledge of larger units is largely limited to idioms, which are regarded as fairly peripheral to "core" language processing.

In this chapter, we propose an alternative view of the mental lexicon that is consistent with evidence from dialogue. We show that interlocutors make use of fixed or semi-fixed expressions during a particular conversation with meanings that are established through that conversation. We argue that they "routinize" these expressions by storing them in the mental lexicon, normally for that conversation alone. This requires a conception of the lexicon in which complex expressions (of all kinds, not just established idioms) can be stored alongside more traditional lexical units. On this view, the lexicon can be constantly and dynamically updated, and the strict division between acquisition and adult usage is removed. It accords with some recent linguistic accounts, particularly that developed by Jackendoff (2002).

We first outline our conception of dialogue as a largely automatic process of alignment between interlocutors. We then explain how routines get established as part of this process of alignment, and interpret routinization in terms of Jackendoff's (2002) conception of the mental lexicon. Finally, we discuss some implications of our account.

DIALOGUE AS ALIGNMENT

It is fairly uncontroversial that the most natural and basic form of language use is dialogue. It is acquired early in life, does not require special training, and appears to be a universal skill. In contrast, producing and even understanding monologue is complex and difficult, and it is by no means always fully mastered. Therefore it is perhaps surprising that psycholinguistics has largely concentrated on the study of monologue, as in experiments concerned with understanding and producing words and utterances in isolation. Even when the task is fairly natural, as in text comprehension during reading, the skill that is used is clearly derivative. Although there is no reason to doubt that the study of monologue will be highly informative about the way that people represent and process language, it would surely be sensible to invest at least equivalent effort into the study of dialogue. In particular, we must be aware that the study of monologue will not necessarily provide a valid account of language use in all its diversity.

Experimental psychology (and cognitive science more generally) seeks to explicate the mechanisms and processes that underlie our mental abilities. In particular, it hopes to develop mechanistic accounts of cognitive processes. These goals, common to most psychological work on memory, perception, reasoning, and so on, are equally accepted by the psycholinguistic community that tends to investigate monologue. When applied to psycholinguistics, this approach has been branded the 'language as product' tradition by H. H. Clark (1996). In the much more limited tradition of research into dialogue, there is less interest in explication of mental mechanisms. In part, this is because of the considerable influence of Clark and his championing of the alternative 'language as action' tradition, which is concerned with the way that language is used, and does not regard a mechanistic model as its primary goal.

Whereas we accept that understanding language use is an important and laudable goal, we hold to the standard mechanistic goals of cognitive psychology. Pickering and Garrod (2004) argue that it is possible to develop a mechanistic psychology of dialogue just as we have developed mechanistic psychologies of memory, perception, reasoning, and indeed monologue. The main part of that article is an attempt to outline such a theory, which we call the interactive-alignment account of dialogue.

According to this account, a conversation is successful to the extent that interlocutors end up with aligned situation models. Informally, this means that they come to understand the relevant aspect of the world in the same way. More formally, we assume that people construct situation models, which capture key elements of the situation under discussion (Sanford & Garrod, 1981; Zwaan & Radvansky, 1998). According to Zwaan and Radvansky, the key dimensions encoded in situation models are space, time, causality, intentionality, and the identity of the main characters. So in a successful conversation, interlocutors will have similar representations of the time and location of events, the main characters involved, and so on.

The central question, therefore, is how do interlocutors achieve this alignment? In contrast to 'intentional' views of conversation, where interlocutors are regularly inferring what they believe their listener knows or does not know and are trying to work out what they should say in order to be informative to their listeners, we assume that alignment proceeds in a largely automatic manner. Although we do not deny a role to intentional processes, and certainly accept that people are in principle capable of extensive modeling of their partners' mental states, we believe that the pressures of actual conversation (having to listen, to plan one's response in a very short time, to determine exactly when to speak, and so on) mean that in practice interlocutors perform very little 'other modeling'.

Pickering and Garrod (2004) argue that interlocutors do not simply align their situation models, but rather align their representations at many (indeed, all) levels of representation at the same time. In itself, this would not lead to alignment of the situation model, but Pickering and Garrod propose that alignment at one level of representation leads inexorably to alignment at other levels of representation. Specifically, alignment at one level is enhanced by greater alignment at other levels.

This leads to alignment of the situation model, without interlocutors needing to formulate the explicit goal of aligning their models. Even if people fail to align their representations in a specific way, Pickering and Garrod argue they make use of an automatic repair mechanism. Explicit repair of misalignment is very much a last resort. This explains why conversation is so much easier than the complexity of the task would suggest (Garrod & Pickering, 2004).

It is best to explain the model with reference to a few specific experimental results. Garrod and Anderson (1987) noticed that interlocutors tend to converge on particular referring expressions in a 'maze game' task where pairs of participants had to negotiate their way around mazes. For example, if one interlocutor referred to the row of the maze as a *floor*, the other would tend to do so too. In a task involving describing cards, Brennan and Clark (1996) found that partners tended to mirror each others' (often idiosyncratic) descriptions, and indeed often retained distinctions (e.g., specific details about the type of object involved) when these distinctions were no longer necessary for identification. These results suggest that interlocutors rapidly converge on names for referring expressions. Importantly, these studies (and others) found that explicit negotiation about what to call an object was extremely rare and certainly not necessary for alignment. Our proposal (in line with Garrod & Anderson, 1987) is that interlocutors are primed by each other to employ the same form. Since the priming takes place between comprehension and production, it is most straightforwardly compatible with a common coding or 'parity' between production and comprehension, as is increasingly assumed in theories of the relationship between perception and action (e.g., Hommel, Müsseler, Aschersleben, & Prinz, 2001).

Interlocutors also tend to align syntactically. Following classic demonstrations that speakers perseverate in their choice of syntactic structure in isolated production (Bock, 1986), Branigan, Pickering, and Cleland (2000) had two participants take it in turns to describe cards to each other and to find those cards in an array. One of the participants was a confederate of the experimenter who produced scripted responses (depending on experimental condition). For example, the confederate might describe a card as either *the cricketer giving the plate to the diver* (the *prepositional object* or *PO* form) or as *the cricketer giving the diver the plate* (the *double object* or *DO* form). The experimental subject tended to mirror the syntactic form used by the confederate, with a PO form being considerably more likely after the PO prime and a DO form being considerably more likely after a DO prime. Similar priming occurs within noun phrases (Cleland & Pickering, 2003) and even between languages, with a Spanish passive increasing the likelihood of an English passive in bilinguals (Hartsuiker, Pickering, & Veltkamp, 2004).

Moreover, repetition of lexical items and semantic relations between lexical items enhances syntactic priming. For example, syntactic alignment is enhanced if prime and target share lexical items. In Branigan et al. (2000), the confederate produced a description using a particular verb (e.g., *the nun giving the book to the clown*). Some experimental subjects then produced a description using the same verb (e.g., *the cowboy giving the banana to the burglar*); whereas other subjects produced a description using a different verb (e.g., *the cowboy handing the banana to the burglar*). The magnitude of priming was considerably greater when the verb was repeated. These results demonstrate a link between lexical and syntactic levels, with lexical alignment enhancing syntactic alignment. Not surprisingly, a 'lexical boost' also occurs in monologue (Pickering & Branigan, 1998). Likewise, Cleland and Pickering (2003) found that a boost also occurs when prime and target contain semantically related words: People tended to produce noun phrases like *the sheep that's red* (rather than *the red sheep*) more often after hearing *the goat that's red* than after hearing *the book that's red*. This demonstrates that semantic relations between lexical items enhance syntactic priming. However, we note that Cleland and Pickering found no comparable boost when prime and target contained phonologically related nouns (specifically, differing by only one or two word-medial phonemes, e.g., *sheep* vs. *ship*). This suggests that there may be some limits to the interconnections between syntax and phonology.

INTERACTIVE ALIGNMENT AND ROUTINIZATION

Real interactive language is extremely repetitive, and the comparison with carefully crafted monologue (as in texts) is striking (Tannen, 1989). See for example Table 6.1, which is taken from Garrod and Anderson (1987) and which we discuss in detail here. Pickering and Garrod (2004) argued that expressions that are repeated become routines for the purposes of the dialogue. A routine is an expression that is "fixed" to a relatively large extent. We assume that it has some fixed lexical content, though it may also contain elements that vary (in which case, we refer to it as semi-productive). It occurs at a much higher frequency than the frequency of its component words would lead us to expect (e.g., Aijmer, 1996). Stock phrases, idioms, and some clichés are routines. Groups of people may develop particular types of routine, perhaps in order to aid their fluency. For example, Kuiper (1996) described the fixed language used by auctioneers and sportscasters. Their use of such expressions certainly is a great aid to their fluency, especially as they are often producing monologues (e.g., horse-racing commentaries).

TABLE 6.1.
Transcript of an extract from a maze-game dialogue taken from Garrod and Anderson (1987).

8-----A: You know the extreme right, there's one box.
9-----B: Yeah right, the extreme right it's sticking out like a sore thumb.
10----A: That's where I am.
11----B: It's like a right indicator.
12----A: Yes, and where are you?
13----B: Well I'm er: that right indicator you've got.
14----A: Yes.
15----B: The right indicator above that.
16----A: Yes.
17----B: Now if you go along there. You know where the right indicator above yours is?
18----A: Yes.
19----B: If you go along to the left: I'm in that box which is like: one, two boxes down O.K.?

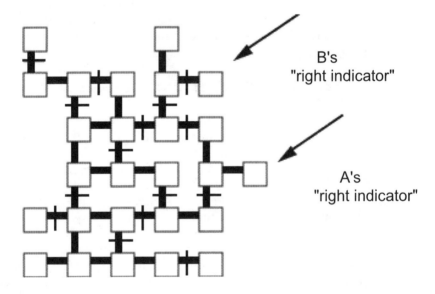

FIG. 6.1. Schematic illustration of the maze being described in the transcript in Table 6.1. The arrows indicate the positions that A and B describe as right indicators.

Most discussion of routines refers to the long-term development of fixed expressions that may well be lexicalized (e.g., Aijmer, 1996; Kuiper, 1996; Nunberg, Sag, & Wasow, 1994). But they may also be established for the purposes of a particular interchange. If one interlocutor starts to use an expression and gives it a particular meaning, the other will most likely follow suit. In other words, routines are set up 'on the fly' during dialogue. We believe that the use of routines contributes enormously to the fluency of dialogue. For example, Pickering and Garrod (2004) give the example *the previous administration*, which can take on a specific meaning (referring to a particular political body) as part of a conversation, and where other interpretations of the individual words (e.g., *administration* meaning work) or of the expression as a whole (e.g., referring to a different political body) are not considered. The establishment of this form of words and meaning as a routine has the effect that interlocutors access it without seriously considering alternatives. In production, they do not make a difficult choice between using the word *administration* or its near-synonym *government*; and in comprehension, they do not consider (non-routinized) interpretations of the words (e.g., of *administration*). After the conversation is over, however, the interlocutors may 'drop' this routine and return to their 'standard' use of the words.

Routines can of course be elicited experimentally, as we illustrate from Garrod and Anderson (1987). Table 6.1 gives a brief transcript of an interaction in which A and B are trying to establish their respective positions in the maze (indicated by arrows in Figure 6.1). Consider the use of *right indicator*, which takes on a specific meaning (referring to a particular configuration within mazes). Once the players have fixed on this expression and interpretation, they do not describe the configuration in alternative ways. Although we can be less certain of what happens during comprehension, the responses to references to *right indicator* strongly suggest that they also understand the expression in its special sense. Similar processes occur when interlocutors agree on a 'shorthand' description of unfamiliar objects, as when referring to a tangram as *an ice skater* (H. H. Clark & Wilkes-Gibbs, 1986).

In the rest of this paper, we provide a first attempt to account for the process of routinization within the linguistic framework developed by Jackendoff (2002), especially Chapter 6 (see also Jackendoff, 1999). We draw a distinction between interactive alignment and routinization. Interactive alignment involves the priming of particular levels of representation and the links between those levels. Producing or comprehending any utterance leads to the activation of those representations, but their activation gradually decays. However, when

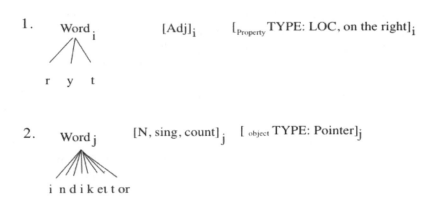

FIG. 6.2. Schematic illustration of the lexical items *right* and *indicator* as accessed before establishing a routine for *right indicator*.

interactive alignment leads to sufficiently strong activation of the links between the levels, routinization occurs. Routinization involves the setting down of new memory traces associated with a particular expression. The expression therefore becomes lexicalized, with a particular semantics, phonology and syntax, in terms of a conception of the lexicon similar to Jackendoff (2002). Routines are comparatively long-lasting and involve a kind of implicit learning. Not surprisingly, the new representations do not normally come about by explicit agreement.

Jackendoff (2002) proposes that linguistic representations (i.e., containing phonological, syntactic, and semantic/conceptual components) may either be stored and accessed directly, or constructed on-line. Anything that is stored and accessed directly he treats as a lexical item. Hence, lexical items can range from morphemes to whole constructions or even stretches of text that have been memorized (e.g., speeches). To explain his account, we need to describe the representation of both traditional lexical items (i.e., words) and more complex lexical items.

Traditional lexical items have a phonological representation linked to a syntactic representation, both of which are linked to a conceptual/semantic representation. Figure 6.2 illustrates the arrangement for the word *right* (in 2.1). The phonology is shown on the left, the syntactic representation in the middle and the conceptual/semantic representation on the right. The three representations are all linked to each other through the subscript *i*. More complex lexical items, such as fixed or semi-productive idioms, are represented as having phonological, syntactic and conceptual/semantic components, but with only partial mappings between the three components. For example, the idiomatic construction *take to task* involves separate mappings between the phonological words and the syntactic structure and between the syntactic structure and the semantic structure (see Figure 6.3). These complex lexicalizations provide a suitable framework for formalizing routines because they represent the fixed aspects of the routines but at the same time allow for variables, such as the variable NP in *take NP to task*. Note that Jackendoff (2002) assumes that the variable NP is inserted by a separate rule, and hence does not form part of the lexical item in Figure 6.3.

We assume that routines are not simply recovered from long-term memory as complete chunks (e.g., in contrast to Kuiper, 1996). There are a number of reasons to suspect that producing routines involves some compositional processes. First, it can straightforwardly explain how people produce semi-productive routines with a variable element, as in *take X to task*, where *X* can be any noun phrase referring to a person or people. Second, the structure of non-idiomatic sentences can be primed by idiomatic sentences in production (Bock, 2004). Third, it is consistent with the production of idiom blends like *That's the way the cookie bounces* (Cutting & Bock, 1997). Note that evidence also suggest syntactic processing of routines in comprehension. For example, syntactically appropriate continuations to phrases are responded to faster than syntactically inappropriate ones when the phrase is likely to be the beginning of an idiom (e.g., *kick the ...*; Peterson, Burgess, Dell, & Eberhard, 2001).

Let us explain routinization in dialogue by examples from the maze-game transcript in Table 6.1. First, consider the use of *right indicator*. When *B* says *it's like a right indicator* (11), the expression *right indicator* is

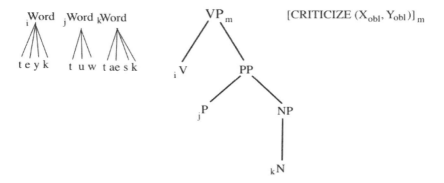

FIG. 6.3. Schematic illustration of how *take to task* is represented as a lexical item in Jackendoff's (2002) framework. By convention, subscripts on the left of a category (here, i, j, k) map the phonology to the syntax, whereas subscripts on the right (here, m) map the syntax onto the semantics.

not a routine, but is composed of two expressions whose interpretations are relatively standard, and whose meaning involves normal processes of meaning composition. So, B accesses the lexical entries in Figure 6.2 and creates a phrase with the structure in Figure 6.4(1). Importantly, however, B does not simply use *right indicator* to refer to any object that can be referred to as a right indicator, but instead uses it to refer to a particular type of object that occurs within this maze (see Figure 6.1). A accepts this description with *yes* (12), presumably meaning that he has understood B's utterance correctly. He then interprets A's utterance at this stage using the normal processes of meaning decomposition corresponding to the compositional processes that A has used in production. The expression *right indicator* now keeps recurring, and is used to refer to positions in the maze. Whereas initially it was used as part of a simile [*it's like a right indicator* in (11)], subsequently it is used referentially [*that right indicator you've got* in (15)]. At some point (we cannot be certain when, but presumably fairly rapidly), it becomes a routine.

How does such routinization occur? We propose that the activation of *right* and *indicator* plus the specific meaning that *right indicator* has in this context leads to the activation of the phonological representation and syntactic representation together with the activation of the specific meaning ("right-hand-protrusion-on-maze"). Therefore the links among the phonology, syntax and semantics are activated (as specified in the interactive alignment model). That increases the likelihood that the

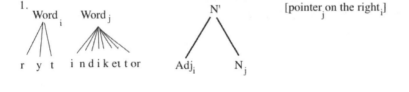

FIG. 6.4. Schematic illustration of (1) the standard interpretation for *right indicator* and (2) the lexicalization of the dialogue routine for *right indicator*.

interlocutors are going to subsequently use *right indicator* with that specific meaning.

But in addition to this basic interactive-alignment process, the activation of the links "suggest" the positing of a new long-term association, essentially that *right indicator* can have the meaning "right-hand-protrusion-on-maze". We propose that when activation is strong enough, a new lexical entry is constructed, as illustrated in Figure 6.4(2). In this representation, the phonology of *right* and *indicator* are linked to the syntactic categories Adj and N in the syntactic component, but crucially there is no direct link between the phonology of the two words and the semantic/conceptual representation at the right of the figure. Instead, a new link is established between the N' (which is the mother node for Adj and N) and the local meaning "right-hand-protrusion-on-maze".

This automatic account of routinization does not require speakers to take into account what they assume their addressees believe about the meaning of *right indicator* in order to determine when they can use this term. There is no need to reason that the addressee would be able to understand *right indicator* before deciding whether to use this expression in contrast to a longer alternative.

Clearly, we cannot specify exactly what makes activation strong enough for routinization to occur, but assume that it depends on at least the frequency of use of the expression with that meaning by both speakers. For example, many uses of *right indicator* meaning "right-hand-protrusion-on-maze" will increase the likelihood that the expression becomes routinized. Importantly, both interlocutors must construct the same routine (i.e., the same new lexical entry) for it to be stable (otherwise the interlocutors would not align). In order for the routine to be established, both interlocutors must accept it, at least implicitly. For example, continuation is sufficient for acceptance, but when the listener questions the term used, for instance saying *right indicator?* with a rising intonation (Ginzburg & Cooper, 2004), the expression and its interpretation are not accepted. When this happens, we propose that activation immediately drops and the expression *right indicator* with the meaning "right-hand-protrusion-on-maze" does not become lexicalized.

Let us now consider another slightly different example from the maze game transcripts. In order to describe their horizontal position in the maze, some players aligned on the term *floor*, to mean a horizontal line or row of boxes. Before beginning the experiment, they presumably did not represent this meaning for *floor*, though they presumably know that it has a related meaning in terms of stories within a building. Again, we assume a process like that for *right indicator*. First, one speaker wishes

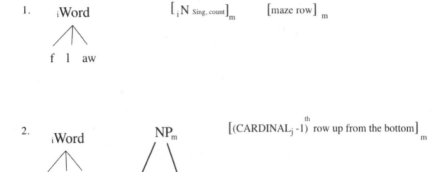

FIG. 6.5. Schematic illustration of the lexicalization of *floor* (1) when routinized to mean "row on the maze" and (2) when routinized to mean "row as ordered from the bottom of the maze".

to refer to a row within the maze and decides to use *floor*. Perhaps he does not access the term *row*, or perhaps he is not happy to use *row* in this particular way. He chooses *floor* (rather than an alternative expression) because the established meaning is in some sense related to the desired meaning. At this point, the desired meaning "row" is simply the speaker's interpretation of this particular use of *floor*, and is not lexicalized. If the speaker is successful, the listener realizes that *floor* is to be interpreted as referring to a row in the maze (presumably she realizes that this is the only sensible interpretation of *floor* at this point). When the listener accepts the speaker's use, we propose the phonological representation of *floor* is activated, as is its local interpretation ("row"). Therefore the link between the phonology and semantics is activated and increases the likelihood that the listener is going to subsequently use *floor* with that specific meaning. When the activation is strong enough, a new lexical entry is constructed along the lines shown in Figure 6.5(1). In this representation the phonology of *floor* is mapped onto the syntactic structure in the normal way, but then there is a separate mapping from this structure to the new meaning of *floor* in the context of the dialogue.

How is this representation of *floor* different from any other lexical representation of *floor*? We suggest that its semantic component is highly specific. In other words, it only applies with respect to a particular situation model, which is associated with this particular context (e.g., maze-game dialogues). Frequently players went beyond this simple routine to align on a more complex one also involving *floor*, exemplified by the descriptions *floor one, floor two, floor three* with the interpretations "bottom row", "one up from the bottom row", "two up from the bottom row". In this case, the routine is *Floor X*, where X is a cardinal number. The mapping between phonology and semantics is more complex than the *right indicator* example, because it involves a compositional mapping from the syntactic structure to the semantic representation [see Figure 6.5(2)]. Here the phonology of floor maps onto the category N in the syntactic representation but does not map directly into the semantic representation because it requires a cardinal number *n* to yield the appropriate semantic interpretation "$(n - 1)^{th}$ up from the bottom row". So the lexical structure reflects both the frozen-in aspect of the interpretation of *floor* together with how it is to be interpreted when combined with the cardinal numeral. Interestingly, players who adopted this routine did sometimes use *top* or *bottom*, but when they did, they did not say *top floor* or *bottom floor*, but instead substituted an alternative term (e.g., *top line, bottom row*). This suggests that the use of *floor* in the routine *floor X* blocked the use of *floor* in a non-routinized way.

Finally, let us consider another example from the maze transcripts that illustrates a routine that fixes the interpretation of an adjective. The example comes from a special use of top or bottom that developed in some of the conversations. Players would commonly set out by describing their position in terms of its relationship to the top of the maze as in *Second row from the top*. However, in some cases they proceeded to align on a more elliptical version of this description of the form *Second top row*, in which *top* is interpreted as "from the top". In other words, *Second top row* corresponds to the second row from the top of the maze. Again, in some cases these descriptions became established as routines, which can be represented as in Figure 6.6. In this representation the phonology for *top* maps onto the Adj in the syntactic NP structure, but there is no direct mapping from the Adj to the semantic representation. Rather, the mapping to the semantic representation comes from the ordinal determiner (e.g., *second, third, fourth*) and the noun (e.g., *row*) with which the adjective has to be combined.

Routinization therefore involves the positing of links between the levels. Routines are objects that have partly or completely fixed interpretations at multiple linguistic levels. For instance, that a particular lexical item gets a particular interpretation for that conversation, or that a particular combination has a particular interpretation (as in *right indicator*). This combination then gets stored and can be accessed as a routine, thereby reducing choice. One prediction is therefore that the difficulty that is associated with determining which expression to use when more than one is available will disappear or at least be greatly

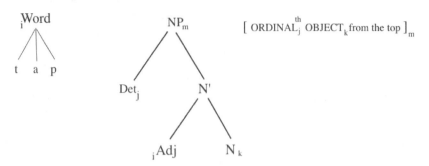

FIG. 6.6. Schematic illustration of the lexicalization of *top* when routinized to mean "as ordered from the top".

reduced when it has become a routine. For example, pictures that have more than one name take longer to describe than pictures that have one dominant name (e.g., Griffin, 2001). But when a particular name has been routinized, accessing that name should be straightforward even if there is an alternative.

IMPLICATIONS OF ROUTINIZATION

In the final section, we consider some implications of our approach to routinization. We have focused on the establishment of temporary routines for the purpose of a particular interchange. This appears to be an important and almost entirely neglected aspect of language use. But routines need not be 'dropped' once the conversation is over. When this happens, the new lexical entry remains in the speaker's lexicon.

In fact, experimental evidence suggests that routines do extend beyond the particular interchange. Garrod and Doherty (1994) had people play the maze game with different partners. When all members of a group played with each other (e.g., A with B, C with D, then A with C, B with D, then A with D, B with C), they converged on description schemes to a much greater extent than when participants played with members of a different group on each interchange (e.g., A with B, C with D, A with C, A with E, B with F). In other words, interlocutors who formed a 'network' converged to a much greater extent than those who did not (and indeed converged more than those who played repeatedly with the same partner). This shows that they converged on description schemes that lasted beyond one interchange, and hence that the routinization of the schemes persisted.

Garrod and Doherty (1994) showed that interlocutors who did not come from the same community failed to converge. In terms of our current proposal, this occurred because of a clash between routinization and priming: One participant's routinized lexical entries may not match with the priming that occurs as a result of the other participant using a different lexical entry. In other words, if A has routinized particular expressions with partner B and now encounters partner C from a different community, then A's routines will not correspond to B's routines. As a consequence each interlocutor's tendency to use different routines will get in the way of the local interactive alignment process.

More speculatively, we suggest that the establishment of routines can be equated with the processes that take place during language acquisition. In particular, the process by which children set down representations for novel words and expressions (which are lexicalized within Jackendoff's account) may be akin to routinization. However, we need to explain why routinization might lead to large-scale vocabulary acquisition, when it clearly extends adults' store of expressions to a much more limited extent.

Of course, children encounter new words much more often than adults. But in addition, we believe that young children are much more "set up" to accept novel pairings between form and meaning (and grammar, though we ignore this here) than adults. In other words, the links between the components of linguistic representations are particularly strong. This can be seen in the strong tendency children have to avoid synonyms (e.g., E. V. Clark, 1993). For example, if a young child refers to particular footwear as *boots* she will tend not to accept the term *shoes* to refer to the same objects. This is compatible with a particularly strong link being set up between the word and a particular meaning. Garrod and Clark (1993) found that children (aged 7 through 8 years) would converge on referring expressions and description schemes to refer to maze positions to at least as strong an extent as adults. But they were much less happy than adults to abandon those referring schemes when it became clear that they were leading to misunderstanding. They interpreted this result as showing that the natural tendency for the children is to converge (as predicted by interactive alignment) and it is only as the child matures that they are able to inhibit this tendency when it is required.

Such commitment to particular form-meaning pairings is efficient both for processing and acquisition. For processing, it means that the space of alternatives that the child has to consider is rapidly reduced. But it has the difficulty that it reduces the ability of the child to express a wider range of concepts (assuming that synonyms can have slight differences in meaning, or can have differences imposed for particular interchanges) and to comprehend the full range of meanings that a speaker expresses. These problems do not of course matter so much if the interlocutor (the parent) is aware of the child's limitations, and (for instance) employs a limited vocabulary.

For acquisition, if novel lexical items follow from the fixation of form-meaning pairings, then children will establish new routines more easily than adults. If a child hears *floor* being used to refer to a row, then she will establish the link between *floor* and its meaning in such a way that she will be unable to accept another term to refer to the same thing. We have argued that this occurs in adults too, but the assumption is that adults can abandon such conventions more straightforwardly than children. This means that adults' conversation is more flexible than children's, but that the establishment of novel items is more straightforward for children.

We have argued for an account of dialogue in which interlocutors align their linguistic representations in a largely automatic manner. One effect of alignment is that it leads to the development of conversational routines (expressions with fixed forms and specialized interpretations). We propose that such routines are represented as lexical items within the framework proposed by Jackendoff (2002), where the lexicon contains complex expressions as well as words. Our account has implications for the processing and development of language.

REFERENCES

Aijmer, K. (1996). *Conversational routines in English: Convention and creativity.* London: Longman.

Bock, J. K. (1986). Syntactic persistence in language production. *Cognitive Psychology, 18*, 355-387.

Bock, J. K. (2004). *Are words all there is?* Paper presented at the 17th annual CUNY conference on human sentence processing. University of Maryland.

Branigan, H. P., Pickering, M. J., & Cleland, A. A. (2000). Syntactic coordination in dialogue. *Cognition, 75*, B13-B25.

Brennan, S. E., & Clark, H. H. (1996). Conceptual pacts and lexical choice in conversation. *Journal of Experimental Psychology: Learning, Memory, and Cognition, 22*, 1482-1493.

Clark, E. V. (1993). *The lexicon in acquisition.* Cambridge: Cambridge University Press.

Clark, H. H. (1996). *Using language.* Cambridge: Cambridge University Press.

Clark, H. H., & Wilkes-Gibbs, D. (1986). Referring as a collaborative process. *Cognition, 22*, 1-39.

Cleland, A. A., & Pickering, M. J. (2003). The use of lexical and syntactic information in language production: Evidence from the priming of noun phrase structure. *Journal of Memory and Language, 49,* 214-230.

Cutting, J. C., & Bock, J. K. (1997). That's the way the cookie bounces: Syntactic and semantic components of experimentally elicited idiom blends. *Memory & Cognition, 25,* 57-71.

Garrod, S., & Anderson, A. (1987). Saying what you mean in dialogue: A study in conceptual and semantic co-ordination. *Cognition, 27,* 181-218.

Garrod, S., & Clark, A. (1993). The development of dialogue co-ordination skills in schoolchildren. *Language and Cognitive Processes, 8,* 101-126.

Garrod, S., & Doherty, G. (1994). Conversation, co-ordination and convention: An empirical investigation of how groups establish linguistic conventions. *Cognition, 53,* 181-215.

Garrod, S., & Pickering, M. J. (2004). Why is conversation so easy? *Trends in Cognitive Sciences, 8,* 8-11.

Ginzburg, J., & Cooper, R. (2004). Clarification, ellipsis, and the nature of contextual updates. *Linguistics and Philosophy, 27,* 297-366.

Griffin, Z. M. (2001). Gaze durations during speech reflect word selection and phonological encoding. *Cognition, 82,* B1-B14.

Hartsuiker, R. J., Pickering, M. J., & Veltkamp, E. (2004). Is syntax separate or shared between languages? Cross-linguistic syntactic priming in Spanish/English bilinguals. *Psychological Science, 15,* 409-414.

Hommel, B., Müsseler, J., Aschersleben, G., & Prinz, W. (2001). The theory of event coding (TEC): A framework for perception and action planning. *Behavioral and Brain Sciences, 24,* 849-937.

Jackendoff, R. (1999). Parallel constraint-based generative theories of language. *Trends in Cognitive Sciences, 3,* 393-400.

Jackendoff, R. (2002). *Foundations of language.* Oxford: Oxford University Press.

Kuiper, K. (1996). *Smooth talkers: The linguistic performance of auctioneers and sportscasters.* Mahwah, NJ: Lawrence Erlbaum Associates.

Nunberg, G., Sag, I. A., & Wasow, T. (1994). Idioms. *Language, 70,* 491-538.

Peterson, R. R., Burgess, C., Dell, G. S., & Eberhard, K. M. (2001). Disassociation between syntactic and semantic processing during idiom comprehension. *Journal of Experimental Psychology: Learning, Memory, and Cognition, 27,* 1223-1237.

Pickering, M. J., & Branigan, H. P. (1998). The representation of verbs: Evidence from syntactic priming in language production. *Journal of Memory and Language, 39,* 633-651.

Pickering, M. J., & Garrod, S. (2004). Toward a mechanistic psychology of dialogue. *Behavioral and Brain Sciences, 27,* 169-225.

Sanford, A. J., & Garrod, S. C. (1981). *Understanding written language.* Chichester: Wiley.

Tannen, D. (1989). *Talking voices: Repetition, dialogue, and imagery in conversational discourse.* Cambridge: Cambridge University Press.

Zwaan, R. A., & Radvansky, G. A. (1998). Situation models in language comprehension and memory. *Psychological Bulletin, 123,* 162-185.

7 Defining the Relation Between Linguistics and Neuroscience

David Poeppel and David Embick
University of Maryland, College Park, and
University of Pennsylvania, USA

The popularity of the study of language and the brain is evident from the large number of studies published since the early 1990s that have used PET, fMRI, EEG, MEG, TMS, or NIRS to investigate aspects of brain and language, in linguistic domains ranging from phonetics to discourse processing. The amount of resources devoted to such studies suggests that they are motivated by a viable and successful research program, and implies that substantive progress is being made. At the very least, the amount and vigor of such research implies that something significant is being learned. In this chapter, we present a critique of the dominant research program, and provide a cautionary perspective that challenges the belief that *explanatorily significant progress* is already being made. Our critique focuses on the question of whether current brain/language research provides an example of interdisciplinary *cross-fertilization*, or an example of *cross-sterilization*. In developing our critique, which is in part motivated by the necessity to examine the presuppositions of our own work (e.g., Embick, Marantz, Miyashita, O'Neil, & Sakai, 2000; Embick, Hackl, Schaeffer, Kelepir, & Marantz, 2001; Poeppel, 1996; Poeppel et al., 2004), we identify fundamental problems that must be addressed if progress is to be made in this area of inquiry. We conclude with the outline of a research program that constitutes an attempt to overcome these problems, at the core of which lies the notion of computation.

PROBLEMS

In principle, the combined study of language and the brain could have effects in several directions. One possibility is that the study of the brain will reveal aspects of the structure of linguistic knowledge. The other possibility is that language can be used to investigate the nature of computation in the brain. In either case, there is a tacit background assumption: Namely that the combined investigation promises to generate progress in one of these two domains. Given the actual current state of research, these two positions—rarely questioned or, for that matter, identified in studies of language and the brain—lack any obvious justification when examined carefully. If asked what to study to learn about the nature of language, surely one would not send a student to study neuroscience; rather, one might recommend a course in phonetics or phonology or morphology or syntax or semantics or psycholinguistics. Similarly, if asked about neurobiology, one typically does not recommend the study of linguistics, or even neurolinguistics. Thus the idea that neuroscience is in a position to inform linguistic theory, and vice versa, is clearly open to question. A third option is that the cognitive neuroscience of language should be pursued as an end in itself. To the extent that this option can be coherently formulated as a program of research (what point is there to a science of language and brain that contributes to the understanding of neither?), results in this domain run the risk of being effectively sui generis; that is, isolated from other research programs in such a way that they do not form the basis for progress beyond the immediate question addressed in any given study. At the very least, then, it is clear that current neurolinguistic research has not advanced—in an *explanatorily significant* way—the understanding of either linguistic theory or of neuroscience. While this failure is by no means necessary, we contend that it will continue until certain fundamental problems are identified, acknowledged, and addressed.

Here we concentrate on two problems. The first problem, which we call the *Granularity Mismatch Problem* (GMP), is that there is a mismatch between the 'conceptual granularity' of the elemental concepts of linguistics and the elemental concepts of neurobiology and cognitive neuroscience (which are, relative to the corresponding linguistic primitives, coarse-grained). This mismatch prevents the formulation of theoretically motivated, biologically grounded, and computationally explicit linking hypotheses that bridge neuroscience and linguistics. Naturally, the GMP applies not just to the linguistics-neuroscience interface, but equally to other experimental disciplines that operate with objects of different sizes.

Granularity Mismatch Problem (GMP): Linguistic and neuroscientific studies of language operate with objects of different granularity. In particular, linguistic computation involves a number of fine-grained distinctions and explicit computational operations. Neuroscientific approaches to language operate in terms of broader conceptual distinctions.

The second problem is called the *Ontological Incommensurability Problem* (OIP): The fundamental elements of linguistic theory cannot be reduced or matched up with the fundamental biological units identified by neuroscience. This problem results from a failure to answer the question of how neurological structures could be specialized to perform specific types of computations, linguistic or otherwise. That is, while our particular focus here is on language, the GMP and OIP could be applied to the entire range of areas in which the relationship between cognition and biology is examined, and thus are general 'interface problems' for the study of cognition.

Illustrating what we take to be the 'contact-problems' or 'interface-problems' between linguistics and neuroscience, consider the central dilemma, illustrated in Figure 7.1. The figure enumerates aspects of the architecture of each domain and directly exemplifies the conceptual mismatches. The natural move given these two distinct sets of categories is to attempt a reduction or a direct mapping between one set of categories and the other.

Linguistics	Neuroscience

Fundamental elements of representation (at a given analytic level)

distinctive feature	dendrites, spines
syllable	neuron
morpheme	cell-assembly/ensemble
noun phrase	population
clause	cortical column

Fundamental operations on primitives (at a given analytic level)

concatenation	long-term potentiation (LTP)
linearization	receptive field
phrase-structure generation	oscillation
semantic composition	synchronization

FIG. 7.1. Some primitives for representation and processing. The two unordered lists enumerate some concepts canonically used to explain neurobiological or linguistic phenomena. There are principled ontology-process relationships within each domain (i.e., vertical connections). However, if we take these lists seriously, the interdisciplinary (i.e., horizontal) connections remain, at best, arbitrary.

A direct reduction would involve connecting linguistic categories on the left to neurobiological categories on the right with an arrow that implies a direct computational connection between the two. To our knowledge, there is not a single case of a successful reduction in these terms in the domain of language; it appears that that the categories on the two sides are simply listed using different alphabets (or 'currencies'):

Ontological Incommensurability Problem (OIP): The units of linguistic computation and the units of neurological computation are incommensurable.

The OIP does not suggest that no progress is being made in either the linguistic or neurobiological ontology; clearly, each of these is becoming increasingly refined, with improved empirical coverage. Rather, the OIP encapsulates the observation that these ontologies are developing independently of each other, with no solid connections linking them. In part this is the result of the fact that the objects/processes in each column (Figure 7.1) have been introduced in order to allow for certain types of generalizations. But the generalizations that these notions permit are different in kind. For example, the *morpheme* is introduced to capture regularities concerning the terminal elements of the syntax, that is, the minimal pieces of word- and sentence-structure; *linearization* operations are introduced to characterize the required process that transforms hierarchical representations into representations suitable for our available input-output machinery; and so on. In contrast, *neuron* is an anatomic unit that can encompass numerous distinct processing subroutines, and *synchronization* is postulated as a hypothesis about how spatially and temporally distributed neural activity might be coordinated in the generation of unified perceptual experience. It is evident that a direct mapping is extremely problematic. Indeed, it is conceivable that the conceptual architecture of linguistics and neurobiology as presently conceived will never yield to any type of reduction, requiring instead substantive conceptual change in one or both of the disciplines (in the sense of Carey, 1985) that might enable unification (in the sense of Chomsky, 2000). This problem, once again, is a more general challenge in the cognitive neurosciences and is exemplified here on the basis of the linguistics-neuroscience interface, although all approaches with interfaces of differing character face these issues.

We suggest a straightforward solution to the GMP and OIP, namely spelling out the ontologies and processes in computational terms that are at the appropriate level of abstraction (i.e., can be performed by specific neuronal populations) such that explicit interdisciplinary linking hypotheses can be formulated. Based on our discussion, we suggest a program of research that pursues the second strategy mentioned above, namely that the use of linguistically motivated categories can support the study of computation in the brain. In other words, rather than pursuing the standard approach in which linguistically postulated categories must be validated by biological data, a position which we argue to be fundamentally flawed, we recommend taking linguistic categories seriously and using them to investigate how the brain computes with such abstract categorical representations. Importantly, our perspective advocates an integrated approach to the study of linguistic computation, in which linguistic theories must be accountable to all forms of evidence, including psycho- and neurolinguistic results. The integrated approach has direct implications both for the cognitive neuroscience of language and for linguistic theory, implications that are identified as the discussion proceeds below. In this and other ways, this approach stands in contrast to the prevailing view in neurolinguistics, to which we now turn.

THE STANDARD RESEARCH PROGRAM IN THE COGNITIVE NEUROSCIENCE OF LANGUAGE

The canonical assumption of the Standard Research Program about research on brain and language is that neurobiological methods are used to validate concepts and categories introduced to the experimental research program by linguistic theory. For example, theoretical linguistic research deals with elemental concepts such as 'root,' 'functional category,' or 'head movement,' and the neurolinguist is supposed to set out to obtain correlative biological measures that provide support for the concept in question. On this view, the data generated by the range of techniques that are used in neurolinguistic research — that is, the neuropsychological deficit-lesion method, EEG, MEG, PET, or fMRI — provide evidence for concepts, representations, and processes that are independently motivated by linguistic research, and the neurolinguistic data give the theoretical-linguistic conceptual apparatus the imprimatur of hard science methodology. This approach constitutes a form of reductionism in which biological evidence is 'better' or more fundamental than other evidence.

Research in this vein has a long and respectable tradition and, to be sure, many important results have been obtained. Indeed, the observation that localized brain lesions or brain activation correlate with specific linguistic domains has been foundational for modern neuroscience research (for review and new perspectives, see Hickok & Poeppel, 2004). Modern studies using contemporary recording techniques show that some of the relatively broad distinctions one can draw in linguistics (e.g., syntax versus lexical semantics versus phonology) are reflected in biological data. While such insights are certainly scientifically interesting, clinically relevant, and receive considerable popular attention, there are clear limitations to this methodology that dampen our enthusiasm about this approach as a comprehensive research program. Although this type of research provides the field with important correlative datapoints, one learns little of explanatory depth about language and little about the brain. That is, while such results might indicate the existence of some correlation between linguistic and biological objects, there is no theory of such correlations, nor do such correlations necessarily lead to any further understanding of how brain structures or linguistic computations operate.

The level of computational detail present in studies of linguistic representations and processes far exceeds our knowledge of how to detect such distinctions in the physiological measurements we understand, as well as our know-how about what to look for in the data. As a result, the (often implicit) belief that linguistic categories are not 'real' until detected in the brain subjects linguistic investigations to a kind of methodological stricture that simply cannot be taken seriously. It is unreasonable to expect that all distinctions relevant to linguistic computation must have visible reflexes in *current* imaging (or lesion, or psycholinguistic) data. For instance, the fact that the sentences *The cat is on the hat* and *The hat is on the cat* are different grammatical objects, each requiring distinct representation/computation by the grammar, is a fact whether or not these sentences can be shown using current techniques to be different in terms of neuronal activation. An explanatory theory of linguistic computation in the brain should employ linguistic categories as a means of exploring neural computation; but the failure to detect distinctions in any particular case does not necessarily imply that the linguistic distinctions are incorrect. The latter type of inference might be possible in the context of an articulated theory of neurolinguistic computation; but we have nothing like that at present.

It is quite generally the case that contemporary linguistic research investigates fine-grained and subtle distinctions among representations and processes, whereas neurobiological data that are concerned with speech and language probe coarser distinctions, for instance, questions such as *Are there differences between phonological and syntactic processing*? In other words, there is a compelling mismatch (GMP) in what we can learn about language by studying language (a lot, judging by the progress of linguistic research since the 1950s) and what we can learn about language by studying the brain (not as much, judging by the progress of neurolinguistic research since the 1850s). Similarly, neurolinguistic research per se rarely leads to principled neurobiological insights. To learn something substantive about brain structure and function, it is necessary that we develop a focused research program that explicitly formulates hypotheses about how particular brain areas execute the complex functions they support. In the specific case of language, it is clear that the standard research program offers relatively little in the necessary direction, and for this reason an alternative research program must be developed.

PROGRESS IN THE STANDARD RESEARCH PROGRAM? IMAGING BROCA'S AREA

The preceding discussion concentrates on the fact that the distinctions made in neurological study of language are coarse in comparison with the distinctions made by linguistics. *Syntax, semantics,* and *phonology* are not the names of explicit computational tasks, as is often implicit in standard research; rather, these terms refer to (often vaguely defined) general domains ('phrase structure'; 'meaning'; 'sound structure'), each of which consists, of course, of numerous computations and representations in any coherent linguistic theory. One consequence of the failure to recognize the coarseness of the categories employed in the cognitive neuroscience of language is that there are instances of false convergence. In the particular case that we briefly examine in this section, the false convergence is one that suggests that 'Broca's Area' is a (more or less monolithic) cortical area whose function is to compute syntax (the latter construed as a more or less monolithic task). While many functional imaging studies have argued for such a conclusion, closer examination reveals that this interpretation is not tenable (Hagoort, this volume, and Thompson-Schill, this volume, discuss Broca's complex and its putative functions) and that the difficulties in this area arise, among other reasons, from the failure to analyze neurolinguistic computation at the correct level of granularity. (We ignore here the additional more technical problems that confront such functional imaging studies, including issues associated with more fine-grained anatomic distinctions, experimental design, analysis, as well as implicit assumptions about the relationship between loci of activation and cognitive systems.)

The activation of Broca's area has been reported in many studies of both syntactic comprehension and production, leading many researchers to conclude that this area has a privileged status in syntax. Elsewhere we review this work in more detail (Embick & Poeppel, in press); here we limit ourselves to a few examples from different techniques (PET, fMRI), designs (block versus single trial), and sensory modalities (auditory versus visual) to illustrate the generality of the issue. Turning to specific studies, Dapretto and Bookheimer (1999), used fMRI in a block design, and presented sentences auditorily to subjects who performed one of two tasks. In a condition labeled 'syntactic', participants were asked to judge whether two sentences — one active (*The policeman arrested the thief*), and one passive (*The thief was arrested by the policeman*) — were the same or different. In the 'semantic' condition, subjects judged whether two sentences in which a single word differed were the same (*The lawyer/attorney questioned the witness*) or different (*The lawyer/driver questioned the witness*). This study reported activation in BA 44 for the comparison syntax minus semantics (as well as syntax minus rest), and activation in BA 47 for semantics minus syntax. Auditory presentation was also used in the event-related fMRI study performed by Ni et al. (2000), in which subjects performed syntactic and semantic oddball tasks, in which a sequence of grammatical sentences contained an occasional deviant oddball (syntactic: *Trees can grew*; semantic: #*Trees can eat*). A subtraction of *semantics* from *syntax* showed activation in BA 44/45. A block design with visual presentation was employed in the PET study of Moro et al. (2001). The study employed silent reading and acceptability judgments on four types of Italian sentences: A baseline of Jabberwocky; word-order violations; morphosyntactic violations; and phonotactic violations. Activation for the syntactic and morphosyntactic conditions minus the phonotactic condition was found in left BA 45, and Right BA 44/45. An fMRI study by Kang, Constable, Gore, and Avrutin (1999) used an event-related design in which subjects were presented visually with phrasal stimuli containing syntactic and semantic violations. The stimuli were verb phrases like *drove cars* (the normal condition). There were two deviant conditions: syntactically deviant, for example, *forgot made*; and semantically deviant, for example, *wrote beers*. Relative to the normal condition, activation was found for both the syntactically and semantically deviant stimuli in BA 44/45; the activation in left BA 44 was greater for syntax than for semantics. In addition to the studies using anomaly detection/judgment outlined above, activation in Broca's area has also been reported in studies of the syntax of artificial language learning (Musso et al., 2003), as well as in studies of syntactic complexity (Caplan, Alpert, & Waters, 1998).

Despite the different tasks and designs in these studies, the fact that Broca's area (defined as BA 44/45) was consistently active in a number of 'syntax' studies seems at first glance to be confirmation of the claim that this area is specialized for syntax. Even limiting ourselves to the imaging literature, however, there are considerations that suggest that this conclusion is at best an oversimplification.

The first additional consideration is that Broca's area has been reported to be active in a number of linguistic tasks that are not (overtly) syntactic. These other tasks range from sub-lexical and lexical tasks, for instance auditory lexical decision (Zatorre, Evans, Meyer, & Gjedde, 1992; Poeppel et al., 2004) to studies of minimal pairs in tone languages (Gandour et al., 2000) to phonetic tasks such as the processing of rapid phonetic transitions or phoneme sequences (Fiez et al., 1995; Gelfand & Bookheimer, 2003). Burton (2001) reviews imaging studies that implicate BA 44/45 in phonetics and phonology. From that review it can be concluded that the claim that Broca's area is exclusively devoted to syntax is incorrect, although it leaves open the possibility (examined below) that Broca's area is specialized for language in some broader sense.

The second consideration that complicates the simple view of a straightforward syntax-Broca's area mapping is the fact that Broca's area is active in a number of entirely non-linguistic tasks; naturally these findings also challenge the more general claim that this area is specialized for language, and not simply syntax. The tasks include motor activation, motor imagery, and rhythmic perception (see Embick & Poeppel, in press, for discussion).

The interpretation that identifies Broca's area as responsible for syntax is, naturally, informed by sources of evidence other than imaging studies, including deficit-lesion studies and electrophysiological studies. Concentrating on imaging studies, to which much recent energy has been devoted, it is clear that a simple mapping between 'Broca's area' and 'syntax' cannot be maintained. While these results generate an apparent contradiction, this situation cannot be surprising given a realistic view of how cognitive functions such as the construction and manipulation of a syntactic representation are computed. In linguistic domains other than syntax, for instance, a complex internal structure is clearly required for processes such as phonetic and phonological analysis, lexical analysis, and so on. Therefore the expectation that syntax should be a simplex, unstructured computation associated with a single undifferentiated cortical region is unrealistic, and probably hopeless as a hypothesis for guiding future research. It is clear that one, or perhaps several of the computational subroutines that are essential for syntactic processing/ production are computed in the Inferior Frontal Gyrus (IFG). But these are not 'syntax' per se—they are computational subcomponents of syntax. What is required is a theory that identifies these operations at the correct level of abstraction or granularity and seeks to associate them with different subparts of 'Broca's complex' (Hagoort, this volume) and other implicated brain areas. For example, two components essential to syntax are the creation of hierarchical structures and a process that linearizes these hierarchical structures. These are the kinds of computations that can be abstracted from syntax in the broad sense, and which are perhaps associated with different subparts of the IFG. The natural assumption is that the differently structured cortical areas are specialized for performing different types of computations, and that some of these computations are necessary for language but also for other cognitive functions. For instance, the activation of 'mirror neurons' (Rizzolatti & Arbib, 1998) in the IFG has a role in motor action/imitation, but also finds a natural place in the linguistic domain in the context of 'forward' models of speech perception (Halle, 2002). Thompson-Schill (this volume) attributes to at least one part of 'Broca's Complex', specifically BA 47, the generic role of "selection between competing sources of information". While this type of operation is so general that it must hold for virtually any cognitive process, one might be able to work out for what specific aspects of language an operation of that type could be relevant.

Based on this brief summary, we cannot conclude that major insights have been obtained concerning the structure of language or our understanding of the brain. This negative conclusion holds in spite of the fact that not all discussions of Broca's Area are subject to the criticisms leveled above (Hagoort, this volume; Thompson-Schill, this volume; Horwitz et al., 2003). That is not to say that the imaging work is not both clinically helpful and potentially informative to theory construction. On the contrary, in conjunction with an appropriately granular theory of the computations performed in the brain, the spatial information provided by imaging has the potential to illuminate aspects of the biological foundation of language by providing the critical link between specialized cortical areas and cognitively relevant types of computations. However, in the broader context of the issues addressed in this paper, it is clear that what look like results linking linguistic and neurological categories in the case of Broca's area are actually *problems*; and these problems result from the limitations that are inherent to the standard research program.

STEPS TOWARD PROGRESS: ELECTROPHYSIOLOGICAL STUDIES?

We have argued that the imaging literature, although rich with important correlative information, is, for the moment, unsatisfying as a source of information likely to enrich explanatory models. What is the status of electrophysiological research? In fact, most of the work builds on the same assumptions as most imaging studies. One aspect of standard electrophysiological work on language processing that underscores this perspective is that the experiments reflect a 'reification' of ERP components. Specifically, many (probably most) studies on the LAN, N400, and P600/SPS components interpret each component as reflecting *syntax* or *semantics* or *phonology*. Indeed, a major goal of many studies, much like in imaging, is to dissociate syntactic from semantic and phonological processing. This may be a useful goal (of an intermediate type), but it again highlights the mismatch between the granularity of linguistic versus neurolinguistic concepts. An ERP component cannot reflect syntax per se, because syntax is not a single computation. Moreover, by not looking to the subroutines involved, it misses the overlap that might occur because computational subroutines are shared by different processes (say, for example, linearization).

There are, of course, numerous exceptions, i.e. studies that attempt to probe in detail how linguistic categories and computations are executed. We merely point out that, typically, the main distinctions being drawn in such electrophysiological studies using EEG or MEG are *syntax* versus *semantics* versus *phonology*, and the standard interpretation is that the LAN 'is' syntactic structure building, the N400 'is' lexical semantic integration, and the P600 'is' syntactic error detection (and perhaps reanalysis and repair processes). In this way, there is no substantive distinction, at the conceptual level, of studying linguistic representation and computation between imaging and electrophysiological approaches.

PROSPECTS: REDEFINING A RESEARCH PROGRAM

Putting aside simple associations like 'syntax is in Broca's area', the next move is to appeal to a finer-grained set of categories derived from ongoing research in linguistic theory and in neuroscience. We take it that the central question of neurolinguistic research is the question of how the grammar of human language is computed in the human brain. Our revised research program diverges from a familiar assumption in linguistic theory, which often proceeds as if experimental evidence — whether from neuroscience or psycholinguistics — is *in principle* irrelevant to theories of how language works. This assumption, which is often tacit in linguistic theory, is made manifest in the idea that there might be notions of 'psychological' or 'neurological' reality that are distinct from the reality that linguistic theory addresses. This view of linguistic reality is incompatible with our approach to language and the brain.

The grammar consists of representation and computations. We assume that linguistic computations are executed in the brain in real time. There is no need for terms like 'psychologically real' or 'neurologically real.' These terms, because they are qualified, imply that there is some other type of reality to linguistic computations beyond being computed in the brain. If a linguistic analysis is correct—that is, identifies something real—it identifies computations/representations that are computed in the minds/brains of speakers. How these computations are implemented at different levels of biological abstraction is the primary analytical question for neurolinguistics. As noted, our perspective requires an integrated theoretical and experimental perspective, something that runs contrary to a current trend in linguistic theory. The tendency in generative syntax, for example, is to speak as if the computations proposed in syntactic analyses need not be regarded as computations that are performed in real time. But why should the null hypothesis be that there is some notion of grammar that is not computed in the brain in real time? This assumption simply makes the link between linguistics and neuroscience harder to bridge, for reasons that are ultimately historical, and not necessarily principled. Just as the research program of neurolinguistics must be informed by linguistic theory, linguistic theory cannot proceed in a way that systematically ignores experimental results. Even if specific instances in which experimental data resolve questions of theory are difficult to come by at present, this is a fact that reflects technical and methodological difficulties and a non-integrated research program; in principle, the forms of evidence on the language faculty that are provided by these methodologies are just as relevant to linguistic theory as, say, native speaker intuitions are.

At the level of the computations referred to in the preceding discussion, our revised research program insists that we restrict our attention to computations that are actually performed by the human brain. That is, the notion of computation that is central to our research program is not an abstract model of computation; we are interested in the question of what computations are performed in the brain, and not some way of modeling behavior. Ultimately if we discover restrictions on the types of abstract computations the brain can perform, we might discover as a result the nature of some of the properties of human language. But this linking is only possible given our assumptions about the grammar and the nature of computation just outlined.

One way to proceed is to stand typical neurolinguistic research on its head. Suppose one abandons the central concern with identifying correlations between biological measurements and previously hypothesized elements of language processing and aims, instead, to explicitly use elemental linguistic units of representation and computation to investigate how the brain encodes complex information. More colloquially, suppose we use language to learn how the brain works. Based on established and empirically well supported distinctions drawn in linguistics (say the notion of 'constituency' or the notion of 'distinctive feature'), we work on the problem of how the brain encodes complex and abstract information, in general, and linguistic information, in particular. Insofar as we learn additional facts about the language system (that were not visible to linguistic or psycholinguistic research per se), we are delighted—and happily take credit for any serendipitous findings. However, the basic assumption is that we study aspects of brain function by relying on a system whose cognitive architecture is well understood (like the visual system, for example).

There are many levels of analysis at which one could proceed from this perspective. In some of our own research, we are beginning at the beginning, that is, with the process of speech perception. Speech perception is of interest because it forms the basis for the transformation of physical signals into the representations that are used for computation in the brain (see Scott, this volume). One fundamental challenge for the system is how to transform continuous physical signals (acoustics) into the abstract, discrete representations that form the basis for further linguistic computation. We can build on the theoretical position that the elementary linguistic constituent is the 'distinctive feature' (e.g., Halle, 2002), and from that perspective the computational challenge is to go from sound to feature. This transformation of information is non-trivial: No automatic speech recognition system comes anywhere close to the performance of a human.

Preliminary results have demonstrated that it is possible to probe neural representation by using linguistically motivated categories like distinctive feature. For instance, Phillips, Pellathy, Yeung, and Marantz (in prep.) investigate the neural response to stimuli that differ in terms of a phonological feature [±voice]. The study employs a paradigm in which all stimuli differ acoustically. Despite these acoustic differences, all stimuli fall into the major categories defined by a phonological feature. The results of this study suggest that the brain can employ phonological (as opposed to acoustic) categories like [±voice] for computation by 180ms. Thus, by making use of *distinctive feature*, motivated by linguistic research, the experimental study is able to derive claims about the timecourse of auditory processing in the brain. Eulitz and Lahiri (2004) take the relevance of abstract features further, providing neurophysiological evidence that the hypothesized abstract primitives at the basis of lexical representation can be probed with such an approach.

Moving from the phonetic/phonological level to the domain of syntax, matters become more complex. The general strategy we have outlined calls for a separation of cognitively realistic computations from more general areas, such as *syntax*. One potentially promising operation of this type is the operation of linearization. The hierarchical representations motivated by syntactic theory must have a linear order imposed on them, because of the requirement that speech be instantiated in real time. In addition to being necessary for syntax, it is quite plausible that linearization operations of this type are also required in other linguistic and cognitive domains (e.g., for phonological sequencing, or for motor planning/execution, respectively). Extracting the computational operation (or operations) of linearization from these different domains amounts to approaching the problem at the correct level of granularity, in the manner we have stressed above: Linearization operations of a specific type have uniform computational properties, and it might be expected that certain brain regions are specialized to perform this type of computation. Ultimately it is possible that the use of (a family of) linearization operations in different cognitive tasks broadly construed is in part responsible for the apparently puzzling activation of Broca's area reviewed above.

There is much work to be done in these areas. To the extent that we have made progress in clarifying a research program that promises to yield substantive results, we still have not come close to the problem of how specific computations are executed by specialized brain regions. But the agenda we have outlined makes it possible to move closer to such questions, by highlighting the importance of concentrating on the nature of computational operations in language at the correct level of granularity.

CONCLUSIONS

The joint study of brain and language—cognitive neuroscience of language—has achieved some basic results correlating linguistic phenomena with brain responses, but has not advanced to any explanatory theory that identifies the nature of linguistic computation in the brain. Results from this area are therefore in some ways both confused and confusing. The absence of an explanatory theory of this type is the result of the conceptual granularity mismatch and the ontological immensurability between the foundational concepts of linguistics and those of neurobiology: The machinery we invoke to account for linguistic phenomena is not in any obvious way related to the entities and computations of the biological systems in question. Consequently, *there is an absence of reasonable linking hypotheses* by which one can explore how brain mechanisms form the basis for linguistic computation. If this critical perspective is on the right track, there is significant danger of (long-term) interdisciplinary cross-sterilization rather than cross-fertilization between linguistics and neurobiology, or, for that matter, linguistics and other empirical disciplines. To defend against being subjected to a poverty-of-the-imagination argument, we suggested a substantive alternative research program. The critical link between disciplines should come from computation, specifically, from computational models that are made explicit at the appropriate level of abstraction to create an interface for linguistics and neurobiology. By hypothesis, in such computational models the primitives and operations must be of the type that they can plausibly be executed by assemblies of neurons—thereby providing the neurophysiological grounding—and must reasonably be constitutive subroutines of linguistic computation—thereby providing the theoretical foundation.

ACKNOWLEDGMENTS

During the preparation of this manuscript, David Poeppel was a Fellow at the Wissenschaftskolleg zu Berlin. David Poeppel is supported by NIH R01 DC05660.

REFERENCES

Burton, M. W. (2001). The role of inferior frontal cortex in phonological processing. *Cognitive Science, 25*, 695–709.
Caplan D., Alpert, N., & Waters, G. (1998). Effects of syntactic structure and propositional number on patterns of regional cerebral blood flow. *Journal of Cognitive Neuroscience, 10*, 541-552.
Carey, S. (1985). *Conceptual change in childhood.* Cambridge, MA: Bradford Books, MIT Press.
Chomsky, N. (2000). Linguistics and brain science. In A. Marantz, Y. Miyashita, & W. O'Neil (Eds.), *Image, language, brain* (pp. 13-28). Cambridge, MA: MIT Press.
Dapretto, M., & Bookheimer, S. Y. (1999). Form and content: Dissociating syntax and semantics in sentence comprehension. *Neuron, 24*, 427-432.
Embick, D., Marantz, A., Miyashita, Y., O'Neil, W., & Sakai, K. L. (2000). A syntactic specialization for Broca's area. *Proceedings of the National Academy of Sciences, USA, 97*, 6150-6154.
Embick, D., Hackl, M., Schaeffer, J., Kelepir, M., & Marantz, A. (2001). A magnetoencephalographic component whose latency reflects lexical frequency. *Cognitive Brain Research, 10*, 345-348.

Embick, D., & Poeppel, D. (in press). Mapping syntax using imaging: Prospects and problems for the study of neurolinguistic computation. In K. Brown (Ed.), *Encyclopedia of language and linguistics* (2nd ed.). Oxford: Elsevier.

Eulitz, C., & Lahiri, A. (2004). Neurobiological evidence for abstract phonological representations in the mental lexicon during speech recognition. *Journal of Cognitive Neuroscience, 16,* 577-583.

Fiez, J., Tallal, P., Raichle, M., Katz, W., Miezin, F., & Petersen, S. (1995). PET studies of auditory and phonological processing: Effects of stimulus type and task condition. *Journal of Cognitive Neuroscience, 7,* 357-375.

Gandour, J., Wong, D., Hsieh, L., Weinzapfel, B., Van Lancker, D., & Hutchins, G. (2000). A crosslinguistic PET study of tone perception. *Journal of Cognitive Neuroscience, 12,* 207-222.

Gelfand, J., & Bookheimer, S. (2003). Dissociating neural mechanisms of temporal sequencing and processing phonemes. *Neuron, 38,* 831-842.

Halle, M. (2002). *From memory to speech and back.* Berlin: Mouton.

Hickok, G., & Poeppel, D. (Eds.). (2004). Towards a new functional anatomy of language. *Cognition, 92* (1-2).

Horwitz, B., Amunts, K., Bhattacharyya, R., Patkin, D., Jeffries, K., Zilles, K., & Braun, A. (2003). Activation of Broca's area during the production of spoken and signed language: A combined cytoarchitectonic mapping and PET analysis. *Neuropsychologia, 41,* 1868-1876.

Kang, A., Constable, R., Gore, J., & Avrutin, S. (1999). An event-related fMRI study of implicit phrase-level syntactic and semantic processing. *NeuroImage, 10,* 555-561.

Moro, A., Tettamanti, M., Perani, D., Donati, C., Cappa, S., & Fazio, F. (2001). Syntax and the brain: Grammar by selective anomalies. *NeuroImage, 13,* 110 - 118.

Musso, M., Moro, A., Glauche, V., Rijntjes, M., Reichenbach, J., Buchel, C., & Weiller, C. (2003). Broca's area and the language instinct. *Nature Neuroscience, 6,* 774-781.

Ni, W., Constable, R., Mencl, W., Pugh, K., Fulbright, R., Shaywitz, S., Shaywitz, B., Gore, J., & Shankweiler, D. (2000). An event-related neuroimaging study distinguishing form and content in sentence processing. *Journal of Cognitive Neuroscience, 12,* 120-133.

Phillips, C., Pellathy, T., Yeung, H., & Marantz, A. (in prep.). Phonological feature representations in auditory cortex.

Poeppel, D. (1996). A critical review of PET studies of phonological processing. *Brain and Language, 55,* 317-351.

Poeppel, D., Guillemin, A., Thompson, J., Fritz, J., Bavelier, D., & Braun, A. R. (2004). Auditory lexical decision, categorical perception, and FM direction discrimination differentially engage left and right auditory cortex. *Neuropsychologia, 42,* 183-200.

Rizzolatti, G., & Arbib, M. A. (1998). Language within our grasp. *Trends in Neurosciences, 21,* 188-194.

Zatorre, R., Evans, A., Meyer, E., & Gjedde, A. (1992). Lateralization of phonetic and pitch discrimination in speech processing. *Science, 256,* 846–849.

Section 2

Biology
and
Behavior

8

Genetic Specificity of Linguistic Heritability

Karin Stromswold
Rutgers University, New Brunswick, USA

TWIN STUDIES OF LANGUAGE

The logic of twin studies

The most common method used to study the role of genetic factors in development is to determine whether monozygotic (MZ) cotwins are linguistically more similar to one another than dizygotic (DZ) cotwins. Because MZ and DZ cotwins share essentially the same pre- and postnatal environment, whereas MZ cotwins share 100% of their DNA and DZ cotwins share only 50% of their DNA, if MZ cotwins are linguistically more similar than DZ cotwins, this suggests that genetic factors play a role in language. If, on the other hand, MZ cotwins are no more similar to one another than DZ cotwins, this suggests that genetic factors play a negligible role for language. Putting aside the possibility of interactions and correlations between genetic and environmental factors, the variation in linguistic abilities in a population (the phenotypic variance) is due to genetic variance plus environmental variance. Heritability is a measure of the proportion of the phenotypic variance that is due to genetic variance. In twin studies, environmental factors that may contribute to phenotypic variance are divided into those environmental factors that cotwins do and do not share. Shared environmental factors include the linguistic input children receive (assuming parents of twins speak the same way to both cotwins), and nonshared environmental factors include illnesses or accidents that only occur to one cotwin.

121

Concordance rates for language disorders

One way to determine whether MZ cotwins are linguistically more similar than DZ cotwins is to compare the MZ and DZ concordance rates for developmental language disorders. Twins are concordant for a language disorder if both cotwins are impaired, and discordant if only one cotwin is language-impaired. If the concordance rate for language disorders is significantly greater for MZ than DZ twins, this suggests that genetic factors play a role in language disorders such as dyslexia and specific language impairment (SLI). Stromswold (2001) performed meta-analyses of 10 twin studies of written or spoken language disorders. In these 10 studies, the mean proband-wise concordance rate was 80% for MZ twins and 46% for DZ twins. In all 10 studies, concordance rates were greater for MZ than DZ twin pairs, with the differences being significant in all but one study. When the twin pairs from the studies were pooled together, the overall concordance rate was significantly higher for MZ twins (80%) than DZ twins (46%). In the 5 twin studies of written language disorders, the mean concordance rate was 76% for MZ twins and 41% for DZ twins, with the overall concordance rate for MZ twins (75%) being significantly greater than for DZ twins (43%). For the 5 twin studies of spoken language disorders, the mean concordance rate was 84% for MZ twins and 52% twins, with the overall concordance rate for MZ twins (84%) being significantly greater than for DZ twins (50%). One can obtain an estimate of the role of heritable factors for a disorder by doubling the difference in MZ and DZ concordance rates for the disorder. For example, if the concordance rate for spoken language impairments is 84% for MZ twins and 50% for DZ twins, the heritability of spoken language impairments is 68%. An estimate of the role of shared environmental factors is obtained by subtracting the heritability estimate from the MZ concordance rate (84% – 68% = 16%), and an estimate of the role of non-shared (twin-specific) environmental factors is obtained by subtracting the MZ concordance rate from 100 (100% – 84% = 16%).

Heritability estimates that are based on concordance analyses have a number of limitations. First, they are only as valid as the diagnoses given to twins. If non-impaired twins are incorrectly diagnosed as being language impaired, or if language-impaired twins fail to be diagnosed, this can dramatically affect heritability estimates. Secondly, the estimates are only as specific as the diagnoses twins receive. If (some of) the twins' linguistic impairments are secondary to non-linguistic deficits, then the estimates obtained will not be good estimates of the heritability of linguistically-specific impairments. A third limitation of heritability estimates obtained from twin concordance analyses is that they are estimates of broad-sense heritability, and as such include the influence of gene dominance, epitasis (interactions between genes) and interactions between genes and environment.

Univariate analyses of normal twins' linguistic abilities

There are two additional drawbacks that are fairly specific to concordance-based heritability estimates. The first drawback has to do with the fact that concordance analyses take what is likely to be a continuous variable (linguistic ability) and artificially categorize people as either impaired or not impaired. Inevitably, there will be cases in which one twin scores just a few points higher than his or her cotwin, but this small difference is enough for one twin be labeled "normal" and the other impaired. The second drawback is that twin concordance studies can only be used to study the heritability of language impairments, and not the heritability of normal linguistic function. This is important because it is becoming increasingly clear that there isn't perfect overlap in heritable factors that affect language development and proficiency in people who have normal language versus impaired language (see Stromswold, 2001). In cases where the data obtained are more or less continuous (e.g., scores on language tests, age of acquisition of linguistic milestones) rather than dichotomous (presence or absence of a language disorder), one can address both of these drawback by comparing the similarity of normal MZ and DZ cotwins' language scores.

In univariate analyses, a twin's performance on test A is compared with his cotwin's performance on that same test. In meta-analyses of 8 studies of typically-developing twins' vocabulary development, Stromswold (2001) found that the mean weighted correlation coefficient was .93 for MZ twins (as compared to .76 for DZ twins). For phonemic awareness, the MZ correlation coefficient was .90 (compared to .56 for DZ twins). For articulation, the correlation coefficient was .92 for MZ twins and .85 for DZ twins. For reading, the coefficient for MZ twins was .86 (as compared to .66 for DZ twins). For spelling, the coefficient was .78 for MZ twins (as compared to .48 for DZ twins). Stromswold (2001) reported the results of 12 twin studies in which 36 tests of morphosyntax were administered. Unfortunately, the variability among these tests precluded calculating mean correlation coefficients. However, it is worth noting that in 33 of the 36 tests, the MZ correlation coefficient was larger than the DZ twins, with the difference being significant for 12 of the 36 morphosyntactic tests. Falconer's (1960) estimate of the effect of heritable factors is calculated by doubling the difference between the MZ and DZ intra-twin correlation coefficients. The role of shared environmental factors is computed by subtracting Falconer's heritability estimate from the MZ correlation coefficient and the role of non-shared environmental factors is calculated by subtracting the MZ correlation from one. We can use these formulas to estimate, for example, that 68% of phonemic awareness is due to heritable factors, 22% is due to shared environmental factors, and 10% is due to nonshared environmental factors.

Univariate analyses clearly reveal that for a wide range of linguistic tasks, normal MZ cotwins perform more similarly to one another than DZ cotwins do. This suggests that heritable factors play a substantial role in the linguistic abilities of normal people. However, like heritability estimates based on twin concordancy, Falconer's heritability estimates are estimates of broad sense heritability. A second limitation of univariate twin analyses is that they do not allow one to tell whether the heritable factors that affect language are specific to language. It is possible, for example, that the heritable factors that affect phonemic awareness also influence other cognitive, linguistic, or motor abilities.

Multivariate analyses of normal twins' linguistic abilities

Bivariate analyses can help determine how specific-to-language the genetic factors that influence language are.[1] In bivariate analyses, a twin's performance on test A is compared with his cotwin's performance on test B. Genetic influence on the phenotypic correlation between test A and B (bivariate heritability) is estimated by the extent to which the MZ cross-twin correlation is greater than the DZ cross-twin correlation. In contrast, the genetic correlation estimates the extent to which the same genetic factors affect A and B regardless of their contribution to the correlation between A and B. Genetic correlation may be high, yet bivariate heritability low and vice versa. For example, genetic factors might play a substantial role for both gross motor abilities and linguistic abilities, but if completely different genetic factors are responsible for gross motor and linguistic abilities, the genetic correlation will be zero. Conversely, genetic factors might play only a modest role for gross motor and linguistic abilities, but if the same genetic factors are responsible for both abilities, the genetic correlation will be high. One limitation of multivariate analyses is that they only allow one to determine the extent to which there is genetic overlap for the particular behavioral traits one has assessed. For example, researchers involved in the U.K. Twins Early Development Study (TEDS) have used multivariate analyses to determine the specificity of genes that affect verbal and nonverbal

---

[1]Using Cholesky decomposition modeling, bivariate analyses can be extended to investigate relationships among more than two variables (see de Jong, 1999).

abilities. In addition to heritable factors that influence both nonverbal cognitive abilities and verbal abilities, there appear to be genetic factors that influence verbal abilities but not nonverbal cognitive abilities (e.g., Price et al., 2000). It is possible, however, that these latter genetic factors affect more than just verbal abilities. For example, genetic factors that affect verbal abilities but not nonverbal cognitive abilities could nonetheless affect oral motor abilities, fine motor abilities, gross motor abilities, social-emotional abilities, short term memory, attention, auditory processing, etc.. The only way to rule this out is to assess all of these abilities in the same group of subjects, and perform the appropriate analyses. Unfortunately, in order to have the statistical power to do so, one must have data from a very large number of twins. We have begun such a twin study and, as of December 2003, we have assessed the gross motor, fine motor, oral-motor, cognitive, personal-social, and linguistic abilities of 400 sets of twins (Stromswold, 2003).

A second limitation is that the estimates of the genetic correlation for two behavioral traits are only as good as the behavioral tests used to assess the two traits. For example, analyses of the TEDS data suggest that the same genes affect vocabulary development and syntactic development, and that no vocabulary- or syntax-specific genetic factors exist (Dale, Dionne, Eley, & Plomin, 2000). However, this might reflect limitations in the way syntax and vocabulary development were assessed. In the TEDS study, parents assessed their twins' vocabularies by indicating whether they said each of 100 words. Parents then assessed their twins' syntax by choosing which sentence in 12 pairs of sentences (e.g., *baby crying, baby is crying*) sounded more like something that their twins might say. It seems plausible that, during the early stages of language learning, parents are fairly good at recalling whether their child says particular words and, hence, that the TEDS vocabulary measure is probably adequate. The same is not necessarily true of the TEDS syntax measure. It is very unlikely that a child has said the exact sentences listed, so to complete the syntax measure, parents must act as amateur developmental linguists. Furthermore, parents complete the syntax section immediately after completing the vocabulary checklist. Therefore, one worry is that parents who check off lots of words on the vocabulary test might (unconsciously) be biased to choose the "better" of the sentences in each pair, whereas parents who check off few words might be biased to choose the "worse" sentence in each pair, and this bias accounts for the high genetic correlation for vocabulary and syntax. In our ongoing twin study (Stromswold, 2003), we address this problem by supplementing parents' reports of when their twins acquired linguistic milestones (babbling, first word, first sentence, and clear articulation) and whether (and how much) written and spoken language therapy their twins received, with direct assessment of key linguistic skills (Stromswold, 2002). For example, articulation is assessed with a word repetition task, lexical access is assessed via a rapid naming task, and syntax is assessed with a picture-pointing comprehension test of semantically reversible sentences. (A sample test may be found at: http://ruccs.rutgers.edu/~karin/PERINATAL/PALS/PAL4.pdf).

The role of environment on language development

Twin studies are usually used to explore whether genetic factors affect a phenotypic trait, but it is equally valid to use twin studies to examine how environmental factors influence a trait. A limitation shared by concordance, univariate, and multivariate twin studies, however, is that estimates of the phenotypic effects of shared and non-shared environment completely conflate the effects of prenatal and postnatal environment. Seventy years of research has confirmed that even when impaired twins are excluded, twins' language development is 2 to 3 months delayed compared to singletons (see Dale et al., 2000). This delay is believed to reflect the special environmental hardships twins face. The (often unspoken) assumption in most twin studies is that when one refers to the role of environmental factors in language development, one is referring to the role of postnatal factors such as the quantity or quality of adult linguistic input that children receive. Indeed, several studies have shown that twins typically receive less adult linguistic input than singletons (for a review, see, Reznick, 1997; Stromswold, 2001).

Conway, Lytton, and Pysh (1980) found that maternal speech variables (amount of maternal speech, amount of maternal child-directed speech, and complexity of maternal speech) accounted for 15% of the variance in twins' language development, whereas neonatal variables (Apgar scores,[2] gestational age, and birth weight) accounted for 8% of the variance. These results are often cited as proof that postnatal factors

---

[2]Apgar scores are commonly used to rate the physical well-being of neonates on a 0 to 10 scale, with 10 being the best score possible. Five physical parameters are given a score of 0, 1, or 2, and these subscores are summed to give a neonate's Apgar score. The word 'Apgar' is both an eponymic tribute to its inventor (Virginia Apgar) and a mnemonic for the five parameters that are assessed (Appearance or color, Pulse rate, Grimace or reflex irritability, Activity or muscle tone, and Respiration). Some studies have shown that low scores (e.g., 5 minute Apgar scores of less than 7) are associated with neurodevelopmental delay (Thorngren-Jerneck & Herbst, 2001) and linguistic delay (Cusson, 2003).

affect language development much more than prenatal factors. However, Conway et al.'s (1980) findings should be viewed with great caution for several reasons. First, the study had only 24 twins. Second, the twins had atypically benign perinatal histories (they were born an average of 2 weeks later and 400 grams heavier than the mean for U.S.-born twins). Third, there was considerably less variance for neonatal variables than maternal variables, and this may have decreased the predictive power of the neonatal variables. Fourth, because the study didn't distinguish between MZ and DZ twins, and twin and singleton data were collapsed in the regression analyses, these data cannot be used to evaluate the relative importance of neonatal versus maternal variables on twins' language. There is another reason to suspect that postnatal environment may not play a major role in language development. If postnatal environment *did* play a major role, we would expect that twins who are reared apart would have less similar linguistic abilities than twins reared together. Contrary to this prediction, Pedersen, Plomin, and McClearn (1994) found that the heritability estimates for vocabulary size were quite similar for elderly twins who were reared together or apart.

The effects of perinatal environment

Since the 1950s, researchers have known that twins suffer from more pre- and perinatal complications than singletons, and MZ are at greater risk for many of these complications than DZ twins (for a historical perspective, see Lenneberg, 1967). Twins are 5 time more likely to be born prematurely (before 37 weeks gestation) and 10 times more likely to be born at low birth weights (less than 2500 grams) than singletons (Center for Disease Control, 1999), both of which are major risk factors for language impairments. Furthermore, twins (especially MZ twins) are more likely to suffer perinatal complications such as hypoxic/ischemic brain injuries, fetal growth restriction, prolonged labor, umbilical cord incidents, and hyperbilirubinemia. The special perinatal environmental factors associated with twinning result in perinatal mortality rates for twins who share a placenta being twice as great as for twins who do not share a placenta[3] and 4 times as high as for singletons; congenital malformations being more common in twins (particularly MZ twins) than singletons; discordance for congenital malformations being more common in MZ twins than DZ twins; and neurodevelopmental disabili-

---

[3]DZ twins never share a placenta, whereas 75% to 80% of MZ twins do share a placenta (see Stromswold, 2004).

ties being more common in twins than singletons, with certain disabilities (e.g., cerebral palsy) being more common in MZ twins than DZ twins. (For a discussion of perinatal risk factors associated with twinning, see Stromswold, 2004 and references therein.)

There are at least two reasons why children who experience perinatal hardships may be more likely to exhibit language delays than children who don't experience these hardships. The first reason is that, because language is one of the most complicated tasks that children must master, children with subtle (but non-specific) neurodevelopmental dysfunction are likely to exhibit language delays. The second reason is that the neural substrates of language may be particularly vulnerable to the effects of these perinatal hardships. Consider, for example, the effects of excess bilirubin. Excess bilirubin causes neonatal jaundice and, in severe cases, can lead to bilirubin encephalopathy in which cerebral grey matter is destroyed (Volpe, 1995). Although hyperbilirubinemia can affect any part of the central nervous system, the auditory pathways are particularly sensitive to the effects of bilirubin (e.g., Shapiro, 2002), and even modestly elevated bilirubin in the neonatal period is associated with mild sensorineural hearing loss and auditory dysfunction (e.g., Amin et al., 2001). Recent studies suggest that children with minimal hearing losses (hearing thresholds of between 16 and 25 dBs) are more likely to suffer from language delays and impairment than children with normal hearing (e.g., Bess, Dodd-Murphy, & Parker, 1998). This is important for genetic studies of SLI because the hearing thresholds generally used to ensure that hearing impaired children aren't labeled SLI would miss some children with minimal hearing losses (see Stromswold, 1997).

Teasing apart the effects of pre- and post-natal environments

Birth weight discrepancies in twin pairs may provide a way of teasing apart the effects of prenatal and postnatal environment. Here's why: Because DZ twins share only 50% of their DNA, birth weight differences in DZ twin pairs reflect differences in the genetic endowment of twin pairs (one twin might be genetically predisposed to be bigger than his cotwin) *and* differences in the prenatal environment. In contrast, because MZ twins share 100% of their DNA, differences in MZ twin pairs' birth weights *solely* reflect differences in the cotwins' prenatal environments. By comparing MZ cotwins who have very similar birth weights with MZ cotwins who have very dissimilar birth weights (i.e., birth weights that differ by at least 15% or 20%, Charlemaine et al., 2000), we can obtain an estimate of the effect of intrauterine environment on later development. To the extent that MZ cotwins who have very similar birth weights are linguistically more similar to one another than MZ cotwins who have very different birth weights, this is a measure of the effect of intrauterine environment on language development. Estimates of the effect of intrauterine environment can be calculated using slight variants of the methods traditionally used to calculated heritability estimates. However, instead of contrasting the linguistic similarity of MZ and DZ cotwins, we compare the linguistic similarity of MZ cotwins who have similar and dissimilar birth weights. The size of interactions between genetic and intrauterine environmental factors can be estimated by comparing how great an effect having very different birth weights has for MZ and DZ cotwins (in essence calculating a difference of a difference score).

The best biologic predictors of developmental delays in prematurely-born and intrauterine growth restricted children are hypoxic-ischemic perinatal brain injuries and subnormal brain growth (see Berg, 1989 and references therein). Brain growth is typically spared in intrauterine growth restriction, but when this protective mechanism fails, the risk of neurodevelopmental delay is high (Kramer et al., 1989). This is especially true when head size (a proxy for brain growth) fails to normalize during infancy and childhood (e.g., Hack et al., 1991). Neonatologists and pediatricians routinely record infants' head circumferences, and it is trivial to obtain this measurement on older children and adults. Therefore, one could investigate the role of perinatal brain injuries on linguistic abilities by testing whether discrepancy in head circumference in MZ cotwins is associated with linguistic discordance in these twins. Because there are well-normed growth curves for head circumference, one could also test whether MZ twins whose head circumferences are persistently discrepant are more likely to be linguistically discordant than MZ twins whose head circumferences become more similar with time. Following the logic outlined for birth weight discrepancy, size of interactions between genetics and intrauterine factors can be estimated by comparing how having very different head sizes affects linguistic similarity in MZ and DZ cotwins. Neonatal neural ultrasounds are routinely obtained on neonates admitted to neonatal intensive care units. Neural ultrasounds are used primarily to detect and determine the severity of intraventricular hemorrhages (IVHs). One can easily tell whether (and how severe) an IVH a neonate has suffered for each side of the brain. Therefore, another way to investigate the extent to which perinatal brain injuries affect language development is to compare the linguistic abilities of MZ cotwins who are concordant or discordant for IVHs.

Mothers are usually able to recall the complications and interventions that occur during labor and delivery. For example, more than 90% of the mothers of twins in our study are able to report whether each of their twins was breech, how long they were in labor, what drugs they received during labor, how much time passed between the delivery of the first twin and the second twin, whether forceps or vacuum extraction was used for each twin, and whether there were any cord complications (Stromswold, 2003). These data could easily be used to estimate the impact of intrapartum complications on language development in twins.

Interactions among genetic and environmental factors

Prenatal factors might affect twins differentially according to their genetic make up. A relatively minor ischemic injury to brain areas involved in language or a mild sensorineural hearing loss might have devastating effects on a twin genetically at risk for language impairments, yet have no discernible adverse affect on a twin who is not genetically at risk. Postnatal environmental factors could also have different effects on different people depending on their genetic makeup. A child who is genetically at risk for developing language disorders may be particularly sensitive to subtly impoverished linguistic environments. Because the genetically-at-risk child is likely to have relatives who are language impaired, he is likely to be reared in linguistically impoverished environments. A child who is linguistically less adept (for genetic and/or environment reasons) may respond less to linguistic input. His parents might unconsciously respond by providing less (or less complex) linguistic input, which might further impede his language acquisition. The less linguistically-adept child might unconsciously avoid linguistically challenging situations, choosing instead activities and friends that make fewer linguistic demands of him, thereby further slowing his language development. At the other end of the spectrum, if there are synergistic interactions between genetic and postnatal environmental factors, a child who has the genetic propensity to succeed at language might benefit more from enriched environments (and better tolerate impoverished environments). Because a genetically well-endowed child is more likely to have relatives who are linguistically able, he is more likely to be reared in linguistically enriched environments. In addition, such a child might seek out environments that are linguistically challenging, thereby further accelerating his language development. Genetic-postnatal environmental interactions do not necessarily have to involve psychosocial environmental factors. A child who is genetically at risk for language delay may be more susceptible to the adverse effects of malnutrition, environmental toxins, or postnatal head injury, whereas a child who is not genetically at-risk may be more resilient to the effects of such insults.

Prenatal and postnatal environmental factors may be correlated (e.g., pre- and postnatal malnutrition in poor families) or interact with one other. For example, as mentioned above, children with mild hearing losses due to perinatal factors may seek out linguistically less challenging environments and/or receive less linguistic input either because they cannot hear what is said to them or their parents limit what they say to their child (Nelson & Soli, 2000). In addition, children with mild hearing losses may be more susceptible to the effects of slightly impoverished linguistic input (prenatal–postnatal interaction).

Gene-gene interactions could also be phenotypically important for language. Bivariate analyses of the data from 1937 same-sex TEDS twin pairs at age 2 reveals that only 21% of the variance in expressive vocabulary size can be explained by scores on a parent-administered nonverbal cognitive test, and the genetic correlation between nonverbal and expressive vocabulary measures is only .30 (Price et al., 2000). At age 4, one-sixth of the TEDS twins were tested on a battery of language and nonverbal cognitive tests. Bivariate analyses of these data reveal a genetic correlation of .46 for language and nonverbal abilities (Colledge et al., 2002). Taken together, these results suggest that, as children get older, the overlap in genetic factors affecting language and nonverbal abilities becomes more apparent. This increase could reflect the impact of gene-gene or gene-environment interactions.

MOLECULAR GENETIC STUDIES OF LANGUAGE

The logic of molecular genetic studies

In most molecular genetic studies of language, parametric and nonparametric linkage analysis techniques are used to compare the genomes of language-impaired people and their normal relatives, and determine how the genomes of affected people differ from those of unaffected relatives. This is usually done by finding large multiplex families (multi-generational families in which several family members suffer from the same disorder, and this disorder appears to have simple Mendelian transmission) and comparing the DNA of affected and unaffected family members. In parametric linkage analyses, the transmission of marker alleles through multiple generations is compared with the transmission of the trait phenotype to determine whether the marker locus and trait locus assort independently, or whether they show decreased recombination (which would indicate that the two loci are near each other on the same chromosome).

Because language-disordered multiplex families are rare (Stromswold, 1998), geneticists also compare the DNA of sibling pairs in which one sibling is affected and the other is unaffected. In non-parametric sibling-pair analyses, the proportion of marker alleles that are identical in pairs of siblings is compared with the phenotypic similarity between the siblings. For example, siblings share 0, 1, or 2 alleles at a particular locus. If the trait locus is closely linked to a marker allele, similarity between the siblings for the marker alleles should correspond to similarity for the trait phenotype, regardless of mode of transmission or penetrance for the disorder.[4] Sibling-pair linkage analyses have several possible advantages over multiplex family analyses. First, because sibling-pair analyses are usually nonparametric, they are more likely to reveal associations, particularly with traits with variable expressivity. Second, one does not need to specify the mode of transmission in sibling-pair analyses. Third, sibling-pair analyses can reveal linkage even when penetrance is incomplete. Fourth, because it is easier to locate affected-unaffected sibling pairs than multiplex families, the sample size (and statistical power) is likely to be greater for sibling-pair than multiplex family analyses. Fifth, because most cases of developmental language disorders do not appear to follow simple Mendelian transmission patterns (Stromswold, 1998), linkage analyses conducted on multiplex families may implicate genes that *can* cause language disorders but rarely do (Stromswold, 2001). This appears to be the case for the FOXP2 gene, the mutation of which is clearly associated with speech dyspraxia (and a myriad of other disorders) in the members of the KE family (Lai et al., 2001). In 4 large studies of people with spoken language impairments (Bartlett et al., 2002; Meaburn, Dale, Craig, & Plomin, 2002; Newbury et al., 2002; O'Brien et al., 2003), the FOXP2 mutation has not been found in a single language impaired person.

Written language impairment loci

To date, at least 8 loci (1p34-36, 2p15-16, 3p12-q13, 6p21.3, 6q12-13, 11p15.5, 15q21, and 18p11.2) and possibly 9 (7q32, Kaminen et al., 2003) have been linked to written language disorders (for a review, see Fisher & DeFries, 2002; Stromswold, 2001).[5] Recently, Taipale et al. (2003) have

---

[4]Mode of transmission refers to the way in which a genetic disorder is passed from one generation to the next (e.g., autosomal dominant, autosomal recessive, X-linked recessive, multifactorial-polygenic). Penetrance is the fraction of individuals with a given genotype who exhibit the disorder.

[5]Humans have 22 pairs of autosomal and 2 sex (X,Y) chromosomes.

identified a candidate gene for dyslexia at the 15q21 locus. If genes at all of these loci can cause dyslexia, what does this say about the genetic specificity of dyslexia? One possibility is that the different dyslexia loci contain genes that affect different aspects or component skills of reading. For example, Grigorenko (2001) has argued that the 15q21 locus is associated with orthographically-based (or surface) dyslexia and the 6p21 locus is associated with phonologically-based dyslexia. This association has not generally been found and, at this point, the preponderance of the evidence does not suggest that there is a simple relationship between dyslexia loci and subcomponents of reading (see Fisher & DeFries, 2002; Stromswold, 2001). The specificity of putative dyslexia loci is further undermined by the observation that *most* of these loci are also linked to other neuropsychological disorders.[6] The 2p15 dyslexia locus is also (weakly) linked to schizophrenia (Shaw et al., 1998), the 6p21 locus is also linked to attention deficit-hyperactivity disorder (ADHD) and schizophrenia (see references in Stromswold, 2001), the 6q13 locus is also linked to schizophrenia (e.g., Cao et al., 1997; Straub et al., 2002), the 7q32 locus is also linked to autism (see Bonora et al., 2002; Collaborative Linkage Study of Autism, 2001 and references therein), the 11p11.5 locus is also linked to ADHD (see Langley et al., 2004 and references therein); bipolar disorder (see Zandi et al., 2003 and references therein) and autism (Trottier, Srivastava, & Walke, 1999); the 15q21 locus is also linked to ADHD (Bakker et al., 2003), and the 18p11 locus is also linked to bipolar disorder and schizophrenia (Kikuchi et al., 2003; Reyes et al., 2002).

Spoken language impairment loci

At least 6 loci or genes have been linked to spoken language impairments: The FOXP2 gene on 7q31 (Lai et al., 2001), a region near the CFTR gene at 7q31 (Bartlett et al., 2004; O'Brien et al., 2003), a region near D7S3052 at 7q31 (Bartlett et al., 2004; O'Brien et al., 2003), 13q21[7] (Bartlett et al., 2004; Bartlett et al., 2002), a locus at 16q24 (SLI Consortium, 2002),

---

Autosomal chromosomes are numbered from 1 to 22 by size, with 1 being the largest. Each chromosome has an asymmetrically placed constriction that is used to define a short arm (p) and a long arm (q) of the chromosome. Thus, for example, 15q21 refers to staining band 21 on the long arm of chromosome 15.

[6]Because loci encompass thousands of genes, the overlap in loci for language disorders and other neurodevelopmental disorders could merely be coincidental.

[7]Fisher, Lai, and Monaco (2003) have argued that the 13q21 locus might be better characterized as a dyslexia locus because the phenotype that links to 13q21 is reading impairment and not spoken language impairment.

and a locus at 19q13 (SLI Consortium, 2002). There are also some data that suggest spoken language impairment loci at 2p22 (Bartlett et al., 2004; Bartlett et al., 2002) and at 1p36, 2p15, 6p21, and 15q21 (Bartlett et al., 2000), and there are case reports of mutations associated with spoken language impairments that implicate loci at 15q13, 1p22, and/or 2q31 (see Stromswold, 2001 and references therein). As is the case with dyslexia loci, many of the spoken language impairment loci are also linked to other neurodevelopmental disorders. The D7S3052 loci on 7q31 is near the IMMP2L gene that has been implicated in Tourette syndrome (Petek et al., 2001). The CFTR region of 7q31 has been implicated in autism (Wassink et al., 2001), as have the loci at 13q21 (Collaborative Linkage Study of Autism, 2001) and 19q13 (Liu et al., 2001). Furthermore, although the FOXP2 mutation segregates perfectly with affectedness in the KE family, it is unclear how phenotypically specific the effects of the mutation are as affected family members suffer from grammatical deficits, speech dyspraxia (difficulty making the complex, oral motor movements necessary for speech), depressed nonverbal IQ, and developmental learning disorders that do not appear to be verbal in nature (see Stromswold, 2001 and references therein).

Problems associated with genotype-phenotype mapping

Phenocopy is the term used to describe the situation when different genotypes can result in the same phenotype. The fact that 9 distinct loci have been linked to dyslexia and a dozen loci have been linked to spoken language impairments clearly indicates that different genotypes can cause at least broadly defined phenotypes such as written and spoken language impairments. Even rather specific language impairment phenotypes may have different causes, and hence may be due to different genotypes. Consider a phenotype that is characterized by the selective omission of grammatical morphemes. This phenotype could be the result of a genetic disorder that selectively impairs syntax, a genetic disorder that specifically impairs control of rapid, complex oral motor movements necessary for language (speech dyspraxia), a genetic disorder that specifically impacts some component of auditory processing (e.g., auditory short term memory, auditory sequencing, rapid auditory processing), or a genetic disorder that affects multiple aspects of language but not nonverbal cognition (see Stromswold, 1997).

Pleiotropy is the term that is used when the same genotype results in different phenotypes. A particularly clear example of pleiotropy is incomplete penetrance, when family members share a mutation for a disorder, but only some of these family members are clinically affected. Another type of pleiotropy is when all family members who have a mutation are affected, but the nature of the disorder varies among family members. Consider again a genetic mutation that affects people's abilities to coordinate complex oral motor movements (oral motor apraxia). A person with such a genotype could present as someone who is unwilling or unable to speak in any situation (mutism) or in selective situations (selective mutism), as someone with speech dyspraxia, as someone who has a dysfluency or stutter, or as someone who omits phonologically unstressed elements (i.e., grammatical morphemes) and, hence, appears to have a grammatical deficit.

In addition to dealing with the problems of phenocopy and pleiotropy, geneticists must grapple with the problem that a genotype may be expressed phenotypically in different ways at different points of development. Returning again to the oral motor apraxia mutation, an infant with such a mutation might have difficulty coordinating suck and swallow, and might present as having a feeding disorder or failing to grow adequately. As a toddler, the child might have outgrown his feeding disorder, but be unwilling to speak. By the time he is school-aged, he might speak but selectively omit phonologically unstressed elements. As an adult, his impairment might not be readily apparent, but he might nonetheless avoid linguistically-taxing social or professional settings, and hence might seem shy. In a similar fashion, a child who starts out with a fairly language-specific deficit might, over time, begin to show additional secondary deficits. For example, because he has difficulty understanding what is said to him, he might appear to have attention deficit disorder. Eventually, the child's difficulty understanding spoken language is likely to result in poor school performance, and perhaps even lowered nonverbal IQ.

FUTURE DIRECTIONS

How can we increase the rate of progress toward greater understanding of the genetic and environmental bases of language?

One way to simplify the task of identifying loci and genes that affect language is by analyzing the DNA of MZ and DZ twins. We can perform fine-grained molecular genetic analyses to determine whether linguistically discordant MZ twin pairs differ more genetically (e.g., in terms of frequency of spontaneous mutations) or epigenetically (e.g., in terms of methylation patterns) than linguistically concordant MZ twin pairs. We can also perform linkage analyses of DZ twins. Although DZ twins are, on average, no more genetically similar than full siblings, linkage analyses of twins are more likely to be fruitful than linkage analyses of siblings for several reasons. First, the environments of DZ twins are almost certainly more similar than the environments of nontwin siblings. Thus, environmental differences between DZ twins are less likely to obscure the effects of genetic factors. Second, because DZ cotwins are the same age, the same tests and measures can be used to evaluate their linguistic function, thus eliminating a huge source of noise in linkage analyses. Third, the concern that the language-disordered genotype may be expressed differently at different ages (the developmental problem) does not apply.

We can use data from twins to simplify the task of identifying which prenatal and postnatal factors affect language development (either acting alone or in concert with genetic factors). We can explore the effects of pre- and perinatal environmental factors by measuring the linguistic similarity of MZ cotwins and DZ cotwins that are concordant and discordant for birth weight, head circumference, brain injuries and intrapartum complications. Similarly, we can explore the impact of postnatal environmental factors on language by measuring the linguistic similarity of MZ and DZ cotwins that have been exposed to different biological (e.g., head injuries, neurological illnesses, neurotoxins), psychosocial, or linguistic environments.

Recently Becker (2004) proposed the Common Variant/Multiple Disease (CV/MD) hypothesis to account for pleiotropy and phenocopy in autoimmune disorders, metabolic disorders (type 2 diabetes and obesity) and schizoid disorders (schizophrenia and bipolar disorders). According to the CV/MD hypothesis, common alleles that contribute to a particular disease under particular genetic and environmental conditions may result in a different disease under other genetic and environmental conditions. For a group of related disorders (e.g., autoimmune disorders such as thyroiditis, systemic lupus erythematosus, and multiple sclerosis), there are some genetic and environmental factors that are unique to a particular disease and other genetic and environmental factors that are shared by several diseases. The CV/MD hypothesis could explain why *most* of the loci that have been linked to written and spoken language disorders have also been linked to other neurodevelopmental disorders, why most cases of familial language disorders do not have simple Mendelian patterns of transmission, why different people with the same genetic mutation have different clinical pictures, and why linkage analyses of people with familial language disorders often fail to identify susceptibility loci, including loci that have been previously identified. By adopting the CV/MD hypothesis that developmental language disorders belong to a larger class of neurodevelopmental disorders, we will have a framework in which we can better explore, understand, and explain how genetic and environmental factors affect language.

ACKNOWLEDGMENTS

Portions of this work were supported by grants from the Bamford-Lahey Children's Foundation, the Busch Biomedical Research Foundation, the National Science Foundation (BCS-9875168, BCS-0042561, BCS-0124095), and a Rutgers University unrestricted research grant. I thank participants at the Brain and Behavior Workshop for their helpful comments and suggestions.

REFERENCES

Amin, S. B., Ahlfors, C., Orlando, M. S., Dalzell, L. E., Merle, K. S., & Guillet, R. (2001). Bilirubin and serial auditory brainstem responses in premature infants. *Pediatrics, 107,* 664-670.

Bakker, S. C., van der Meulen, E. M., Buitelaar, J. K., Sandkuijl, L. A., Pauls, D. L., Monsuur, A. J., van 't Slot, R., Minderaa, R. B., Gunning, W. B., Pearson, P. L., & Sinke, R.J. (2003). A whole-genome scan in 164 Dutch sib pairs with attention-deficit/hyperactivity disorder: Suggestive evidence for linkage on chromosomes 7p and 15q. *American Journal of Human Genetics, 72,* 1251-1260.

Bartlett, C. W., Flax, J., Yabut, O., Li, W., Tallal, P., & Brzustowicz, L. M. (2000). A Genome-scan for linkage of Specific Language Impairment: Report on chromosomes, 1, 6, and 15. *American Journal of Human Genetics, 67,* 1710 (abstract).

Bartlett, C. W., Flax, J. F., Logue, M. W., Smith, B. J., Vieland, V. J., Tallal, P., & Brzustowicz, L. M. (2004). Examination of potential overlap in autism and language loci on chromosomes 2, 7, and 13 in two Independent samples ascertained for Specific Language Impairment. *Human Heredity, 57,* 10-20.

Bartlett, C. W., Flax, J. F., Logue, M. W., Vieland, V. J., Bassett, A. S., Tallal, P., & Brzustowicz, L. M. (2002). A major susceptibility locus for specific language impairment is located on 13q21. *American Journal of Human Genetics, 71,* 45-55.

Becker, K. G. (2004). The common variants/multiple disease hypothesis of common complex genetic disorders. *Medical Hypotheses, 62,* 309-317.

Berg, A. T. (1989). Indices of fetal growth-retardation, perinatal hypoxia-related factors and childhood neurological morbidity. *Early Human Development, 19,* 271-283.

Bess, F. H., Dodd-Murphy, J., & Parker, R. A. (1998). Children with minimal sensorineural hearing loss: Prevalence, educational performance and functional status. *Ear & Hearing, 19,* 339-354.

Bonora, E., Bacchelli, E., Levy, E. R., Blasi, F., Marlow, A., Monaco, A. P., & Maestrini, E. (2002). Mutation screening and imprinting analysis of four candidate genes for autism in the 7q32 region. *Molecular Psychiatry, 7,* 289-301.

Cao, Q., Martinez, M., Zhang, J., Sanders, A. R., Badner, J. A., Cravchik, A., Markey, C. J., Beshah, E., Guroff, J. J., Maxwell, M. E., Kazuba, D. M., Whiten, R., Goldin, L. R., Gershon, E. S., & Gejman, P. V. (1997). Suggestive evidence for a schizophrenia susceptibility locus on chromosome 6q and a confirmation in an independent series of pedigrees. *Genomics, 43*, 1-8.

Center for Disease Control (1999). Births: Final data for 1997. *National Vital Statistics Report, 47*, 1-94.

Charlemaine, C., Duyme, M., Ville, Y., Aurengo, A., Tremblay, R., Frydman, R., & Pons, J. (2000). Fetal biometric parameters, twin type and birth weight difference: A longitudinal study. *European Journal of Obstetrics, Gynecology, & Reproductive Biology, 93*, 27-32.

Collaborative Linkage Study of Autism (2001). An autosomal genomic screen for autism. *American Journal of Medical Genetics, 105*, 608-615.

Colledge, E., Bishop, D. V. M., Dale, P. S., Koeppen-Schomerus, G., Price, T. S., Happé, F., Eley, T. C., Dale, P. S., & Plomin, R. (2002). The structure of language abilities at 4 years: A twin study. *Developmental Psychology, 38*, 749-757.

Conway, D., Lytton, H., & Pysh, F. (1980). Twin-singleton language differences. *Canadian Journal of Behavioral Science, 12*, 264-271.

Cusson, R. M. (2003). Factors influencing language development in preterm infants. *Journal of Obstetric, Gynecologic, & Neonatal Nursing, 32*, 402-409.

Dale, P. S., Dionne, G., Eley, T. C., & Plomin, R. (2000). Lexical and grammatical development: A behavioural genetic perspective. *Journal of Child Language, 27*, 619-642.

de Jong, P. F. (1999). Hierarchical regression analysis in structural equation modeling. *Structural Equation Modeling, 6*, 198-211.

Falconer, D. S. (1960). *Introduction to quantitative genetics.* New York: Ronald Press Company.

Fisher, S. E., & DeFries, J. C. (2002). Developmental dyslexia: Genetic dissection of a complex cognitive trait. *Nature Review Neuroscience, 3*, 767-780.

Fisher, S. E., Lai, C. S. L., & Monaco, A. P. (2003). Deciphering the genetic basis of speech and language disorders. *Annual Review of Neuroscience, 26*, 57-80.

Grigorenko, E. L. (2001). Developmental dyslexia: An update on genes, brains, and environments. *Journal of Child Psychology & Psychiatry & Allied Disciplines, 42*, 91-125.

Hack, M., Breslau, N., Weissman, B., Aram, D., Klein, N. K., & Borawski, E. (1991). Effect of very low birth weight and subnormal head size on cognitive abilities at school age. *The New England Journal of Medicine, 325*, 231-237.

Kaminen, N., Hannula-Jouppi, K., Kestila, M., Lahermo, P., Mulle, K., Kaaranen, M., Myllyluoma, B., Voutilainen, A., Lyytinen, H., Nopola-Hemmi, J., & Kere, J. (2003). A genome scan for developmental dyslexia confirms linkage to chromosome 2p11 and suggests a new locus on 7q32. *Journal of Medical Genetics, 40*, 340-345.

Kikuchi, M., Yamada, K., Toyota, T., Itokawa, M., Hattori, E., Yoshitsugu, K., Shimizu, H., & Yoshikawa, T. (2003). Two-step association analyses of the chromosome 18p11.2 region in schizophrenia detect a locus encompassing C18orf1. *Molecular Psychiatry, 8*, 467-469.

Kramer, M. S., McLean, F. H., Olivier, M., Willis, D. M., & Usher, R. H. (1989). Body proportionality and head and length 'sparing' in growth-retarded neonates: A critical reappraisal. *Pediatrics, 84,* 717-723.

Lai, C. S. L., Fisher, S. E., Hurst, J. A., Vargha-Khadem, F., & Monaco, A. P. (2001). A forkhead-domain gene is mutated in a severe speech and language disorder. *Nature, 413,* 519-523.

Langley, K., Marshall, L., van den Bree, M., Thomas, H., Owen, M., O'Donovan, M., & Thapar, A. (2004). Association of the Dopamine D4 Receptor Gene 7-Repeat Allele with neuropsychological test performance of children with ADHD. *American Journal of Psychiatry, 161,* 133-138.

Lenneberg, E. H. (1967). *Biological foundations of language.* New York: John Wiley.

Liu, J., Nyholt, D. R., Magnussen, P., Parano, E., Pavone, P., Geschwind, D., Lord, C., Iversen, P., Hoh, J., Ott, J., & Gilliam, T. C. (2001). A genomewide screen for autism susceptibility loci. *American Journal of Human Genetics, 69,* 327-340.

Meaburn, E., Dale, P. S., Craig, I. W., & Plomin, R. (2002). Language-impaired children: No sign of the FOXP2 mutation. *NeuroReport, 13,* 1075-1077.

Nelson, P., & Soli, S. (2000). Acoustical barriers to learning: Children at risk in every classroom. *Language, Speech and Hearing Services in Schools, 31,* 356-361.

Newbury, D., Bonora, E., Lamb, J., Fisher, S., Lai, C., Baird, G., Jannoun, L., Slonims, V., Stott, C. M., Merricks, M. J., Bolton, P. F., Bailey, A., & Monaco, A. P. (2002). FOXP2 is not a major susceptibility gene for autism or specific language impairment. *American Journal of Human Genetics, 70,* 1318-1327.

O'Brien, E. K., Zhang, X., Nishimura, C., Tomblin, J. B., & Murray, J. C. (2003). Association of specific language impairment (SLI) to the region of 7q31. *American Journal of Human Genetics, 72,* 1536-1543.

Pedersen, N. L., Plomin, R., & McClearn, G. E. (1994). Is there G beyond g? (Is there genetic influence on specific cognitive abilities independent of genetic influence on general cognitive ability?) *Intelligence, 18,* 133-143.

Petek, E., Windpassinger, C., Vincent, J. B., Cheung, J., Boright, A. P., Scherer, S. W., Kroisel, P. M., & Wagner, K. (2001). Disruption of a novel gene (IMMP2L) by a breakpoint in 7q31 associated with Tourette syndrome. *American Journal of Human Genetics, 68,* 848-858.

Price, T. S., Eley, T. C., Dale, P. S., Stevenson, J., Saudino, K., & Plomin, R. (2000). Genetic and environmental covariation between verbal and nonverbal cognitive development in infancy. *Child Development, 71,* 948-959.

Reyes, G. D., Esterling, L. E., Corona, W., Ferraren, D., Rollins, D. Y., Padigaru, M., Yoshikawa, T., Monje, V. D., & Detera-Wadleigh, S. D. (2002). Map of candidate genes and STSs on 18p11.2, a bipolar disorder and schizophrenia susceptibility region. *Molecular Psychiatry, 7,* 337-339.

Reznick, J. S. (1997). Intelligence, language, nature and nurture in young twins. In R. J. Sternberg & E. L. Grigorenko (Eds.), *Intelligence, heredity and environment* (pp. 483-504). New York, NY: Cambridge University Press.

Shapiro, S. M. (2002). Somatosensory and brainstem auditory evoked potentials in the Gunn rat model of acute bilirubin neurotoxicity. *Pediatric Research, 52,* 844-849.

Shaw, S. H., Kelly, M., Smith, A. B., Shields, G., Hopkins, P. J., Loftus, J., Laval, S. H., Vita, A., De Hert, M., Cardon, L. R., Crow, T. J., Sherrington, R., & DeLisi, L. E. (1998). A genome-wide search for schizophrenia susceptibility genes. *American Journal of Medical Genetics, 81,* 364-376.

SLI Consortium (2002). A genomewide scan identifies two novel loci involved in specific language impairment. *American Journal of Human Genetics, 70,* 384-398.

Straub, R. E., MacLean, C. J., Ma, Y., Webb, B. T., Myakishev, M. V., Harris-Kerr, C., Wormley, B., Sadek, H., Kadambi, B., O'Neill, F.A., Walsh, D., & Kendler, K. S. (2002). Genome-wide scans of three independent sets of 90 Irish multiplex schizophrenia families and follow-up of selected regions in all families provides evidence for multiple susceptibility genes. *Molecular Psychiatry, 7,* 542-559.

Stromswold, K. (1997). Specific language impairments. In T. E. Feinberg & M. J. Farah (Eds.), *Behavioral neurology and neuropsychology* (pp. 755-772). New York: McGraw-Hill.

Stromswold, K. (1998). The genetics of spoken language disorders. *Human Biology, 70,* 297-324.

Stromswold, K. (2001). The heritability of language: A review and meta-analysis of twin, adoption and linkage studies. *Language, 77,* 647-723.

Stromswold, K. (2002). *The Parent Assessment of Language (PAL) tests.*

Stromswold, K. (2003). Perinatal risk factors study twin data: December, 2003.

Stromswold, K. (2004). Why aren't identical twins linguistically identical? Genetic, prenatal and postnatal factors. *Rutgers University Center for Cognitive Science Technical Report, 76,* 1-35.

Taipale, M., Kaminen, N., Nopola-Hemmi, J., Haltia, T., Myllyluoma, B., Lyytinen, H., Muller, K., Kaaranen, M., Lindsberg, P. J., Hannula-Jouppi. K., & Kere, J. (2003). A candidate gene for developmental dyslexia encodes a nuclear tetratricopeptide repeat domain protein dynamically regulated in brain. *Proceedings of the National Academy of Sciences, USA, 100,* 11553-11558.

Thorngren-Jerneck, K., & Herbst, A. (2001). Low 5-minute Apgar score: A population-based register study of 1 million term births. *Obstetrics & Gynecology, 98,* 65-70.

Trottier, G., Srivastava, L., & Walke, C.-D. (1999). Etiology of infantile autism: A review of recent advances in genetic and neurobiological research. *Journal of Psychiatry & Neuroscience, 24,* 103-115.

Volpe, J. J. (1995). *Neurology of the newborn, 3rd ed.* Philadelphia: W. B. Saunders.

Wassink, T. H., Piven, J., Vieland, V. J., Huang, J., Swiderski, R. E., Pietila, J., Braun, T., Beck, G., Folstein, S. E., Haines, J. L., & Sheffield, V. C. (2001). Evidence supporting WNT2 as an autism susceptibility gene. *American Journal of Medical Genetics, 105,* 406-413.

Zandi, P., Willour, V., Huo, Y., Chellis, J., Potash, J., MacKinnon, D., Simpson, S. G., McMahon, F. J., Gershon, E., Reich, T., Foroud, T., Nurnberger, J., Jr., DePaulo, J. R., Jr., & McInnis, M. G. (2003). Genome scan of a second wave of NIMH genetics initiative bipolar pedigrees: Chromosomes 2, 11, 13, 14, and X. *American Journal of Medical Genetics, 119B,* 69-76.

9 The Neurobiology of Speech Perception

Sophie K. Scott
Department of Psychology and Department of Phonetics and Linguistics, University College London, UK

Speech is a striking human skill, both in terms of the precision of the motor acts which production involves, and the complexity of the acoustic signal that we perceive as meaningful words. Our perception of speech is both robust and flexible: We are able to follow speakers with a wide variety of different accents and moods, in very adverse auditory environments. This perceptual ability is all the more impressive when the actual nature of the speech signal is considered. Speakers do not produce simple strings of regular phonemes which are then sequenced into words by the listener. There is a lot of variability in the acoustic signal, resulting from speaker differences, co-articulation and assimilation effects. This variability precludes a simple linear mapping between the acoustic signal and the identity of the phone that is expressed (Bailey & Summerfield, 1980). It is also important to note that the 'surface', acoustic representation of speech is not wholly separable from the intended meaning: Coarticulation has been suggested to have a communicative quality (Whalen, 1990) in addition to its role in making speech production more fluid, assimilation effects are constrained by syntactical features (Hawkins, 2003), prosody influences the linguistic information in speech at many levels. The aim of this chapter is to delineate the neural systems involved in speech perception, rather than the whole language system. I argue that neurally, robust and flexible speech perception is supported by multiple, parallel processing streams. I argue that these streams bear some relation to the anatomy of primate auditory cortex. I also address the basis of functional asymmetries between the left and right temporal

141

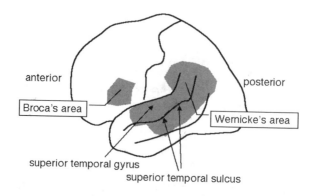

FIG. 9.1. Lateral surface of the left cerebral hemisphere. The regions of Broca's area (historically associated with speech production) and Wernicke's area (associated with speech perception), are shaded. The regions are taken from Gray and Williams (1995).

lobes, which have often been invoked to explain the left hemispheric dominance in speech perception.

Information in speech is carried by the source—either voiced or unvoiced—that is produced by the controlled release of breath through the larynx, and the filtering of this source by the articulators (tongue, jaw, lips and soft palate). The resulting signal is highly complex, and of course it conveys not only phonetic information, but also information about age, sex, mood and speaker identity. In terms of speech perception, no one acoustic cue is critical for the intelligibility of speech: There is a great deal of redundancy in the speech signal, and therefore a multiplicity of acoustic cues to phonetic identity. Thus at least sixteen distinct acoustic properties distinguish the phonemes /b/ or /p/ in the sequences /aba/ and /apa/, which differ only in voicing from a phonetic perspective. Indeed, across the world's languages, no phonemic contrasts exist which can be distinguished on just one acoustic attribute (Kluender, 2002). At the level of the acoustic signal, if one cue is removed, listeners will rely on another. Thus both spectral and amplitude envelope information can be independently degraded to some degree, with little impact on intelligibility (Shannon, Zeng, Kamath, Wygonski, & Ekelid, 1995; Drullman, Festen, & Plomp, 1994). Likewise speech can still be understood with little or no pitch information (the main cue to the 'speech melody' in intonation). Importantly, the comprehension of speech is not a bottom up process, driven solely by acoustics: There are top down linguistic effects, such that transformed speech is more easily understood in predictable sentences than in unpredictable sentences, and both are better understood than word lists (Stickney & Assmann, 2001). Speech perception is also flexible. Listeners seem to reset their phonetic boundaries after relatively short exposure to speakers who produce consistently intermediate speech sounds (e.g., producing an intermediate fricative phone instead of either /f/ or /s/; Norris, McQueen, & Cutler, 2003). This complexity and flexibility means that the neural processing of speech may depend on multiple, integrated perceptual systems.

THE ORGANIZATION OF PRIMATE AUDITORY CORTEX

Speech perception and production can be characterized as the first 'cognitive' processes to be localized in the human brain. Speech production has been intimately linked to Broca's area, in the posterior third of the left inferior frontal gyrus (Figure 9.1). Speech perception, in contrast, has been traditionally associated with the left posterior superior temporal sulcus (STS), the core of Wernicke's area (Bogen & Bogen, 1976). However, functional imaging and patient studies have implicated quite extensive regions in the left temporal lobe and inferior parietal lobe in speech perception (Figure 9.1), to the extent that the concept of Wernicke's area as a single processing module has been called into question (Wise, Scott, Blank, Mummery, & Warburton, 2001). Relating the anatomy and connectivity of the dorsolateral temporal lobes to functional aspects of speech perception is one way to start to fractionate Wernicke's area, following the assumption that the perceptual processing of speech will rest (initially) upon auditory processing substrates. Since little is known about human auditory neuroanatomy, parallels will be drawn with non-human primate studies. Pioneering developments in studies of primate auditory anatomy and physiology indicate that, as in the primate visual system, there is hierarchically organized processing of auditory information. This hierarchical processing is seen both in the connectivity of the different auditory regions, and in the complexity of the processing associated with these regions, for example, the processing of progressively more complex sounds is associated with increasing synaptic distance from primary auditory cortex. There is a tonotopic organization of neurons in A1, with distinct neuronal responses to pure tones of different frequencies. Responses to progressively more wideband stimuli are maximal in cortex (so called belt and parabelt) lateral to A1 (Rauschecker, 1998) (Figure 9.2). As in the visual system, there appear to be at least two streams of processing, in terms of both anatomical connectivity (Kaas & Hackett, 2000) and stimulus response characteristics (Rauschecker & Tian, 2000), running anterior and posterior to primary auditory cortex.

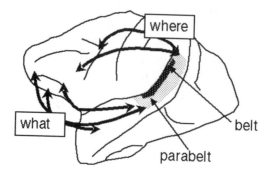

FIG. 9.2. The what and where pathways in the non-human primate brain. The belt and parabelt auditory cortical fields are outlined in the shaded areas. Posterior belt and parabelt fields project to prefrontal cortex along a different pathway than the anterior route for rostral belt and parabelt regions. These connections converge in adjacent prefrontal and premotor regions.

Anterior auditory association cortex has been found to be sensitive to conspecific vocalizations—a 'what pathway' for auditory processing. In contrast, posterior auditory fields show responses selective to the location of a sound—an auditory 'where pathway'. These differences are a matter of degree rather than absolute (Tian, Reser, Durham, Kustov, & Rauschecker, 2001). The 'what' and 'where' pathways converge in adjacent but non-overlapping regions of prefrontal cortex (Romanski et al., 1999; Figure 9.2). Thus, as in the visual system, multiple parallel processing streams support different aspects of auditory perceptual processing. Functional imaging techniques that enable some degree of precision in localization—PET and fMRI—have allowed the elaboration of this model in human auditory cortical regions. Hierarchically organized processing of the features of acoustic signals can be seen in early auditory cortex, with greater responses to pure tones in primary auditory cortex, and greater responses to noise bursts in non-primary auditory areas (Wessinger et al., 2001). Hierarchically organized processing can also be seen with responses to increasing degrees of structure such as temporal regularity (Griffiths, Buchel, Frackowiak, & Patterson, 1998), harmonic structure (Hall et al., 2002), amplitude modulation (Giraud et al., 2000), frequency modulation (Hall et al., 2002), and spectral modulation (Thivard, Belin, Zilbovicius, Poline, & Samson, 2000) being associated with activity lateral, anterior and posterior to primary auditory cortex (PAC) and spreading down towards the superior temporal sulcus (STS), the dorsal bank of which, at least in the non-human primate, is heteromodal cortex. There is also evidence supporting the anterior–posterior distinction described in the primate literature. Several studies have outlined a role for posterior auditory (Warren, Zielinski, Green, Rauschecker, & Griffiths, 2002) and inferior parietal (Zatorre, Bouffard, Ahad, & Belin, 2002) regions in the spatial location of sound cues—a putative 'where' pathway (Warren & Griffiths, 2003). In contrast to the traditional emphasis on posterior auditory regions in speech perception, the anterior 'what' pathway appears to dominate the processing of spoken language (Scott & Wise, 2004; Scott & Johnsrude, 2003). This is addressed in the following section.

SPEECH PERCEPTION: FROM SOUND TO MEANING

Speech perception was one of the first topics studies with functional imaging (e.g., Wise et al., 1991), partly due to the expected left hemispheric dominance in speech processing. However, such studies, which typically contrasted the neural response to speech to a silent baseline, generally revealed extensive activation in *bilateral* STG and STS (e.g., Wise, Greene, Büchel, & Scott, 1999) to speech. This was in stark contrast to the expected left hemispheric activation. Functional imaging studies are crucially influenced by the 'baseline' condition chosen, as measured activation is only meaningful relative to some other condition, and of course speech relative to silence is a strong and complex acoustic stimulus, in addition to its linguistic identity. To control for this, some studies compared the neural responses to speech with that seen for tones, but is not a satisfactory control for the spectral and envelope variation in speech (e.g., Binder et al., 1997). Other studies used stimuli that controlled for speech envelope modulation, but not the spectral variation present in speech (e.g., Mummery, Ashburner, Scott, & Wise, 1999). Use of such amplitude modulated baselines still found bilateral activation, but the regions involved were more constrained in distribution, tending to reveal 'speech' responses lateral, posterior, and anterior to PAC, in the STG and STS. The pattern of activation that might be seen with a baseline stimulus that more closely controlled for the spectro-temporal aspects of the speech signal remained unclear. To try and address this, we used spectrally rotated speech (Blesser, 1972), in which speech is low pass filtered (e.g., at 4KHz) and then spectrally inverted (e.g., at 2KHz), to give a signal with all the spectro-temporal structure of the original speech, without intelligibility (Scott, Blank, Rosen, & Wise, 2000). This rotated speech sounds rather like an alien speaking, and preserves the intonation profile of the original speech, though the overall signal is less strong in its sense of pitch (Blesser, 1972).

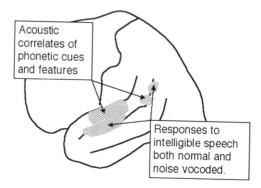

FIG. 9.3. The regions in the left temporal lobe that respond to intelligible speech, and to stimuli with the acoustic correlates of phonetic detail (Scott et al., 2000, Narain et al., 2003).

We also used another form of intelligible speech—noise vocoded speech (Shannon et al., 1995), and its spectrally rotated equivalent. Noise vocoded speech simulates the percept of a cochlear implant, and sounds like a harsh whisper. This allowed us to distinguish the neural regions which responded to intelligible speech, relative to an acoustically matched baseline, regardless of the degree to which the speech sounded like a human speaker. The dominant neural response to intelligible speech lay in the left anterior superior temporal sulcus (STS) (Scott et al., 2000) (Figure 9.3). Lying lateral and anterior to primary auditory cortex (PAC), this was the first unambiguous evidence of a left lateralized response to intelligible speech. This result is in direct contrast to the previous emphasis on posterior temporal cortex, established by neuropsychological studies of speech and language processing (Wise, Scott, Blank, Mummery, & Warburton, 2001). The result of an anteriorly directed response to intelligible speech has been replicated and extended using fMRI (Narain et al., 2003; Specht & Reul, 2003). In our original study (Scott et al., 2000), STG lateral to PAC showed a sensitivity to the rotated speech, in addition to the speech and noise vocoded speech (Figure 9.3). This suggested a role for lateral STG (parabelt in the primate brain) in the processing of phonetic cues and features. More recent work using non-words has demonstrated that, indeed, the lateral STG is sensitive to language specific phonologically relevant contrasts, relative to acoustic change (Jacquemot, Pallier, LeBihan, Dehaene, & Dupoux, 2003). Jacquemot et al. were thus able to demonstrate that speech specific effects can be seen in early acoustic areas, prior to later neural responses to the intelligibility of speech. There is thus apparently hierarchically organized processing of the speech signal, running lateral and anterior to

PAC. Such hierarchical processing and rostral direction is consistent with the 'what' pathway described in non-human primate studies (Rauschecker, 1998).

There is also a role for posterior temporal regions in speech processing (Figure 9.3). There are posterior STS/inferior parietal lobe activations associated with intelligible speech (Davis & Johnsrude, 2003; Narain et al., 2003). These are more easily detected with fMRI than with PET, where they tend to remain sub-threshold (Narain et al., 2003). The reasons for this difference between PET and fMRI in sensitivity to posterior activations is not clear. One possible reason is methodological: Good fMRI studies of speech perception utilize sparse scanning designs (Hall et al., 1999), to attempt to overcome the loud scanner noise, such studies are necessarily event related. In contrast, all PET designs use blocked presentation. Since event related designs are more sensitive to transient responses than blocked designs (since this is the function specifically modeled), this may implicate the posterior temporal lobe regions in rather more transient responses to heard speech, than the response in the anterior STS. This difference may have more than a technical implications: There could be distinctly different profiles of responses in the posterior and anterior STS. While Wise et al. (2001) speculated that these more posterior temporal regions are important in aspects of the episodic transient representation of speech input, other groups (Hickok & Poeppel, 2000) have emphasized the role of these regions in semantic processing. A recent study demonstrated functional differences in the response of anterior and posterior STS regions to the amount of speech related spectro-temporal information. Lateral and anterior left STG/STS regions show sensitivity to increasing numbers of channels in noise vocoded speech, but not to spectrally rotated equivalents. Thus these regions show sensitivity to the amount of speech-relevant information in the signal. In contrast, the posterior STS regions are activated by *any* speech-related properties in the signal, regardless of the overall level of intelligibility (Scott, Rosen, Lang, & Wise, under review). This suggests that as identified in rapid fMRI paradigms (Specht & Reul, 2003), posterior and anterior temporal lobe regions may be involved in distinctly different aspects of speech processing.

SPEECH PERCEPTION: FROM SOUND TO ARTICULATION

Speech production and perception are intimately linked; this can be seen in our difficulty when we encounter speech sounds from outside our phonemic repertoire—the classic example being that native Japanese speakers differentiate little between the English phonemes /r/ and /l/, with 'red' and 'led' sounding like the same word, since these are allophonic sounds in Japanese. When native Japanese speakers first learn English, it can be difficult for them to use /r/ and /l/ contrastively, both in perception and production. This effect can be seen for vowels as well as consonants: German listeners find it hard to distinguish the English words 'cattle' and 'kettle'. Language specific effects of the perception of phonological and acoustic change have been shown in the lateral STG (Jacquemot et al., 2003). Other studies have tried to identify neural regions that are activated both by speaking and by listening to speech, which might link speech perception and production. Wise et al. (2001) showed that a region on the left superior temporal lobe, posterior and medial to primary auditory cortex, is activated by when subjects articulate, even when they articulate silently: The activation is thus independent of the sound of their own utterance. This response in *auditory* cortex to a speech *motor* act was hypothesized to be important in sensory-motor integration, and suggests that speech production might be guided by knowledge of the sounds of speech, as well as providing a route for integrating motor information when processing heard speech. This activation has been interpreted as showing, as in the visual system in man, that there is a 'how' pathway for sensori-motor integration in auditory processing (Wise et al., 2001; Hickok & Poeppel, 2000). The 'how' route can be contrasted with the 'what' stream involved in speech perception, and the two might be conceived of as synthesis versus analysis: One stream processes speech with respect to the encoded motor information (synthesis) and one analyses the linguistic information (analysis). Heard speech is processed as both a sound and as an action (Scott & Johnsrude, 2003). Of course, both streams of information are related. This can be seen behaviorally: Silently mouthing a word primes later acoustic lexical decision, but not visual lexical decision (Monsell, 1987). How this system might relate to the 'where' pathway is still unclear, but may represent the encoding of motoric information in a spatio-temporal framework. The 'where' pathway, if it can be distinguished functionally from the 'how' pathway still affects speech perception—sounds can only be grouped as a vowel if they can also be grouped by location (Darwin & Hukin, 1998).

SPEECH PERCEPTION: THE ROLE OF PREFRONTAL CORTEX

As mentioned earlier, both the 'what' stream and the 'where/how' stream(s) converge in frontal cortical regions (Romanski et al., 1999; Scott & Johnsrude, 2003); (Figure 9.2; Figure 9.4). Can a role for such anterior brain regions be seen in speech perception? Certainly, if the speech task is made explicit—such as phoneme monitoring—then left prefrontal and premotor regions are robustly involved (Demonet et al., 1992). Can a frontal involvement be distinguished in more basic speech comprehensions tasks? Davis and Johnsrude (2003) associated left lateral prefrontal cortical regions with 'effort' in speech perception, as it was activated more by varieties of distorted speech than by normal, clear speech. However, their speech perception task incorporated an explicit task, which may over emphasize prefrontal involvement. Using a passive listening task, we have shown that responses in left ventral prefrontal cortex and dorsal premotor cortex vary with the loudness of the speech relative to continuous background noise—the louder the noise, the greater the activity (Scott, Rosen, Wickham, & Wise, 2004). This does suggest that frontal regions are recruited when the speech is difficult to hear, though what precise mechanisms this might involve remain unclear.

The existence of frontal cortical fields that respond when speech is heard – a putative 'mirror neuron system' involved in speech perception – has been of particular interest, not least as this has been postulated to be a driving force in the evolution of language (Rizzolatti & Arbib, 1998). There is evidence of populations of purely auditory fields in non-human primate frontal cortex (Poremba et al., 2003), and there is evidence for mirror neurons that respond to hearing actions (e.g., tearing paper) (Kohler, Umilta, Keysers, & Gallese, 2001). With respect to human speech perception, there is also evidence, from a TMS study, that watching a speaker or hearing speech activates left lateralized mouth regions in motor cortex (Watkins, Strafella, & Paus, 2003). This is consistent with a mirror neuron system for speech perception, but needs further work to establish the degree to which it is caused by speech *specific* influences. Assuming that this can be determined, the left anterior insula is a premotor region that may show such mirror neuron properties. A region important for accurate articulation, it can be shown to respond during repetition (Wise et al., 1999) and free speech production (Blank, Scott, Murphy, Warburton, & Wise, 2002), but also shows a response to heard speech (Wise et al., 1999), and has been implicated in top down influences in speech-based perceptual learning (Narain, Wise, Rosen, Matthews, & Scott, under review). More studies are needed investigating the link between speech perception and speech production both in posterior auditory and anterior premotor regions, a framework which will help the development of the 'how' pathway.

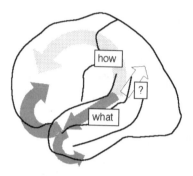

FIG. 9.4. A schematic diagram of the 'what' and 'how' pathways in the left hemisphere. The what pathway projects to ventral and polar regions associated with long term storage of semantic knowledge, as well as to prefrontal cortex. The precise role of the route toward lateral inferior parietal regions (marked with a question mark) — semantic processing, or transient representations important in repetition — remains to be determined.

SPEECH PERCEPTION: CONNECTIONS TO SEMANTIC KNOWLEDGE

The links between auditory areas in the temporal neocortex have been emphasized in this chapter by the analogy with the auditory streams of processing in the non-human primates. However the human language system extends beyond superior temporal and prefrontal cortex. In addition to connections between auditory and prefrontal/premotor regions, there are connections from rostral STS to temporal pole and inferior temporal lobe regions, including the basal language area (Luders et al., 1991; Figure 9.4). In functional terms, spoken language probably maps onto widely distributed representations of conceptual knowledge from unimodal auditory processing, through higher association cortex to heteromodal regions. These heteromodal regions are found in the STS, temporal pole and inferotemporal cortex, particularly perirhinal cortex in the collateral sulcus, regions which have been associated with semantic and knowledge based representations (Scott & Johnsrude, 2003). The reciprocal projections between these regions and the dorsolateral temporal lobes may, for example, form a route for the linguistic modulation of speech perception. Behaviorally, sentences which are highly semantically predictable are more easily comprehended than those of low predictability, and both are better understood than lists of isolated words. Such effects can be enhanced when the speech is degraded to some degree (Stickney & Assmann, 2001). The neural basis of such linguistic top-down modulation remains unclear.

SPEECH PERCEPTION: THE ROLE OF
HEMISPHERIC ASYMMETRIES

The results discussed in this chapter have generally shown a clear left lateralization for the processing of intelligible speech. Why spoken language should be a left hemispheric phenomenon, however, is harder to establish (though it should be noted that the left anterior STS/STG is also activated by environmental noises (Giraud & Price, 2001) and paralinguistic expressions of emotion (Morris, Scott, & Dolan, 1999)). In terms of speech processing, there has been a long-standing interest in identifying acoustic, non-speech-specific bases for this difference, partly as a response to accounts which postulate a 'speech is special' model. Indeed, establishing a non-linguistic basis for this 'left brain' dominance would be parsimonious. Non-linguistic approaches have tended to be expressed in a left = fast, temporal and a right = slow, spectral/pitch framework (where the terms 'pitch' and 'spectral' are often used interchangeably). The problems with this general position are three-fold. First, spoken language does not mainly consist of 'fast' acoustic cues and features: These are found in the formant transitions associated with plosives, but not in those associated with fricatives, liquids, nasal obstruents, lexical tone or vowels (Nittrouer, 1999; Scott & Wise, 2004). Second, the auditory system is not easily characterized along a dimension with temporal processing at one end and spectral/pitch processing at the other, a dimension which is typically described by such models (Poeppel, 2001; Zatorre, Belin, & Penhune, 2002). The spectral detail available for cortical processing is limited by the non linear representation of frequency at the cochlear: Fine spectral detail is not present in the signal passed to the auditory pathways. In addition, pitch itself is not a simple acoustic property; it is not dependent on good spectral resolution, and it appears to be bilaterally computed (e.g., Griffiths et al., 1998). Temporal acuity is preserved in the signal transmitted to the acoustic nerve, and it declines with synaptic distance from the cochlea. This means that acuity on a very fine temporal scale (such as that used for interaural differences) is not available at the auditory cortex without recoding. Finally, there is a dearth of functional imaging data to support a simple distinction between the way the left and right hemisphere respond to acoustic manipulations. Thus the introduction of frequency modulation, amplitude modulation, harmonic structure and spectral dynamics do not, relative to an unmodulated signal, result in left/right asymmetries (Hall et al., 2002; Thivard et al., 2000; Giraud et al., 2000). The explicit variation of temporal properties of the signal, such as iteration rate of rippled noise (Griffiths et al., 1998), modulations in spectral ripples (Langers, Backes, &

van Dijk, 2003), or inter-stimulus interval in click trains (Harms & Melcher, 2002), also does not lead to changes in the response profiles of the left and right auditory cortices. One study explicitly contrasting contrast fast and slow spectral change in speech-like stimuli showed a left temporal lobe response to both fast *and* slow spectral variation (Belin et al., 1998): A recent study has failed to replicate this effect in auditory areas (Temple et al., 2000). Naturally, the lack of a difference between the left and right auditory cortices could be a result of a lack of power, or the resolution of fMRI and PET: However to echo Sherlock Holmes, this does remain a striking, repeated instance of a dog *never* barking in the night.

In contrast to this lack of a clear left/right asymmetry of processing change or low level structure (fast or slow) in acoustic signals, there are acoustic manipulations that reliably lead to hemispheric asymmetries in auditory areas. The right STG/STS shows robust and reliable response to dynamic pitch variation, be this rate and amount of pitch change (Zatorre & Belin, 2001), melodic structure (Patterson, Uppenkamp, Johnsrude, & Griffiths, 2002), or speech melody (Scott et al., 2000). This is consistent with neuropsychological findings that patients with right, not left, temporal lobe resections can detect the presence of pitch change, but not discriminate pitch direction (Johnsrude, Owen, White, Zhao, & Bohbot, 2000). This, along with the finding that pitch itself is bilaterally computed (Griffiths et al., 1998), implicates the right STG/STS is the processing of structured pitch sequences, in tones sequences, music and speech. All languages use pitch variation to convey intonation, a key property of spoken language, and there is a clear asymmetry in the processing of this higher-level acoustic property. Thus we can probably state that there is at least one acoustic basis for hemispheric asymmetries in speech perception: Structured pitch variation is processed predominantly in the right STG/STS. But this does not seem to be one end of a dimension of processing across the two hemispheres, and it remains to be determined whether such a property can be identified for the left temporal lobe, that can be measured without truly speech like properties being present in the signal. Further bases of asymmetries, such that attention may differentially affect left and right hemispheres in speech perception, or that speech perception might be lateralized because the speech production system is left lateralized, or that this might reflect perceptual expertise in processing linguistic information, must also be investigated further. However, the picture that we can build from existing data is that the left temporal lobe is predominantly driven by linguistic information in the acoustic input (Narain et al., 2003, under review; Scott et al., 2000; Jacquemot et al., 2003), rather than simple acoustic features. Speech may indeed be processed in a 'special' way.

CONCLUSIONS

Speech perception is robust and automatic, and there is considerable evidence that it is mediated neurally by (at least) two streams of processing, one driven by a sound to meaning processing (the 'what' pathway), and other from sound to articulation (the 'how' pathway). These appear to share anatomical and functional similarities with the 'what' and 'where' pathways described in non-human primate auditory processing. Frontal lobe involvement in speech perception (both prefrontal and premotor) can be distinguished, and such involvement is emphasized when the speech is hard to hear, or an active task is being performed on the heard input. The left anterior insula in particular is emerging as a premotor region with involvement in both speech perception and production. The elaboration of our understanding of these pathways will go some of the way to help us conceive of the neural basis of speech perception without an uncritical dependence on Wernicke's area as an explanatory construct.

REFERENCES

Bailey, P. J., & Summerfield, Q. (1980). Information in speech: Observations on the perception of [s]-stop clusters. *Journal of Experimental Psychology: Human Perception and Performance, 63*, 536-563.

Belin, P., Zilbovicius, M., Crozier, S., Thivard, L., Fontaine, A., Masure, M. C., & Samson, Y. (1998) Lateralization of speech and auditory temporal processing. *Journal of Cognitive Neuroscience, 10*, 536-540.

Binder., J. R., Frost, J. A., Hammeke, T. A., Cox, R. W., Rao, S. M., & Prieto, T. (1997). Human brain language areas identified by functional magnetic resonance imaging. *Journal of Neuroscience, 17*, 353-362.

Blank, S. C., Scott, S. K., Murphy, K., Warburton, E., & Wise, R. J. S. (2002). Speech production — Wernicke, Broca and beyond. *Brain, 125*, 1829-1838.

Blesser, B. (1972). Speech perception under conditions of spectral transformation. I. Phonetic characteristics. *Journal of Speech and Hearing Research, 15*, 5-41.

Bogen, J. E., & Bogen, G. M. (1976). Wernicke's region — where is it? *Annals of the New York Academy of Sciences, 280*, 834-843.

Darwin, C., & Hukin, R. (1998). Perceptual segregation of a harmonic from a vowel by interaural time difference in conjunction with mistuning and onset asynchrony. *Journal of the Acoustical Society of America, 103*, 1080-1084.

Davis, M. H., & Johnsrude, I. S. (2003). Hierarchical processing in spoken language comprehension. *Journal of Neuroscience, 23*, 3423-3431.

Demonet, J. F., Chollet, F., Ramsay, S., Cardebat, D., Nespoulous, J. D., Wise, R., & Frackowiak, R. (1992). The anatomy of phonological and semantic processing in normal subjects. *Brain, 115*, 1753-1768.

Drullman, R., Festen, J. M., & Plomp, R. (1994). Effect of temporal envelope smearing on speech reception. *Journal of the Acoustical Society of America, 95,* 1053-1064.

Giraud, A. L., Lorenzi, C., Ashburner, J., Wable, J., Johnsrude, I., Frackowiak, R., & Kleinschmidt, A. J. (2000). Representation of the temporal envelope of sounds in the human brain. *Neurophysiology, 84,* 1588-1598.

Giraud, A. L., & Price, C. J. (2001). The constraints functional neuroimaging places on classical models of auditory word processing. *Journal of Cognitive Neuroscience, 13,* 754-765.

Gray, H., & Williams, P. L. (1995). *Gray's Anatomy: The anatomical basis of medicine and surgery* (38th ed.). London: Churchill Livingstone.

Griffiths, T. D., Buchel, C., Frackowiak, R. S., & Patterson, R. D. (1998). Analysis of temporal structure in sound by the human brain. *Nature Neuroscience, 1,* 422-427.

Hall, D. A., Haggard, M. P., Akeroyd, M. A., Palmer, A. R., Summerfield, A.Q., Elliott, M. R., Gurney, E. M., & Bowtell, R. W. (1999). "Sparse" temporal sampling in auditory fMRI. *Human Brain Mapping, 7,* 3-23.

Hall, D. A., Johnsrude, I. S., Haggard, M. P., Palmer, A. R., Akeroyd, M. A., & Summerfield, A. Q. (2002). Spectral and temporal processing in human auditory cortex. *Cerebral Cortex, 12,* 140-149.

Harms, M. P., & Melcher, J. R. (2002). Sound repetition rate in the human auditory pathway, representations in the waveshape and amplitude of fMRI activation. *Journal of Neurophysiology, 88,* 1433-1450.

Hawkins, S. (2003). Roles and representations of systematic fine phonetic detail in speech understanding. *Journal of Phonetics, 31,* 373-405.

Hickok, G., & Poeppel, D. (2000). Towards a functional neuroanatomy of speech perception. *Trends in the Cognitive Sciences, 4,* 131-138.

Jacquemot, C., Pallier, C., LeBihan, D., Dehaene, S., & Dupoux, E. (2003). Phonological grammar shapes the auditory cortex, a functional magnetic resonance imaging study. *Journal of Neuroscience, 23,* 9541-9546.

Johnsrude, I. S., Owen, A. M., White, N. M., Zhao, W. V., & Bohbot, V., (2000). Impaired preference conditioning after anterior temporal lobe resection in humans. *Journal of Neuroscience, 20,* 2649 –2656.

Kaas, J., & Hackett, T. (2000). Subdivisions of auditory cortex and processing streams in primates. *Proceedings of the National Academy of Sciences, USA, 97,* 11793-11799.

Kohler, E., Umilta, M. A., Keysers, C., & Gallese, V. (2001). Auditory mirror neurons in the ventral premotor cortex of the monkey. *Society for Neuroscience Annual Meeting* (Vol. 27), pp. 129.9.

Kluender, K. R. (2002). Speech. In V.S. Ramachandran (Ed.), *Encyclopedia of the Human Brain* (Vol. 4, pp. 433-448). San Diego: Academic Press.

Langers, D. R., Backes, W. H., & van Dijk, P. (2003). Spectrotemporal features of the auditory cortex, the activation in response to dynamic ripples. *Neuroimage, 20,* 265-275.

Luders, H., Lesser, R. P., Hahn, J., Dinner, D. S., Morris, H. H., Wyllie, E., & Godoy, J. (1991). Basal temporal language area. *Brain, 114,* 743-754.

Monsell, S. (1987). On the relation between lexical input and output pathways for speech. In A. Allport, D. G. Mackay, W. Prinz, & E. Scheerer (Eds.), *Language perception and production: Relationships between listening speaking reading and writing* (pp. 273-311). London: Academic Press.

Morris, J. S., Scott, S. K., & Dolan, R. J. (1999). Saying it with feeling: Neural responses to emotional vocalizations. *Neuropsychologia, 37*, 1155-1163.

Mummery, C. J., Ashburner, J., Scott, S. K., & Wise, R. J. S. (1999). Functional neuroimaging of speech perception in six normal and two aphasic patients. *Journal of the Acoustical Society of America, 106*, 449-457.

Narain, C., Scott, S. K., Wise, R. J. S., Rosen, S., Leff, A. P., Iversen, S. D., & Matthews, P. M. (2003). Defining a left-lateralised response specific to intelligible speech using fMRI. *Cerebral Cortex, 13*, 1362-1368.

Narain, C., Wise, R. J. S., Rosen S., Matthews P., & Scott S. K. (under review). Plasticity in auditory processing: Neural correlates of perceptual reorganisation in speech perception. *Cerebral Cortex.*

Nittrouer, S. (1999). Do temporal processing deficits cause phonological processing problems? *Journal of Speech, Language and Hearing Research, 42*, 925-942.

Norris, D., McQueen, J. M., & Cutler, A. (2003). Perceptual learning in speech. *Cognitive Psychology, 47*, 204-238.

Patterson, R. D., Uppenkamp, S., Johnsrude, I. S., & Griffiths, T. D. (2002). The processing of temporal pitch and melody information in auditory cortex. *Neuron, 36*, 767-776.

Poeppel, D. (2001). Pure word deafness and the bilateral processing of the speech code. *Cognitive Science, 25*, 679-693.

Poremba, A., Saunders, R.C., Crane, A.M., Cook, M., Sokoloff, L., & Mishkin, M. (2003). Functional mapping of the primate auditory system. *Science, 299*, 568-572.

Rauschecker, J. P. (1998). Cortical processing of complex sounds. *Current Opinions in Neurobiology, 8*, 516-521.

Rauschecker, J. P., & Tian, B. (2000). Mechanisms and streams for processing of "what" and "where" in auditory cortex. *Proceedings of the National Academy of Sciences, USA, 97*, 11800-11806.

Rizzolatti, G., & Arbib, M. A. (1998). Language within our grasp. *Trends in Neurosciences, 21*, 188-194.

Romanski, L. M., Tian, B., Fritz, J., Mishkin, M., Goldman-Rakic, P. S., & Rauschecker, J. P. (1999). Dual streams of auditory afferents target multiple domains in the primate prefrontal cortex. *Nature Neuroscience, 2*, 1131-1136.

Scott, S. K., Blank, S. C., Rosen S., & Wise, R. J. S. (2000). Identification of a pathway for intelligible speech in the left temporal lobe. *Brain, 123*, 2400-2406.

Scott, S. K., & Johnsrude, I. S. (2003). The neuroanatomical and functional organization of speech perception. *Trends in Neurosciences, 26*, 100-107.

Scott, S. K., Rosen, S., Lang, H., & Wise R. J. S (under review). Neural correlates of intelligibility in speech investigated with noise vocoded speech. *Journal of the Acoustical Society of America.*

Scott, S. K., Rosen, S., Wickham, L., & Wise, R. J. S. (2004). A positron emission tomography study of the neural basis of informational and energetic masking effects in speech perception. *Journal of the Acoustical Society of America.*

Scott, S. K., & Wise, R. J. S. (2004). The functional neuroanatomy of prelexical processing of speech. *Cognition, 92,* 13-45.

Shannon, R. V., Zeng, F. G., Kamath, V., Wygonski, J., & Ekelid, M. (1995). Speech recognition with primarily temporal cues. *Science, 270,* 303-304.

Specht, K., & Reul, J. (2003). Functional segregation of the temporal lobes into highly differentiated subsystems for auditory perception, an auditory rapid event-related fMRI-task. *Neuroimage, 20,* 1944-1954.

Stickney, G. S., & Assmann, P. F. (2001). Acoustic and linguistic factors in the perception of bandpass-filtered speech. *Journal of the Acoustical Society of America, 109,* 1157-1165.

Temple, E., Poldrack, R. A., Protopapas, A., Nagarajan, S., Salz, T., Tallal, P., Merzenich, M. M., & Gabrieli, J. D. (2000). Disruption of the neural response to rapid acoustic stimuli in dyslexia, evidence from functional MRI. *Proceedings of the National Academy of Sciences, USA, 97,* 13907-13912.

Thivard, L., Belin, P., Zilbovicius, M., Poline, J. B., & Samson, Y. (2000). A cortical region sensitive to auditory spectral motion. *Neuroreport, 11,* 2969-2972.

Tian, B., Reser, D., Durham, A., Kustov, A., & Rauschecker, J. P. (2001). Functional specialization in rhesus monkey auditory cortex. *Science, 292,* 290-293.

Warren, J. D., Zielinski, B. A., Green, G. G., Rauschecker, J. P., & Griffiths, T. D. (2002). Perception of sound-source motion by the human brain. *Neuron, 34,* 139-148.

Warren, J. D., & Griffiths, T. D. (2003). Distinct mechanisms for processing spatial sequences and pitch sequences in the human auditory brain. *Journal of Neuroscience, 23,* 5799-5804.

Watkins, K. E., Strafella, A. P., & Paus, T. (2003). Seeing and hearing speech excites the motor system involved in speech production. *Neuropsychologia, 41,* 989-994.

Wessinger, C. M., VanMeter, J., Tian, B., Van Lare, J., Pekar, J., & Rauschecker, J. P. (2001). Hierarchical organization of the human auditory cortex revealed by fMRI. *Journal of Cognitive Neuroscience, 13,* 1-7.

Whalen, D. (1990). Coarticulation is largely planned. *Journal of Phonetics, 18,* 3-35.

Wise, R., Chollet, F., Hadar, U., Friston, K., Hoffner, E., & Frackowiak, R. (1991). Distribution of cortical neural networks involved in word comprehension and word retrieval, *Brain, 114,* 1803-1817.

Wise, R. J. S., Greene, J., Büchel, C., & Scott, S. K. (1999). Brain systems for word perception and articulation. *The Lancet, 353,* 1057-1061.

Wise, R. J. S., Scott, S. K., Blank, S. C, Mummery, C. J., & Warburton, E. (2001). Identifying separate neural sub-systems within 'Wernicke's area.' *Brain, 124,* 83-95.

Zatorre, R. J., & Belin, P. (2001). Spectral and temporal processing in human auditory cortex. *Cerebral Cortex, 10,* 946-953.

Zatorre, R. J., Belin, P., & Penhune, V. B. (2002). Structure and function of auditory cortex: Music and speech. *Trends in Cognitive Sciences, 6,* 37-46.

Zatorre, R. J., Bouffard, M., Ahad, P., & Belin P. (2002). Where is 'where' in the human auditory cortex? *Nature Neuroscience, 5,* 905-909.

10 Broca's Complex as the Unification Space for Language

Peter Hagoort
F.C. Donders Centre for Cognitive Neuroimaging, Nijmegen, The Netherlands

The 1990s saw an enormous increase in studies investigating the brain correlates of language processing. With the advent of techniques for in-vivo scanning of the human brain in action (e.g., PET, fMRI, MEG), we no longer need to rely on the experiments of nature in the form of a brain lesion, to study the relation between brain and language. One could thus argue that a solid bridge between psycholinguistics and neurobiology has been established. In addition to the classical behavioral measures such as reaction times, speech errors, acceptability ratings, etc., we are nowadays able to measure the neuronal responses that underlie specific language tasks. Psycholinguistics and neurobiology are on common ground, so one could think.

However, there is also another perspective on the relation between psycholinguistics and neurobiology. Many in the field of psycholinguistics feel a deep dissatisfaction about the psycholinguistic quality of most neuroimaging studies on language. The sophistication in psycholinguistics in carefully controlling for numerous potential confounds in the materials (frequency, familiarity, morphological structure, phonological structure, etc., etc.) and in addressing issues based on explicit models of speaking, listening, reading or writing, is very often not present in neuroimaging studies on language. I had the privilege to review the language abstracts for the annual meeting of the Organization for Human Brain Mapping for a number of years. Overall, the psycholinguistic quality of the majority of these submissions is disappointing. In short,

157

although the bridge between psycholinguistics and neurobiology is there, more traffic back and forth is needed to shape an integrated cognitive neuroscience of language.

In order to define the criteria that an adequate neurobiology of language has to meet, we first need to clarify what we take our *explanandum* to be. If, like myself, one is interested not only in the cognitive architecture of language, but also in the only machinery that so far has been able to instantiate natural language (i.e., the human brain), it is obvious that the bridge between psycholinguistics and neurobiology has to be crossed. However, it is a perfectly valid position to restrict one's explanandum to the *cognitive* architecture of language functions. For a psycholinguist of that kind the brain facts will only be relevant in so far as they can be used to develop, select or constrain a cognitive architecture model for the language function of interest. The cognitive architecture then specifies the levels of representation needed and the processing steps required for accessing representational structures, and for performing the necessary computational operations on them, such that unification of all the relevant bits and pieces results. Even in this case, I believe that brain facts are relevant. Let me give two examples. Recently, Kempen (2003) has proposed an explicit computational model of syntactic processing that deals with both syntactic encoding and grammatical decoding (parsing). For a number of reasons (such as speaker-hearer alignment during dialog (Garrod & Pickering, 2004; Pickering & Garrod, this volume) a common mechanism for grammatical encoding and decoding is attractive. Nevertheless, the common mechanism view goes against the standard view that assumes separate mechanisms for encoding and parsing. To decide empirically between the one vs. two mechanisms architecture, brain facts might be relevant. For instance, a common mechanism view would be hard to reconcile with neuroimaging data that show a clear segregation of areas activated by encoding and areas activated by decoding. Under the reasonable assumption that a common mechanism view and a separate mechanism view have consequences for the hypothesized neural organization of grammatical encoding/decoding, brain facts do contribute to the body of empirical data that might guide the choice for one cognitive architecture option over the other.

A second example relates to the nature of the information flow. For instance, strictly feedforward models of language processing (e.g., Cutler & Clifton, 1999) predict a fixed spatio-temporal pattern of brain activity that is not seriously modulated by attention or output related factors (e.g., task parameters). It is compatible with a serial model of perception and action, in which a perceptual stage is followed by central cognition (e.g., executive function), which is then followed by appropriate action (cf Fodor, 1983). Recent findings in cognitive neuroscience (e.g., Rizzolatti, Fogassi, & Gallese, 2002) raise serious doubts about the general tenability of the serial model. Whoever's model may finally turn out to be the right one for language perception, it seems that a strictly feedforward model of language perception predicts another spatio-temporal profile of brain activity under various task conditions than an interactive model. Again evidence from MEG/EEG and/or fMRI studies could provide relevant empirical evidence to select among alternative architectural options.

In summary, an adequate neurobiology of language can provide data that are of relevance for specifications in terms of the cognitive architecture of language functions. At the same time, the relevant brain facts can only be obtained in neuroscience research that is strongly guided by state of the art psycholinguistics in terms of theoretical models and experimental materials. Finally, explicit computational models are helpful in achieving the necessary precision in specifying the consequences of particular principles of both cognitive and neural architectures. This is what I refer to as the triangle of cognitive neuroscience, with mutual constraints operating at the levels of the computational models, the cognitive architectures and the neural architectures. The criteria for an integrated neurobiology of language are thus specifications of the neural principles of language functions that are adequate in relation to behavioral data and the cognitive architectures derived from these data (*upward adequacy*), and specifications of the cognitive architectures that are adequate in the light of our understanding of the principles of brain function (*downward adequacy*). The underlying assumption is of course that there is a systematic relation between cognitive states and brain states. Despite claims made in the past that these two levels of description and explanation might not be related in a lawful or transparent way (e.g., Fodor, 1975; Mehler, Morton, & Jusczyk, 1984), the recent success of cognitive neuroscience is seen as an indication that this assumption is valid.

In the remainder of this chapter I outline how in a neurobiological account of language one can specify the contribution of the classical language area, Broca's area, in a way that does justice to both psycholinguistic models of language and our general understanding of this part of the brain.

BROCA'S COMPLEX

Despite some disagreement in the literature, most authors agree that Broca's area comprises Brodmann Areas 44 and 45 of the left hemisphere.

In the classical textbooks these areas coincide at the macroscopic level with the pars opercularis (BA 44) and the pars triangularis (BA 45) of the third frontal convolution. However, since there is much anatomical variability, in many brains these areas are not easy to identify (Uylings, Malofeeva, Bogolepova, Amunts, & Zilles, 1999). Furthermore, cytoarchitectonic analysis (Amunts, Schleicher, & Zilles, 1997) shows that the borders of areas 44 and 45 do not neatly coincide with the sulci that were assumed to form their boundaries in gross anatomical terms. More fundamentally, one has to ask what the justification is to subsume these two cytoarchitectonic areas under the overarching heading of Broca, rather than, say, areas 45 and 47. Areas 44 and 45 show a number of clear cytoarchitectonic differences, one of which is that 45 has a granular layer IV, whereas 44 is dysgranular. In contrast, like area 45, area 47 is part of the heteromodal component of the frontal lobe, known as the granular cortex (Mesulam, 2002). In addition, areas 44 and 45 have clearly distinct postnatal developmental trajectories and show a difference in their patterns of lateral asymmetry. Using an observer-independent method for delineating cortical areas, Amunts and colleagues (1999) analyzed histological sections of 10 human brains. They found a significant left-over-right asymmetry in cell density for area 44, whereas no significant left-right differences were observed for area 45.

From a neuroanatomical perspective, there thus seems to be no strong motivation to treat Broca's area as a natural kind. There is not (yet) convincing neuroanatomical evidence that necessitates the marriage of BA 44 and BA 45 into one unified area that is motivated from a cytoarchitectonic, histological, and receptor-architectonic point of view. On the basis of imaging studies, it is not unlikely that the pars orbitalis of the third frontal convolution (roughly corresponding to BA47) is part of the frontal language network as well (Devlin, Metthews, & Rushworth, 2003; Hagoort, Hald, Bastiaansen, & Petersson, 2004). From a functional anatomical perspective it thus makes sense to use the term *Broca's complex* for this set of areas. Most of Broca's complex (especially BA 45 and 47) is part of prefrontal cortex, the remainder (especially BA 44) is classically seen as belonging to premotor cortex, just as ventral BA6, which might be involved in language processing as well.

The account that I propose hereafter is based on an embedding of Broca's complex in the overall functional architecture of prefrontal cortex, and a general distinction between memory retrieval of linguistic information and combinatorial operations on information retrieved from the mental lexicon. These operations are referred to as unification or binding.

Broca's complex as part of prefrontal cortex

Integration is an important part of prefrontal cortex function. This holds especially for integration of information in the time domain (Fuster, 1995). To fulfill this role, prefrontal cortex needs to be able to hold information online (Mesulam, 2002), and to select among competing alternatives (Thompson-Schill, D'Esposito, & Kan, 1999; Thompson-Schill, this volume). Electrophysiological recordings in the macaque monkey have shown that this area is important for sustaining information triggered by a transient event for many seconds (Miller, 2000). This allows prefrontal cortex to select among and to establish unifications between pieces of information that are perceived or retrieved from memory at different moments in time. Recent neuroimaging studies indicate that Broca's complex contribute to the unification operations required for binding single word information into larger structures. In psycholinguistics, integration and unification refer to what is usually called post-lexical processing. These are the operations on information that is retrieved from the mental lexicon. It seems that prefrontal cortex is especially well suited to contribute to post-lexical processing. In the context of language processing, integration includes selection among competing unification possibilities, so that one unified representation spanning the whole utterance remains.

In this chapter I do not review the rapidly increasing number of neuroimaging studies on different aspects of language processing, and on the role of the left inferior frontal cortex in this context. However, what I do is highlight a few points of what I take to be lessons to be learnt from this recent body of evidence.

A first important lesson is that it would be a serious mistake to assume that Broca's area is a language-specific area, and that within the language domain it only subserves one very specific function. As Mesulam has argued in a series of classical papers (Mesulam, 1998, 1990), "many cortical nodes are likely to participate in the function of more than one network. Conceivably, top-down connections from transmodal areas could differentially recruit such a cortical node into the service of one network or another." (1998: 1040). In this conception, a particular cognitive function is most likely served by a distributed network of areas, rather than by one local area alone. In addition, the local area participates in more than one function. For instance, Broca's area has also been found activated when subjects had to search for a target hidden within a complex geometric pattern (Fink et al., in press), or during mental imagery of grasping movements (Decety et al., 1994). A one-to-one mapping between Broca's area and a specific functional component of the language system would thus be a highly unlikely outcome. Nevertheless, many neurolinguistic accounts of the role of Broca's area still presuppose such a one-to-one mapping (e.g., Grodzinsky, 2000). Data from neuroscience argue against such a kind of organization. Even for the visual system, it is claimed that the representations of, for example, objects and faces in ventral temporal cortex are widely distributed and overlapping (Haxby et al., 2001). It would indeed be highly surprising if the different representational domains in the language network would behave according to more localist principles than the visual system.

The second lesson to be learnt is that within Broca's complex, there might be functionally defined subregions. By now, there is some indication that this complex shows a ventral to dorsal gradient (Bookheimer, 2002). Roughly speaking, BA 47 and BA 45 are involved in semantic processing, BA 45, 44, and 46 contribute to syntactic processing (see Figure 10.1). Finally BA 44 and BA 6 have a role in phonological processing. Broca's complex is thus involved in at least three different domains of language processing (semantic, syntactic, phonological), with, presumably, a certain level of relative specialization within different subregions of Broca's complex. However, the overlap of activations between these three different types of information is substantial. Subregional specificity within Broca's complex for any of these information types can thus not be concluded.

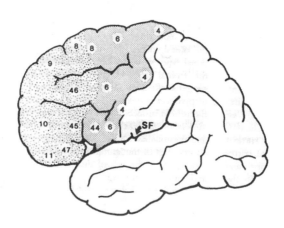

FIG. 10.1. Lateral view of the left hemisphere. Brodmann areas (BA) are marked by number. Classically, Broca's area comprises BA 44 and BA 45. (after Mesulam, 2002). SF: Sylvian Fissure. Sparsely dotted areas: Heteromodal association cortex, including BA 45 and BA 47. Densely dotted area: Motor-premotor cortex, including BA 44 and BA 6.

From a cognitive neuroscience perspective, the conclusion must be that neither at the level of brain structure nor at the level of cognitive function is Broca's area a natural kind. Instead, within the left inferior frontal cortex, it refers to a conglomerate of related but cytoarchitectonically distinct areas with a responsivity to distinct information types within the domains of language comprehension and production. Almost certainly, the conglomerate contributes to other cognitive functions as well. In what follows I propose a role of Broca's complex in what I refer to as binding or unification of information retrieved from the mental lexicon.

Broca's complex as the unification space for language

Recent accounts of the human language system (Jackendoff, 1999, 2002; Levelt, 1999) assume a cognitive architecture, which consists of separate processing levels for conceptual/semantic information, orthographic/phonological information, and syntactic information. Based on this architecture, most current models of language processing agree that, in on-line sentence processing, different types of constraints are very quickly taken into consideration during speaking and listening/reading. Constraints on how words can be structurally combined operate alongside qualitatively distinct constraints on the combination of word meanings, on the grouping of words into phonological phrases, and on their referential binding into a discourse model.

Moreover, in recent linguistic theories, the distinction between lexical items and traditional rules of grammar is vanishing. For instance, Jackendoff (2002) proposes that the only remaining rule of grammar is UNIFY PIECES, "and all the pieces are stored in a common format that permits unification." (p. 180). The unification operation clips together lexicalized patterns with one or more variables in it. The operation MERGE in Chomsky's Minimalist Program (Chomsky, 1995) has a similar flavour. Thus, phonological, syntactic, and semantic/pragmatic constraints determine how lexically available structures are glued together. In Jackendoff's recent account (2002), for all three levels of representation (phonological, syntactic, semantic/conceptual) information that is retrieved from the mental lexicon has to be unified into larger structures. In addition, interface operations link these three levels of analysis. The contribution of Broca's complex can be specified in terms of the unification operations at these three levels. In short, the left inferior frontal cortex recruits lexical information, mainly stored in temporal lobe structures, and unifies them into overall representations that span multiword utterances. Hereafter, I show in more detail how this could work for the syntactic level of analysis (for more details, see Hagoort, 2003).

According to the Unification Model for parsing (see Vosse & Kempen, 2000) each word form in the lexicon is associated with a structural frame. This structural frame consists of a three-tiered unordered tree, specifying the possible structural environment of the particular lexical item (see Figure 10.2).

The top layer of the frame consists of a single phrasal node (e.g., NP). This so-called root node is connected to one or more functional nodes (e.g., Subject, Head, Direct Object) in the second layer of the frame. The third layer contains again phrasal nodes to which lexical items or other frames can be attached.

This parsing account is 'lexicalist' in the sense that all syntactic nodes (e.g., S, NP, VP, N, V, etc.) are retrieved from the mental lexicon. In other words, chunks of syntactic structure are stored in memory. There are no syntactic rules that introduce additional nodes. In the on-line comprehension process, structural frames associated with the individual word forms

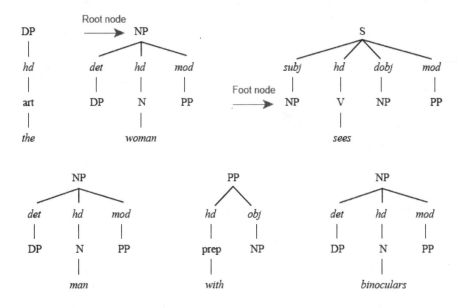

FIG. 10.2. Syntactic frames in memory (the mental lexicon), retrieved on the basis of the word form input for the sentence "The woman sees the man with the binoculars." DP: Determiner Phrase; NP: Noun Phrase; S: Sentence; PP: Prepositional Phrase; art: article; hd: head; det: determiner; mod: modifier; subj: subject; dobj: direct object.

incrementally enter the unification workspace. In this workspace constituent structures spanning the whole utterance are formed by a unification operation. This operation consists of linking up lexical frames with identical root and foot nodes, and checking agreement features (number, gender, person, etc.).

The resulting unification links between lexical frames are formed dynamically, which implies that the strength of the unification links varies over time until a state of equilibrium is reached. Due to the inherent ambiguity in natural language, alternative binding candidates will usually be available at any point in the parsing process. That is, a particular root node (e.g., PP) often finds more than one matching foot node (i.c. PP) with which it can form a unification link (for examples see Hagoort, 2003).

Ultimately, one phrasal configuration results. This requires that among the alternative binding candidates only one remains active. The required state of equilibrium is reached through a process of lateral inhibition between two or more alternative unification links. The outcome of the unification process is thus achieved via a selection mechanism (i.e. lateral inhibition) that 'chooses' between different unification options (cf. Thompson-Schill, this volume). In general, due to gradual decay of activation more recent foot nodes will have a higher • level of activation than the ones that entered the unification space earlier. In addition, strength levels of the unification links can vary in function of plausibility (semantic!) effects. For instance, if instrumental modifiers under S-nodes have a slightly higher default activation than instrumental modifiers under an NP-node, lateral inhibition can result in overriding the recency effect.

The Unification Model accounts for sentence complexity effects known from behavioral measures, such as reading times. In general, sentences are harder to analyze syntactically when more potential unification links of similar strength enter into competition with each other. Sentences are easy when the number of U-links is small and of unequal strength.

The advantage of the Unification Model is that it is computationally explicit, it accounts for a large series of empirical findings in the parsing literature and in the neuropsychological literature on aphasia, and it belongs to the class of lexicalist parsing models that have found increasing support in recent years (Bresnan, 2001; Jackendoff, 2002; Joshi & Schabes, 1997; MacDonald, Pearlmutter, & Seidenberg, 1994).

This model also nicely accounts for the two classes of syntax-related ERP-effects that are consistently reported over recent years in ERP studies on language. One type of ERP effect related to syntactic processing is the P600/SPS (Hagoort, Brown, & Groothusen, 1993). The P600/SPS is reported in relation to syntactic violations, syntactic ambiguities, and syntactic complexity. Another syntax-related ERP is a left anterior negativity, referred to as LAN or, if earlier in latency than 400 ms as ELAN (Friederici, Hahne, & Mecklinger, 1996). In contrast to the P600/SPS, the (E)LAN has so far only been observed to syntactic violations. In the Unification Model, binding (unification) is prevented in two cases. One case is when the root node of a syntactic building block (e.g., NP) does not find another syntactic building block with an identical foot node (i.c. NP) to bind to. The other case is when the agreement check finds a serious mismatch in the grammatical feature specifications of the root and foot nodes. The claim is that the (E)LAN results from a failure to bind, as a result of a negative outcome of the agreement check or a failure to find a matching category node. For instance, the sentence "The woman sees the man because with the binoculars" does not result in a completed parse, since the syntactic frame associated with "because" does not find unoccupied (embedded) S-root nodes that it can bind to. As a result, unification fails.

In the context of the Unification Model, I have proposed that the P600/SPS is related to the time it takes to establish unification links of sufficient strength (Hagoort, 2003). The time it takes to build up the unification links until the required strength is reached is affected by ongoing competition between alternative unification options (syntactic ambiguity), by syntactic complexity, and by semantic influences. The amplitude of the P600/SPS is modulated by the amount of competition. Competition is reduced when the number of alternative binding options is smaller, or when lexical, semantic or discourse context modifies the strengths of the unification links in a particular direction, thereby shortening the duration of the competition. Violations result in a P600/SPS because unification attempts are still made. For instance, a mismatch in gender or agreement features might still result in weaker binding in the absence of alternative options. However, in such cases the strength and build-up of U-links will be affected by the partial mismatch in syntactic feature specification. Compared to less complex or syntactically unambiguous sentences, in more complex and syntactically ambiguous sentences it takes longer to build up U-links of sufficient strength. The latter sentences, therefore, result in a P600/SPS in comparison to the former ones.

In summary, it seems that the Unification Model provides an acceptable account for the collective body of ERP data on syntactic processing. It is the most explicit computational model account of these data that is currently around.

The Unification Model also seems to be compatible with PET/fMRI studies on syntactic processing. In a recent meta-analysis of 28 neuroimaging studies, Indefrey (2003) found two areas that were critical for syntactic processing, independent of the input modality (visual in reading, auditory in speech). These two supramodal areas for syntactic processing were the left posterior superior temporal gyrus and the left posterior inferior frontal cortex, substantially overlapping with left prefrontal cortex. The left posterior temporal cortex is known to be involved in lexical processing (Indefrey & Cutler, 2004). In connection to the Unification Model, this part of the brain might be important for the retrieval of the syntactic frames that are stored in the lexicon. The Unification Space where individual frames are connected into a phrasal configuration for the whole utterance might be localized in the left frontal part of the syntax-relevant network of brain areas.

However, unification operations take place not only at the syntactic processing level. Combinatoriality is a hallmark of language across representational domains. That is, it holds equally for syntactic, semantic and phonological levels of analyses. In all these cases lexical bits and pieces have to be combined and integrated into larger structures. The need for combining independent bits and pieces into a single coherent percept is not unique for language comprehension. It also holds for the visual system. In visual neuroscience this is referred to as the *binding problem*. However, the tricks that the brain might use for solving the binding problem in vision most likely don't work for language. The central question in vision is how the different attributes of an object, that are known to be processed in different cortical areas within visual cortex, are brought together so that they result in a unified visual percept. One solution that has gained popularity in recent years, although it is still controversial, is that the mechanism of visual binding is related to the synchronicity of firing in the cell assemblies that code for the individual visual features (Varela, Lachaux, Rodriguez, & Martinerie, 2001).

The major difference between visual perception and language comprehension is that visual binding is more or less instantaneous, whereas language comprehension is extended in time. The relevant areas in visual cortex deliver their specific outputs (e.g., color information, motion information, etc.) within a very narrow time window. On the basis of the available experimental evidence, it is assumed that synchronous networks emerge and disappear at time scales between 100 ms and 300 ms (Varela et al., 2001). In contrast, one of the hallmarks of language processing is that information is spread out over relatively extended time periods. For instance, in parsing the auditory sentence "Noam thought of a couple of nice example sentences for his linguistics class but by accident wrote them down in his political diary," the information of Noam as the subject of the sentence still has to be available some second or so later when the acoustic information encoding the finite verb form "wrote" has reached auditory cortex.

Crucially, the binding problem for language is how information that is not only processed in different parts of cortex, but also at different time scales and at relatively widely spaced parts of the time axis, can be unified into a coherent representation of a multiword utterance.

One requirement for solving the binding problem for language is, therefore, the availability of cortical tissue that is particularly suited for maintaining information on-line, while binding operations take place. As we have seen, prefrontal cortex seems to be especially well-suited for doing exactly this. It has reciprocal connections to almost all cortical and subcortical structures, which puts it in a unique neuroanatomical position for binding operations across time, both within and across different domains of cognition.

The unification operations at semantic and phonological levels share the extended time characteristics with syntactic processing. Therefore, Broca's complex is also suited for these types of unification operations. Figure 10.3 shows how semantic/conceptual unification and phonological unification could be worked out along similar lines, with BA 47 and 45 involved in semantic binding, BA 45 and 44 in syntactic binding, and BA 44 and 6 in phonological binding. However, one has to realize that the overlap of activations for these different information types is substantial, and the ventral-to-dorsal gradient cannot be taken as solid evidence for a subregional specificity within Broca's complex.

BROCA'S AREA REVISITED

As I have tried to make clear, despite the large appeal of Broca's area, it is not a very well defined concept. Instead of Broca's area I have therefore proposed the use of the term Broca's complex, to refer to a series of related but distinct areas in the left inferior frontal cortex, at least encompassing BA 47, 45, 44, and ventral BA6. This set of areas subserves more than one function in the language domain, and presumably other non-language functions as well. In the context of language processing the common denominator of Broca's complex is its role in selection and unification operations by which individual pieces of lexical information are bound together into representational structures spanning multiword utterances. One can thus conclude that Broca's complex plays a pivotal role in solving the binding problem for language.

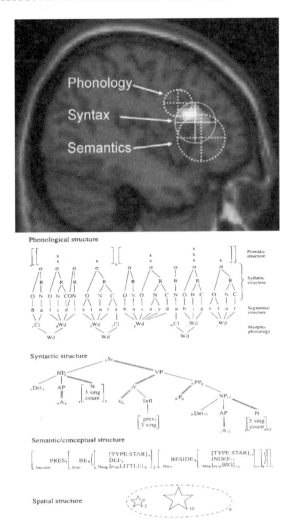

FIG. 10.3. The gradient in left inferior frontal cortex for activations and their distribution, related to semantic, syntactic and phonological processing, based on the meta-analysis in Bookheimer (2002). The centers represent the mean coordinates of the local maxima, the radii represent the standard deviations of the distance between the local maxima and their means (courtesy of Karl Magnus Petersson). The activation shown is from artificial grammar violations in Petersson, Forkstam, and Ingvar (2004). Below, the phonological, syntactic, and semantic/ conceptual structures for the sentence "The little star's beside the big star" (Jackendoff, 2002). The unification operations involved are suggested to require the contribution of Broca's complex.

REFERENCES

Amunts, K., Schleicher, A., Burgel, U., Mohlberg, H., Uylings, H. B., & Zilles, K. (1999). Broca's region revisited: Cytoarchitecture and intersubject variability. *Journal of Comparative Neurology, 412,* 319-341.

Amunts, K., Schleicher, A., & Zilles, K. (1997). Persistence of layer IV in the primary motor cortex (area 4) of children with cerebral palsy. *Journal für Hirnforschung, 38,* 247-260.

Bookheimer, S. (2002). Functional MRI of Language: New approaches to understanding the cortical organization of semantic processing. *Annual Review of Neuroscience, 25,* 151-188.

Bresnan, J. W. (2001). *Lexical-functional syntax.* Oxford: Blackwell.

Chomsky, N. (1995). *The minimalist Program.* Cambridge, MA: MIT Press.

Cutler, A., & Clifton, C. E. (1999). Comprehending spoken language: A blueprint of the listener. In C. M. Brown & P. Hagoort (Eds.), *The neurocognition of language* (pp. 123-166). Oxford: Oxford University Press.

Decety, J., Perani, D., Jeannerod, M., Bettinard, V., Tadardy, B., Woods, R., Mazziotta, J. C., & Fazio, F. (1994). Mapping motor representations with positron emission tomography. *Nature, 371,* 600-602.

Devlin, J. T., Metthews, P. M., & Rushworth, M. F. S. (2003). Semantic processing in the left prefrontal cortex: A combined functional magnetic resonance imaging and transcranial magnetic stimulation study. *Journal of Cognitive Neuroscience, 15,* 71-84.

Fink, G. R., Manjaly, Z. M., Stephan, K. E., Gurd, J. M., Zilles, K., Amunts, K., & Marshall, J. C. (in press). A role for Broca's area beyond language processing: Evidence from neuropsychology and fMRI. In K. Amunts & Y. Grodzinsky (Eds.), *Broca's area.* Oxford: Oxford University Press.

Fodor, J. A. (1975). *The language of thought.* New York: Thomas Y. Crowall

Fodor, J. A. (1983). *The modularity of mind.* Cambridge, MA: MIT Press.

Friederici, A. D., Hahne, A., & Mecklinger, A. (1996). Temporal structure of syntactic parsing: Early and late event-related brain potential effects. *Journal of Experimental Psychology: Learning, Memory, and Cognition, 22,* 1219-1248.

Fuster, J. M. (1995). Temporal processing. *Annals of the New York Academy of Sciences, 769,* 173-181.

Garrod, S., & Pickering, M. J. (2004). Why is conversation so easy? *Trends in Cognitive Sciences, 8,* 8-11.

Grodzinsky, Y. (2000). The neurology of syntax: Language use without Broca's area. *Behavioral and Brain Sciences, 23,* 1-21; discussion 21-71.

Hagoort, P. (2003). How the brain solves the binding problem for language: A neurocomputational model of syntactic processing. *NeuroImage, 20,* S18-S29.

Hagoort, P., Brown, C. M., & Groothusen, J. (1993). The Syntactic Positive Shift (SPS) as an ERP measure of syntactic processing. *Language and Cognitive Processes, 8,* 439-483.

Hagoort, P., Hald, L., Bastiaansen, M., Petersson, K. M. (2004). Integration of word meaning and world knowledge in language comprehension. *Science, 304,* 438-441.

Haxby, J. V., Gobbini, M. I., Furey, M. L., Ishai, A., Schouten, J. L., & Pietrini, P. (2001). Distributed and overlapping representations of faces and objects in ventral temporal cortex. *Science, 293*, 2425-2430.

Indefrey, P. (2003). Hirnaktivierungen bei syntaktischer Sprachverarbeitung: Eine Meta-Analyse. In H. M. Müller & G. Rickheit (Eds.), *Neurokognition der Sprache* (pp. 31-50). Tübingen: Stauffenburg Verlag.

Indefrey, P., & Cutler, A. (2004). Prelexical and lexical processing in listening. In M. S. Gazzaniga (Ed.), *The cognitive neurosciences* (III) (pp. 759-774). Cambridge, MA: MIT Press.

Jackendoff, R. (1999). The representational structures of the language faculty and their interactions. In C. M. Brown & P. Hagoort (Eds.), *The neurocognition of language* (pp. 37-79). Oxford: Oxford University Press.

Jackendoff, R. (2002). *Foundations of language: Brain, meaning, grammar, evolution.* Oxford: Oxford University Press.

Joshi, A. K., & Schabes, Y. (1997). Tree-adjoining grammars. In G. Rozenberg & A. Salomaa (Eds.), *Handbook of formal languages. Vol. 3: beyond words* (pp. 69-123). Berlin: Springer Verlag.

Kempen, G. (2003). Generation. In W. J. Frawley (Ed.), *International Encyclopedia of Linguistics. Second Edition* (Vol. 1, pp. 362-364). New York: Oxford University Press.

Levelt, W. J. M. (1999). Producing spoken language: A blueprint of the speaker. In C. M. Brown & P. Hagoort (Eds.), *The neurocognition of language* (pp. 83-122). Oxford: Oxford University Press.

MacDonald, M. C., Pearlmutter, N. J., & Seidenberg, M. S. (1994). Lexical nature of syntactic ambiguity resolution. *Psychological Review, 101*, 676-703.

Mehler, J., Morton, J., & Jusczyk, P. W. (1984). On reducing language to biology. *Cognitive Neuropsychology, 1*, 83-116.

Mesulam, M.-M. (1990). Large-scale neurocognitive networks and distributed processing for attention, language, and memory. *Annals of Neurology, 28*, 597-613.

Mesulam, M.-M. (1998). From sensation to cognition. *Brain, 121*, 1013-1052.

Mesulam, M.-M. (2002). The human frontal lobes: Transcending the default mode through contingent encoding. In D. T. Stuss & R. T. Knight (Eds.), *Principles of frontal lobe function* (pp. 8-31). Oxford: Oxford University Press.

Miller, E. K. (2000). The prefrontal cortex and cognitive control. *Nature Review Neuroscience, 1*, 59-65.

Petersson, K. M., Forkstam, C., & Ingvar, M. (2004). Artificial syntactic violations activate Broca's region. *Cognitive Science, 28*, 383-407.

Rizzolatti, G., Fogassi, L., & Gallese, V. (2002). Motor and cognitive functions of the ventral premotor cortex. *Current Opinions in Neurobiology, 12*, 149-154.

Thompson-Schill, S. L., D'Esposito, M., & Kan, I. P. (1999). Effects of repetition and competition on activity in left prefrontal cortex during word generation. *Neuron, 23*, 513-522.

Uylings, H. B. M., Malofeeva, L. I., Bogolepova, I. N., Amunts, K., & Zilles, K. (1999). Broca's language area from a neuroanatomical and developmentsl perspective. In C. M. Brown & P. Hagoort (Eds.), *The neurocognition of language* (pp. 319-336). Oxford: Oxford University Press.

Varela, F., Lachaux, J.-P., Rodriguez, E., & Martinerie, J. (2001). The brainweb: Phase synchronization and large-scale integration. *Nature Reviews Neuroscience, 2,* 229-239.

Vosse, T., & Kempen, G. A. M. (2000). Syntactic structure assembly in human parsing: A computational model based on competitive inhibition and lexicalist grammar. *Cognition, 75,* 105-143.

11

Dissecting the Language Organ: A New Look at the Role of Broca's Area in Language Processing

Sharon L. Thompson-Schill
Departments of Psychology and Neurology,
Cognitive Center for Neuroscience,
University of Pennsylvania, Philadelphia, USA

Early in the 19th century, the notion that a mental faculty could be localized to a particular region of the brain was associated with the palpation of the scalps of Victorian men and women in their parlors—hardly the basis for serious scientific pursuits. Reports of selective language impairments following frontal lobe damage (consistent with the phrenologists' localization of language) were largely ignored. But resistance to localism in the scientific community was waning in 1861, when Paul Broca first described the case of Leborgne, rendered speechless (except for the recurrent use of the syllable "tan") by a condition that Broca subsequently attributed to progressive softening of "the middle part of the frontal lobe of the left hemisphere" (1861a: 237). Following Broca's reports, and for much of the twentieth century, lesions to the left frontal operculum were linked to a constellation of linguistic deficits affecting the production of words and sentences and the comprehension of certain syntactic structures (i.e., Broca's aphasia). In his argument for a functionally distinct system for articulated language, Broca also laid the foundations for modern cognitive neuropsychology, when he proposed that the independence of a cognitive faculty can be investigated by the careful functional analysis of impaired and spared deficits and by the precise description, "by name and by row [of] the affected convolutions and the degree of alteration of each" (p. 340). Thus, we see in 1861 both a delineation of the general approach of lesion-deficit analyses of the functional independence of cognitive processes and the specific description of the seat of a "language organ."

173

THE FACULTY SEARCH: CANDIDATE FUNCTIONS
OF BROCA'S AREA

Although the general impact of Broca's work on the field of neuro-psychology is immeasurable, the specific question of the function of Broca's area has been reopened in recent years. Systematic investigations of the neural correlates of language disorders generally have found only weak support for historical associations between lesion location and aphasia syndromes; in particular, these methods have revealed that infarction of Broca's area is neither necessary nor sufficient for the syndrome of Broca's aphasia (e.g., Mohr et al., 1978). In contrast to failed attempts to localize aphasia syndromes, lesion analysis of specific deficits has proven to be a more promising way to study the relationship between brain structure and function. Accordingly, recent hypothesized functions of Broca's area have tended to be more narrowly defined than is the syndrome of Broca's aphasia. In this chapter, I briefly review some current hypotheses about the role of Broca's area in articulation, syntax, selection, and verbal working memory. While it is easy to view these as mutually exclusive, this need not be the case; throughout the chapter, I will highlight points of theoretical contact between these hypotheses. In addition, there may not be a *single* function of Broca's area, if simply for the fact that Broca's "area" is not an anatomical area *per se*: The frontal operculum includes at least two cytoarchitecturally distinct regions (Brodmann's areas 44 and 45) and perhaps even more subregions (Amunts et al., 1999; see also Hagoort, this volume). However, for the purposes of simplicity here, I will refer to these regions collectively as Broca's area as I review candidate functions of the frontal operculum in language. Finally, I will consider linguistic impairments that would result from the loss of one putative function: the ability to guide selection among competing sources of information.

The Articulation Organ?

Broca described Leborgne's impairment as a loss of speech (i.e., aphemia), following damage to the organ controlling "the faculty of articulated language, which must not be confused with the general faculty of language" (1861b: 331). It was subsequent investigators who saddled Broca's area with the burden of a host of other linguistic functions and dubbed the disorder a loss of language, or aphasia. While it appears that this expansion of the functions of Broca's area may have been overexuberant, what about Broca's original claim? Is there an

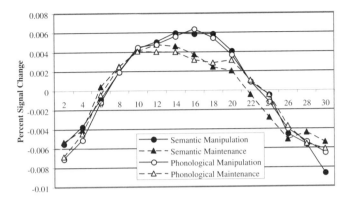

FIG. 11.1. Delay-period activity in Broca's area during maintenance (triangles) or manipulation (circles) of either semantic (filled) or phonological (unfilled) information. Results indicate that the fMRI response in Broca's area is affected by processing demands but not the type of information that is being processed (adapted from Barde & Thompson-Schill, 2002).

independent "faculty of articulated language", and if so, is it controlled by Broca's area?

Some recent neuroimaging studies have supported a role of the left frontal operculum in aspects of speech production (e.g., Indefrey et al., 2001) or phonological processing (Poldrack et al., 1999). Laura Barde and I recently argued against the hypothesis that Broca's area is specialized for phonological processing based on the results of an fMRI study that compared the maintenance and manipulation of semantic and phono-logical information in a delayed recognition working memory paradigm (Barde & Thompson-Schill, 2002). As shown in Figure 11.1, we observed modulation of activity in Broca's area as a function of processing de-mands (i.e., more activity when subjects had to manipulate information during the memory delay than when they passively maintained that in-formation), but no differences between semantic and phonological processing conditions (cf. Gold & Buckner, 2002). Thus, neuroimaging studies are mixed in their support of the claim that Broca's area has a specialized role in speech production or phonology.

Neuropsychological investigations have also failed to support a link between Broca's area and articulatory processes. In a group of patients categorized as Broca's aphasics, impairments in articulation and prosody and the presence of phonemic errors were associated with lesions outside of Broca's area; patients with lesions restricted to Broca's area displayed normal articulation (Alexander, Naeser, & Palumbo, 1990). Dronkers and colleagues (1996) reported a striking correlation between lesion location and apraxia of speech, an articulatory deficit commonly associated with Broca's aphasia. However, the lesion location they identified was *not* Broca's area. Rather, it was a discrete region of the left precentral gyrus of the insula. It was recently confirmed that Leborgne, too, had extensive subcortical damage including the insula (Dronkers, Plaisant, Iba-Zizen, & Cabanis, 2000). A number of neuroimaging studies also support the role of the anterior insula in overt articulation (e.g., Wise, Greene, Buchel, & Scott, 1999). These findings indicate that Broca may have been correct about the notion of an independent faculty for articulation, although it appears that his localization of that faculty to the left frontal operculum was in error.

The Syntax Organ?

The dominant theoretical and clinical analyses of aphasia in the twentieth century were focused on deficits in language activities (i.e., production and comprehension). The shift away from this description might be credited to the discovery that patients with Broca's aphasia could neither produce *nor comprehend* grammatically complex utterances (Caramazza & Zurif, 1976). Although a group of investigators in the late nineteenth century (including Arnold Pick and Henry Head) had discussed notions of syntax and grammar with regard to aphasia, the most powerful impetus for a reformulation of language deficits came from work in linguistics and psycholinguistics beginning in the 1950s. For example, Chomsky (1981) not only asserted that there was a "language organ" in the mind, but he went on to characterize specific operations, such as those described in his government-binding theory, that were integral to this organ. The loss of these operations is, to some investigators, the defining characteristic of Broca's aphasia (e.g., Grodzinsky, 2000).

As a result of this redefinition of Broca's aphasia, Broca's area now has been hypothesized to be the seat of syntax or, in more recent characterizations, of a specific syntactic operation. Grodzinsky and colleagues have argued that Broca's area "is now thought to house mechanisms that compute dependencies among nonadjacent sentential constituents, established by transformational relations" (2000: 83), based not only on their analysis of the syntactic deficits in patients with Broca's aphasia, but also on converging evidence from neuroimaging studies. However, recent reviews of the relevant neuroimaging literature (Friederici, 2002; Kaan & Swaab, 2002) revealed that this structure-function relation is neither specific to Broca's area (i.e., similar patterns of activation are seen throughout frontal and temporal cortices of both hemispheres) nor to syntactic processing (i.e., activation is also observed during non-syntactic, and even non-linguistic, processing). Furthermore, some of the

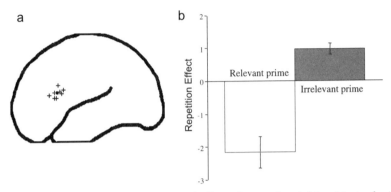

FIG. 11.2. (a) Foci of fMRI activation in Broca's area in eight subjects during retrieval of color words or action words associated with a target noun (in comparison to word reading); the filled circle indicates the centroid of activation across subjects. (b) The effect of item repetition on activity in Broca's area during word retrieval, when the prime was relevant (unfilled) or irrelevant (filled) information about the item. Priming irrelevant information increased activation in Broca's area (but not in other cortical regions) during word retrieval. Adapted from Thompson-Schill et al., 1999.

neuropsychological evidence for this hypothesis has been questioned on the grounds that agrammatic sentence comprehension can result from limitations to general processing capacities (e.g., Dick et al., 2001).

The Selection Organ?

In any step along an information-processing stream, an appropriate representation must be selected for further processing. In some cases, selection of a representation may proceed successfully based entirely on local constraints (e.g., bottom-up inputs to a system). However, in other cases, conflict among competing representations may require top-down modulation of the selection process. For example, consider the task of retrieving an action word associated with a given stimulus. In response to the target "scissors", the strongly-associated action "cut" might be activated from the input. In contrast, in response to the target "cat", the activation of many weakly associated actions (e.g., "scratch", "purr") and/or of a strongly associated non-action (e.g., dog) might fail to produce sufficient activation to select any action representation. Both of these situations (underdetermined representations and prepotent representations) can induce conflict among active representations in working memory that requires top-down intervention (Botvinick, Braver, Barch,

Carter, & Cohen, 2001). We suggest that this intervention comes in the form of a modulatory signal from prefrontal cortex that aids in the selection of an appropriate representation (cf. Fletcher, Shallice, & Dolan, 2000; Miller & Cohen, 2001). This domain-general mechanism is necessary for the successful performance of many tasks, including the ability to identify typeface color instead of reading a word (i.e., the Stroop task; Perret, 1974), to reduce interference during working memory (Thompson-Schill et al., 2002), to maintain fixation instead of making a saccade to a target (i.e., the anti-saccade task; Guitton, Buchtel, & Douglas, 1985), and, as I argue below, for many language tasks as well. That is not to say that the function of Broca's area is domain-general. Rather, we propose that the *mechanism* which enables an organism to select between competing sources of information is a general mechanism implemented by prefrontal cortex that is recruited in different functional domains, both linguistic and non-linguistic; but that may have been harnessed by linguistic systems, perhaps subject to modifications, and perhaps, in this domain-specific form, linked to Broca's area specifically. That is, the ability to select between competing representations may be an example of what Hauser, Chomsky, and Fitch recently dubbed the "faculty of language—broad sense"—a mechanism that is shared with nonhuman animals, that interacts with a more narrowly-defined language system, and that, as such, is responsible for "many of the details of language that are the traditional focus of linguistic study" (2002: 1574). Thus, an impairment in this function, which is necessary for some (but not all) linguistic tasks, could be the source of some of the specific symptoms commonly associated with Broca's aphasia.

For nearly a decade, my colleagues and I have been investigating this mechanism and its link to Broca's area. Initially, we observed that the systematic manipulation of selection demands during semantic processing effectively modulated the fMRI response in Broca's area (Thompson-Schill, D'Esposito, Aguirre, & Farah, 1997). Subsequent studies have shown that this effect is not found in other cortical areas involved in language, such as temporal cortex (Thompson-Schill, D'Esposito, & Kan, 1999), is not limited to production tasks or to certain stimulus types, such as verbs (Thompson-Schill et al., 1997), is not an effect of response conflict (Barch, Braver, Sabb, & Noll, 2000), and is not simply a reflection of task difficulty (Thompson-Schill et al., 1999). Rather, it appears that activity in Broca's area is modulated by increasing demands to select a representation among competing sources of information.

Most relevant to the current discussion are studies we conducted examining the effects of competition during word retrieval both on activation in Broca's area in normal subjects and on performance in

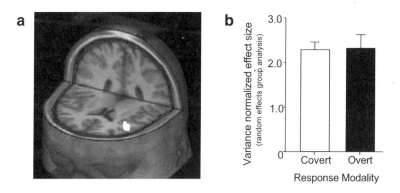

FIG. 11.3. (a) Activation in Broca's area during a picture naming task. (b) The magnitude of activation in this region was affected by picture-name agreement. Shown here is the magnitude of the name agreement effect in Broca's area during covert (unfilled) and overt (filled) picture naming.

patients with focal lesions to Broca's area. During a word retrieval task, priming of irrelevant information was associated with increased activity in Broca's area (see Figure 11.2; Thompson-Schill et al., 1999). Similarly, Irene Kan and I recently asked subjects to retrieve the name of pictured objects that varied in name agreement (Kan & Thompson-Schill, 2004). As shown in Figure 11.3, we observed increased activity in Broca's area when subjects named pictures with low name agreement (e.g., a picture of a sofa, which was also called a couch, a loveseat, etc.) than those with high name agreement (e.g., a picture of an apple was uniformly called an apple). Both of these effects could reflect the response in Broca's area to increased demands for selection among competing representations. We tested the necessity of Broca's area for selection during word retrieval in patients with lesions to the left inferior frontal gyrus. Patients with lesions including Broca's area were impaired during word retrieval under high selection demands but unimpaired during word retrieval under low selection demands (Thompson-Schill et al., 1998). Furthermore, the degree of impairment was strongly correlated with the extent of damage in Broca's area (but not with overall lesion volume; see Figure 11.4). These observations demonstrate the necessity of Broca's area for selection among competing alternatives, in this case, during word retrieval.

The Verbal Working Memory Organ?

The advent of neuroimaging has revealed many findings that were, in some cases, unanticipated by the neuropsychological literature. While it

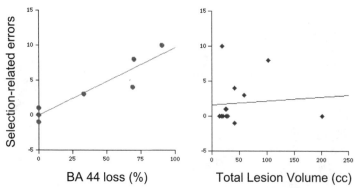

FIG. 11.4. Selection-related errors (high selection items — low selection items) on a word retrieval task, as a function of damage to pars opercularis (Brodmann's area 44; left panel; $r^2 = 0.91$) and as a function of overall lesion volume (right panel; $r^2 = 0.01$) in patients with focal, frontal lesions. Adapted from Thompson-Schill et al. (1998).

is easy to offer the widely repeated disclaimer "neuroimaging and neuropsychology address different problems", this avoids the question of why the two methodologies have not converged. One case of an apparent divergence in neuroimaging and neuropsychology is the study of working memory. Almost any neuroimaging paper on the topic of working memory will report activation in prefrontal cortex. In a recent review of neuroimaging studies, Cabeza and Nyberg (2000) noted activation in prefrontal cortex in all but 2 of 60 working memory comparisons (i.e., some condition requiring working memory compared to some baseline condition). In many of these comparisons, particularly with verbal tasks, activation was observed in Broca's area.

In contrast to the seemingly clear interpretation of these neuroimaging findings, a recent meta-analysis of neuropsychological studies of working memory showed that, in contrast to lesions in temporoparietal cortex, lesions to prefrontal cortex did not reliably lead to impairments in working memory capacity (D'Esposito & Postle, 1999). The authors suggested that frontal patients have deficits on working memory tasks that "require the mediation of other PFC-supported processes" (e.g., tasks with distractor-filled delay intervals; p. 1315). One such candidate process is selection: Activation in Broca's area is observed during working memory trials in a proactive interference paradigm, in which probe familiarity is a competing source of information at response (Jonides, Smith, Marshuetz, Koeppe, & Reuter-Lorenz, 1998). We reported data from a patient with a lesion to Broca's area who had a selective impairment in his ability to inhibit proactive interference in working memory (see Figure 11.5;

Thompson-Schill et al., 2002); we interpreted this deficit as a failure to select among competing sources of information. According to this account, activation in Broca's area might be observed during the delay period of working memory tasks as a precaution against potentially interfering stimuli; however, this activation would only prove to be necessary in working memory tasks where interference actually occurred. In other words, activation in Broca's area during working memory tasks is consistent with the hypothesis that the function of Broca's area is to guide selection when there are competing sources of information.

This hypothesis may have implications for a long-standing debate in the study of sentence comprehension: Do the tasks of assigning syntactic structure and interpreting the meaning of a sentence using that structure require a domain-specific separate-sentence-interpretation resource (e.g., Caplan & Waters, 1999) or do these tasks depend on a single verbal working memory capacity resource (e.g., Just & Carpenter, 1992)? We suggest that sentence comprehension depends on a resource that is better characterized as a non-mnemonic process than as a mnemonic capacity. That is, the single resource may be the ability to select between competing sources of information, which is necessary both for some working memory tasks and for some sentence processing tasks.

WHEN SELECTION FAILS: LANGUAGE PROCESSING WITHOUT BROCA'S AREA

The hypothesis that Broca's area subserves selection among competing sources of information was not developed in the domain of language per se. However, certain symptoms would be expected to arise from the operation of a language system that is unable to select between competing sources of information. These symptoms should be observed in patients with lesions affecting Broca's area. Notice that this does not lead to the hypothesis that all patients with a selection-impairment will have Broca's aphasia, nor does it lead to the hypothesis that all patients with Broca's aphasia will have a selection impairment. As reviewed above, there is neither a necessary nor sufficient relation between Broca's area lesions and Broca's aphasia; as such, this is not a hypothesis about Broca's aphasia per se. Rather, the claim is that certain *symptoms* should be observed in patients with damage to Broca's area as a result of an inability to select between competing sources of information. Although few experiments have explicitly tested this idea, here I review those findings that are consistent with this hypothesis, and outline a strategy for testing these ideas further.

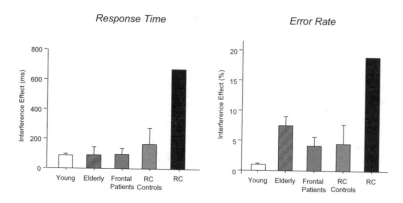

FIG. 11.5. A patient (RC) with left prefrontal damage including pars triangularis (Brodmann's area 45) showed an exaggerated interference effect in response time (left panel) and error rate (right panel) on working memory trials with recently-presented foils. Patients with frontal lesions sparing BA45 exhibited an interference effect comparable to age-matched control subjects. Adapted from Thompson-Schill et al., 2002.

Language Production

An impairment in word retrieval is a ubiquitous deficit in all types of aphasia and could result from failures at any stage in the word production process. In cases where a word retrieval failure is the result of a selection deficit, performance should be modulated by competition. Luria described the language production deficit associated with frontal lobe syndromes as "dynamic aphasia", reflecting that the linguistic deficits come and go as a function of context (Luria, 1973). Other investigators have reported that restricted lesions of Broca's area result in a syndrome that resembles transcortical motor aphasia, in which production impairments are primarily evident on generative language tasks such as verbal fluency or storytelling. These types of deficits could result from a selection failure in unconstrained settings. There are several sources of experimental evidence that damage to prefrontal cortex (and in some cases, specifically to Broca's area) results in a word retrieval impairment that is best characterized as a failure to select among competing alternatives.

First, damage to prefrontal cortex is associated with selection-related impairments on verbal fluency tasks (e.g., retrieving the names of animals, or of words that start with F). A patient with a bilateral, frontal lesion was impaired at generating exemplars of the superordinate category "animals" but was normal at generating exemplars of the subordinate category "farm animals" (Randolph, Braun, Goldberg, & Chase, 1993). Presumably, the cue "farm animals" activates a more restricted set of representations, resulting in less competition among the set of candidate responses. Similarly, my colleagues and I reported that patients with early Alzheimer's disease (also associated with frontal dysfunction) were more impaired at generating words given a one-letter cue (e.g., words that start with "F") than at generating words given a two-letter cue (e.g., words that start with "FL"); in fact, one-third of the patients were able to produce more words in the latter case, again, presumably as a result of decreased competition among candidate responses (Tippett, Gendall, Farah, & Thompson-Schill, 2004). The ability to initiate a switch between two semantic categories on a fluency task (e.g., from farm animals to jungle animals) has been linked to frontal lobe functioning (e.g., Troyer, Moscovitch, Winocur, Alexander, & Stuss, 1998); switching may require the inhibition of active (but already reported) representations using the same mechanisms required to override a prepotent response. Although selection in these cases has not been explicitly linked to Broca's area, these observations suggest a potentially fruitful line of future investigation.

Second, damage to prefrontal cortex is associated with selection-related word retrieval impairments on confrontation naming tasks (i.e., retrieving a word solely in response to a picture cue). In order to identify cases where confrontation naming fails as the result of a selection impairment, one would have to show that naming performance was affected by the number of competing alternatives. One way to experimentally introduce conflict among competing alternatives during confrontation naming is to present pictures in semantically-related blocks, which is known to exert an interfering effect in normal speakers (e.g., Damian, Vigliocco, & Levelt, 2001). An exacerbation of this interference effect was observed in a nonfluent aphasic patient with anterior damage (but critically, not in a patient with a posterior lesion) who exhibited a context-sensitive word-retrieval impairment that was interpreted as a failure of competitive selection (Wilshire & McCarthy, 2002).

The most detailed investigation of selection-related deficits in language production following damage to Broca's area comes from Robinson and colleagues (1998), who recently reported a case study of a patient with dynamic aphasia following a lesion of the left frontal operculum; this patient had an impairment confined to generative tasks with high selection demands. For example, when given a stem of a sentence and asked to generate a single word to complete it, the patient would fail with a sentence such as "Bob went to the store to buy some…" although she would succeed with "Bob takes his coffee with milk and …"

In a second patient (Robinson, Shallice, & Cipolotti, in press), the selection deficit was confined to the language domain, indicating that the impairment was an inability to select between competing *verbal* representations.

Language Comprehension

As reviewed above, impairments in the syntactic analysis of sentences have been attributed to lesions of Broca's area; however, similar deficits have been observed in many types of aphasia (Dick et al., 2001), and among agrammatic Broca's aphasics, the pattern of deficits may vary (Badecker & Caramazza, 1985). Thus, we can ask (as here), what would a deficit in sentence comprehension caused by a selection impairment look like? Following from the idea that sentence interpretation involves a dynamic competition among multiple sources of information (e.g., Trueswell & Tanenhaus, 1994), we propose that selection demands are increased when these various sources do not converge on a unique interpretation (e.g., passive sentences, which pit syntactic and word order cues against each other). An inability to select between competing sources of information may have particular implications for syntactic cues, as some psycholinguists have argued that "a preliminary semantic interpretation is defined on an incomplete syntactic representation and is maintained unless inconsistent information arrives; thus syntax acts more like a filter for proposed interpretations" (Carlson & Tanenhaus, 1988: 286); patients with selection deficits may have an inability to "undo" these provisional interpretations (cf. Saffran, Schwartz, & Linebarger, 1998). In addition, this framework may explain why some patients with Broca's aphasia fail to comprehend simple sentences (e.g., active sentences; Schwartz, Saffran, & Marin, 1980), a phenomenon which has thus far been poorly explained by both syntactic theories (e.g., Grodzinsky, 1986) and limited resource theories (e.g., Dick et al., 2001). By our account, impairments might occur in comprehension of any sentence with competing interpretations, including reversible active sentences. At present, there has been no direct test of the claim that Broca's area is associated with selection-related impairments in sentence comprehension; however, as many available data are consistent with this claim (e.g., Schwartz et al., 1980), it would be a potentially productive line of future investigation.

Another way to increase competition during sentence comprehension is to introduce ambiguity, either at the level of lexical (e.g., homonyms) or syntactic (e.g., garden path sentences) interpretation. Ambiguity that occurs when one word has two distinct meanings is a model case for understanding how semantic selection is necessary for normal language comprehension. For instance, in order to understand the sentence "He dug with a spade," the meaning of spade associated with shovel must be selected over the meaning associated with card games. Several studies have indicated that patients exhibiting symptoms of Broca's aphasia show a delay in selecting context-appropriate meanings of ambiguous words (e.g., Swaab, Brown, & Hagoort, 1998). More recently, the failure to select a context-appropriate interpretation has been linked to lesions of left prefrontal cortex (Metzler, 2001). Syntactic ambiguity resolution has not been investigated in brain-damaged patients, although the ability to resolve syntactically ambiguous sentences has been linked to working memory in normal subjects (MacDonald, Just, & Carpenter, 1992), and has been shown to be insensitive to context in young children (Trueswell, Sekerina, Hill, & Logrip, 1999), who often behave in a qualitatively similar way as patients with frontal lobe damage (e.g., Diamond & Doar, 1989). The investigation of these processes in patients with damage to Broca's area is the next logical step.

SUMMARY

As we approach the sesquicentennial of Broca's seminal paper, we have numerous hypotheses about the function (or functions) of Broca's area to consider and a slate of methods with which to do so. The proposal that Broca's area is involved in selecting information among competing sources of information provides a framework for studying both linguistic and non-linguistic deficits associated with damage to prefrontal cortex. This putative mechanism potentially relates to other hypotheses about language impairments, such as reduced lexical activation (Utman, Blumstein, & Sullivan, 2001), impaired contextual selection (Swaab et al., 1998), and even trace deletion hypotheses (see Zurif, 1995 for a discussion of the role of processing resources that sustain lexical activation during gap-filling). This mechanism may also play a role in unification operations linked to Broca's area (see Hagoort, this volume). In addition, the framework outlined here has the added advantage of continuity with other hypothesized functions of prefrontal cortex (e.g., Miller & Cohen, 2001) and thus with mechanisms that can be studied in our pre-linguistic primate cousins. Returning briefly to the question of language evolution, it is tempting to note that both the communication of patients with lesions to Broca's area and the communication of nonhuman primates have been described as situation-specific (Jackendoff, 2002). The ability to select among competing sources of information may serve as example of "a trait present in nonhuman animals [that] did not evolve specifically for human language, although it may be part of the language faculty and play an intimate role in language processing" (Hauser et al., 2002: 1572).

That is, perhaps the evolution of processes subserved by Broca's area was indeed critical for modern human communication, but not in the way that Broca initially envisioned.

ACKNOWLEDGMENTS

The preparation of this chapter was supported by NIH R0160414, NIH R01067008, and the Searle Scholars Program. The following people contributed in meaningful ways to many of the ideas and experiments described here: Geoff Aguirre, Laura Barde, Laurel Buxbaum, Anjan Chatterjee, Branch Coslett, Mark D'Esposito, Lila Gleitman, Amishi Jha, John Jonides, Irene Kan, Dan Kimberg, Martha Farah, Bob Knight, Jared Novick, Tatiana Schnur, Myrna Schwartz, Geeta Shivde, Ed Smith, Marianna Stark, Diane Swick, and John Trueswell.

REFERENCES

Alexander, M. P., Naeser, M. A., & Palumbo, C. (1990). Broca's area aphasias: Aphasia after lesions including the frontal operculum. *Neurology, 40,* 353-362.

Amunts, K., Schleicher, A., Burgel, U., Mohlberg, H., Uylings, H. B., & Zilles, K. (1999). Broca's region revisited: Cytoarchitecture and intersubject variability. *The Journal of Comparative Neurology, 412,* 319-341.

Badecker, W., & Caramazza, A. (1985). On considerations of method and theory governing the use of clinical categories in neurolinguistics and cognitive neuropsychology: The case against agrammatism. *Cognition, 20,* 97-125.

Barch, D. M., Braver, T. S., Sabb, F. W., & Noll, D. C. (2000). Anterior cingulate and the monitoring of response conflict: evidence from an fMRI study of overt verb generation. *Journal of Cognitive Neuroscience, 12,* 298-309.

Barde, L. H. F., & Thompson-Schill, S. L. (2002). Models of functional organization of the lateral prefrontal cortex in verbal working memory: Evidence in favor of the process model. *Journal of Cognitive Neuroscience, 14,* 1054-1063.

Botvinick, M. M., Braver, T. S., Barch, D. M., Carter, C. S., & Cohen, J: D. (2001). Conflict monitoring and cognitive control. *Psychological Review, 108,* 624-652.

Broca, P. P. (1861a). Loss of speech, chronic softening and partial destruction of the anterior left lobe of the brain. Translation by Christopher D. Green, retrieved from http://psychclassics.yorku.ca, September 10, 2003. *Bulletin de la Société Anthropologique, 2,* 235-238.

Broca, P. P. (1861b). Remarks on the seat of the faculty of articulated language, following an observation of aphemia (loss of speech) Translation by Christopher D. Green, retrieved from http://psychclassics.yorku.ca, September 10, 2003. *Bulletin de la Société Anatomique, 6,* 330-357.

Cabeza, R., & Nyberg, L. (2000). Imaging cognition II: An empirical review of 275 PET and fMRI studies. *Journal of Cognitive Neuroscience, 12.* http://mitpress.

Caplan, D., & Waters, G. S. (1999). Verbal working memory and sentence comprehension. *Behavioral & Brain Sciences, 22*, 77-126.

Caramazza, A., & Zurif, E. B. (1976). Dissociation of algorithmic and heuristic processes in language comprehension: Evidence from aphasia. *Brain & Language, 3*, 572-582.

Carlson, G., & Tanenhaus, M. K. (1988). Thematic roles and language comprehension. In W. Wilkins (Ed.), *Thematic relations: Syntax and semantics* (Vol. 21, pp. 263-288). New York: Academic Press.

Chomsky, N. (1981). *Lectures on government and binding*. Dordrecht, Netherlands: Foris.

D'Esposito, M., & Postle, B. R. (1999). The dependence of span and delayed-response performance on prefrontal cortex. *Neuropsychologia, 37*, 1303-1315.

Damian, M. F., Vigliocco, G., & Levelt, W. J. M. (2001). Effects of semantic context in the naming of pictures and words. *Cognition, 81*, 77-86.

Diamond, A., & Doar, B. (1989). The performance of human infants on a measure of frontal cortex function, the delayed response task. *Developmental Psychobiology, 22*, 271-294.

Dick, F., Bates, E., Wulfeck, B., Utman, J. A., Dronkers, N. F., & Gernsbacher, M. A. (2001). Language deficits, localization, and grammar: Evidence for a distributive model of language breakdown in aphasic patients and neurologically intact individuals. *Psychological Review, 108*, 759-788.

Dronkers, N. F. (1996). A new brain region for coordinating speech articulation. *Nature, 384*, 159-161.

Dronkers, N. F., Plaisant, O., Iba-Zizen, M. T., & Cabanis, E. A. (2000). "Tan" revisited and agrammatic sentence production. *Brain and Language, 74*, 553-555.

Fletcher, P. C., Shallice, T., & Dolan, R. J. (2000). "Sculpting the response space" — An account of left prefrontal activation at encoding. *Neuroimage, 12*, 404-417.

Friederici, A. D. (2002). Toward a neural basis of auditory sentence processing. *Trends in Cognitive Science, 6*, 78-84.

Gold, B. T., & Buckner, R. L. (2002). Common prefrontal regions coactivate with dissociable posterior regions during controlled semantic and phonological tasks. *Neuron, 35*, 803-812.

Grodzinsky, Y. (1986). Language deficits and the theory of syntax. *Brain and Language, 27*, 135-159.

Grodzinsky, Y. (2000). The neural substrate of the language faculty: Suggestions for the future. *Brain and Language, 71*, 82-84.

Guitton, D., Buchtel, H. A., & Douglas, R. M. (1985). Frontal lobe lesions in man cause difficulties in suppressing reflexive glances and in generating goal-directed saccades. *Experimental Brain Research, 58*, 455-472.

Hauser, M. D., Chomsky, N., & Fitch, W. T. (2002). The faculty of language: What is it, who has it, and how did it evolve? *Science, 298*, 1569-1579.

Indefrey, P., Brown, C. M., Hellwig, F., Amunts, K., Herzog, H., Seitz, R. J., & Hagoort, P. (2001). A neural correlate of syntactic encoding during speech production. *Proceedings of the National Academy of Sciences, USA, 98*, 5933-5936.

Jackendoff, R. (2002). *Foundations of language*. Oxford: Oxford University Press.

Jonides, J., Smith, E. E., Marshuetz, C., Koeppe, R. A., & Reuter-Lorenz, P. A. (1998). Inhibition in verbal working memory revealed by brain activation. *Proceedings of the National Academy of Sciences, USA, 95,* 8410-8413.

Just, M. A., & Carpenter, P. A. (1992). A capacity theory of comprehension: Individual differences in working memory. *Psychological Review, 99,* 122-149.

Kaan, E., & Swaab, T. Y. (2002). The brain circuitry of syntactic comprehension. *Trends in Cognitive Science, 6,* 350-356.

Kan, I. P., & Thompson-Schill, S. L. (2004). Effect of name agreement on prefrontal activity during overt and covert picture naming. *Cognitive, Affective, & Behavioral Neuroscience, 4,* 43-57.

Luria, A. R. (1973). *The Working Brain.* New York: Basic Books.

MacDonald, M. C., Just, M. A., & Carpenter, P. A. (1992). Working memory constraints on the processing of syntactic ambiguity. *Cognitive Psychology, 24,* 56-98.

Metzler, C. (2001). Effects of left frontal lesions on the selection of context-appropriate meanings. *Neuropsychology, 15,* 315-328.

Miller, E. K., & Cohen, J. D. (2001). An integrative theory of prefrontal cortex function. *Annual Review of Neuroscience, 24,* 167-202.

Mohr, J. P., Pessin, M. S., Finkelstein, S., Funkenstein, H. H., Duncan, G. W., & Davis, K. R. (1978). Broca aphasia: Pathologic and clinical. *Neurology, 28,* 311-324.

Perret, E. (1974). The left frontal lobe of man and the suppression of habitual responses in verbal categorical behavior. *Neuropsychologia, 12,* 323-330.

Poldrack, R. A., Wagner, A. D., Prull, M. W., Desmond, J. E., Glover, G. H., & Gabrieli, J. D. (1999). Functional specialization for semantic and phonological processing in the left inferior prefrontal cortex. *Neuroimage, 10,* 15-35.

Randolph, C., Braun, A. R., Goldberg, T. E., & Chase, T. N. (1993). Semantic fluency in Alzheimer's, Parkinson's, and Huntington's disease: Dissociation of storage and retrieval failures. *Neuropsychology, 7,* 82-88.

Robinson, G., Blair, J., & Cipolotti, L. (1998). Dynamic aphasia: An inability to select between competing verbal responses? *Brain, 121,* 77-89.

Robinson, G., Shallice, T., & Cipolotti, L. (in press). A failure of high level verbal response selection in progressive dynamic aphasia. *Cognitive Neuropsychology.*

Saffran, E. M., Schwartz, M. F., & Linebarger, M. C. (1998). Semantic influences on thematic role assignment: Evidence from normals and aphasics. *Brain & Language, 62,* 255-297.

Schwartz, M. F., Saffran, E. M., & Marin, O. S. (1980). The word order problem in agrammatism. I. Comprehension. *Brain & Language, 10,* 249-262.

Swaab, T. Y., Brown, C., & Hagoort, P. (1998). Understanding ambiguous words in sentence contexts: Electrophysiological evidence for delayed contextual selection in Broca's aphasia. *Neuropsychologia, 36,* 737-761.

Thompson-Schill, S. L., D'Esposito, M., Aguirre, G. K., & Farah, M. J. (1997). Role of left inferior prefrontal cortex in retrieval of semantic knowledge: A reevaluation. *Proceedings of the National Academy of Sciences, USA, 94,* 14792-14797.

Thompson-Schill, S. L., D'Esposito, M., & Kan, I. P. (1999). Effects of repetition and competition on activity in left prefrontal cortex during word generation. *Neuron, 23,* 513-522.

Thompson-Schill, S. L., Jonides, J., Marshuetz, C., Smith, E. E., D'Esposito, M., Kan, I. P., Knight, R. T., & Swick, D. (2002). Effects of frontal lobe damage on interference effects in working memory. *Cognitive, Affective, and Behavioral Neuroscience, 2,* 109-120.

Thompson-Schill, S. L., Swick, D., Farah, M. J., D'Esposito, M., Kan, I. P., & Knight, R. T. (1998). Verb generation in patients with focal frontal lesions: A neuropsychological test of neuroimaging findings. *Proceedings of the National Academy of Sciences, USA, 26,* 14792-14797.

Tippett, L. J., Gendall, A., Farah, M. J., & Thompson-Schill, S. L. (2004). Selection ability in Alzheimer's disease: Investigation of a component of semantic processing. *Neuropsychology, 18,* 163-173.

Troyer, A. K., Moscovitch, M., Winocur, G., Alexander, M. P., & Stuss, D. (1998). Clustering and switching on verbal fluency: The effects of focal frontal- and temporal-lobe lesions. *Neuropsychologia, 36,* 499-504.

Trueswell, J. C., Sekerina, I., Hill, N. M., & Logrip, M. L. (1999). The kindergarten-path effect: Studying on-line sentence processing in young children. *Cognition, 73,* 89-134.

Trueswell, J. C., & Tanenhaus, M. K. (1994). Toward a lexicalist framework for constraint-based syntactic ambiguity resolution. In C. Clifton, K. Rayner & L. Frazier (Eds.), *Perspectives on sentence processing* (pp. 155-179). Hillsdale, NJ: Lawrence Erlbaum Associates.

Utman, J. A., Blumstein, S. E., & Sullivan, K. (2001). Mapping from sound to meaning: Reduced lexical activation in Broca's aphasics. *Brain and Language, 79,* 444-472.

Wilshire, C. E., & McCarthy, R. A. (2002). Evidence for a context-sensitive word retrieval disorder in a case of nonfluent aphasia. *Cognitive Neuropsychology, 19,* 165-186.

Wise, R. J., Greene, J., Buchel, C., & Scott, S. K. (1999). Brain regions involved in articulation. *Lancet, 353,* 1057-1061.

Zurif, E. B. (1995). Brain regions of relevance to syntactic processing. In L. R. Gleitman & M. Liberman (Eds.), *An invitation to cognitive science* (2nd ed., Vol. 1, pp. 381-397). Cambridge, MA: MIT Press.

12 Biology and Behavior: Insights from the Acquisition of Sign Language

Gary Morgan
Language and Communication Science,
City University, London, UK

INTRODUCTION: LANGUAGE ACQUISITION

Evidence from the acquisition of spoken language has fuelled centuries of debate on the biological bases of language behavior. But language may be acquired through more than one modality. Sign language is acquired in a visual-spatial modality, and as evidence from the course of acquisition of sign languages becomes increasingly available it is possible to ask what parts of language acquisition are modality-general and what aspects are specific to speech or sign. Data on the influence of modality on language acquisition provides important new insights and makes further progress in elucidating the relationship of biology to language behavior.

One of the major debates in the study of children's language development is the relative influence of nature and nurture (e.g., Tomasello, 2000; Fisher, 2002). What is inside of the child (in their nature) versus what is outside of the child (in their nurture) that shapes development? Many researchers (Newport & Supalla, 1980; Newport & Meier, 1985; Meier, 2002; Petitto, 1997; Petitto et al., 2001) have argued that the nature part of language acquisition is the same for children exposed to a sign or spoken language, while the nurture part is radically different between modalities. The modality of sign impacts on how children will exploit their biological capacities for language acquisition.

Additionally, in the same way that research into reasons why some children fail to acquire language has provided valuable evidence for

191

understanding normal language acquisition (e.g., van der Lely, Rosen, & McClelland, 1998; Leonard, 1998), the documentation of developmental sign language impairments will open up a new window onto the debate into the origins of specific language impairment (SLI).

THE GRAMMAR OF BRITISH SIGN LANGUAGE: AN OVERVIEW

Once linguists began to seriously study sign languages they were faced with the inevitable conclusion that language was not synonymous with speech. British Sign language (BSL) is as expressively rich as any spoken language and is unrelated to English. As a natural human language, it has all the linguistic ingredients characteristic of any other language: a lexicon and a 'computational system' (Chomsky, 1995: 6, 221) with syntax, semantics, phonology and morphology. In this section I provide a brief overview of selected parts of BSL (for more details see Morgan, Smith, Tsimpli, & Woll, 2002; Sutton-Spence & Woll, 1999).

Phonology

A sign can be decomposed into three sets of features: hand configuration, movement, and place of articulation. Hand configuration describes the particular shape the hand makes, including the extension or flexion of the fingers and the orientation of the hand relative to the body. This parameter is often labeled simply 'handshape'. The parameter of hand configuration can be described in terms of a hierarchy of complexity, where the 'simplest' handshapes involve the fewest number of features (selection of fingers, contact between fingers, etc.) and so have been termed 'unmarked'. In BSL the four main unmarked handshapes have the labels B, 5, G, and A and are shown in the context of lexical signs in figures 12.1-12.4. [1]

Signs differ in their primary movement (e.g., straight vs. arced) or absence of movement (holds). They may also differ in their local or secondary movement, such as finger wiggling, or opening and closing of

---

[1]Signed sentences that appear in the text follow standard notation conventions. Signs are represented by upper-case English glosses. When more than one English word is needed to capture the sign's full meaning this is indicated through a hyphenated gloss. Repetition of signs is marked by '+'. 'IX' is a point to an area of sign space which acts as a syntactic index for referring to an argument in the sentence. Subscripted lower-case letters indicate coindexation.

Fig. 12.1. 'B' — 'BOOK'

Fig. 12.2. '5' — 'MIRROR'

Fig. 12.3. 'G'—'UNDERSTAND'

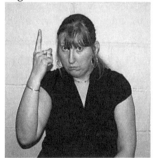

Fig. 12.4. 'A'—'MY'

FIG. 12.1. to 12.4. Still images of four signs which use unmarked handshapes in BSL labeled B, 5, G, and A.

the hand during transitions between one location and another. Signs are also contrastive in their place of articulation. Some signs make contact with the signer's body, arms, head or face (e.g., figure 12.4 MY), while in other signs the hands touch each other (e.g., figure 12.1 BOOK). All signs in BSL are made up of a handshape in combination with the other sign parameters, i.e. different handshapes at different places of articulation with different movements or holds. Signs can share one or more parameter. For example, the signs NAME and AFTERNOON are minimal pairs in BSL as they have identical handshape and movement, but differ in place of articulation (forehead and chin, respectively). For more details of sign phonology see Brentari (2002).

Morpho-syntax

In sign languages, morphological person agreement is realized by the movement of the verb stem between locations in front of the signer,

_kASK_j
'(she) asks (him)'

FIG. 12.5. Movement of the verb ASK between two locations in sign space to encode morphological person agreement. Syntactic arguments are given in the previous sentence.

which have been previously indexed as BOY and GIRL. Thus spatial locations act as referential indexes (either the spatial location of the present referent or an arbitrary location assigned to a non-present referent). An example of an utterance with arbitrary syntactic locations is shown in (1). The first IX point is directed towards a location to the front and right of the signer. The signer then signs GIRL and directs the movement of the sign ASK from her own body location. The movement of the verb between locations in sign space is shown in the photo still in figure 12.5.

(1) BOY_j   IX_j   GIRL_k _kASK_j
'There is a girl and there is a boy (she) asks (him)'

BSL also uses classifiers or polycomponential forms comprising of both spatial and syntactic information. Classifiers appear in BSL with verbs to encode location and movement of nouns. For example a noun coming from the class of long thin animates, such as a vertically erect person, can be described as moving rightward in a zigzag manner by selecting a G handshape (with the index finger pointing upward) and articulating the path of that form through sign space. In addition, signers use classifiers as anaphoric devices. The sentence in English, 'The boy just managed to clear the top of the fence' is produced in BSL by spreading the information across the two hands and face. This simultaneity of production depends on the use of antecedent nouns which licence the classifiers for BOY and FENCE. The face articulates the manner of the movement ('just managed'), the right hand signs the movement of the boy with a classifier and the left hand shows the wall, again through a classifier (see Emmorey, 2003 for more details on sign language classifiers). With this brief background on BSL grammar complete, I turn to discuss the role of modality in sign language acquisition.

Topic 1: Phonological processing

It is argued that children are better language learners than adults despite their limited cognitive abilities (e.g., Newport, 1990). Some have suggested one reason for this is because of their early sensitivity to the prosody of language (Jusczyk, 1997). When the language to be learned is perceived through the eyes, do children continue to be better learners than adults? How are children's abilities in the processing of phonology and their first attempts at producing language altered when the input and phonetics are radically different?

A related line of research to this set of questions is to do with the robustness of children's language acquisition abilities. Many deaf children experience late and impoverished exposure to a first language.[2] The reasons for this are numerous but one major factor is that 90% to 95% of deaf children are born to hearing parents who have no knowledge of sign language or how to modify their communication when interacting with a young deaf child. The question is, if you are in a critical period for language but there is no accessible input, how long can that sensitivity last?

Studying the behavioral differences between late and early sign learners allows one to observe the impact of environment on the biological capacity for language acquisition in an otherwise normal socially stimulating nurture. It is known that deaf children can create the rudiments of a gesture based communication system with their non-signing hearing parents (Goldin-Meadow, 2003) and that if enough individuals come together a full-blown language is created (Kegl, 2002; Senghas, 2003). But what are the outcomes for language processing of late first language acquisition? Mayberry, Lock, and Kazmi (2002) addressed this question using a sign 'shadowing' task (repeating a sentence while watching it). Subjects were more able to shadow what they were seeing if they were able to predict signs based on grammatical knowledge and pragmatic context. In order to do this it is crucial that subjects get beyond the phonological level of processing and further into accessing semantic content; however, the high processing demands of the task make this difficult.

---

[2]'Deaf' here means born with a hearing loss that significantly impacts on the ability to acquire spoken language.

Mayberry compared three groups of signing adults. Each group had had at least 30 years experience of American Sign Language (ASL) but differed in their age of first exposure to the language. The early learners were exposed to ASL during 0-3 years, child learners at 5-8 years, and late learners between 9-13 years. Mayberry measured the level of sign processing by comparing what the signers saw with what they produced themselves. The results of the study showed that all groups substituted signs either for semantically similar vocabulary (e.g., BROTHER for SISTER) or phonologically similar signs (e.g., the (ASL) minimal pairs, AND for SLEEP). Mayberry found that the late learners made many more phonological substitutions even when the resulting utterances were ungrammatical while the early learners made more semantic errors but still produced grammatically correct sentences.

The results of this study indicate that the effects of late exposure to first language are long lasting. Late sign learners process sign slower and at a more superficial level than native signers. We can interpret these results in relation to the question of whether children are superior to adults as sign learners. It is better to learn a sign language within an early-activated critical period for sign language (see Newport, Bavelier, & Neville, 2001, for a wider discussion of critical period). This suggests that the advantage over adults that children have in acquiring a language extends into sign language acquisition also. Children appear to benefit from limited cognitive resources at the start of language acquisition as this forces them to carry out a componential rather than holistic analysis of their language and presumably lay down more robust phonological representations in the process. These differences surface in processing abilities 30 years after first exposure and discriminate between different groups of otherwise fluent signers (see Morford & Mayberry, 2000; Kegl, 2002 for more discussion of these effects). Early exposure to sign is crucial in allowing the biological component of language acquisition to switch on and maximize processing abilities. As well as the developing phonological system, phonetic constraints appear during early language acquisition. The phonetic inventories of sign and speech differ radically but for both modalities children have to master complex motoric behaviors to communicate successfully.

Research on children acquiring a native sign language has revealed systematic differences between the child's production and the input to the child from surrounding adult models. These differences have been documented in relation to handshape, place of articulation and type of movement (e.g., Cheek, Cormier, Repp, & Meier, 2001). During the first period of language acquisition signing children substitute marked forms with unmarked. This is especially observable in the development of handshapes. Stoneham (2003) in a case study of BSL acquisition reported that the child signed COW at 1;5 but substituted a G handshape for the citation Y hand (thumb and little finger extended). The G handshape is simpler in the phonological system as it has fewer finger selection features. As well as substitutions children may insert gesture fillers into signs. This happens by the child modifying or inserting a new movement between handshape transitions, which require local or internal movements. These meaningless pauses and gesture movements embedded within signs are not observed in the adult model. Sign fillers are similar to phonological processes in spoken language acquisition and are used by the young child to make the job of sign segmentation easier. In a separate study of a child of the same age, more substitutions of handshape appeared with signs that were at the periphery of the child's field of vision: That is, more handshape substitutions were found in signs located on the head, compared with signs articulated on the forearm (Bakker, 2003). This result suggests that young children acquiring sign language are less able to monitor their own signing when they have less visual feedback.

These results indicate that in the acquisition of sign phonology and phonetics, the types of simplification processes for managing and representing language are similar across modalities. This suggests that children at the start of language acquisition approach segmentation, representation and early production with similar motivations. The major effect of modality is in how these child strategies get expressed differently through simplifications of movement, or handshape substitutions rather than a preference for simple over complex sounds or the substitution of stops for fricatives in early speech development. Modality moves limitations in the perceptual system from hearing to vision. These underlying abstract similarities between what children do with signs and words in the beginning of language acquisition forces consideration of the strong biological component acting on these processes.

Topic 2: Development of grammar

Children developing spoken language between ages 2;6 and 4;0 are reported to produce the different verb argument structures of their language with minimal errors (Pinker, 1989). When errors appear they are generally rule-governed; for example, children may over-generalize verb argument structures from the adult language to verbs whose meanings and structures do not fit that pattern, saying things like: 'Daddy go me round' (Bowerman, 1982).

Across different language typologies, children work out the specific way their target language links meaning to form (e.g., Allen, 1996). In spoken languages this may be through word order and/or case and/or inflectional morphology. Sign languages use the same grammatical devices but map meanings onto spatial contrasts. In a series of studies we have been documenting the emergence, longitudinal acquisition and overgeneralization of inflectional morphology for encoding person agreement in children natively acquiring BSL (Morgan, Barrière, & Woll, in press; Morgan, Herman, & Woll, 2002). This work has highlighted the influence of modality in terms of both language typology and input in the acquisition of BSL grammar. The influence of modality on the unfolding of grammar provides us with a window on the relationship between biology and behavior. In work on longitudinal acquisition of BSL person agreement morphology we have highlighted two effects of modality in this domain (Morgan et al., in press). Verb inflections are not simple to segment in sign languages, and Meier (2002) has argued that in ASL, since inflections are not suffixal, syllabic or stressed, the markers of agreement are not discrete affixal language units. The relatively late onset of verb agreement morphology in children's signing, compared with similarly morphologically rich spoken languages, reflects this segmentation difficulty. Coupled with typology is the crucial effect of the visual environment in which children learn to sign.

The input to signing children is dependent on adults timing their language to match children's visual attention. Deaf children do not see the same amount of adult sign language as hearing children listen to or overhear in the ambient spoken language. This is simply because once they look away from the adult signer their access to the input disappears. This is not the case for hearing children acquiring spoken language. The use by adults of simplified child-directed signing makes it more visually salient but qualitatively different to adult-adult sign. Adults address quantitatively less obligatory inflectional morphology to children than when signing to other adults (Morgan et al., in press). The type of inflectional morphology sign languages use, as well as differences between seeing and hearing language, influence the rate of development of specific features of BSL grammar. Despite deaf children experiencing significantly less language directed to them or in the ambient environment than hearing age peers they go on to develop sign fluency at approximately the same ages. In specific aspects of grammar there are cross-modality differences but these modality effects are local and not global. This developmental parity between deaf and hearing language acquisition with very different *amounts* of input may mean that much of the speech addressed to hearing children is redundant. The acquisition of language can take place with significantly less raw material to analyze and with significantly more of a biological component.

199

Topic 3: Specific language impairment

Specific language impairment (SLI) in hearing children acquiring spoken language is diagnosed where there is a deficit in normal language acquisition with no apparent cognitive, social or neurological cause (Leonard, 1998). Since hearing loss is specifically excluded in diagnosing SLI, it has been impossible to explore SLI in deaf children. Frequently problems are reported with phonology, syntax and inflectional morphology (e.g., van der Lely et al., 1998; Leonard, 1998). SLI encompasses many different subtypes including language perception and production difficulties as well as higher order semantic/pragmatic problems. There is much debate about the underlying core cause of language impairment. Current explanations include an auditory processing deficit (Bishop, 1992) or an impairment of a grammar-processing module (van der Lely et al., 1998). Although there are different explanations for different impairments and for different children, the common prevailing hypothesis has been that 'most children with SLI have some auditory processing problems' (Bishop, 1992). More recently there has been an attempt to separate out auditory processing difficulties from cases of impairments in the processing of grammatical relations.

There are very few reported studies of atypical development in children acquiring a sign language in the literature (Woll, Morgan, & Herman, 2003). One reason for this is that up until recently language pathologists have known little about sign language acquisition and consequently SLI was not normally considered if the child's primary mode of communication was sign. Additionally sign was considered perfectly learnable by deaf children who had previously failed to learn a spoken language, but there was little understanding of the difference between a sign language and gestures, or sign supported English vs. British Sign Language.

However, if the incidence of language impairment is the same in children who are born deaf (or are the hearing offspring of deaf signing parents) as it is in the general population, then at least 7% of children learning sign language *will have* language impairment (figure from Leonard, 1998). It may even be the case that the incidence of sign SLI is higher in the deaf population because of the more generalized neurological insults which may accompany deafness (e.g., sequelae of meningitis, rubella, or cytomegalovirus). We are interested in finding out what language impairment looks like in a sign language and what parts of the language are affected. Is it the same as or different from SLI in spoken language development?

This area of research, while of great importance to current debates, is difficult to carry out for several reasons:

1. Characteristics of the signing population. Because late learners represent the biggest group within the signing community (they are typically atypical) much care is needed in distinguishing language delay caused by language deprivation and delay from language disorder. Individuals who experience late exposure to a first language are **not** language impaired. The subtle differences between native and non-native signers seen in high demand contexts (such as Mayberry's shadowing task) are more similar to the differences between fluent native and non-native speakers, although the non-native signers differ from non-native speakers in that they have no native first language. It is of course possible that late language learning children are at more risk of a language disorder if they are already on the borderline for impairment. Deaf children are rarely referred for specialist sign language intervention and therapy, and this only occurs after a protracted time in other types of speech and language therapy, thus exacerbating the problem. The signing population is very heterogeneous and therefore controlling for other cognitive differences between impaired and un-impaired groups (e.g., language mediated memory, visual-spatial processing) is crucial.

2. Design of tests. Aside from the abilities of the testers,[3] the tests used to measure sign language impairment need to distinguish between poor performance because of late language learning and poor performance as a result of a language disorder. The late sign language learner may exhibit a normal developmental path but with delays (same sequence of milestones but different ages) or a different developmental path which cannot be explained by considering deficits outside the language faculty (e.g., deficits in non-verbal cognition). We are currently working with the hypothesis that errors with language structure in children with sign SLI will show a different pattern than typical first language acquisition or second language development.

This prediction is supported by recent findings from research on unimpaired but late sign exposed deaf children (Lillo-Martin & Berk, 2003). In this longitudinal study of two children aged 5;6−6;0 when first exposed to ASL, language acquisition unfolded in the same sequence as in children who experience typical early exposure to language (a one sign stage followed by a two sign stage followed by the expansion of morphology, etc.).

---

[3]When evaluating language development in signing children testers must be sensitive enough to identify children who use very skilled communication strategies (e.g., gesture) to compensate or disguise poor linguistic development.

Previous research has documented developmentally impaired signing in individuals with additional impairments (e.g., Atkinson, Woll, & Gathercole, 2002; Morgan et al., 2002; Woll & Grove, 1996). In general across these individuals impairments outside of the language faculty have produced atypical sign language development. Current work is focusing on cases of atypical development stemming from impairments within language rather than with associated systems.

In a series of clinical case studies we are developing a battery of tests for sub-types of sign language developmental impairments. Up to now these tests are based on our experience with different language disorders in children acquiring spoken languages. We maintain a clinic, which receives referrals of deaf and hearing signing children with apparent problems in BSL grammar (Morgan & Herman, 2002), sign processing, pragmatic difficulties, and expressive sign disfluencies (Morgan & Herman, in prep). The goal of this research is to understand how atypical sign language development can be measured and explained. This involves the development of tests, which can accurately pinpoint where the specific language problem lies (sign phonology, morpho-syntax, pragmatics, etc). These tests need to be based within standard developmental scores for non-impaired signing children. Using data from adult signing, normal acquisition and atypical cases we are building a model of normal sign language processing in order to arrive at some understanding of the origins of different sign impairments.

As an example of this work, some preliminary findings are presented for a child with problems in BSL and English grammar. The child (JA) is a hearing male aged 5;11 at testing. He communicates at home in BSL with his deaf mother and deaf father. He was referred for an assessment because of reported difficulties with English and poor behavior at school. JA's English was assessed using the Clinical Evaluation of Language Fluency (CELF). He scored poorly in the comprehension of sentences in English with spatial prepositions, tenses, and pronouns. His expressive skills and single word vocabulary were relatively strong. We assessed JA's signing abilities using the BSL Reception Skills Test (Herman, Holmes, & Woll, 1999). The assessment involves watching an adult signer on video sign short sentences; after each item the child has to point to a corresponding picture from a choice of four (due both semantic and phonological distracters). The sentences cover a range of grammatical constructions including: negation; pluralisation through the use of lexical signs and classifiers; different verbs of movement and location again involving different types of classifiers and their sentential predicates. This test is the only published BSL assessment battery available at present. Results can be compared with age-normed standard scores for children between 3 and 12 years. In the BSL test JA scored appropriately on single vocabulary items, as in the English assessment, but he scored very low on signed sentences which contained BSL grammatical information for encoding plurality, negation and sentences involving classifiers.

What marked JA's poor performance out as atypical was the erratic profile of passes and fails on test items. His performance did not follow a typical pattern either for a child of his age or for a non-native signing child with a language delay (i.e., a performance like a child from a younger age-group). He failed several early items in the test (which are designed to be linguistically simple) and passed several of the more difficult items. We concluded from this assessment that JA's patterns of problems in language are: similar in English and BSL; and not like those found in normal development or typical second language processing problems. Some current research on spoken language SLI in bilinguals has shown that impairments appear in both the children's languages (Paradis, Crago, Genesee, & Rice, 2003). Because BSL and English differ in how they encode grammatical rules it is not possible to say that JA's performed poorly on exactly the same linguistic items in both languages but the areas in which he had difficulty were comparable.

Sign language impairments and implications for SLI

The fact that an impairment surfaces in a hearing signing child in both modalities and in similar linguistic domains is evidence for difficulties with more abstract features of language than those based in auditory processing. We are currently investigating what might underlie language impairment in BSL. Perhaps what links SLI in signed and spoken language is a difficulty with the processing of speeded sequential stimuli. Rather than being modality-specific, the stimuli may be either visual or sound based. Explanations of SLI based on a processing deficit argue that poor processing or problems with language segmentation prevent the child from forming robust phonological representations. This has consequences throughout the system into higher hierarchical units e.g., morpho-syntactic structures. This difficulty might not be unique to sound. Children with a problem in laying down sign language phonological representations because of a visual processing deficit (specific to the patterns and frequencies common to language) would also be at a disadvantage in their development of sign grammar. A difference between the modalities argues against this explanation. The transition between phonological contrasts in sign language is slower than in spoken languages (Emmorey, 2002) which means that if an impairment lies at the level of speed of processing it would be circumvented by the sign modality.

Alternatively what may unite sign and spoken language SLI is the existence of an impaired amodal linguistic module (e.g., for computing grammatical dependencies). Whatever we find as a plausible cause of sign SLI we suggest that these studies of developmental sign language impairments will show that the general role of auditory processing in SLI is overstated.

CONCLUSIONS

Language acquisition can be explored from different perspectives when instead of study children exposed to sound-based languages we study languages perceived through the eyes and articulated through movements of the hands and face. The remarkable similarities in the way language emerges and is acquired in signing and speaking children points to robust internal forces as driving a set of language dedicated processes. However, across the areas of phonology, grammar, and language impairment, the patterns of acquisition are not identical across modalities. As with any cross-linguistic comparison, language-specific features come to bear on the nature of children's rule-governed errors and their speed of mastery of specific linguistic structures. The phonology and grammar of BSL coupled with specific perceptual limitations in the visual spatial domain influence how children act on the available evidence. At the start of language use, at around age one year, we see that children simplify handshape and movement parameters in rule-governed ways. Currently however we know very little about how infants perceive sign language and how they visually segment the sign-stream in order to isolate cues to syntactic structures. Our preliminary research into SLI in child users of sign language has revealed that impairments in the acquisition of grammar are not modality specific. The more work we do on normal and atypical sign language acquisition, the more subtypes of impairment we will be able to document and the more able we will be to understand universal features of acquisition and impairment across modalities. By identifying the origins and explaining the specific impairments in atypical sign language development, this work can provide a means to deciding what is the biological contribution to SLI (is it auditory processing or the computation of grammatical dependencies). Therefore the study of normal and atypical sign language acquisition is more important than ever for understanding what is so special about children's most amazing developmental achievement.

ACKNOWLEDGMENTS

I would like to thank Bencie Woll for the several hours of discussion we have had about ideas contained in this chapter. Thanks also to Ros Herman, Victoria Joffe, Neil Smith, Isabelle Barrière, and especially, Karen Emmorey for advice in the preparation of this work. I am also indebted to the audience and other speakers at the 'four corners' workshop at MPI.

REFERENCES

Allen, S. E. M. (1996). *Aspects of argument structure acquisition in Inuktitut.* Amsterdam: John Benjamins.

Atkinson, J. A., Woll, B., & Gathercole, S. (2002). The impact of developmental visuo-spatial learning difficulties on British Sign Language. *Neurocase, 8,* 424-441.

Bakker, D. (2003). *The development of the handshape parameter in British Sign Language: A dependency phonology approach.* Unpublished master's thesis, University of Amsterdam.

Bishop, D. V. M. (1992). The underlying nature of specific language impairment. *Journal of Child Psychology and Psychiatry, 33,* 1-64.

Bowerman, M. (1982). Evaluating competing linguistic models with language acquisition data: Implications of developmental errors with causative verbs. *Quaderni di Semantica, 3,* 5-66.

Brentari, D. (2002). Modality differences in sign language phonology and morphophonemics. In R. Meier, K. Cormier, & D. Quinto (Eds.), *Modality and structure in signed and spoken languages.* New York: Cambridge University Press.

Cheek, A., Cormier, K., Repp, A., & Meier, R. P. (2001). Prelinguistic gesture predicts mastery and error in the production of early signs. *Language, 77,* 292-323.

Chomsky, N. (1995). *The minimalist program.* Cambridge, MA: MIT Press.

Emmorey, K. (2002). *Language, cognition, and the brain: Insights from sign language research.* Mahwah, NJ: Lawrence Erlbaum Associates.

Emmorey, K. (2003). *Perspectives on classifier constructions in sign language.* Mahwah, NJ: Lawrence Erlbaum Associates.

Fisher, C. (2002). The role of abstract syntactic knowledge in language acquisition: A reply to Tomasello (2000). *Cognition, 82,* 259-278.

Goldin-Meadow, S. (2003). *The resilience of language: What gesture creation in deaf children can tell us about how all children learn language.* New York: Psychology Press.

Herman, R., Holmes, S., & Woll, B. (1999). *Assessing British sign language development: Receptive skills test.* Gloucestershire, UK: Forest Bookshop.

Jusczyk, P. W. (1997). *The discovery of spoken language.* Cambridge, MA: MIT Press.

Kegl, J. (2002). Language emergence in a language-ready brain: Acquisition. In G. Morgan & B. Woll (Eds.), *Directions in sign language acquisition* (pp. 207-254). Amsterdam: John Benjamins.

Leonard, L. (1998). *Children with specific language impairment.* Cambridge, MA: MIT Press.

Lillo-Martin, D., & Berk, S. (2003). Acquisition of constituent order under delayed language exposure. In B. Beachley, A. Brown, & F. Conlin (Eds.), *Proceedings of the 27th Annual Boston University Conference on Language Development* (pp. 484-495). Cascadilla Press.

Mayberry, R. I., Lock, E., & Kazmi, H. (2002). Linguistic ability and early language exposure. *Nature, 417,* 38.

Meier, R. P. (2002). The acquisition of verb agreement in ASL: Pointing out arguments for the linguistic status of agreement in signed languages. In G. Morgan & B. Woll (Eds.), *Directions in sign language acquisition* (pp. 115-142). Amsterdam: John Benjamins.

Morford, J. P., & Mayberry, R. (2000). A reexamination of "early exposure" and its implications for language acquisition by eye. In C. Chamberlain, J. P. Morford, & R. Mayberry (Eds.), *Language acquisition by eye* (pp. 111-127). Mahwah, NJ: Lawrence Erlbaum Associates.

Morgan, G., Smith, N. V., Tsimpli, I.-M., & Woll, B. (2002). Language against the odds: The learning of British Sign Language by a polyglot savant. *Journal of Linguistics, 38,* 1-41.

Morgan, G., & Herman, R. (in prep.). *Stuttering into sign language.* Manuscript, City University, London.

Morgan, G., & Herman, R. (2002). *Specific sign language impairment: Deprivation or disorder?* Paper presented at IASCL Madison, July 2002.

Morgan, G., Herman, R., & Woll, B. (2002). The development of complex verbs in British Sign Language. *Journal of Child Language, 29,* 655-675.

Morgan, G., Barrière, I., & Woll, B. (in press). The influence of typology and modality in the acquisition of verb agreement in British Sign Language. First Language.

Newport, E. L. (1990). Maturational constraints on language learning. *Cognitive Science, 14,* 11-28.

Newport, E. L., & Supalla, T. (1980). The structuring of language: Clues from the acquisition of signed and spoken language. In U. Bellugi & M. Studdert-Kennedy (Eds.), *Signed and spoken language: Biological constraints on linguistic form* (pp. 187-212). Dahlem-Workshop. Weinheim: Chemie Verlag.

Newport, E., & Meier, R. (1985). The acquisition of American Sign Language. In D. Slobin (Ed.), *The crosslinguistic study of language acquisition.* Vol. 1: The data (pp. 881-938). Hillsdale, NJ: Lawrence Erlbaum Associates.

Newport, E. L., Bavelier, D., & Neville, H. J. (2001). Critical thinking about critical periods: Perspectives on a critical period for language acquisition. In E. Dupoux (Ed.), *Language, brain, and cognitive development: Essays in honor of Jacques Mehler* (pp. 481-502). Cambridge, MA: MIT Press.

Paradis, J., Crago, M., Genesee F., & Rice, M. (2003). French-English bilingual children with specific language impairment: How do they compare with their monolingual peers. *Journal of Speech Language and Hearing Research, 36,* 113-127.

Petitto, L. (1997). In the beginning: On the genetic and environmental factors that make early language acquisition possible. In M. Gopnik (Ed.), *The inheritance and innateness of grammars* (pp. 45-69). Oxford: Oxford University Press.

Petitto, L. A., Katerelos, M., Levy, B., Gauna, K., Tétrault, K., & Ferraro, V. (2001). Bilingual signed and spoken language acquisition from birth: Implications for the mechanisms underlying early bilingual language acquisition. *Journal of Child Language, 28,* 453-496.

Pinker, S. (1989). *Learnability and cognition: The acquisition of argument structure.* Cambridge: Cambridge University Press.

Senghas, A. (2003). Intergenerational influence and ontogenetic development in the emergence of spatial grammar in Nicaraguan Sign Language. *Cognitive Development, 18,* 511-531.

Stoneham, H. (2003). *Phonological processes in the acquisition of British Sign Language: A case study.* Unpublished doctoral dissertation, City University, London, UK.

Sutton-Spence, R. L., & Woll, B. (1999). *An introduction to the linguistics of BSL.* Cambridge: Cambridge University Press.

Tomasello, M. (2000). Do young children have adult syntactic competence? *Cognition, 74,* 209-253.

van der Lely, H. K. J., Rosen, S., & McClelland, A. (1998). Evidence for a grammar specific deficit in children. *Current Biology, 8,* 1253-1258.

Woll, B., & Grove, N. (1996). On language deficits and modality in children with Down Syndrome: A case study of twins bilingual in BSL and English. *Journal of Deaf Studies and Deaf Education, 1,* 271-278.

Woll, B., Morgan, G., & Herman, R. (2003). *Sign language acquisition: Typical and atypical development.* Paper presented at SRCD Pre-conference, Tampa, FL, April 2003.

Section 3

Production and Comprehension

13 Maximal Input and Feedback in Production and Comprehension

Gabriella Vigliocco
University College London, UK

Robert J. Hartsuiker
Ghent University, Belgium

Since the 1980s, a fundamental question in psycholinguistics has been whether the processes engaged during language production and comprehension should be conceived as modular or not. In both domains, two fundamental properties of the processing system have been debated: Whether the flow of information from a level n to a subsequent level $n+1$ is *maximal* or *minimal* (e.g., does information cascade from one processing level to the next or is only the end result at each level transmitted to the following level?); and whether the flow of information from a level n to a level $n+1$ is *bidirectional* or *unidirectional* (does information at a given level feed back to a previous level?).

As discussed in Boland and Cutler (1996), when we consider spoken word recognition and sentence comprehension, there is substantial evidence for maximal flow of information from one level to the next, and maximal flow is assumed by most theories (an exception is the Garden Path Model, e.g., Frazier, 1987). The "great divide" in comprehension research is between theories that only assume unidirectional flow of information and theories that assume feedback (e.g., in spoken word recognition: Shortlist, Norris, McQueen, & Cutler, 2000, vs. TRACE, McClelland & Elman, 1986; in sentence comprehension: Incremental Interactive Theory, e.g., Altmann & Steedman, 1988 vs. Constraint-

Satisfaction, e.g., Tanenhaus & Trueswell, 1995). The situation is somewhat different in language production research where the divide is rather between theories that assume minimal and unidirectional flow of information (e.g., Levelt, Roelofs, & Meyer, 1999) and theories that assume both maximal flow and bidirectional flow of information (e.g., Dell, 1986).

However, from a review of the production literature (Vigliocco & Hartsuiker, 2002), we have concluded that maximal input is supported by a plethora of evidence, both in word and sentence production. Although this interpretation of the findings, when applied to the production system as a whole may still be controversial (see McQueen, this volume), it is a challenge for defenders of minimalist views to explain the different experimental results without invoking maximal input. However, just as in spoken word recognition, the current evidence does not clearly support the existence of bidirectional flow of information, because results that appear to argue for feedback can also be explained by invoking alternative mechanisms (Vigliocco & Hartsuiker, 2002).

On the basis of our review, we concluded that two options were viable. First, one can abandon the notion of feedback altogether and embrace a model of production that allows only for maximal input (along the lines of the model of word production discussed by Lloyd-Jones & Humphreys, 1997). Second, one can maintain both maximal input and feedback. In the comprehension literature, the first option has been advocated by certain theories of spoken word recognition (Norris et al., 2000) and sentence comprehension (Altmann & Steedman, 1988). But this option may not be as readily viable when we consider production. Although it would certainly be parsimonious to have the same constraints on information flow for both production and comprehension, there are important differences in task demands between the two: Producing language implies implementing language-specific dependencies from one type of information to another ("getting the details of the form right", Garrett, 1980) in every utterance. In contrast, understanding a sentence can dispense with getting the details of the form right if sufficient information to achieve an interpretation is available (e.g., from the context). Because of the constraints posed by having to "get the details of the form right", production may require more precise information-handling in order to avoid errors. As discussed in Vigliocco and Hartsuiker (2002), allowing for maximal input may help increasing efficiency in the system (by virtue of preactivating representations at subsequent levels), however, without feedback, or other monitoring mechanisms, maximal input could increase the likelihood of committing errors.

For these reasons, we have chosen to follow the second option thus maintaining both maximal input and feedback, proposing a maximalist, levels of integration, view of sentence production. In this chapter, we outline this framework, presenting illustrative examples of evidence favoring maximal input and of evidence compatible with bidirectional flow of information between some of the assumed levels of integration. We further introduce alternative accounts for the reported evidence for bidirectional flow, alternative accounts that dispense with feedback. We conclude by presenting arguments for why these alternative accounts of the evidence do not score any better than feedback accounts. As we move along, we draw parallels with similar assumptions in spoken word recognition and sentence comprehension. A more intimate link (making production and comprehension regular but not inseparable bedfellows) is discussed when we present our arguments in support of feedback.

LEVELS OF INTEGRATION

Just as in comprehension, a number of processing steps are assumed to underlie sentence production. Figure 13.1 presents a sketch of the levels of representation that we assume are involved in going from intention to articulation (corresponding to those proposed by Garrett, 1984). A brief discussion of these levels is necessary to set the stage for addressing the issue of information flow.

The *message level* representation is conceived as a level at which non-linguistic cognitive processes (e.g., information about the visual environment, encyclopedic knowledge, the discourse record, and a person's intentions) converge in preparation for verbal expression. At this level many of the details present in our perceptual/conceptual experience of the world are stripped, leaving an abstract representation that, by virtue of being abstract, can effectively interface with language (e.g., Druks & Shallice, 2000; Levelt, 1989). The message guides lexical retrieval as well as phrasal integration. Following a long-standing tradition in production research, we assume that lexical retrieval proceeds in two main steps: First, an abstract lexico-semantic representation (also referred to as a *lemma*, Kempen & Huijbers, 1983) is selected corresponding to the meaning to be expressed, and specifying some syntactic properties of the words; during a second step, the corresponding word form is retrieved. These distinct lexical representations are closely involved in phrasal integration processes: Lexico-semantic representations guide the unfolding of frames for sentences at the functional level of processing; word form representations are involved in positional level processes. *Functional level* processes are assumed to realize the mapping between the message and a bound-sentence level frame that corresponds to that message. The domain on which functional level processes operate is syntactic: Representations at this level honor hierarchical syntactic relationships among words. *Positional level* processes are concerned with the mapping between a hierarchically specified representation to a linearly ordered frame. Such a mapping involves two steps: First, word forms are inserted in slots corresponding to linear positions; second, phonological segments are linearized within phonological words. The domain of frames at this level is prosodic. Thus, for both lexical retrieval and phrasal integration the main distinction is between a level guided by a message in which semantic and syntactic relationships determine the structure of the representation and a level in which the content of those representations is specified for linear word order and segmental content.

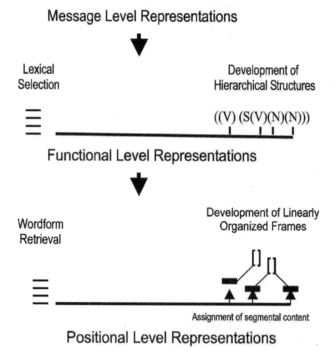

FIG. 13.1. Levels of integration in sentence production according to Garrett (1984). The figure does not include the processes of phonetic encoding. For simplicity, the arrows indicate only the general flow of information from message to positional level representations (i.e., maximal input and bidirectional flow are not depicted).

INFORMATION FLOW

Given this basic architecture for production, we have proposed maximal input and bidirectional flow of information at four central interfaces (or as we prefer to call them, *joints*) in the system: (1) between retrieving lemmas and retrieving word form information; (2) between lexical selection and phrasal integration; (3) between message and functional level processing and, finally, (4) between functional level processes and positional level processes.

It is important to note that our framework is only one version of the set of possible maximalist frameworks for production: a structured and constrained version. First, distinct levels of processing are maintained each of which is characterized by different computations and units (primary information). Information from other levels (secondary information) can nonetheless affect processing. Interactions among levels are allowed, but they are only "local" (e.g., Dell, 1986; Rapp & Goldrick, 2000) as maximal input and bidirectional flow of information is only assumed between adjacent levels.

Thus, while our proposal is in continuity with the proposal by Dell (1986), it contrasts with other interactive views, for example, the constraint-satisfaction framework in which levels of processing are not as clearly distinguished and in which different types of information are brought to bear on processing at different times. Constraint-satisfaction views could be considered as fully interactive systems in which the result of processing is determined by the interaction of multiple graded probabilistic constraints. Such an approach to sentence production has been recently advocated to account for non-syntactic effects on agreement processing (which has been considered by many accounts to be a prototypical syntactic operation, encapsulated from non-syntactic information) in English (e.g., Haskell & MacDonald, 2003). These effects, however, can be also be captured by a locally interactive system (Vigliocco & Hartsuiker, 2002). A locally-interactive lexical retrieval system has also been argued to provide a better fit to aphasic patients' naming data than a fully interactive model (Rapp & Goldrick, 2000). Moreover, assuming distinct levels of integration and a locally interactive system allows us to capture data from spontaneously occurring errors that might prove to be difficult to accommodate without assuming hierarchically organized levels of integration (Garrett, 1980). Finally, it is worth noting that constraint-satisfaction accounts of sentence production have been developed as a direct extension of similar models developed for sentence comprehension. As we have discussed above, differences in task demands between production and comprehension need to be taken into account because they seem to require different degrees of temporal overlap of different processes. It is an open question whether they also require architectural differences in the systems.

Maximal Input

As just mentioned, in production there is substantial evidence in support of maximal input from one level to another at the different joints. As much of this evidence is comprehensively reviewed in Vigliocco and Hartsuiker (2002), we limit our presentation here to examples from two joints: the joint between lexical retrieval and phrasal integration and the joint between message and functional level integration (for review of evidence supporting maximal input in spoken word recognition and sentence comprehension, see e.g., McQueen, this volume; Boland & Cutler, 1996). Regarding the first joint, evidence compatible with maximal input is provided by work by Vigliocco, Vinson, Indefrey, Levelt, & Hellwig (2004). They investigated semantic substitution errors (e.g., saying *hand* when *foot* is intended) in German. In this language, all nouns have grammatical gender (masculine, feminine, or neuter) and, considering words referring to objects and abstract entities, gender has no obvious conceptual force. Nonetheless, observations from spontaneously occurring errors suggest that when German speakers make semantic substitution errors, the produced nouns more often have the same gender as the intended nouns relative to chance rate (Marx, 1999). For example, if the intended word is *Boot* [boat-neuter] a semantic error such as *Auto* [car-neuter] which preserves gender is more likely than an error such as *Zug* [train-masculine], which has a different gender. Vigliocco et al. (2004) induced semantic substitution errors in the laboratory by presenting German speakers with pictures to name in quick succession. In one condition, speakers were asked to name the pictures using a *bare noun* (e.g., "Fuss" [foot-masc]). In a second condition speakers were asked to name the same pictures using a *noun phrase* (e.g., "Der Fuss" [the-masc foot-masc]). Gender preservation (i.e., significantly more errors with the same gender than with a different gender) was observed when speakers produced phrases, but not when they produced bare nouns. The difference between bare noun and phrase production indicates that gender preservation does not occur solely because of greater semantic similarity between the target and the intruding words, but that it requires the engagement of phrasal integration processes. In particular, the results suggest that a syntactic frame for the target is retrieved/built, even if the target is not actually selected for production. Thus, frames for different highly activated lemmas would be available in parallel and would affect the lexical selection process. This finding is problematic for models that assume minimal input at this joint (e.g., WEAVER++, Levelt, Roelofs, & Meyer, 1999; Roelofs, this volume); they would predict that syntactic frames are only retrieved/built for the selected lemma, and not for highly activated but unselected lemmas (see Vigliocco et al., 2004: 492).

As a second example of evidence supporting maximal input in the system, consider the interface between message and functional level. Vigliocco and Franck (1999) investigated agreement in gender between sentential subjects and predictive adjectives in French and Italian in order to test whether non-necessary message level (conceptual) information affects functional level (syntactic) integration. In critical experiments in French and Italian, speakers were presented with sentence beginnings such as (examples are in Italian only) "*La ragazza nel parco*"[the-fem girl-fem in-the-masc park-masc] and "*La panchina nel parco*"[the-fem bench-fem in-the-masc park-masc]. Speakers were asked to complete the sentence beginnings using a predicative adjective (producing for example "*La ragazza nel parco e' bionda*", [the-fem girl-fem in-the-masc park-masc is blonde-fem]). In both languages all nouns are marked for gender (masculine or feminine) and predicative adjectives must agree in gender with the noun, that is, the subject of the sentence. They found that speakers were more likely to commit agreement errors (for example producing a masculine adjective when the subject was feminine) for nouns such as "*panchina*" [bench-fem] than for nouns such as "*ragazza*" [girl-fem]. These results were explained as follows. Although nouns of both types are syntactically marked as feminine, and this information is necessary and sufficient for agreement, the word "*ragazza*" is also conceptually feminine (referring to a female entity), while "*panchina*" is only syntactically feminine. The message-level information concerning the sex of the referent is taken into account for agreement processing beyond establishing the syntactic specification of the noun (maximal input), resulting in the difference between these two types of nouns.

Bidirectional Flow of Information

Despite the many studies in the literature that have been argued to provide evidence for bidirectional flow of information, most of this evidence can be explained without requiring feedback. Again, the situation here is analogous to the comprehension domain, in particular spoken word recognition where findings of lexical effects on pre-lexical representations have been attributed to feedback, but which can also be explained without feedback (see McQueen, this volume). Let us consider two examples that illustrate alternative accounts in production: The first concerns the joint between the message and the lexical and functional level, and the second concerns the joint between the functional and the positional level.

In a series of experiments Kita and Özyürek (2003) provided evidence that message-level representations are tuned to language-specific properties, a finding that can be taken to suggest that functional level information can feed back to affect message level representations. In a critical experiment, they investigated cross-linguistic differences in the spontaneous gestures that accompany speech for speakers of English, Japanese and Turkish. Co-speech gestures convey imagistic information (reflecting visuo-spatial properties of a referent) but are also tightly linked to speaking as, for example, they are synchronized to speech. Turkish, Japanese and English speakers were presented with video clips depicting motion events (for example, swinging) and were asked to describe the events. Crucially, whereas English is a language in which the manner of motion is expressed in the verb itself, Turkish and Japanese tend to have fewer verbs expressing manner; verbs instead tend to encode the direction of the motion event. Of interest was whether the spontaneously produced gestures would follow the cross-linguistic differences, namely whereas English speakers' gestures would depict an arc trajectory (the manner of motion), the Turkish and Japanese speakers' gestures would depict the direction of motion, but not the manner (despite the fact that the gestures, encoding imagistic information, can easily encode the manner of motion in all three languages). Indeed, English speakers produced arc gestures when describing the swinging event more often than speakers of Turkish and Japanese, thus suggesting feedback at this joint, in line with the *thinking for speaking* hypothesis put forward by Slobin (1996).

It has been argued, however, that such a language-specific effect on gestures does not provide evidence for on-line feedback at this joint for the adult production system, as it may have arisen during development. Along these lines, Levelt (1989: 103) wrote: "*Although conceptualizing and grammatical encoding are interacting for the language-acquiring child, the mature speaker knows what to encode... in short the system has become autonomous*".[1] Thus feedback would be used by the language-learning child, but it would then disappear in the language processing adult. A

---

[1]Note that these findings also cannot simply be accounted for as being due to interactions between lexical concepts and lemmas (an interface at which feedback is assumed, for example, in Levelt et al., 1999): The produced gestures did not solely follow the linguistic pattern, but importantly also expressed properties of the visual scene that were never verbalized, thus suggesting the engagement of a richer message level representation than a single lexical concept.

similar proposal in which feedback is assumed for learning but not for language processing, has been put forward by Norris, McQueen, and Cutler (2003) in the domain of spoken word recognition. These authors suggest that interactivity in the system is used for learning: not just during language development in childhood, but also in adulthood, serving the fundamental function of adjusting for variability in the acoustic signal. Interactivity, however, would not be part of processing. By posing discontinuity between language learning and language processing, data that have been argued to provide evidence for feedback can be accommodated in strictly feedforward models.

Let us now consider a different joint: the interface between functional and positional level processing. A number of studies investigating agreement in different languages have reported effects of morpho-phonological realization of agreement markers (e.g., Vigliocco, Butterworth, & Semenza, 1995). These effects have been argued to be compatible with feedback at this joint. However, they can also be accounted for without invoking feedback by assuming that the different error rates arise as a consequence of the ability of a comprehension-based monitor to detect and correct erroneous speech. For example, Hartsuiker, Schriefers, Bock, and Kikstra (2003) elicited verb agreement errors in Dutch and German, following preambles of the type *"the protest against the demonstrations"*. In German, the case of the local noun phrase *"the demonstrations"* depends on the preposition; some prepositions license dative case, others, accusative case. Depending on the particular case, and on the gender of the noun, the determiner is either unambiguously marked as dative or ambiguously marked: Its form is compatible with both nominative and accusative case. In the study by Hartsuiker et al., the verb more often incorrectly agreed with a plural local noun (relative to a singular baseline) if the determiner was ambiguous between accusative and nominative, than if it was unambiguously dative. They argued that this finding was compatible with two possible feedback explanations. One explanation entails that the morphophonological form of the determiner activates syntactic feature information at the lexico-syntactic level (such as nominative case), and that verb number is incorrectly assigned on the basis of this information. Another explanation entails that the effects occur when morphemes are integrated with a syntactic frame, and that the morpheme's number specification feeds back and overrides the number marking on the frame (Bock, Eberhard, Cutting, Meyer, & Schriefers, 2001). A third explanation, however, does not require feedback. Under the assumption that errors are detected and corrected on the fly by a monitor that uses the comprehension system (Levelt, 1989), errors in which determiner, noun, and verb are incompatible (because the noun phrase is unambiguously dative) are easier to detect through an internal monitoring loop, and that these errors are therefore more often filtered out before articulation.

Thus, these examples illustrate two important manners in which evidence *prima facie* supporting bidirectional flow of information has been accounted for within strictly feedforward architectures. In the next section we present a critical discussion of these alternative accounts of feedback-like effects.

WHAT IS FEEDBACK GOOD FOR?

Defenders of strictly feedforward processing systems (both in production and comprehension research) have provided alternative accounts for feedback-like effects; they further argue that bidirectional flow of information serves no clear function in language processing. Below we discuss two functions of feedback: feedback for learning and feedback for accuracy.

Feedback for Learning

We have discussed how feedback during language development is necessary in order to establish which parts of a message are to be encoded in a particular language (Levelt, 1989) specifically at the joint between message and functional level processing. The effects of this language-specific tuning occurring during language development would produce the cross-linguistic differences in gestures we have described above (Kita & Özyürek, 2003) for adult speakers (see Slobin, 1982, 1996 for developmental data showing language-specific tuning of message level representations).

Feedback during language development can also be beneficial at other joints in the system. Consider for example the joint between functional and positional level processing. Here, implicitly learning and taking advantage of regularities between phonological markers and syntactic properties can help the child learn syntactic categories. For the adult language user, such sensitivity would translate into stronger connections between the syntactic and phonological properties. These stronger connections can affect both production and comprehension. Sensitivity to phonological cues to grammatical classes and sub-classes has been established for grammatical class and gender of nouns. With respect to grammatical class, Kelly (1992) showed that English language users are sensitive to position of the main stress, and use it to help make noun/verb decisions (see also Arciuli & Cupples, 2003). These cues also influence novel uses of words, such that a given verb is more likely to be creatively used as a noun if its stress pattern is noun-like than if it is verb-like. With respect to grammatical sub-classes (such as gender) phonological correlates are used by children to determine gender classes in different languages (e.g., Karmiloff-Smith, 1978; Levy, 1983). Phonological correlates have been shown to affect the speed with which adult native speakers of Italian categorize a word according to gender (Bates, Devescovi, Pizzamiglio, D'Amico, & Hernandez, 1995) and agreement errors in production (see Vigliocco & Hartsuiker, 2002). Thus, feedback is, if not necessary, certainly useful for learning. Nonetheless, it has been argued that assuming feedback for learning does not imply that feedback is used for processing: Either because feedback would be strictly limited to language development in childhood, or, more generally, because (although not limited to language learning in childhood) it would only be triggered in learning circumstances. For example, for spoken word recognition, Norris et al. (2003) suggested that feedback for learning can be implemented in Merge (a feedforward cascading architecture) by adding a back-propagation algorithm sending an error-correcting training signal between lexical and sub-lexical representations. The learning mechanism would help listeners to adjust to differences in pronunciation (e.g., differences in how a non-word initial /t/ is pronounced in UK and US English) but feedback would not be used during online processing. Note here that, as discussed in McQueen (this volume), feedback for learning at this phonological/phonetic interface may be far better motivated in perception than in production.

There is not, however, compelling evidence that the mechanisms underlying feedback for learning qualitatively differ from those that have been assumed to underlie feedback for processing. Norris et al. (2003), in fact, acknowledge that feedback subserving learning could be implemented in a manner also affecting online processing, specifically in Hebbian networks, in which connections could be modified by feedback. In this latter scenario, feedback during online processing would exist as a *consequence* of being part of a system that serves both learning and processing. Importantly, a proposal of this kind poses continuity between language learning and language processing instead of discontinuity (see Seidenberg & MacDonald, 1999, for a number of arguments favoring continuity between language learning and language processing). Likewise, in the domain of language production, syntactic priming effects (the tendency to re-use a recently processed syntactic structure, e.g., Bock, 1986; Hartsuiker & Kolk, 1998; Pickering & Branigan, 1998) have been explained by postulating continuity between learning and processing (Bock & Griffin, 2000; Chang, Dell, Bock, & Griffin, 2000).

Feedback for Accuracy

A textbook function of feedback (for example in visual perception) is to ensure that variable and possibly degraded input will converge upon representations for sharply defined categories. Textbook examples are letters that are ambiguous between an <A> and a <H> being categorized appropriately, depending on linguistic context, or the correct visual recognition of a word, even though one of its letters is visually degraded (see McClelland & Rumelhart, 1981, for discussion of interactive effects in letter and word perception). Feedback can ensure accuracy of perception or production, and we suggest it can do so in two ways. We will refer to these ways as "staying on the right track" and "getting back on track" respectively. The former indicates that feedback can steer the activational dynamics; the latter indicates that feedback can aid the monitoring function (e.g., "*Am I saying what I meant to?*").

Staying on the right track

As an illustration of the first putative function of feedback, take the *lexical bias effect* (i.e., the phenomenon that phonological speech errors tend to result in real words more often than chance predicts). Researchers in the interactive tradition have viewed this phenomenon as evidence for feedback between sublexical and lexical representations. Since feedback would never converge on a representation for a nonsense word (since by definition there are no such representations in the mental lexicon), only erroneous *words* would be activated by feedback, and hence would be produced relatively more often than nonwords (Dell, 1986; Dell & Kim, in press; Hartsuiker, Corley, & Martensen, in press; Humphreys, 2002). While such feedback will sometimes converge on an incorrect lexical representation (i.e., a phonological neighbor of the target, especially if this neighbor has been primed by the context; Baars, Motley, & MacKay, 1975), it is important to note that this feedback will also activate the correct representation, and during the course of *normal* processing it will mainly activate the correct representation. In other words, it will steer processing, so that the correct lexical representation is relatively more active than competitors, and the sets of phonemes corresponding to the target are more active than sets of phonemes that do not correspond to any real word. Feedback thus keeps the production system on the right track.

Turning to language comprehension, we have already mentioned the classical examples from letter and word perception, in which feedback has an analogous function: Enhancing the perception of discrete categories by compensating for the variability in the input, and both in production and comprehension such findings have been simulated using feedback-based models (Dell, 1986; McClelland & Rumelhart, 1981). Interestingly, the function of "staying on the right track" is not restricted to the processing of words and letters or sounds. It also appears to play a role early in the processing of sentences. For example, Hagoort, Brown, and Osterhout (1999) reported a study that presented temporarily ambiguous sentences in an ERP paradigm. Sentences such as *"The sheriff saw the indian and the cowboy noticed the horse"* yielded a P600 component after "cowboy" (relative to a unambiguous control with a comma after "indian"), suggesting that readers had drifted off the right track and initially constructed an NP compound (the indian and the cowboy). But no P600 was observed in the structurally identical sentence *"The boatsman repaired the sail and the skipper furnished the mast"*. This suggests strongly that early on, readers exploit a later level (semantics) in order to avoid being led down the garden path. Converging evidence comes from studies using the visual world paradigm. For example, Tanenhaus et al. (1995) showed that information from the visual environment (e.g., is there an empty towel in the context) also prevents listeners from garden path effects on sentences such as *"put the apple on the towel in the box"*.

Getting back on track

Of course, both speakers and listeners sometimes do lose the right track; we sometimes produce slips of the tongue, or misread a word or sentence. How do we get back on track? In other words, how do we notice that we have made a mistake and correct the mistake? Let us return to the example of the lexical bias effect. According to discrete-level theorists, this phenomenon can be explained exclusively as the result of self-monitoring. On such an account, speakers inspect their own speech (in particular, the phonological representation as it unfolds, before articulation) using the normal mechanisms of speech perception in order to detect abnormalities. There is indeed substantial evidence for an "inner" monitoring loop, and computational simulations (Hartsuiker & Kolk, 2001) showed that an inner loop, through speech perception, is compatible with data on the time course of speech error interruptions and repairs (Oomen & Postma, 2001).

Our contention is that the divide between monitoring and feedback explanations is not necessarily a divide. While "feedback" and "monitoring" are sometimes presented as mutually exclusive alternatives, this is misleading, because there are no *a priori* reasons for why a feedback-based production system could not have a self-monitoring component. Hartsuiker et al. (in press) recently reported data which they explain by a combination of feedback and monitoring, and in fact, several theories of monitoring in production exploit feedback precisely for the purpose of monitoring. Most of these theories assume a monitoring device or devices localized within the language production system or in a connectionist network used for perception as well as production. Recent work provides some evidence that can be interpreted as supporting a production-based monitor (Postma, 2000; Oomen, Postma, & Kolk, in press), possibly in combination with a perceptual loop for overt repairs. For example, Oomen et al. present the case of patient G, a patient with Broca's aphasia, whose monitoring deficits mimic his production deficits, suggesting a deficit at a level subserving both production and production *monitoring*.

Why would a connectionist production monitor use feedback? The most important reason is that the pattern of feedback is informative about the occurrence of an error, and provides details about the error which can be used in repairing. For example, the connectionist model proposed by Schade and Laubenstein (1993), stipulates a link-verification procedure. Once a unit is selected at level *n+1*, the link-verification mechanism checks whether that unit is connected to an active node at level *n*. Thus, if /r/ is selected as an onset consonant, but the intended word was "*cat*", the verification mechanism fails; an error is detected. This implies an upward flow of information (that is, based on events at a later level, an earlier level is inspected), although not necessarily of an upward flow of activation. It is interesting to note that WEAVER++ (Levelt, et al., 1999) uses a similar verification procedure, but that it is used to *prevent* errors rather than to correct them; if verification fails in WEAVER++, selection of the erroneous unit simply does not take place. In other words, in WEAVER++, feedback of information is used for staying on the right track.

Other models exploit the fact that feedback of *activation* is abnormal when an error is made. For example, MacKay (1992) argues that an error will often result in a novel combination. If the speaker's goal is to say "*cat*", but instead says, "*crat*", a series of phonemes is produced that the speaker may have never before produced in that sequence. In MacKay's proposal, this novel combination also provides a novel pattern of feedback, and since the feedback does not converge on an existing node (there was no morpheme node for "*crat*" in the speaker's mental lexicon), a new node will be immediately instantiated. Activation of that new node provides a cue to the error detection mechanism.

The account put forward by Postma and Kolk (1993) also exploits the fact that error processing results in an abnormal feedback flow of activation. They argued that if the goal morpheme was "*cat*", but if the phonemes /r/, /æ/ and /t/ are selected, the morpheme unit receives too little feedback relative to its own activation. That is, if the encoding had gone well, there would have been feedback from three units; instead there is feedback from only two units. In this view, the monitor compares the amount of outgoing activation from the target unit with the amount of incoming activation (through feedback) to that unit.

As these proposals demonstrate, feedback can be informative about the occurrence of an error in different ways. This does not mean, however, that feedback is *necessary* for a connectionist production monitor. Mattson and Baars (1982) for example, pointed out that during error processing there are also abnormalities in the feedforward flow of activation. That is, if an error is produced, the corresponding unit will have a higher activation level than the unit representing the correct response; but since the "correct" unit was the target unit, it will also have a relatively high activation. So instead of having one highly active unit (the normal case), there will be two active units (with the correct unit possibly on its way, but too late, to overtake the error unit). This activation pattern could be detected, for example by having a "trouble unit", to which all representational units are connected by excitatory connections with small weights and a threshold. The "trouble unit" would be activated only when more than one of the representational units has a high activation level (see Botvinick, Braver, Barch, Carter, & Cohen, 2001, for a similar proposal with respect to performance monitoring)

What would be the advantage of having a feedback production monitor? One important reason is that a feedforward monitor, as just described, is sensitive only to a global parameter of the output layer (its total amount of activation). In contrast to the proposals made by Postma and Kolk (1993) and by Schade and Laubenstein (1993), it provides no information about *which* unit was incorrectly encoded. But a monitoring system detecting that a given target unit (e.g., "*cat*") receives too little feedback from the sublexical level, or one detecting that a selected unit (e.g., /r/) is not connected to the target unit, could immediately repair by re-activating the target unit. A device specifying what was wrong about an error seems particularly useful for language production, as many different things can go wrong at many different levels when we speak. In contrast, in performance monitoring (cf. Botvinick et al., 2001) the information that something was wrong is sufficient, since the participant usually has a choice between only two actions (i.e., press the left button or press the right button).

Before concluding, let us return to language comprehension again. Much of the debate that has occupied this field for the past decades is whether higher-level information (semantics, world knowledge) exerts an immediate influence on sentence parsing or whether there is only a late influence, for example to resolve an initial garden path effect. We have argued above for early effects (i.e., feedback steering analysis), but this is not universally accepted (e.g., Frazier, 1987; Friederici, 2002, for serial models). Crucially, even those authors rejecting a role of feedback initially, do subscribe to the second role of feedback: getting back on the right track. It is interesting to note that Kolk, Chwilla, Van Herten, and Oor (2003) ascribe a functional significance to the P600 component in ERPs in terms of monitoring. According to these authors, a P600 is typically observed following unexpected linguistic input (such as a garden path sentence, a syntactic violation, or in their case, a syntactically correct sentence with an implausible meaning). They argue that, from the perspective of the processor, this can mean one of two things: The linguistic input is really deviant, or a comprehension mistake was made along the way. The P600 would reflect a monitoring process (*is this really what the sentence says, or did I make a mistake?*).

In summary, feedback can aid comprehension and production in maintaining accuracy in two ways. It can sharpen representations in normal processing, and it can aid in recovery when something has gone wrong.

CONCLUSIONS

In contrast to comprehension, the task demands of producing language (the complexities involved in realizing speech corresponding to our intentions) provide a strong rationale for assuming a production system in which the flow of information from one level to the next is minimal, and in which there is no feedback from one level to a previous one. Allowing for maximal input and feedback would necessarily increase noise in the system. We have argued in this chapter, however, that just as in comprehension, maximal input must be part of the model, as it is supported by existing evidence. Feedback, which allows the language learner to tune to language specific properties and to take advantage of regularities in the linguistic environment, can be used in order to ensure accuracy in the mature system. Both functions (helping learning and helping accuracy) are not special to production, but are common to production and comprehension.

REFERENCES

Altmann, G. T. M., & Steedman, M. (1988). Interaction with context during human sentence processing. *Cognition, 30,* 191-238.

Arciuli, J., & Cupples, L. (2003). Effects of stress typicality during speeded grammatical classification. *Language and Speech, 46,* 353-374.

Baars, B. J., Motley, M. T., & MacKay, D. G. (1975). Output editing for lexical status in artificially elicited slips of the tongue. *Journal of Verbal Learning and Verbal Behavior, 14,* 382-391.

Bates, E., Devescovi, A., Pizzamiglio, L., D'Amico, S., & Hernandez, A. (1995). Gender and lexical access in Italian. *Perception and Psychophysics, 57,* 847-862.

Bock, J. K. (1986). Syntactic persistence in language production. *Cognitive Psychology, 18,* 355-387.

Bock, J. K., Eberhard, K. M., Cutting, J. C., Meyer, A. S., & Schriefers, H. (2001). Some attractions of verb agreement. *Cognitive Psychology, 43,* 83-128.

Bock, J. K., & Griffin, Z. M. (2000). The persistence of structural priming: Transient activation or implicit learning? *Journal of Experimental Psychology: General, 129,* 177-192.

Boland, J. E., & Cutler, A. (1996). Interaction with autonomy: Multiple Output models and the inadequacy of the Great Divide. *Cognition, 58,* 309-320.

Botvinick, M. M., Braver, T. S., Barch, D. M., Carter, C. S., & Cohen, J. D. (2001). Conflict monitoring and cognitive control. *Psychological Review, 108,* 624-652.

Chang, F., Dell, G. S., Bock, K., & Griffin, Z. M. (2000). Structural priming as implicit learning: A comparison of models of sentence production. *Journal of Psycholinguistic Research, 29,* 217-229.

Dell, G. S. (1986). A spreading-activation theory of retrieval in sentence production. *Psychological Review, 93,* 283-321.

Dell, G. S., & Kim, A. E. (in press). Speech errors and word form encoding. In R. Hartsuiker, R. Bastiaanse, A. Postma, & F. Wijnen (Eds.), *Phonological encoding and monitoring in normal and pathological speech.* Hove, UK: Psychology Press.

Druks, J., & Shallice, T. (2000). Selective preservation of naming from description and the "restricted preverbal message." *Brain and Language, 72,* 100-128.

Frazier, L. (1987). Sentence processing: A tutorial review. In M. Coltheart (Ed.), *Attention and Performance XII: The psychology of reading* (pp. 559-586). Hove, UK: Erlbaum.

Friederici, A. D. (2002). Towards a neural basis of auditory sentence processing. *Trends in Cognitive Sciences, 6,* 78-84.

Garrett, M. F. (1980). Levels of processing in sentence production. In B. Butterworth (Ed.), *Language production, Vol. 1: Speech and talk* (pp. 177-220). London: Academic Press.

Garrett, M. F. (1984). The organization of processing structure for language production: Application to aphasic speech. In D. Caplan, A. R. Lecours, & A. Smith (Eds.), *Biological perspectives on language* (pp. 172-193). Cambridge, MA: MIT Press.

Hagoort, P., Brown, C. M., & Osterhout, L. (1999). The neurocognition of syntactic processing. In C. M. Brown & P. Hagoort (Eds.), *The neurocognition of language.* Oxford: Oxford University Press.

Hartsuiker, R. J., Corley, M., & Martensen, H. (in press). The lexical bias effect is modulated by context, but the standard monitoring account doesn't fly:

Belated reply to Baars, Motley, & MacKay (1975). *Journal of Memory and Language.*

Hartsuiker, R. J., & Kolk, H. H. J. (1998). Syntactic persistence in Dutch. *Language & Speech, 41,* 143-184.

Hartsuiker, R. J., & Kolk, H. H. J. (2001). Error monitoring in speech production: A computational test of the perceptual loop theory. *Cognitive Psychology, 42,* 113-157.

Hartsuiker, R. J., Schriefers, H. J., Bock, J. K., & Kikstra, G. M. (2003). Morphological influences on the construction of subject-verb agreement. *Memory and Cognition, 31,* 1316-1326.

Haskell, T. R., & MacDonald, M. C. (2003). Conflicting cues and competition in subject-verb agreement. *Journal of Memory and Language, 48,* 760-778.

Humphreys, K. R. (2002). *Lexical bias in speech errors.* Unpublished doctoral dissertation, University of Illinois, Urbana–Champaign.

Karmiloff-Smith, A. (1978). *A functional approach to child language. A study of determiners and reference.* Cambridge, UK: Cambridge University Press.

Kelly, M. H. (1992). Using sound to solve syntactic problems: The role of phonology in grammatical category assignments. *Psychological Review, 99,* 349-364.

Kempen, G., & Huijbers, P. (1983). The lexicalization process in sentence production and naming: Indirect election of words. *Cognition, 14,* 185-209.

Kita, S., & Özyürek, A. (2003). What does cross-linguistic variation in semantic coordination of speech and gesture reveal? Evidence for an interface representation of spatial thinking and speaking. *Journal of Memory and Language, 48,* 16-32.

Kolk, H. H. J., Chwilla, D. J., Van Herten, M., & Oor, P. J. W. (2003). Structure and limited capacity in verbal working memory: A study with event-related potentials. *Brain and Language, 85,* 1-36.

Levelt, W. J. M. (1989). *Speaking: From intention to articulation.* Cambridge, MA: MIT Press.

Levelt, W. J. M., Roelofs, A., & Meyer, A. S. (1999). A theory of lexical access in speech production. *Behavioral and Brain Sciences, 22,* 1-75.

Levy, Y. (1983). It's frogs all the way down. *Cognition, 15,* 75-93.

Lloyd-Jones, T. J., & Humphreys, W. G. (1997). Perceptual differentiation as a source of category effects in object processing: Evidence from naming and object decision. *Memory and Cognition, 25,* 18-35.

MacKay, D. G. (1992). Awareness and error detection: New theories and research paradigms. *Consciousness and Cognition, 1,* 199-225.

Marx, E. (1999). Gender processing in speech production: Evidence from German speech errors. *Journal of Psycholinguistic Research, 28,* 601-621.

Mattson, M. E., & Baars, B. J. (1992). Error-minimizing mechanisms: Boosting or editing? In B. J. Baars (Ed.), *Experimental slips and human error: Exploring the architecture of volition* (pp. 263-287). New York: Plenum.

McClelland, J. L., & Elman, J. L. (1986). The TRACE model of speech perception. *Cognitive Psychology, 18,* 1-86.

McClelland, J. L., & Rumelhart, D. E. (1981). An interactive activation model of context effects in letter perception: Part 1. An account of basic findings. *Psychological Review, 88*, 375-407.

Norris, D., McQueen, J., & Cutler, A. (2000). Merging information in speech: Feedback is never necessary. *Behavioral and Brian Sciences, 23*, 299-370.

Norris, D., McQueen, J., & Cutler, A. (2003). Perceptual learning in speech. *Cognitive Psychology, 47*, 204-238.

Oomen, C. C. E., & Postma, A. (2001). Effects of time pressure on mechanisms of speech production and self-monitoring. *Journal of Psycholinguistic Research, 30*, 163-184.

Oomen, C. C. E., Postma, A., & Kolk, H. H. J. (in press). Speech monitoring in aphasia: Error detection and repair behaviour in a patient with Broca's aphasia. In R. Hartsuiker, R. Bastiaanse, A. Postma, & F. Wijnen (Eds.), *Phonological encoding and monitoring in normal and pathological speech.* Hove, UK: Psychology Press.

Pickering, M. J., & Branigan, H. P. (1998). The representation of verbs: Evidence from syntactic priming in language production. *Journal of Memory and Language, 39*, 633-651.

Postma, A. (2000). Detection of errors during speech production: A review of speech monitoring models. *Cognition, 77*, 97-131.

Postma, A., & Kolk, H. H. J. (1993). The covert repair hypothesis: prearticulatory repair processes in normal and stuttered disfluencies. *Journal of Speech and Hearing Research, 36*, 472-487.

Rapp, B., & Goldrick, M. (2000). Discreteness and interactivity in spoken word production. *Psychological Review, 107*, 460-499.

Roelofs, A. (in press). Spoken word planning, comprehending, and self-monitoring: Evaluation of WEAVER++. In R. Hartsuiker, R. Bastiaanse, A. Postma, & F. Wijnen (Eds.), *Phonological encoding and monitoring in normal and pathological speech.* Hove, UK: Psychology Press.

Schade, U., & Laubenstein, U. (1993). Repairs in a connectionist language-production model. In R. Kohler & B. B. Rieger (Eds.), *Contributions to quantitative linguistics* (pp. 79-90). Dordrecht: Kluwer.

Seidenberg, M., & MacDonald, M. C. (1999). A probabilistic constraints approach to language acquisition and processing. *Cognitive Science, 23*, 569-588.

Slobin, D. I. (1982). Universal and particular in the acquisition of language. In E. Wanner & L. R. Gleitman (Eds.), *Language acquisition: The state of the art* (pp. 128-172). Cambridge: Cambridge University Press.

Slobin D. I. (1996). From "thought and language" to "thinking for speaking." In J. J. Gumperz & S. C. Levinson (Eds.), *Studies in the social and cultural foundations of language: No. 17. Rethinking linguistic relativity* (pp. 70-96). New York: Cambridge University Press.

Tanenhaus, M. K., Spivey-Knowlton, M. J., Eberhard, K. M., & Sedivy, J. C. (1995). Integration of visual and linguistic information in spoken language comprehension. *Science, 268*, 1632-1634.

Tanenhaus, M. K., & Trueswell, J. C. (1995). Sentence comprehension. In J. Miller & P. Eimas (Eds.), *Handbook of perception and cognition: Speech, language and cognition* (pp. 217-262). San Diego, CA: Academic Press.

Vigliocco, G., Butterworth, B., & Semenza, C. (1995). Computing subject verb agreement in speech: The role of semantic and morphological information. *Journal of Memory and Language, 34,* 186-215.

Vigliocco, G., & Franck, J. (1999). When sex and syntax go hand in hand: Gender agreement in language production. *Journal of Memory and Language, 40,* 455-478.

Vigliocco, G., & Hartsuiker, R. J. (2002). The interplay of meaning, sound & syntax in language production. *Psychological Bulletin, 128,* 442-472.

Vigliocco, G., Vinson, D., Indefrey, P., Levelt, W., & Hellwig, F. (2004). Role of grammatical gender and semantics in German word production. *Journal of Experimental Psychology: Learning, Memory and Cognition, 30,* 483-497.

14

Spoken-Word Recognition and Production: Regular but not Inseparable Bedfellows

James M. McQueen
Max Planck Institute for Psycholinguistics, Nijmegen, The Netherlands

Speech comprehension and speech production have a very intimate relationship. First, talking entails listening to spoken language: When we converse, when we give a speech, even when we talk to ourselves. Second, the encoding and decoding components of speech processing are of course linked via the speech code: The physical speech signal. Third, the production and comprehension systems are necessarily also internally bound together at potentially several different levels of processing. Without such internal links, it would be impossible to learn to speak a language.

These appear to be arguments that, in psycholinguistic research, production and comprehension should not be studied in isolation. If speaking and listening to speech are so intimately bound together, surely they must be treated as a single object of enquiry? It is certainly valuable to examine the system as a whole, as, for example, in research on the interplay between talkers and listeners in interactive dialogue settings (Pickering & Garrod, this volume). But progress in understanding the complex skills that underlie speech processing also requires a more compartmentalized approach, in which the speech processing system is carved at its joints and its parts examined separately. Comprehension processes can be separated from production processes in carefully designed experiments. This is in fact the most common approach in the discipline. Indeed, it is usually the case that speech processing is chopped up into even smaller pieces, with the hope that individual subcomponents of the comprehension system (or the production system) can successfully be studied in isolation.

I illustrate this kind of approach here, by examining two specific properties of speech decoding. I argue, however, that this divide and conquer approach should not be too blinkered. Such research should respect the special relationship that exists between comprehension and production. I suggest that, irrespective of the level of detail within the comprehension (or production) process at which a given experiment is addressed, it is always valuable to keep the linkage between comprehension and production in mind. If successful, this type of research strategy will lead to insights into the component process under direct investigation. But, when viewed from the broader perspective of the full speech-processing system, such research may also be revealing about the inner workings of other components of that system.

DECODING SPOKEN WORDS

There is now considerable evidence that, during spoken-word recognition, listeners evaluate multiple lexical hypotheses in parallel (see McQueen, 2004, for review). As a listener hears an utterance, a number of candidate words, varying in their goodness of fit to the current input, will be considered. Although word-recognition models vary in many other ways, there is broad consensus across models on some kind of multiple evaluation process. In activation-based models such as Shortlist (Norris, 1994, this volume) and TRACE (McClelland & Elman, 1986), for example, the goodness of fit of a given candidate word is reflected in a continuously varying activation value associated with the phonological (form-based) representation of that word. Thus, for instance, as the second and third words in the phrase *He spied a deer* are heard, the words *spider, pie, eider, spine, slide* (etc.) will be activated alongside the words that the speaker actually intended. There is also considerable evidence, and a corresponding theoretical consensus, that there is some form of competition among these activated candidates. In Shortlist and TRACE, for example, there are inhibitory connections between word nodes; activated words thus compete directly with each other. Somewhat more controversial is whether there is a stage of processing which precedes the lexical stage, where information in the speech signal is normalized into some form of abstract phonological representation prior to lexical access. Nevertheless, most models of word recognition include a prelexical processing stage. In Shortlist, the input to lexical access is phonemic (but see Norris, this volume). In TRACE, there are prelexical levels corresponding to acoustic-phonetic features and to phonemes.

During the activation and competition process underlying word recognition, information must flow from the signal, through the prelexical level, up to the lexical level (see Figure 20.1 in Norris, this volume, for a sketch of these processing stages in Shortlist). Two key questions about flow of information during speech decoding can be asked, however. First, how does information flow bottom-up through the system — serially, or in cascade? Second, does information from the lexical level feed back to the prelexical level?

Cascade?

One way to ask whether bottom-up flow of information during speech decoding is serial or cascaded is to examine what kind of information in the speech signal influences processing at the lexical level. A large body of data suggests that fine-grained phonetic detail influences lexical processing. Here, I briefly describe just three of our lines of research on this topic: a study on kidneys and onions, one on pans and pandas, and one on bears and pears.

Spinelli, McQueen, and Cutler (2003) examined French utterances that were lexically ambiguous because of the phonological process of liaison. For example, the final [ʁ] of the word *dernier* is not realized when the following word begins with a consonant (e.g., in *le dernier rognon*, 'the last kidney'). But when the next word is vowel-initial, the [ʁ] is spoken, and is resyllabified: It appears at the onset of that next word (e.g., in *le dernier oignon*, 'the last onion'). As these examples show, liaison can create lexically ambiguous utterances. Although such utterances contain the same sequences of phonemes, they do contain subtle phonetic differences. For example, at normal speaking rates, liaison consonants (e.g., [ʁ] in *dernier oignon*) tend to be about 10 ms shorter than genuinely word-initial consonants (e.g., [ʁ] in *dernier rognon*).

Spinelli et al. (2003) showed, using the cross-modal identity-priming task, that the acoustic differences between liaison and non-liaison utterances influenced lexical disambiguation. Significant priming was observed only when the visual target matched the speaker's intention (i.e., lexical decisions to the visual target OIGNON were significantly faster, relative to an unrelated control condition, when the subject heard *le dernier oignon*, but not when the subject heard *le dernier rognon*). There was however also evidence of weak activation of the unintended words (e.g., *oignon* in *le dernier rognon*). These results suggest that fine-grained differences in the speech signal are not sufficient to block activation of unintended words in potentially ambiguous sequences, but nonetheless can be used in disambiguating such utterances.

Salverda, Dahan, and McQueen (2003) examined a different kind of lexical ambiguity: words embedded in longer words (e.g., *pan* in *panda*). Dutch listeners took part in an eye-tracking experiment in which they saw a screen displaying four pictures (e.g., a ladder, a pan, a shell, and a panda). They heard sentences as they saw these displays (e.g., *Ik zag dat de panda er niet meer was*, 'I saw that the panda wasn't there any more'). They were asked to use a computer mouse to click on the picture corresponding to the entity mentioned in the sentence. The sentences were made by cross-splicing either two tokens of that sentence (*Ik zag dat de pan [da ...]* plus *[... pan] da er niet meer was*) or the first part of a matched sentence where the speaker intended the embedded monosyllabic word (*Ik zag dat de pan [dadels bevatte]*, 'I saw that the pan [contained dates]') plus the same second part. Subjects looked more at the picture of the pan when the sentence was made from the utterance with the shorter word.

Although the critical syllables (e.g., [pɑn]) were phonemically identical across conditions, the monosyllabic words were, on average, 20 ms longer than the first syllables of the longer words. A subsequent experiment showed that this durational difference appeared to be the cause of the difference in eye-tracking performance. The same sentences were made using the same cross-splicing procedure, but this time by selecting, from the set of utterances recorded by the speaker, those with polysyllabic words with the longest first syllables and those with monosyllabic words with the shortest durations. The durational difference in the critical syllables across conditions was thus reversed. Subjects now looked longer at the picture of the pan when the sentence was made from the utterance with the polysyllabic word.

The findings of Spinelli et al. (2003) suggest that fine phonetic detail influences processing at least at the level of phonological word forms (i.e., competition between the lexical representations of the forms *rognon* and *oignon*). Eye-tracking data, however, necessarily reflects semantic activation (the listener must retrieve knowledge about the visual properties of entities mentioned in the sentences in order to be able to find the target pictures). The findings of Salverda et al. (2003) have thus shown that phonetic fine detail also influences processing at the semantic level. The view which emerges from these and other studies on the use of fine-grained phonetic detail in lexical disambiguation (see McQueen, Dahan, & Cutler, 2003, for review), is that there is continuous flow of information from the prelexical level, via representations of lexical form, to representations of word meaning.

There are limitations, however, in the way bottom-up information influences lexical processing. Work in English has suggested that variation in Voice Onset Time (VOT; the time between the burst release of a stop consonant and the onset of vocal fold vibration) in syllable-initial stop consonants influences lexical processing. Andruski, Blumstein, and Burton (1994) showed that, as the duration of positive VOT in word-initial stops was shortened, activation of the words was reduced (e.g., as the [k] in *king* was shortened and thus became more like a [g], priming of responses to *queen* became weaker). Dutch offers a way to test whether such effects depend on the informational value of the VOT variation. Syllable-initial stops in Dutch with prevoicing (i.e., with negative VOT) are always underlyingly voiced, but those without prevoicing may be voiced or voiceless (van Alphen, 2004; van Alphen & Smits, 2004). If only useful phonetic variation significantly influences lexical processing, then the difference between 6 and 0 periods of prevoicing in a word such as *beer*, 'bear', should influence the relative degree of activation of *beer* and *peer*, 'pear'. This is because the presence or absence of prevoicing is critical to the distinction between these two words. However, exactly the same physical difference in amount of prevoicing, but between 6 and 12 periods, should have a weaker effect on lexical processing. This is because the amount of prevoicing is not critical to the [b]/[p] distinction in Dutch; if prevoicing is present, the stop must be voiced.

These predictions were tested in a series of cross-modal priming experiments (van Alphen, 2004; van Alphen & McQueen, submitted). Visual targets such as PEER were preceded by five different kinds of auditory primes, for example: *beer* with 12, 6, or 0 periods of prevoicing, *peer* itself, and an unrelated word. Lexical decision Reaction Times (RTs) to PEER were fastest after the identical prime *peer*, and slowest after *beer* with either 6 or 12 periods of prevoicing. As predicted, there was no difference between the 6- and 12-period conditions. Also as predicted, however, responses to PEER after *beer* with 0 periods of prevoicing were intermediate: RTs were faster than those after *beer* with 6 or 12 periods of prevoicing, but slower than those after *peer*. The influence of fine-grained phonetic detail on the word recognition system is therefore not indiscriminate. Only information that is of value for lexical distinctions appears to have a significant influence on processing at the lexical level.

There are therefore no serial stages in spoken-word recognition. If prelexical processing were to reach categorical decisions about each phoneme that was present in an utterance in a discrete, sequential fashion prior to lexical access, then there would be no way in which fine-grained differences (such as the length of [ʁ] or of the syllable [pɑn]) could influence lexical-level processes. Instead, it appears that spoken-word recognition is graded and continuous; information flows in cascade through the system as it becomes available in the signal.

There are potentially two types of information in cascade: segmental information (that which distinguishes between segments, such as amount of positive VOT in English; Andruski et al., 1994) and suprasegmental information (that which distinguishes between structures larger than the segment, such as words or larger prosodic units). Both in the liaison and embedded word cases, the lexical ambiguity is, at a phonemic level of description, perfect (i.e., the same sequence of segments has two different lexical interpretations). It is thus possible that the durational differences in these cases provide cues not to individual segments, but to prosodic structures, which are then used in lexical disambiguation. Thus, for example, the longer duration of [pɑn], when the monosyllabic word was intended, signals that there is a prosodic word boundary after the syllable, which in turn lends support for the *pan* reading of the utterance (see Salverda et al., 2003 for further discussion).

One possibility, therefore, is that there are two prelexical processes, operating in parallel: One extracting segmental structure from the signal, and one extracting suprasegmental structure. The available evidence suggests that both such processes act in cascade. The work on prevoicing in Dutch, however, suggests that there are limits on the kind of segmental information that is passed to the lexical level: Only that which is useful for lexical distinctions appears to influence lexical processing substantially (van Alphen, 2004). It remains to be seen whether similar constraints apply to the suprasegmental route.

Feedback?

There could be no role for feedback in a strictly serial model. Given the evidence that there is cascade of information from the prelexical to the lexical level, however, it is worth asking whether there is also feedback from the lexicon to prelexical processing during word recognition. In Norris, McQueen, and Cutler (2000), we argued that there is no such feedback. One of our arguments was that the data on lexical effects in phonemic decision-making can be explained without feedback. In phoneme monitoring, for example, listeners can detect target phonemes more rapidly in real words than in nonwords (e.g., /b/ can be detected more quickly in *bat* than in *bal*; Rubin, Turvey, & van Gelder, 1976). In TRACE, phonemic decisions are based on the activation of prelexical phoneme nodes, and lexical effects are due to the feedback connections that exist between word nodes and those prelexical nodes. But in Shortlist and the Merge model (Norris et al., 2000), there is no such feedback. Phonemic decisions in Merge are based on the activation of phonemic decision nodes, which receive input from the prelexical and lexical levels. Responses are faster to /b/ in *bat*, for example, because the decision node for /b/ receives activation from both the prelexical representation of [b] and the lexical representation of *bat*. In *bal*, there is similar flow of information from the prelexical level, but not from the lexical level because there is no strongly activated word. Norris et al. showed how Merge can explain all such standard demonstrations of lexical effects in phonetic tasks.

A second part of our argument was that models with feedback, such as TRACE, cannot explain dissociations that exist between perceptual and lexical effects. It is widely agreed that, as the listener hears a fricative-stop sequence such as [st] or [ʃk], a prelexical mechanism compensates for the influence of the articulation of the fricative on the articulation of the stop. This perceptual compensation for coarticulation process can be seen in how listeners identify ambiguous stops in the context of fricatives: More stops on a [t-k] continuum are identified as [k] after [s] than after [ʃ] (Mann & Repp, 1981). This process is implemented in TRACE as follows: Changes in the activation of prelexical fricative nodes modulate processing of prelexical stop nodes, and hence influence stop identification performance (Elman & McClelland, 1988). Because of the feedback connections, these modulations should occur whether the fricative information comes from the speech signal or from the lexicon.

Pitt and McQueen (1998) asked listeners to identify ambiguous fricatives and ambiguous stops in sequences such as [dʒu? ?eɪps] (e.g., *juice capes*) and [bu? ?eɪps] (e.g., *bush tapes*). Although there was a lexical bias in fricative identification (i.e., more [s] responses in the context based on *juice* than in the context based on *bush*), there was no lexically biased compensation effect on identification of the subsequent stops. There was, however, a compensation effect after unambiguous fricatives (e.g., [dʒus] and [buʃ]). According to the TRACE account, if the compensation mechanism was thus active, and the prelexical fricative nodes were receiving feedback in the ambiguous fricative contexts, as the lexical effect on fricative identification would suggest, there ought to have been a lexically-biased compensation effect on stop identification in those contexts. The Merge model explains this dissociation because the lexicon can bias fricative decisions at the phoneme decision nodes without having any influence on the prelexical compensation mechanism.

A third argument we made in Norris et al. (2000) against lexical-prelexical feedback (see also Norris, this volume) was that it can be of no help to word recognition. If the prelexical level operates optimally, then the lexical level can select the word which best matches any given input. Feedback would act to inform the prelexical level of this decision, but would not be able to alter it. If feedback is of no benefit to spoken-word recognition, we asked, why would it exist?

Our more recent research on feedback arose directly from this question. There *is* a situation where feedback can be of benefit to lexical access, namely, in perceptual learning. Consider what happens if you encounter a speaker who speaks in an unusual way—perhaps that speaker has a speech impediment, or is a non-native speaker of your language, or talks in an unfamiliar dialect. You would be able to understand that speaker better if you could adjust your phonetic categories to match those of the speaker. The lexicon could provide a valuable training signal for this kind of adjustment. If, for example, you were to hear a speaker say [kəræ?], with an ambiguous final fricative midway between [f] and [s], your lexical knowledge could help you interpret the ambiguous sound as [f] (*carafe* is an English word, but there is no word [kəræs]). Norris, McQueen, and Cutler (2003), in a series of experiments in Dutch, showed that listeners do indeed use their lexical knowledge to retune phonetic categories in this way. Exposure in a lexical decision phase to a fricative that was ambiguous between [f] and [s] in lexically biased contexts led to large shifts in subsequent fricative identification. Listeners who heard the ambiguous sound in [f]-biased contexts identified more sounds on an [ɛf]-[ɛs] test continuum as [f] than those who had heard the ambiguous sound in [s]-biased contexts.

McQueen, Cutler, and Norris (2003) showed that this type of perceptual learning generalizes to the processing of words that have not been heard before. For this to occur, the retuning of fricative categories must occur prelexically. The lexical influence on perceptual learning must in turn therefore be due to feedback to the prelexical level. It is important, however, to distinguish this kind of feedback from that discussed earlier. In TRACE, for example, feedback operates as an utterance is heard, such that the activation of prelexical representations always reflects a combination of what was present in the physical utterance and lexical biases. This "on-line" feedback should be distinguished from feedback for perceptual learning (even though it is possible that on-line feedback emerges as an epiphenomenon of the learning mechanism; Norris et al., 2003). Critically, it is only feedback for learning which appears to be of value to word recognition.

ENCODING SPOKEN WORDS

I argue that there is continuous flow of useful fine-grained evidence through the speech decoding system, in cascade all the way up to the meaning level. I also argue that there is feedback for perceptual learning in this system, but not for on-line processing. It might appear that speech production was ignored in these lines of research. But that is far from true. In particular, the work on uptake of fine-grained phonetic detail in perception depends on acoustic analyses of utterances. If the subtle phonetic differences revealed by such analyses were not systematic features of speaker behavior, it is highly unlikely that listeners could have learned to use those differences in lexical disambiguation. Furthermore, knowledge of how articulation of a fricative sound influences articulation of a subsequent stop sound is critical to an understanding of the perceptual data on compensation for coarticulation. The account of perceptual learning in speech perception also depends on production data. If all speakers spoke in the same way, the perception system would not need to be flexible, and there would be no theoretical motivation for the role of feedback in perceptual learning.

While speech production was not the focus of any of these lines of research, its role could not be ignored. Research on comprehension, no matter how narrow, thus depends in part on a production-based perspective. It is also possible, however, to ask whether there is anything that can be learned about production from the perspective of these perception studies. Specifically, is spoken-word production cascaded or serial, and is there feedback during lexical access in production?

Cascade?

In lexical access in comprehension, there is a large body of evidence on continuity and gradedness (see McQueen et al., 2003). There is hence a consensus that there is widespread cascade from word-form to word-meaning representations during word recognition. Although Vigliocco and Hartsuiker (this volume) present a strong case for cascaded processing at other stages of the production process, the evidence on cascade during lexical retrieval in production (i.e., from the lemma level to the word-form level; Levelt, Roelofs, & Meyer, 1999) is more limited than that in perception. The production evidence appears to be largely restricted to lexical retrieval in specific situations (e.g., in retrieval of close synonyms such as *couch/sofa*, Peterson & Savoy, 1998, or in the picture/picture interference situation, e.g., having to retrieve the name *bell* from a picture of a bell when a picture of a bed is also present, Morsella & Miozzo, 2002). Under these circumstances, two lemmas may erroneously be selected instead of one (this sub-optimal behavior may also be the source of blend errors such as *clear* arising from *close* and *near*; see Levelt et al., 1999). Other evidence for cascade in production (e.g., Damian & Martin, 1999) may in fact reflect cascaded processing in the comprehension system. Similarly, mixed semantic/phonological errors (e.g., saying *cat* when *rat* was intended) may reflect self-monitoring of production via the comprehension system. (See Levelt et al. and Vigliocco & Hartsuiker, 2002, for discussion.) Interactions of sentence context and word frequency effects in production do however suggest that there is graded flow of information from the lemma to the word-form level (Griffin & Bock, 1998). But even in production models with cascade, limitations are imposed on its effects (cf. the "activation jolt" in the Dell, Schwartz, Martin, Saffran, & Gagnon, 1997, model).

In short, lexical access in production seems to be less cascaded than that in comprehension. This difference reflects different task demands. Since speech encoding involves generating a single phonological structure from a given message, widespread cascade would make speaking harder. In contrast, cascade can be of benefit in solving the many-to-one mapping problem in speech decoding. If fine-grained information is passed through the recognition system as soon as it becomes available, comprehension will be faster, not just because bottom-up information can be used at higher levels more rapidly, but because higher-level constraints can then also be used more quickly in the process of settling on the correct utterance interpretation.

A more detailed examination of the production process in the light of the perceptual evidence on cascade is also valuable (see also McQueen et al., 2003). As I noted earlier, the durational difference between, for example, the [pɑn] syllables in *panda* and *pan* must be a systematic feature of speaker behavior. Such systematic differences appear to pose problems for the concept of the mental syllabary in the Levelt et al. (1999) theory of lexical access in production. One locus in the theory for a mechanism that would create the difference between *pan* and the first syllable of *panda* is post-lexical, at the interface between phonological and phonetic encoding (see also Cholin, Schiller, & Levelt, 2004). Segments are retrieved in serial order from the lexicon, but syllabic structure is not specified in the lexicon. Instead, syllables are built post-lexically. During this post-lexical "prosodification" stage, durational differences as a function of prosodic structure could be specified (there is a prosodic word boundary after the monosyllabic word *pan*, but not after the first syllable of *panda*). After prosodification, the articulatory gestures for each syllable are retrieved from the syllabary. But, since it is assumed that there is only one gestural program for each common syllable in the speaker's language, the distinction between the two [pɑn] syllables would be obliterated during syllabary access. An alternative explanation might be that the syllables are stored separately (i.e., that for any one abstract syllable, there is a separate gestural program for each prosodic context in which that syllable appears). Then the prosodic difference would be preserved during syllabary look-up. But this explanation is also unsatisfactory, since it undermines the proposed benefit of the syllabary — that only a very limited number of precompiled motor programs would need to be stored. Levelt et al. estimate, for example, that 500 syllables are enough to produce 80% of all English utterances. This estimate would be less impressive if each syllable had to be stored several times.

My main point here, however, is not whether subtle differences such as that between *pan* and *panda* are consistent with the concept of the mental syllabary. Instead, I wanted to illustrate that research on comprehension can also be of value in advancing our understanding of production. Systematicities in phonetic detail that are present in the speech signal and are used by listeners must derive from mechanisms in speech production. Comprehension-oriented research can thus reveal patterns of data that must be explained by theories of speech production.

Feedback?

In the field of speech comprehension, the feedback issue is still hotly debated, and is certainly not yet resolved (see for example, the recent exchange between Magnuson, McMurray, Tanenhaus, & Aslin, 2003, and McQueen, 2003). Similarly, the question of feedback during lexical retrieval in production has been pursued vigorously in the literature (see e.g., Levelt et al., 1999, and accompanying commentaries), and this debate is still going on (see e.g., Vigliocco & Hartsuiker, this volume). As Levelt et al. have argued, if it is assumed that some apparent demonstrations of feedback in production in fact reflect self-monitoring processes (via the speech comprehension system), then there is no need to assume that there is feedback within the production system.

If the production data do not require feedback, are there theoretical arguments in its favor? As I described earlier, there is a good argument to be made *against* on-line feedback in the speech perception system: It would not be of benefit to word recognition. In contrast, there are arguments motivating feedback in on-line production. Dell et al. (1997), for example, suggest that feedback from the phonological form level to the conceptual level in production could help speakers choose words whose phonological forms are currently available. That is, it could act to reduce the incidence of tip-of-the-tongue states. Vigliocco and Hartsuiker (this volume) provide other arguments about the benefits of feedback for production-internal monitoring of speaking.

Interestingly, this situation reverses when we consider feedback for learning at the phonological/phonetic interface; here there is good motivation for feedback in perception, but not in production. (Note, however, that feedback for learning at other levels in the production system may well be beneficial; Vigliocco & Hartsuiker, this volume.) As I suggested earlier, lexical-prelexical feedback for phonetic learning could be of considerable benefit to comprehension. The equivalent in production would be in the context of motor learning due to dialect alterations. Perhaps the links between words and particular articulatory programs could be strengthened via feedback as a speaker changes dialect. But such alterations are unnecessary. If an abstract phonological structure is built before articulatory planning, as in WEAVER++ (Levelt et al., 1999; Roelofs, this volume), dialect alterations would not need to be coded lexically. The changes could be made at the articulatory level, and feedback about these changes to the lexical level would be redundant.

The reason for this difference between perception and production is again that the two systems have fundamentally different tasks. Comprehension has a many-to-one mapping problem (selecting the correct words out of an infinite set of possible utterances). Prior knowledge about words can thus usefully be employed to improve that mapping over time (e.g., in the context of a speaker of an unfamiliar dialect). In production, in contrast, the problem is to build a phonological structure based on a single message. Alterations at the articulatory periphery due to dialect changes can offer no help to the lexical selection process or even to the generation of abstract phonological structures. The comparison between perception and production can therefore be fruitful. In particular, it illustrates how mechanisms in one system may be very different from those in the other because the systems have different computational problems to solve.

ENCODING AND DECODING SPEECH

By way of a coda, I briefly discuss the relationship between comprehension and production in a slightly different way. So far, I have treated listening and speaking as separable but intimately linked objects of study. But are the comprehension and production systems themselves separable, or is there only one speech processing system?

The vocal tract and the muscles controlling it are obviously different from the sensory systems (ears and eyes) involved in speech perception. At the periphery, the comprehension and production systems must be different. But how far in from the sensory and motor periphery is this distinction preserved? If on-line lexical access in comprehension and production are both feedforward processes, then the two systems are likely to be separate at least up to and including the level of phonological word forms in comprehension, and down from this level in production (cf. Figure 19.3 in Roelofs, this volume). That is, if there were only one system, one would expect feedback effects in comprehension (due to the connections used in production) and, vice versa, in production (due to comprehension connections; see also Roelofs, 2003). The evidence that cascade is more widespread during lexical access in comprehension than during lexical retrieval in production also suggests that the systems are separate (because they operate in different ways).

There are a number of other arguments for separate input and output systems. I will mention only two. First, Shallice, McLeod, and Lewis (1985) examined this issue using the dual-task paradigm. Participants were asked to read aloud (a task requiring at least the operation of the speech production system) at the same time as they had to detect first names (e.g., *Mary*) in lists of other spoken words (a task requiring at least the operation of the spoken-word recognition system). Relative to single-task control conditions, there was very little dual-task interference. Such results can be more easily explained if the two systems are separate than if there is only one system performing both tasks. Second, Patterson and Shewell (1987) present dissociations in the performance of an aphasic patient. Her performance in auditory lexical decision was better for content words than for function words. But in a task which again used spoken input but now also required speech production (a repetition task), she performed better on function words than on content words. It is hard to explain this pattern of performance in a single system account; it can easily be explained in one with separate input and output components.

In line with many other authors, I therefore conclude that, at least up to (down from) the level of phonological form representations, the comprehension and production systems are separate. (For further data and arguments, see e.g., Dell et al., 1997; Monsell, 1987; Roelofs, 2003; Zwitserlood, 2003.) At higher levels of syntactic and conceptual processing, however, there may be a more integrated system (see e.g., Garrett, 2000; Kempen, 2000; Roelofs, 2004). It is possible that the representations that are used in building an utterance interpretation in comprehension (i.e., in processing that takes place after phonological decoding) are also used in building a conceptual message in production (i.e., in processing that precedes phonological encoding).

Even if the lower-level input and output components of speech processing are separate, they must still be closely linked. The data on self-monitoring (Schiller, this volume) suggest that the comprehension system receives phonological input from the production system. The reverse also appears to be true. A striking demonstration of the tightness of the comprehension-production link comes from a speech shadowing experiment (Porter & Castellanos, 1980; see also Fowler, Brown, Sabadini, & Weihing, 2003). Participants were asked to listen to an extended vowel of unpredictable duration, which was followed by one of five consonant-vowel (CV) sequences (e.g., [aaaba], [aapa], [aaaama], [aaka], [aaaga]). Their task was to repeat the initial vowel as they heard it, and then either to repeat the final CV as rapidly as possible (a choice RT condition) or to say a fixed CV, irrespective of the CV sequence in the input (a simple RT condition). RTs were computed by measuring the lags between the onset of consonant closure in the stimuli and the corresponding onset in the responses. Participants were only 50 ms slower in the choice RT condition than in the simple RT condition. This difference is much smaller than that normally observed in comparisons of simple and choice RT tasks (Luce, 1986, presents differences in the range 100–150 ms). The speed of the choice RT responses in the shadowing task thus suggests that there is very rapid flow of information from the comprehension system to the production system.

CONCLUSION

The relation between speech comprehension and speech production should not only be approached by studying talking and listening in fully interactive settings, but also by examining individual components of the speech decoding and encoding systems in isolation. This type of approach was exemplified here by an examination of two aspects of the flow of information through the phonological decoding component of the comprehension system. I also argued that the available evidence suggests that it is correct to consider that this component is distinct from (but tightly linked to) the phonological encoding component of the production system. Examination of specific sub-components of the speech processing system should however not be blind to the larger view of the complete system. I illustrated that knowledge about speech production feeds our understanding of comprehension data, and in turn, that work on perception can inform theories of production. This kind of research strategy respects the intimate relationship that exists between comprehension and production by acknowledging, as it were, that they sleep in the same bed. But it also violates that relationship by recognizing that they are not inseparable bedfellows.

REFERENCES

van Alphen, P. M. (2004). *Perceptual relevance of prevoicing in Dutch.* Ph.D. dissertation, University of Nijmegen. MPI Series in Psycholinguistics, 25.

van Alphen, P. M., & McQueen, J. M. (submitted). The effect of Voice Onset Time differences on lexical access in Dutch. Manuscript submitted for publication.

van Alphen, P. M., & Smits, R. (2004). Acoustical and perceptual analysis of the voicing distinction in Dutch initial plosives: The role of prevoicing. *Journal of Phonetics, 32,* 455-491.

Andruski, J. E., Blumstein, S. E., & Burton, M. (1994). The effect of subphonetic differences on lexical access. *Cognition, 52,* 163-187.

Cholin, J., Schiller, N. O., & Levelt, W. J. M. (2004). The preparation of syllables in speech production. *Journal of Memory and Language, 50,* 47-61.

Damian, M. F., & Martin, R. M. (1999). Semantic and phonological codes interact in single word production. *Journal of Experimental Psychology: Learning, Memory, and Cognition, 28,* 345–361.

Dell, G. S., Schwartz, M. F., Martin, N., Saffran, E. M., & Gagnon, D. A. (1997). Lexical access in aphasic and nonaphasic speakers. *Psychological Review, 104,* 801–838.

Elman, J. L., & McClelland, J. L. (1988). Cognitive penetration of the mechanisms of perception: Compensation for coarticulation of lexically restored phonemes. *Journal of Memory and Language, 27,* 143–165.

Fowler, C. A., Brown, J. M., Sabadini, L., & Weihing, J. (2003). Rapid access to speech gestures in perception: Evidence from choice and simple response time tasks. *Journal of Memory and Language, 49,* 396–413.

Garrett, M.F. (2000). Remarks on the architecture of language processing systems. In Y. Grodzinsky, L. Shapiro, & D. Swinney (Eds.), *Language and the brain: Representation and processing* (pp. 31–69). San Diego, CA: Academic Press.

Griffin, Z. M., & Bock, K. (1998). Constraint, word frequency, and the relationship between processing levels in spoken word production. *Journal of Memory and Language, 38,* 313–338.

Kempen, G. (2000). Could grammatical encoding and grammatical decoding be subserved by the same processing module? *Behavioral and Brain Sciences, 23,* 38–39.

Levelt, W. J. M., Roelofs, A., & Meyer, A. S. (1999). A theory of lexical access in speech production. *Behavioral and Brain Sciences, 22,* 1–75.

Luce, R. D. (1986). *Response times.* New York: Oxford University Press.

Magnuson, J. S., McMurray, B., Tanenhaus, M. K., & Aslin, R. N. (2003). Lexical effects on compensation for coarticulation: The ghost of Christmash past. *Cognitive Science, 27,* 285–298.

Mann, V. A., & Repp, B. H. (1981). Influence of preceding fricative on stop consonant perception. *Journal of the Acoustical Society of America, 69,* 548–558.

McClelland, J. L., & Elman, J. L. (1986). The TRACE model of speech perception. *Cognitive Psychology, 18,* 1–86.

McQueen, J. M. (2003). The ghost of Christmas future: Didn't Scrooge learn to be good? Commentary on Magnuson, McMurray, Tanenhaus and Aslin (2003). *Cognitive Science, 27,* 795–799.

McQueen, J. M. (2004). Speech perception. In K. Lamberts & R. Goldstone (Eds.), *The handbook of cognition* (pp. 255–275). London: Sage Publications.

McQueen, J. M., Cutler, A., & Norris, D. (2003). *Perceptual learning in speech generalises over words.* Presented at the 9th Wintercongres of the Nederlandse Vereniging voor Psychonomie, Egmond aan Zee, December 2003.

McQueen, J. M., Dahan, D., & Cutler, A. (2003). Continuity and gradedness in speech processing. In A. S. Meyer & N. O. Schiller (Eds.), *Phonetics and phonology in language comprehension and production: Differences and similarities* (pp. 39–78). Berlin: Mouton de Gruyter.

Monsell, S. (1987). On the relation between lexical input and output pathways for speech. In A. Allport, D. MacKay, W. Prinz, & E. Sheerer (Eds.), *Language*

Perception and production: Relationships between listening, speaking, reading, and writing (pp. 273–311). London: Academic Press.

Morsella, E., & Miozzo, M. (2002). Evidence for a cascade model of lexical access in speech production. *Journal of Experimental Psychology: Learning, Memory, and Cognition, 28,* 555–563.

Norris, D. (1994). Shortlist: A connectionist model of continuous speech recognition. *Cognition, 52,* 189–234.

Norris, D., McQueen, J. M., & Cutler, A. (2000). Merging information in speech recognition: Feedback is never necessary. *Behavioral and Brain Sciences, 23,* 299–325.

Norris, D., McQueen, J. M., & Cutler, A. (2003). Perceptual learning in speech. *Cognitive Psychology, 47,* 204–238.

Patterson, K., & Shewell, C. (1987). Speak and spell: Dissociations and word-class effects. In M. Coltheart, G. Sartori, & R. Job (Eds.), *The cognitive neuropsychology of language* (pp. 237–294). Hillsdale, NJ: Lawrence Erlbaum Associates.

Peterson, R. R., & Savoy, P. (1998). Lexical selection and phonological coding during language production: Evidence for cascaded processing. *Journal of Experimental Psychology: Learning, Memory, and Cognition, 24,* 539–557.

Pitt, M. A., & McQueen, J. M. (1998). Is compensation for coarticulation mediated by the lexicon? *Journal of Memory and Language, 39,* 347–370.

Porter, R. J., & Castellanos, F. X. (1980). Speech-production measures of speech perception: Rapid shadowing of VCV syllables. *Journal of the Acoustical Society of America, 67,* 1349–1356.

Roelofs, A. (2003). Modeling the relation between the production and recognition of spoken word forms. In A. S. Meyer & N. O. Schiller (Eds.), *Phonetics and phonology in language comprehension and production: Differences and similarities* (pp. 115–158). Berlin: Mouton de Gruyter.

Roelofs, A. (2004). Error biases in spoken word planning and monitoring by aphasic and nonaphasic speakers: Comment on Rapp and Goldrick (2000). *Psychological Review, 111,* 561–572.

Rubin, P., Turvey, M. T., & van Gelder, P. (1976). Initial phonemes are detected faster in spoken words than in nonwords. *Perception & Psychophysics, 19,* 394–398.

Salverda, A. P., Dahan, D., & McQueen, J. M. (2003). The role of prosodic boundaries in the resolution of lexical embedding in speech comprehension. *Cognition, 90,* 51–89.

Shallice, T., McLeod, P., & Lewis, K. (1985). Isolating cognitive modules with the dual-task paradigm: Are speech perception and production separate processes? *Quarterly Journal of Experimental Psychology, 37A,* 507–532.

Spinelli, E., McQueen, J. M., & Cutler, A. (2003). Processing resyllabified words in French. *Journal of Memory and Language, 48,* 233–254.

Vigliocco, G., & Hartsuiker, R. J. (2002). The interplay of meaning, sound, and syntax in sentence production. *Psychological Bulletin, 128,* 442–472.

Zwitserlood, P. (2003). The internal structure of words: Consequences for listening and speaking. In A. S. Meyer & N. O. Schiller (Eds.), *Phonetics and phonology in language comprehension and production: Differences and similarities* (pp. 79–114). Berlin: Mouton de Gruyter.

15 Verbal Self-Monitoring

Niels O. Schiller
Universiteit Maastricht, The Netherlands

INTRODUCTION

Serial action involves planning, and planning can be controlled or monitored. For instance, when we reach for a cup, we can adapt the trajectory of our reaching movement in case there is an obstacle, like a milk bottle. Similarly, speakers can monitor their own speech. Speech monitoring is usually viewed as intimately related to ongoing speech planning: Speakers monitor what they will say and what they have just said. Moreover, in order to hold a conversation, tell a story, or give a talk, speakers must keep records of their utterances over seconds or minutes. This suggests cross talk between the production and the comprehension system. In this chapter, I focus on one of the levels of representation that is involved in this cross talk.

It has been proposed that there are at least two routes for speech monitoring, that is, an external and an internal monitoring route. The external route undoubtedly involves the speech comprehension system: Speakers listen to their own verbal output. However, it is also known from several empirical sources that speakers are able to monitor their own speech before it has been uttered. This is called internal monitoring, and I will review the most compelling evidence supporting the existence of an internal monitoring system below. However, the functioning of this internal monitoring system is largely unknown, although it has been proposed that the comprehension system is involved as well.

There is general consensus that one type of representation that is accessible to internal monitoring is the phonological representation of the planned utterance, and I present new evidence that further supports this view. It is less clear whether speakers can also monitor more abstract syntactic representations and/or more fully specified phonetic representations of their planned speech. I review data from different paradigms that have some bearing on this question. I also discuss how the representations we access during self-monitoring are related to representations we generate when we listen to others.

COGNITIVE ASPECTS OF VERBAL MONITORING IN SPEECH PRODUCTION

A large part of human behavior consists of the execution of action such as walking, driving, reaching and grasping, or speaking (Rosenbaum, 1991). Human beings monitor their actions constantly to correct them in the course of their execution if necessary. We are able to detect obstacles and adapt our kinematic motor planning within fractions of a second, lending flexibility to our action system (Desmurget et al., 1999). Similarly, when speaking we constantly monitor the coordination of processes such as the selection of meanings, retrieval of words, syntactic and phonological encoding, and articulation. Perturbation experiments (e.g., unexpected alterations in lip or jaw position caused by a weight attached to the articulatory organ in question) conducted while participants were producing speech revealed compensatory adjustments in the articulatory-motor system within 60 ms demonstrating an active role of tactile and proprioceptive feedback during speech production (Abbs & Gracco, 1984). However, not only proprioceptive but also auditory-sensory feedback can lead to modifications of the speech plan supporting the idea of a self-monitoring speech perception system. Fairbanks and Guttman (1958) demonstrated that delayed auditory feedback could efficiently disrupt the fluency of speaking. When the delay is in the order of 200 ms, speech output is severely disturbed transforming it into some sort of stuttering, suggesting connections between speech production and perception (Schiller & Meyer, 2003).

Each time we open our mouths to utter a word, we make use of mutual connections between production and perception. When we produce a speech error, we can interrupt ourselves and self-correct the error because we listen to our own speech while we speak (auditory-sensory feedback). This is called *external monitoring*. An example for external monitoring would be "They haven't been married ... uh, measured with the precision you're using" (Garrett, 1982: 207). However, we can even self-correct an error before the unintended word has been completely uttered. For instance, in a task involving the description of visual patterns, Levelt (1983) found self-repairs such as "[...] is a *v*-, a horizontal line" (Levelt, 1983: 64). In this example, too little of the word *vertical* was pronounced to make recognition via the external monitoring system possible. In order to interrupt oneself after the articulation of only the first segment of an intended word, the error must have been detected before the onset of articulation, suggesting the existence of an *internal monitoring* system. Moreover, when recordings of telephone calls to a radio talk show were analyzed, Blackmer and Mitton (1991) found that almost 20% of the overt error repairs had a 0 ms cut-off-to-repair time, that is, the speaker repaired a previously produced error without any pausing as in "and you/somebody said". This suggests that an internal monitor had detected the error before it was overtly produced—but too late to stop it from being articulated. The editing system seems to start repairing the error without interrupting the speech flow. Moreover, when speakers are completely deprived from external monitoring, they are still able to monitor their own speech output for errors (Lackner & Tuller, 1979), supposedly via an internal monitor. Maybe the most impressive evidence for an internal monitor is that when speech errors are induced in the laboratory, errors resulting in taboo words (e.g., *tool kits* becoming *cool tits*) occur significantly less often than other errors. However, elevated Galvanic skin responses recorded simultaneously suggest that participants actually generate the taboo word errors internally but detect them before they are overtly uttered, supporting the existence of a prearticulatory self-monitor system for speaking (Motley, Camden, & Baars, 1982).

Why would it be helpful to internally self-monitor one's own speech? Producing speech errors hampers the fluency of speech in a conversation and can often be embarrassing (e.g., when a socially non-appropriate speech error is produced). A self-monitoring system that checks the speech output even before overt articulation and detects as well as repairs non-intended output might therefore prove extremely useful. In the last decade, our knowledge about verbal self-monitoring became much more detailed (see Postma, 2000, for a recent overview). Theories of speech production incorporate mechanisms for self-monitoring and self-repair (Hartsuiker & Kolk, 2001; Laver, 1980; Levelt, 1989; MacKay, 1987). One of the most detailed theories to date is provided by Levelt (1983, 1989; Levelt, Roelofs, & Meyer, 1999; Wheeldon & Levelt, 1995). Levelt's model of speech production distinguishes three different monitoring systems: a conceptual monitor that checks the preverbal message for appropriateness, as well as an internal and an external monitor. In what follows, I focus on the external and internal monitor.

The external monitor is used when we self-perceive our own acoustic speech signals. Whether we listen to our own overt speech or to speech generated by somebody else, the speech is processed through the same perceptual system, as shown, for instance, by recent imaging studies (e.g., Price et al., 1996). Levelt (1989; Levelt et al., 1999) assumes that the internal monitor also proceeds through the general comprehension system. A central perception-based monitor would be economical since two different types of monitoring (internal and external) could be processed by the capabilities of one single perceptual system (see Figure 15.1).

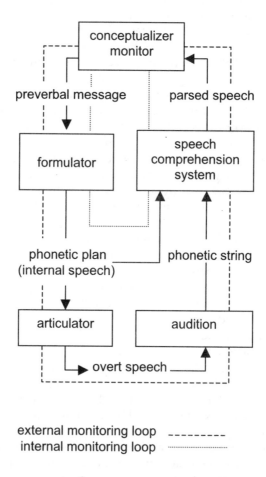

external monitoring loop   ‒ ‒ ‒ ‒ ‒ ‒ ‒ ‒
internal monitoring loop   ⋯⋯⋯⋯⋯⋯⋯

FIG. 15.1. The perceptual loop theory of self-monitoring (after Levelt, 1989).

However, there is agreement that even in Levelt's model, it is not entirely clear how the speech monitor precisely works (Oomen & Postma, 2001, 2002). Originally, the internal monitoring system in Levelt's theory could only access the *phonetic plan*, that is, the output of the speech planning process immediately prior to articulation (Levelt, 1989). In their most recent version of the theory, Levelt et al. (1999: 3) describe self-monitoring as occurring in parallel to phonological and phonetic encoding. However, a clear distinction between internal and external self-monitoring is not made, due to lack of empirical data. Nevertheless, it has been suggested that the internal monitoring system has access to a more abstract code of the planning process, that is, the *phonological planning level* (Levelt et al., 1999; Wheeldon & Levelt, 1995). This theoretical modification is based on a study by Wheeldon and Levelt (1995), in which they asked participants to monitor for pre-specified segments when internally generating the Dutch translation of an English word. Participants heard, for instance, the word *hitchhiker* and generated the Dutch translation *lifter*. When their task was to monitor for /t/, they would press a button because *lifter* contains the phoneme /t/. In contrast, when their task was to monitor for /k/, they would refrain from button pressing. Wheeldon and Levelt found that participants were faster in monitoring for the phoneme /t/ in *tuinmuur* ('garden wall') than in *fietser* ('cyclist'), and they were faster in monitoring for /t/ in *fietser* than in *lifter* ('hitchhiker'). Wheeldon and Levelt (1995) took their result to confirm the hypothesis about the incremental encoding of segments during phonological encoding in speech production. Furthermore, these authors suggested that the monitoring difference between the target segments at the syllable boundary (e.g., *fiet.ser* vs. *lif.ter*) might be due to the existence of a marked syllable boundary or a syllabification process that slows down the encoding of the second syllable.

However, the study by Wheeldon and Levelt (1995) had a number of shortcomings, which I address in this study. First, their materials contained not only monomorphemic but also derived words and compounds. In half of the items, the syllable boundary coincided with a morphological boundary. According to the model by Levelt et al. (1999), morphological structure should have no effect on the monitoring latencies because morphological processing occurs before the phonological encoding level. However, if morphology does exert an effect in the monitoring task, the presumed syllable boundary effect reported by Wheeldon and Levelt (1995) may in fact be due to morphological boundaries. To disentangle syllable boundary and morphological boundary effects I present the results of an experiment in which the two types of boundaries were manipulated independently.

Second, some of the words used by Wheeldon and Levelt (1995) had lexical stress on the first syllable (e.g., *lifter*) while others had lexical stress on the second syllable (e.g., *garnaal* 'shrimp'). In another experiment of the same study, Wheeldon and Levelt showed that stress could influence monitoring latencies—as the theory would predict, because metrical encoding is part of phonological encoding. Here, I will investigate the effect of word stress on segmental monitoring more systematically.

Finally, I will investigate Wheeldon and Levelt's proposal about incremental encoding of segments in an interesting test case. There is evidence that groups of segments may function as single units. For example, 10% of the speech errors include groups of consonants (e.g., /st/ or /tr/) at the beginning of words (so-called *onset clusters*) (Dell, 1986). Treiman and colleagues (Stemberger & Treiman, 1986; Treiman, 1985, 1986) provided further evidence from meta-linguistic awareness tasks for the claim that syllable onsets are independent phonological units. Finally, Santiago, MacKay, Palma and Rho (2000) as well as Kinoshita (2000) provide on-line evidence from picture and word naming suggesting that onset clusters form a unit (but see Schiller, 2004). If it is true that onsets form a unit, one may not expect a monitoring difference between two consonants included in a cluster. In contrast, the incremental encoding hypothesis by Wheeldon and Levelt (1995) would predict a difference.

To summarize, I report the results of testing three previously untested aspects of the monitoring task, that is, the role of morphological boundaries, the influence of lexical stress, and the status of consonant clusters. If only absolute position plays a role in monitoring, morphological boundaries, lexical stress, and complex segments should not have an influence on incremental encoding. If, however, these factors do play a role, the pattern of monitoring may be different when morphological boundaries, varying lexical stress, or complex onsets are included in the test items. Theoretically, morphological boundaries should not show any effect since morphological encoding precedes phonological encoding. In contrast, metrical stress should have an effect on monitoring latencies because metrical encoding forms an integral part of phonological encoding. Finally, whether or not onset complexity should yield an effect is dependent on theoretical assumptions of phonological representation.

INVESTIGATING THE NATURE OF THE INTERNAL SPEECH CODE

Participants in the study by Wheeldon and Levelt (1995) as well as in my study were asked to monitor their own internal speech. This task was used to obtain information about the time course of phonological encoding and the nature of the code being monitored. However, how can I be sure that participants are in fact monitoring an abstract phonological level of representation when performing this task? Theoretically, several levels of representation may be possible for self-monitoring. First, speakers may have access to the abstract word forms in the mental lexicon. Word form representations are claimed to contain information about a word's phonemes, its number of syllables, and its stress pattern (if deviating from default). Second, speakers may have direct access to a word's phonological segments. That is, they might be able to monitor the process of segmental retrieval in isolation. Third, speakers may monitor the output of the process of segment-to-frame association, that is, a syllabified phonological-word representation or possibly an orthographic (graphemic) code. Finally, they might be monitoring some articulatory-phonetic representation.

Levelt (1983, 1989) argued against the last option and proposed that during internal monitoring a pre-articulatory speech output code is monitored by means of an internal loop to the comprehension system. This proposal is supported by the fact that internal speech is produced at a faster rate than overt speech suggesting that the internal speech code is more abstract than the overt one (Anderson, 1982). For example, in the study by Wheeldon and Levelt (1995) the increases in spoken duration were significantly larger than the increases in monitoring latencies, and they yielded a different pattern.

Further evidence against an articulatory-phonetic code comes from a monitoring experiment that included articulatory suppression. Articulatory suppression is known to interfere with phonetic and articulatory encoding processes (Murray, 1968), but not so much with phonological encoding processes (Besner, Davis, & Daniels, 1981). Wheeldon and Levelt (1995) used this phenomenon and showed that articulatory suppression had little influence on monitoring latencies. In the first experiment of their study, Wheeldon and Levelt (1995) established that first syllable onsets could be monitored faster than second syllable onsets. A control experiment for Experiment 1 including an articulatory suppression task showed similar results indicating that participants were not monitoring a phonetic/articulatory code but some abstract (syllabified) phonological planning level.

Furthermore, segmental speech errors are known to occur also in internal speech (Dell & Repka, 1992). Therefore, the internal speech code cannot consist only of whole lexical items but presumably involves similar phonological encoding processes as overt speech. Moreover, the fact that Wheeldon and Levelt (1995) found a syllable effect and an effect of stress position in monitoring internal speech codes (Experiments 1 and

2 of their study) suggests that speakers are monitoring a syllabified, pre-articulatory speech code. In the model proposed by Levelt and colleagues (1999), this would be the phonological word level. At the phonological word level, the abstract speech plan is phonologically specified and prosodified. As a working hypothesis for the current study, I will make the assumption that speakers use this phonological word level for internal monitoring.

One may want to argue that participants do not monitor a speech code at all but rather construct some sort of graphemic representation of the Dutch word. There are several arguments that speak against this, however. First, visualizing letters takes significantly longer than internally saying their names (Weber & Bach, 1969; Weber & Castleman, 1970). Second, although their orthographic representation can affect the processing of auditorily presented words (Jakimik, Cole, & Rudnicky, 1985; Seidenberg & Tanenhaus, 1979), participants presumably did not monitor an orthographic string in the phoneme monitoring experiments for the following reason. Some Dutch words of the current study included segments with irregular spelling-to-sound correspondences (e.g., the letter <c> in *pincet* is pronounced like an /s/) and Wheeldon and Levelt's (1995) study included words with devoiced word-final consonants (e.g., *avond* pronounced with a final /t/). However, even in these words, participants successfully monitored for the target phonemes /s/ and /t/, respectively. Finally, Wheeldon and Levelt (1995) found effects of stress location in syllable onset monitoring, which cannot be explained if an orthographic representation was monitored because stress is not marked orthographically in Dutch.

THE EXPERIMENTS

Next, I present data from four experiments testing the above-mentioned aspects of internal monitoring. The methodology of the experiments to be reported was similar to the one used by Wheeldon and Levelt (1995). Bilingual Dutch-English participants were presented with an English word and requested to generate the Dutch translation. The Dutch target word had to be monitored for a previously specified phoneme. If the phoneme was present in the target word, participants pressed a button as quickly as possible. Otherwise, they did not do anything.

Experiment 1

In the first experiment, I tested words with a simple onset ($C_1VC_2.C_3VC_4$ where C stands for consonant and V stands for vowel, dots mark syllable boundaries (e.g., *pincet* 'tweezers') and words with a complex onset

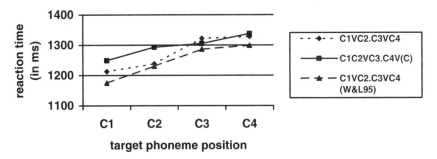

FIG. 15.2.   Button-press latencies from Experiment 1. The three shapes represent three different sets of materials. Diamonds = simple onset words (e.g., *pincet*). Squares = complex onset words (e.g., *bliksem*). Triangles = words used in the Wheeldon and Levelt (1995) study.

($C_1C_2VC_3.C_4VC$; e.g., *bliksem* 'lightening'). As can be seen in Figure 15.2, results of this first experiment showed that the monitoring latencies of the four target positions increased from beginning to end of the Dutch words replicating Wheeldon and Levelt's (1995) result. The differences between C_1 and C_2 were clearly visible, not only for the simple onset words ($C_1VC_2.C_3VC_4$) but also for complex onset words ($C_1C_2VC_3.C_4VC$). This supports the incremental encoding hypothesis but it does not support theories that assume onset clusters are indivisible units. The increase from C_2 to C_3 was only significant for simple onset words. For these words, there was a syllable boundary between C_2 and C_3, and Wheeldon and Levelt (1995) suggested that this might be the reason for the increase in monitoring latencies between these two target positions. Furthermore, when a syllable boundary intervened in complex onset words (between C_3 and C_4), the increase in monitoring latencies was again pronounced (though not significant), suggesting that syllable boundaries presumably do influence the monitoring process (but see Wheeldon & Morgan, 2002 for a slightly different pattern in English). Furthermore, it seems that the monitoring process somehow speeds up towards the end of words because for simple onset words the difference between C_3 and C_4 was negligible. Wheeldon and Levelt (1995) gave a possible account for this effect: They assumed that the setting of a syllable boundary after the encoding of the first syllable's segment delays the initiation of assignment of phonemes to the following syllable. Furthermore, they assumed that the constituent phonemes of a word continue to be made available while the syllabification process takes place. Consequently, when the assignment of segments to the second syllable begins (most of the) phonemes of the second syllable are already available and their left-to-right assignment to the frame can occur at higher speed.

Experiment 2

In the second monitoring experiment, I included morphologically complex words of different CV-structures, that is, $C_1VC_2.C_3VC_4$; for example, *dakpan* 'roof tile'; $C_1C_2VC_3.C_4VC$; for example, *kraambed* 'childbed'; or $C_1VC_2C_3.C_4VC$; for example, *borgsom* 'deposit'. The results of the second experiment were very similar to those of the first experiment (see Figure 15.3). Monitoring latencies increased as a function of the position of the target segment in the word – the earlier the segment occurs in the carrier word, the shorter the reaction times. Interestingly, the intervals between C_2 and C_3 were negligible for words with complex onsets or codas, but not for simple $C_1VC_2.C_3VC_4$ words. Increases in monitoring latencies were again especially pronounced at the syllable boundary, independent of syllable structure. However, morphological boundaries might have emphasized the effect of syllabic boundaries since both coincide in compounded Dutch words. Therefore, we carried out Experiment 3 to disentangle the individual contributions of syllable and morphological boundaries.

Experiment 3

In this third experiment, we contrasted two types of morphologically complex words with identical CV structures, that is, $C_1VC_2.C_3VC_4$; for example, *geurloos* 'odorless' and *fietser* 'bicyclist'. For words of the type *geurloos*, syllable and morphological boundary coincided between C_2 and

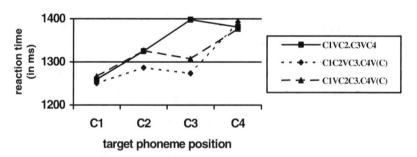

FIG. 15.3. Button-press latencies from Experiment 2. The three shapes represent three different sets of materials. Squares = complex onset words (e.g., *kraambed*). Diamonds = simple onset words (e.g., *dakpan*). Triangles = complex coda words (e.g., *borgsom*).

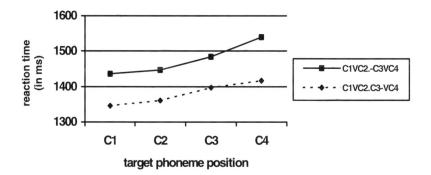

FIG. 15.4. Button-press latencies from Experiment 3. The two shapes represent two different sets of materials. Squares = words with matching syllabic and morphological boundaries (e.g., *geurloos*). Diamonds = words with mismatching syllabic and morphological boundaries (e.g., *fietser*).

C_3 (e.g., *geur.-loos*; hyphens mark morphological boundaries) while they occurred at different positions for words of the type *fietser*. The syllable boundary was also between C_2 and C_3 (e.g., *fiet.ser*) but the morphological boundary was between C_3 and C_4 (e.g., *fiets-er*). If morphological boundaries exhibit a similar effect to syllable boundaries, monitoring latencies between C_2 and C_3 might be larger for words of the type *geurloos* than for words of the type *fietser*. Furthermore, monitoring latencies between C_3 and C_4 should be larger for words of the type *fietser* than for words of the type *geurloos*. As can be seen in Figure 15.4, results revealed no significant role of morphology in monitoring. The monitoring interval between C_2 and C_3 was just as large for words with a morphological boundary at that position (37 ms) than for words without a morphological boundary (36 ms). As for the interval between C_3 and C_4, this is even larger for words without a morphological boundary (55 ms) than for words with a morphological boundary (20 ms). However, this might have to do with the fact that the latter type of words was restricted to derivations and inflections in Dutch constraining the choice of target segments in position C_4 (i.e., either /r/ or /n/).

Experiment 4

In the last experiment to be reported in this chapter I investigated the role of metrical stress in segmental monitoring. As just mentioned, Wheeldon and Levelt (1995) found that word onset monitoring was delayed for words with metrical stress on the second syllable relative to words with metrical stress on the first syllable. In this last experiment, I test whether

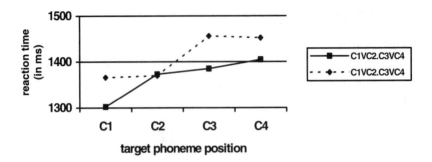

FIG. 15.5. Button-press latencies from Experiment 4. The two shapes represent two different sets of materials. Squares = words with initial stress (e.g., *kermis*). Diamonds = words with final stress (e.g., *fornuis*).

metrical stress influences the monitoring of target phonemes in all positions of a word, that is, from onset to offset. I selected words with identical CV structures, that is, $C_1VC_2.C_3VC_4$, but different stress patterns. Words could either have stress on the first syllable, for example, *kermis* 'fair', or on the second syllable, for example, *fornuis* 'oven'. If metrical stress has no effect on segmental monitoring, the monitoring pattern for both types of words should be very similar. However, as can be seen in Figure 15.5, this was not the case. Whereas the difference between C_1 and C_2 was significant for words with initial stress (e.g., *kermis*), the monitoring difference between C_2 and C_3 was significant for words with final stress (e.g., *fornuis*).

DISCUSSION OF THE RESULTS

Results from four monitoring experiments were presented. One general result was the increase of monitoring latencies across target positions in the word. This replicates earlier results of Wheeldon and Levelt (1995) and supports their view of incremental encoding. When morphological structure was manipulated, no effects over and above syllable structure were observed. Importantly, when metrical stress was manipulated in the item set, significant monitoring differences for words with initial stress were observed at earlier positions than for words with final stress.

This last result could be accounted in the following way. For words with initial stress, stress has to be computed for the first syllable. Stress is realized on the nucleus (i.e., the vowel), therefore monitoring the offset of the first syllable (C_2) is delayed. However, while stress is computed, the remaining segments continue to become available. Therefore, they can be assigned at a higher rate. Similarly, for words with final stress, the computation of the syllable boundary between C_2 and C_3 takes time (see also Wheeldon & Levelt, 1995). While the syllable boundary is computed, the following segments continue to be retrieved and can be inserted at a faster rate. That is why no syllable boundary effect is visible for words with initial stress (because the computation of stress delayed the assignment process of the remainder of the word), and no stress effect is visible for words with final stress (because the computation of the syllable boundary delayed the assignment process of the remainder of the word).

However, there are some data points that apparently do not fit this account. For instance, Levelt and Wheeldon (1995) found significant differences both between C_1 and C_2 (which I argue might be due to the computation of metrical stress for words with initial stress) and between C_2 and C_3 (which might be due to the computation of syllable boundaries)—according to the account given above only one of these events, that is, the first one, should exert an influence because following segments continue to become available but the assignment process is delayed. When this process resumes, segments, syllable boundaries, and stress can be assigned at a faster rate, and monitoring differences may no longer be measurable with the paradigm used here. A potential answer to this puzzle might be that Wheeldon and Levelt's materials included both words with initial and final stress. Words with initial stress might be responsible for the first difference, while words with final stress might be responsible for the second difference. Furthermore, the compounded words in Experiment 2 above showed effects between C_1 and C_2 and also between C_3 and C_4. One might argue, however, that the constituents of a compound were treated as independent phonological words and therefore effects of stress and syllable boundary could be observed in the same word. However, the assumption of such an assignment process during phonological encoding in which stress, syllable boundaries, and segments are included needs further empirical evidence.

In summary, the results of my segmental monitoring experiments have replicated and extended the study by Wheeldon and Levelt (1995) for Dutch. Whereas the study by Wheeldon and Levelt (1995) showed that the monitoring latencies increased with the position of the target segment in the word, my experiments demonstrated that neither syllable structure (i.e., onset complexity) nor morphological structure influenced this incremental pattern. However, syllable boundaries and metrical stress exerted an influence on the monitoring pattern. An account to capture the whole data set presented in this paper was provided.

However, a word of caution might be appropriate. Theoretically, it is possible that participants in such monitoring experiments encode the whole word phonologically and only after phonological encoding has been completed, they monitor the encoded word form—for example, in some sort of phonological buffer—for certain segments. If this were the case, the monitoring latencies would not reflect speech production processes per se. However, the latter kind of monitoring is not able to account for certain patterns in the latencies, such as the increased monitoring speed after a syllable boundary or stress has been computed, which production-based views can account for by assuming that the computation of syllable boundaries and metrical stress takes time and processing resources.

Recently, I extended the just-mentioned results by providing evidence that even *word stress* could be internally monitored during speech production (Schiller, Schmitt, Peters, & Levelt, 2005). In the first experiment of that study, participants were asked to judge whether bisyllabic picture names had initial or final stress. Results showed significantly faster decision times for initially stressed targets (e.g., *KAno* 'canoe') than for targets with final stress (e.g., *kaNON* 'cannon'; capital letters indicate stressed syllables) and revealed that the monitoring latencies are not a function of the picture naming or object recognition latencies to the same pictures. Further experiments replicated this result with trisyllabic picture names (see Figure 15.6 for a summary). Interestingly, the overall pattern of monitoring latencies for metrical stress largely resembles the pattern of latencies for segmental monitoring, namely relatively shorter latencies when earlier parts of the word form are processed. These data might be interpreted as evidence that metrical information of words is encoded rightward incrementally during phonological encoding in speech production.

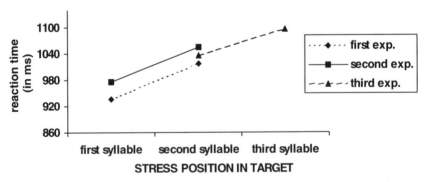

FIG. 15.6. Button-press latencies from three stress monitoring experiments. First experiment: Bisyllabic targets stressed on the first syllable (e.g., *toren* 'tower') or on the second syllable (e.g., *tomaat* 'tomato'). Second experiment: Identical to first experiment but different targets. Third experiment: Trisyllabic targets stressed on the second syllable (e.g., *asperge* 'asparagus') or on the third syllable (e.g., *artisjok* 'artichoke').

SUMMARY AND CONCLUSION

In this chapter, I discussed some of the evidence suggesting that the representation speakers are accessing when they monitor a verbal stimulus is phonological in nature. My own data shows that onset complexity does not play a role in monitoring demonstrating that the incremental effect of verbal monitoring holds not only for relatively, simple syllable structures, but also for more complex ones. Furthermore morphological complexity does not exert any influence on the monitoring pattern, as expected if a phonological code is accessed for monitoring. However, phonological representations themselves, such as syllable boundaries or metrical stress, do show pronounced effects in the monitoring pattern. A sequential, multi-tiered, phonological assignment process could account for this pattern.

I am inclined to interpret the above-mentioned results as speech production effects, although a comprehension locus of the effects cannot be excluded completely. However, it can certainly not be denied that there are strong connections between the production and the comprehension system at the level of phonological planning. The phonological plan (internal speech) as part of the production system must have a connection to the speech comprehension system, otherwise internal monitoring would not be feasible. Apparently, relatively abstract phonological segments can be directly fed into the comprehension system where these segments can be further processed. In fact, a direct connection in the reverse direction, that is, from comprehension to production, has already been assumed for some time to account for phonological priming effects in speech production (Levelt et al., 1999). Future work on verbal monitoring can potentially broaden our knowledge about the relation between speech production and comprehension.

ACKNOWLEDGMENTS

I would like to thank Suzan Kroezen for running Experiments 1 and 2 and Steffie Vroomen for running Experiments 3 and 4.

REFERENCES

Abbs, J. H., & Gracco, V. L. (1984). Control of complex motor gestures: Orofacial muscle responses to load perturbations of the lip during speech. *Journal of Neurophysiology, 51,* 705-723.
Anderson, R. D. (1982). Speech imagery is not always faster than visual imagery. *Memory & Cognition, 10,* 371-380.

Besner, D., Davis, J., & Daniels, S. (1981). Reading for meaning: The effects of concurrent articulation. *Quarterly Journal of Experimental Psychology, 33A,* 415-437.

Blackmer, E. R., & Mitton, J. L. (1991). Theories of monitoring and the timing of repairs in spontaneous speech. *Cognition, 39,* 173-194.

Dell, G. S. (1986). A spreading-activation theory of retrieval in sentence production. *Psychological Review, 93,* 283-321.

Dell, G. S., & Repka, R. J. (1992). Errors in inner speech. In B. J. Baars (Ed.), *Experimental slips and human error: Exploring the architecture of volition* (pp. 237-262). New York: Plenum Press.

Desmurget, M., Epstein, C. M., Turner, R. S., Prablanc, C., Alexander, G. E., & Grafton, S. T. (1999). Role of the posterior parietal cortex in updating reaching movements to a visual target. *Nature Neuroscience, 2,* 563-567.

Fairbanks, G., & Guttman, N. (1958). Effects of delayed auditory feedback on articulation. *Journal of Speech and Hearing Research, 1,* 12-22.

Garrett, M. F. (1982). Levels of processing in sentence production. In B. Butterworth (Ed.), *Language production: Speech and talk* (Vol. 1, pp. 177-220). New York: Academic Press.

Hartsuiker, R. J., & Kolk, H. H. J. (2001). Error monitoring in speech production: A computational test of the perceptual loop theory. *Cognitive Psychology, 42,* 113-157.

Jakimik, J., Cole, R. A., & Rudnicky, A. I. (1985). Sound and spelling in spoken word recognition. *Journal of Memory and Language, 24,* 165-178.

Kinoshita, S. (2000). The left-to-right nature of the masked onset priming effect in naming. *Psychonomic Bulletin and Review, 7,* 133-141.

Lackner, J. R., & Tuller, B. H. (1979). Role of efference monitoring in the detection of self-produced speech errors. In W. E. Cooper & E. C. T. Walker (Eds.), *Sentence processing* (pp. 281-294). Hillsdale, NJ: Lawrence Erlbaum Associates.

Laver, J. D. M. (1980). Monitoring systems in the neurolinguistic control of speech production. In V. A. Fromkin (Ed.), *Errors in linguistic performance: Slips of the tongue, ear, pen, and hand* (pp. 287-305). New York: Academic Press.

Levelt, W. J. M. (1983). Monitoring and self-repair in speech. *Cognition, 14,* 41-104.

Levelt, W. J. M. (1989). *Speaking: From intention to articulation.* Cambridge, MA: MIT Press.

Levelt, W. J. M., Roelofs, A., & Meyer, A. S. (1999). A theory of lexical access in speech production. *Behavioral and Brain Sciences, 22,* 1-75.

MacKay, D. G. (1987). *The organization of perception and action: A theory for language and other cognitive skills.* New York: Springer.

Motley, M. T., Camden C. T., & Baars, B. J. (1982). Covert formulation and editing of anomalies in speech production: Evidence from experimentally elicited slips of the tongue. *Journal of Verbal Learning and Verbal Behavior, 21,* 578-594.

Murray, D. J. (1968). Articulation and acoustic confusability in short-term memory. *Journal of Experimental Psychology, 78,* 679-684.

Oomen, C. C. E., & Postma, A. (2001). Effects of time pressure on mechanisms of speech production and self-monitoring. *Journal of Psycholinguistic Research, 30,* 163-184.

Oomen, C. C. E., & Postma, A. (2002). Limitations in processing resources and speech monitoring. *Language and Cognitive Processes, 17,* 163-184.

Postma, A. (2000). Detection of errors during speech production: a review of speech monitoring models. *Cognition, 77,* 97-131.

Price, C. J., Wise, R. J., Warburton, E. A., Moore, C. J., Howard, D., Patterson, K., Frackowiak, R. S. J., & Friston, K. J. (1996). Hearing and saying. The functional neuro-anatomy of auditory word processing. *Brain, 119,* 919-931.

Rosenbaum, D. A. (1991). *Human motor control.* San Diego: Academic Press.

Santiago, J., MacKay, D. G., Palma, A., & Rho, C. (2000). Sequential activation processes in producing words and syllables: Evidence from picture naming. *Language and Cognitive Processes, 15,* 1-44.

Schiller, N. O. (2004). The onset effect in word and picture naming. *Journal of Memory and Language, 50,* 477-490.

Schiller, N. O., & Meyer, A. S. (2003). Introduction to the relation between speech comprehension and production. In N. O. Schiller & A. S. Meyer (Eds.), *Phonetics and phonology in language comprehension and production. Differences and similarities* (pp. 1-7). Berlin, New York: Mouton de Gruyter.

Schiller, N. O., Schmitt, B. M., Peters, J., & Levelt, W. J. M. (2005). Monitoring metrical stress in polysyllabic words. *Language and Cognitive Processes.*

Seidenberg, M. S., & Tanenhaus, M. K. (1979). Orthographic effects on rhyme monitoring. *Journal of Experimental Psychology: Human, Learning and Memory, 5,* 546-554.

Stemberger, J.-P., & Treiman, R. (1986). The internal structure of word-initial consonant clusters. *Journal of Memory and Language, 25,* 163-180.

Treiman, R. (1985). Onsets and rimes as units of spoken syllables: Evidence from children. *Journal of Experimental Child Psychology, 39,* 161-181.

Treiman, R. (1986). The division between onsets and rimes in English syllables. *Journal of Memory and Language, 25,* 476-491.

Weber, R. J., & Bach, M. (1969). Visual and speech imagery. *British Journal of Psychology, 60,* 199-202.

Weber, R. J., & Castleman, J. (1970). The time it takes to imagine. *Perception & Psychophysics, 8,* 165-168.

Wheeldon, L. R., & Levelt, W. J. M. (1995). Monitoring the time course of phonological encoding. *Journal of Memory and Language, 34,* 311-334.

Wheeldon, L. R., & Morgan, J. L. (2002). Phoneme monitoring in internal and external speech. *Language and Cognitive Processes, 17,* 503-535.

16

The Production and Comprehension of Resumptive Pronouns in Relative Clause "Island" Contexts

Fernanda Ferreira and Benjamin Swets
Michigan State University, USA

Many investigators working on language processing are coming around to the idea that the field should adopt a more naturalistic and ecological approach to psycholinguistics (Pickering & Garrod, 2004; Trueswell & Tanenhaus, 2005). The trick is to hold on to the insights and rigorous methodology associated with the formal, representation-based psycholinguistic tradition while expanding the range of phenomena to include those found particularly in naturalistic speech and human conversation. For instance, people gesture while they talk, but there is little work on the way that linguistic representations are built and coordinated with the production of gestures (for an important exception, see Levelt, Richardson, & La Heij, 1985). Similarly, when people talk, they are often disfluent (Clark, 1996): They produce fillers such as *uh* and *um*, and they repeat words, backtrack, abandon utterances, start them over, and so on. In our recent work, we have begun to investigate how disfluencies affect the parser's structure-building operations (Bailey & Ferreira, 2003, 2005; Ferreira & Bailey, 2004). We have not only demonstrated that disfluencies have a systematic effect on parsing, but we have also shown that it is possible to study a phenomenon of the "wild" like disfluencies in a way that retains the assumption that formal linguistic structures are built during processing, and in real time.

How might this more ecological approach be applied to language production? One idea is to relax the assumption that people produce sentences that conform perfectly to the grammar of their language. Of course, we know that speakers of English will virtually never say some-

263

thing like *the cat black is asleep*, while speakers of Portuguese will say exactly the Portuguese equivalent of this, because of the fundamental word order constraints given by the grammars of the two languages. At the same time, we also know that people often produce utterances that contain "mistakes" such as subject-verb agreement errors. More interestingly, because of the demanding nature of conversation, people sometimes produce a certain sentence type that has a number of interesting properties. Here is an example, heard on the United States' National Public Radio on September 16, 2001:

(1) We're afraid of things that we don't know what they are.

[matrix clause*We're afraid of things*[relative clause *that we don't know*[complement clause*what they are*]]]

Sentences of this type occur reasonably often in conversation (Tony Kroch estimates that one may expect to hear one or two of them every day — personal communication). Thus, although people do not ignore strict grammatical rules such as those that describe sequencing within noun phrases, they do appear to relax other sorts of constraints, such as those that determine the kinds of long-distance dependencies that are legal (Bock & Miller, 1991).[1]

It could be very useful to study what takes place in the language production system when it creates utterances such as (1). One reason these structures are potentially illuminating is that they are ungrammatical or at least marginal in English, but they are nevertheless produced on a fairly frequent basis. What makes these sentences illicit is that they violate the subjacency constraint on wh-movement. The position in (1) occupied by the pronoun *they* is the original source for the wh-element that moves to form the relative clause, but the clause in which it is housed is an "island" (Ross, 1967), meaning that no subconstituent is supposed to leave it. This illicit movement of the wh-element leaves behind a gap (between *what* and *are*), resulting in *we're afraid of things that we don't know what <gap> are*. Typically, when utterances like this are said, the speaker plugs up the gap with what is termed a "resumptive pronoun", resulting in something that is clearly still marginal but much better than the version with just a gap. We will refer to sentences like (1)

---

[1]It is important to note that this structure is grammatical in some languages – for example, in Hebrew and Arabic (Prince, 1990). Thus, this constraint on long-distance dependencies is language specific.

as "islands plus resumptives", to capture their two key properties: They violate an island constraint, and they contain a resumptive pronoun.

Another reason that it might be productive to investigate the island + resumptive structure is that it is much more complex than the forms that are typically investigated in studies of language production. Almost all work up to now has been done on single clause sentences, but (1) contains three: the matrix clause (the entire sentence), the relative clause (*that we don't know what they are*), and the complement clause of *know* (*what they are*). It seems likely that considering structurally more complex forms might shed greater light on how grammatical encoding works; at the very least, more aspects of the grammatical encoder's mechanisms will be on display in a more demanding structure. But the island + resumptive form is not just quantitatively more challenging; it also has a property that allows us to address a critical issue in theories of language production, and that is incrementality. The question of incrementality concerns how much look-ahead the production system requires during utterance encoding (Levelt, 1989). Applying it specifically to the case of syntactic processing, we can ask whether the system plans several words in advance before passing the syntactic representation to the phonological encoder, or is it more of a cascading architecture, where a minimal syntactic unit such as a word is sent off for further processing? The reason the island + resumptive structure is potentially useful for examining this question is that the locus of the ultimate flaw in the sentence is several words downstream and buried in the lowest of the three clauses. A sentence such as (1) does not go wrong until *what*, as revealed by the perfect acceptability of *We're afraid of things that we don't know very much about*. Therefore, if the system is highly incremental, it should not "know" about the island and the gap/resumptive pronoun until it is essentially at that point in the sentence or one word before. Even a less incremental model which assumes that processing is essentially clause-based (Garrett, 1988; Bock & Cutting, 1992) would predict that any effects of the gap/resumptive pronoun would be seen fairly late during articulation—specifically, inside the complement (lowest) clause.

What we can do, then, is see whether speakers give off any clues to suggest that the system is aware of the funny property of island + resumptive structures before the most embedded clause. For example, are initiation times for such sentences longer than for comparable controls? Or is the duration of the first word or two longer? The results we report suggest that the answer to these questions is "yes". Moreover, if the durational properties of such marginal sentences are somewhat distinctive (and the results we report below indicate that they are), it could also turn out that the **perceiver** is sensitive to these cues and can use them to anticipate the marginal structure. At this stage of our research this idea is an untested hypothesis, but the studies that McQueen presents in this volume demonstrate that listeners are sensitive to subtle phonetic timing differences that distinguish lexical identities in short phrases (e.g., *dernier rognon* and *dernier oignon*). In future work we might be able to show that listeners can tell at the start of a sentence like (1) that it will turn out to include an island violation because of its signature durational properties.

Before turning to the details of our study to examine these issues, we should address the issue of incrementality in a bit more detail. Space limitations do not allow us to review here the entire literature relevant to this question (but see Ferreira, 2000; Griffin & Bock, 2000), but we can mention that at the moment the evidence is mixed. Some experiments seem to suggest that the system plans no more than one phrase at a time (for example, Smith & Wheeldon, 2001), but other work implies that there is a fair bit of look-ahead (such as Ford & Holmes, 1978). We describe in some detail one study that provided support for only limited incrementality, in part because the methodology that was used is similar to what we will present here (Ferreira & Swets, 2002). Participants were undergraduates at Michigan State University who were asked to answer arithmetic problems and who gave their answers in the form of an utterance (*The answer is fifty-eight*). The problems always included at least one two-digit addend (e.g., 53+5), so participants were highly unlikely to be able to simply retrieve the sum. The logic of the study was that if the production system is incremental, then the difficulty of the sum should show up while it is being articulated, but difficulty should not influence initiation times for the utterance as a whole. In one experiment, participants were allowed to begin to speak whenever they felt ready, and what we found was no evidence for incremental production: Only initiation times were affected by problem difficulty, not the duration of any part of the utterance. In a follow-up experiment, speakers were required to begin to speak quickly to avoid hearing the sound of a "beep". That sound was their punishment for waiting too long to begin talking. This manipulation reduced initiation times overall from over 2 seconds in the first experiment to about 700 ms in the one with the deadline. But even with this pressure to begin to speak quickly, initiation times still reflected the difficulty of computing the sum. But at the same time, the duration of the earlier part of the utterance was similarly affected, suggesting that speakers did plan the sum to some extent during articulation. Thus, this evidence suggests that the degree to which the system is incremental depends on the speaker's goals and strategies for managing the communicative situation; if a premium is placed on beginning to speak quickly, then the production system does indeed become more incremental, but if there is time to plan, speakers seem to prefer to do so. Note that this tradeoff does not affect the quality of the utterance: We were surprised to find that the accuracy of the sums was just as high when speakers were under time pressure as it was when they controlled when they began to speak. This finding suggests that there is a dimension to human information processing related to intensity of effort (Just & Carpenter, 1993), and clearly participants in experiments only want to work so hard; but this is a topic for another paper.

One limitation of this study is that most of the utterances we say in our day to day lives can be produced without the need for arithmetic computations. The task is not entirely unnatural, of course (consider a situation in which you're telling your dinner companion what his contribution to the bill is), but it is important to see if the same pattern holds with an entirely different kind of utterance. Moreover, as mentioned earlier, it would be useful to assess how incremental the system is when it produces not just simple one-clause sentences (which the arithmetic utterances were) but also multi-clausal utterances with some syntactic complexity. In addition, because the island + resumptive structure is multi-word and multi-clausal, speakers have the opportunity to revise it while they are talking. This mechanism is implicit in the idea of incrementality; speakers do not plan very far ahead, so if they find themselves in the middle of an utterance that looks like it will turn out odd or wrong, they use their knowledge of the grammar online to try to come up with something better. In the case of (1), the speaker could begin with *We're afraid of things that we don't* … and, realizing that an illicit structure is about to emerge, change the utterance to something like (2):

(2) We're afraid of things that we don't understand

The study we report here allowed us to investigate these major questions: First, how incremental is the production system? Second, and related to the first question, do speakers reformulate online as a consequence of making early syntactic commitments that will lead to ungrammaticality? Third, how does the production system balance its desire to encode the true, communicative intentions of the speaker with the requirements and constraints imposed by the grammar of the language? And finally, what is the relation between the production and comprehension of this structure?

ELICITING ISLAND PLUS RESUMPTIVE SENTENCES

Consider a situation in which someone sees a certain species of dog and describes it to another person in this way: *That's a dog that comes from California*. Then imagine she sees another breed of dog (perhaps the interlocutors are at a dog show) and she says (somewhat contrastively), *That's a dog that comes from Brazil*. Now imagine that a dog appears which the speaker is not familiar with. Because of the utterances she produced earlier (i.e., possibly because of structural priming; Bock, 1986; Pickering & Branigan, 1998), she might find herself saying *Geez, that's a dog that I don't know where it comes from*. This general scenario is the basic idea behind our paradigm. Speakers see pictures of people, animals, or cartoon figures, and the pictures are grouped so that three examples of the same category (e.g., three brides, three dogs, three muppets) appear together, in sequence. The first two instances have a descriptor; the last picture of the three is specified as lacking information. The pattern set in motion by the first two utterances is expected to lure our participants into producing the desired island + resumptive structure on the majority of trials. The initiation times for the utterances and the durations of the words that make them up can then be measured and compared to appropriate controls (to be described shortly).

Two experiments will be reported, as well as the results of two follow-up grammaticality judgment studies. In the first production experiment, speakers produced utterances as soon as they felt they were ready. Results showed that the earliest words were longer in the island + resumptive condition, suggesting that the production system uses a great deal of lookahead. In the second production experiment, speakers were given a deadline to respond. This change in procedure reduced response latencies and yielded evidence for more incremental production (because effects on word duration were found in a sentential location closer to the resumptive pronoun). The grammaticality judgment experiments show that comprehenders indeed find these sentences unacceptable. The implications of the experiments as a whole is that incrementality is a parameter of the production system that changes depending on speakers' goals. In addition, the production system appears to be unaware of grammatical constraints to which the comprehension system is quite clearly sensitive, suggesting a production—comprehension asymmetry.

Both experiments consisted of just two conditions: the island + resumptive condition and what we will term the surface-structure control. The same stimuli were used for both experiments. Two different stimulus lists were created; a given participant saw only one of those lists. In each list there were 48 arrays, and each array consisted of three pictures next to three short descriptions of the pictures. The description for the first picture of the trio was a short verb phrase such as *lives in California*. The description for the second was identical, except that the location was changed (e.g., *lives in Brazil*). For the third picture of the trio, the descriptor was either *I don't know* (for the island + resumptive condition) or *doesn't know* (for the surface-structure control condition).

Participants were told that on a computer monitor they would see three pictures next to three descriptors, and their task was to learn the pictures and brief descriptions one by one and then hit the space bar to begin each trial. After they studied the trio, they struck the space bar again, and the question "What is this?" replaced the first descriptor. Figure 16.1 shows this stage in an experimental trial. Participants were instructed to answer the question with a full-sentence response that included at least a noun, a verb, and the content of the descriptor. Although they were instructed to begin speaking as quickly as possible, it was emphasized that it was important to use good sentences that appropriately answered the questions. An example was provided (e.g., *This is a cat that likes fish*). An example of an inappropriate response given the question was also given: (*This cat likes fish*). After describing the first picture of the trio (e.g., *This is a donkey that lives in Brazil*), participants answered the same question for the next two pictures in each slide. After they described the third item from the trio, the trial ended.

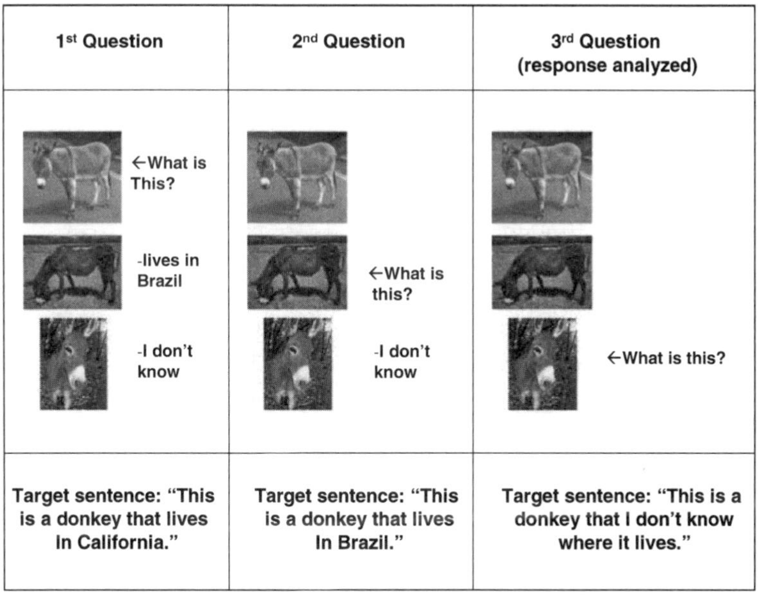

1st Question	2nd Question	3rd Question (response analyzed)
←What is This?		
-lives in Brazil	←What is this?	
-I don't know	-I don't know	←What is this?
Target sentence: "This is a donkey that lives In California."	Target sentence: "This is a donkey that lives In Brazil."	Target sentence: "This is a donkey that I don't know where it lives."

FIG. 16.1. Paradigm to Elicit Island + Resumptive Sentences.

The island + resumptive and the surface-structure control conditions were created as follows. The trials were identical except for the descriptor associated with the third picture of the trio. For the island + resumptive condition, it was the sequence *I don't know*, which entices the participant to say something like *This is a donkey that I don't know where it lives*. For the surface-structure control, the descriptor was *doesn't know*, and so the analogous utterance was expected to be *This is a donkey that doesn't know where it lives*. Notice that the utterances are almost the same except for the words between *that* and *know where it lives*, and even that material has the same number of syllables. This feature of the design means that the utterances to be compared are similar in most essential ways.

Each list consisted of 48 trios; half of those were experimental items, and so half of those (12) were in the island + resumptive condition and half (12) in the surface-structure control condition. The remaining 24 trios were filler trials.

For the first experiment, the data from 30 participants were analyzed, and for the second, 30 people's data were analyzed. Participants proceeded through the trials at their own pace. In the first experiment with no deadline, they were told to speak as soon as they were ready, but they were also encouraged to make sure their utterances were "good". In the second experiment, which employed a deadline procedure, participants were told that as soon as they struck the spacebar to describe the picture, three exclamation points would appear to the right of the screen. The exclamation points would begin disappearing rapidly until, after the third exclamation point disappeared, a "beep" sounded. At any point during the countdown, the participants' voice would terminate the countdown procedure until they had completed their utterance. The countdown was programmed to beep 1750 ms after the onset of the question "What is this?" We pilot-tested various times that were less than the mean initiation time in Experiment 2 (2216 ms) in order to arrive at a timing deadline that would make speakers feel rushed without adversely disrupting performance. As soon as the participant answered the first question, the experimenter pressed a button to start the deadline timer for the answer to the second question (about the second pictured item). The same countdown bars appeared to the right until the participant deactivated them by triggering a voicekey. After the same procedure took place for the third, target sentence description, the participant terminated the trial by pressing the space bar.

Participants' utterances were transcribed and then each one was coded into categories, including the two that were of specific interest (island + resumptive, surface-length control). To be included in the initiation time and durational analyses, target utterances of both types had to meet these criteria: First, the sentences had to begin with a deictic subject followed by *is* (*This is* …). Then a determiner/noun phrase had to follow, and then a complementizer or wh-phrase that initiated the relative clause (… *a donkey who/that* …).

Only utterances that described the third picture of the trio and that met the target criteria described above were included in waveform analyses. Initiation time was defined as the time between the second utterance for each array and the onset of the third and final utterance. Duration was defined as the total time taken to complete the utterance once it has been initiated. To investigate where in the utterances speakers slowed down, we analyzed utterance durations into subparts as follows:

(3) a. [This is a] [donkey] [that] [I don't know] [where it lives].
     b. [This is a] [donkey] [that] [doesn't know] [where it lives].

At the most simple-minded level, we predicted that if the system is incremental, then durations in the two conditions would not diverge until late in the last clause *where it lives*. In contrast, the more non-incremental the production system is, the earlier in the utterance the durations should differ. In addition, if speakers' subjective sense that they are under time pressure affects the extent to which the production system uses look-ahead, then we also predicted that durations would diverge later in the utterance in the deadline condition compared to the no-deadline condition.

In addition, the kinds of utterances that were produced in the two conditions and the two experiments were also examined. We were interested to see whether participants in the resumptive + island condition might find creative ways to prevent themselves from producing these marginal structures, particularly after the first couple of trials. We also speculated that participants would be more successful at reformulating when they were not under time pressure, because it likely takes time and effort to come up with an alternative structure.

Presentation of the findings will be organized as follows. First, we consider the initiation time and duration results for the no-deadline experiment, followed by those same results in the deadline experiment. We will compare performance in the island + resumptive and the surface-structure control conditions, but including only those trials on which the target sentence was actually produced (that is, (3a) in the island + resumptive condition, (3b) in the other). Also, trials were excluded if the initiation time was too short (< 100 ms), too long (> 15 seconds), or if the overall duration of the sentence was longer than 15 seconds. Second, we describe the kinds of utterances that were produced in the experimental conditions in each experiment. Finally, we compare the results for the two experiments, focusing especially on utterance types.

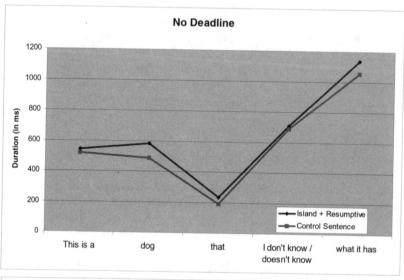

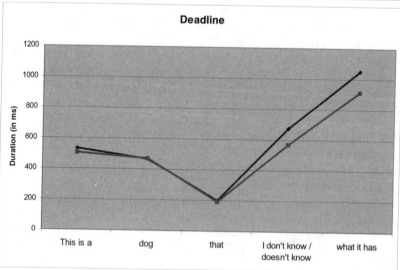

FIG. 16.2. Durations of Island + Resumptive Sentences and Surface-Structure Controls, in Regions.

In the no-deadline experiment, processing times were longer across the board when people produced the island + resumptive sentences compared to the surface-structure controls. Initiation times were 2328 and 2104 respectively. The means for utterance duration are shown in Figure 16.2. The part of the sentence where differences in duration reached conventional levels of statistical significance was at the head noun of the relative clause (i.e., immediately after *This is a*) and on the complementizer (e.g., *that*). In addition, the overall duration of the utterances was longer for the island + resumptive sentences, consistent with the idea that they are harder to produce than are the surface-structure controls.

Results for the second experiment, which required participants to respond before a deadline, are also shown in Figure 16.2. Clearly, the deadline caused people to begin to speak more quickly than they did in the first experiment: Overall initiation times dropped from over two seconds to less than one. As in the no-deadline experiment, those initiation times did not differ significantly between conditions (853 and 797 ms in the island + resumptive and surface-structure control conditions, respectively). Total utterance duration was longer for the island + resumptive sentences. There also were significant effects in the analyses in which the utterances were broken down into parts. In the island + resumptive condition, it took people longer to say *I don't know* than it took people in the surface-structure control condition to say *doesn't know* (674 versus 570 ms). Given that these two phrases have the same number of syllables and stress pattern, it is likely that the difference is due to the greater difficulty of producing the island + resumptive sentences. The duration of *what it has* was also longer for the island + resumptive sentences than the controls.

Comparing the findings across conditions and experiments, two points clearly emerge. One is that the island + resumptive sentences take more processing resources to produce than do the acceptable controls. But more interestingly, it also appears that the difficulty of producing these sentences shows up fairly early in their production, especially when the speaker is not under pressure to respond quickly. In the no-deadline experiment, latencies diverged right at the beginning of the relative clause containing the island, which is one clause before the part of the sentence that contains the resumptive pronoun. And even in the deadline experiment, durations were longer a little further into that relative clause (at the *I don't know* portion). At the same time, it also appears that speakers are more incremental in their production when there is a deadline to begin to speak, consistent with what we observed in our arithmetic study (Ferreira & Swets, 2002). The locus of the difference moved further out into the utterance, suggesting that the production system was using less look-ahead. These results overall suggest that the production system is only somewhat incremental, and the extent to which incrementality is observed depends on the speakers' strategies for managing the communicative situation (in this case, the relatively impoverished one associated with participating in psychological experiments).

Let us now turn to the types of utterances that speakers produced, beginning with the no-deadline experiment. In the island + resumptive condition that was designed to elicit island + resumptive sentences, about 67% of all utterances were of the desired type. This finding is actually quite striking considering that the form is not very acceptable (more on this point later). In the deadline experiment, the percentage of sentences of this type dropped to 56%. Surprisingly, then, people are **less** likely to produce this marginal structure when they are under time pressure, a finding which goes against the general belief that the island + resumptive structure is produced when people do not plan properly and so essentially paint themselves into a syntactic corner (Creswell, 2002). Consistent with this idea are the findings for alternative structures. These other forms can be viewed as ways that speakers avoided producing a marginal form like the island + resumptive. The strategies included coordination (e.g., *This is a donkey and I don't know where it lives*) and left-dislocation (e.g., *This donkey I don't know where it lives*). In the no-deadline experiment, these alternative, licit structures occurred on 18% of trials; but in the experiment in which people spoke under time pressure, alternatives were actually produced **more often**: 21% of the time. We conclude that the island + resumptive form is not a mistake; it is a structure that the production system intends to produce. Moreover, its generation clearly requires significant processing resources. Under time pressure, the grammatical encoder opts not to create this form, perhaps because it is a hard structure.

The unexpected finding that the island + resumptive structure is intentionally produced has two further interesting theoretical implications. One is that it seems to support a modular architecture for the production system. The argument goes like this: The reason the grammatical encoder ends up stuck with the job of producing a marginal form is that the message level does not know about grammatical constraints (especially language-specific ones) and so it gives the grammatical encoder a communicative intention that is not easily accommodated syntactically. The second implication is that the production system is somewhat egocentric, in the sense that it does not take into account the needs of the listener when it formulates utterances. For this point to be more convincing, we need to describe the results of our grammaticality judgment experiments. We turn to those next.

JUDGMENTS OF ACCEPTABILITY

We wanted to obtain clear-cut evidence that the island + resumptive structure is indeed fairly marginal. After all, it is possible that we obtained the results we did in the production experiments because in the sociolinguistic community to which our participants belong, the form is gaining acceptance. Accordingly, in one experiment, people were visually presented sentences like (3) (repeated below as (4)), and their task was to indicate on a scale from 1 (perfect) to 5 (awful) whether the sentences were acceptable in English.

(4) a. [This is a] [donkey] [that] [I don't know] [where it lives].
     b. [This is a] [donkey] [that] [doesn't know] [where it lives].

Consistent with the idea that the comprehension system does not like the island + resumptive structure, sentences such as (4a) were given average ratings of 3.3, and controls like (4b) were given average ratings of 1.9. But perhaps sentences like (4a) are from a spoken register; that is, they are not sentences that tend to occur in written English, so an auditory judgment task might yield more meaningful data. Accordingly, this experiment was re-run, but we used spoken materials with normal prosody. The values for (4a) and (4b) were 3.0 and 1.7 — essentially the same. (Both pairs of means are significantly different.)

Based on these findings, we have begun conducting experiments to examine in more detail the way island + resumptive sentences are comprehended, using eye movement monitoring and detailed follow-up questions to obtain information about how they are interpreted online and how they are ultimately understood. This work is currently in progress, but we expect it to provide results consistent with those of the grammaticality judgment studies: Participants find the sentences harder to understand than controls.

CONCLUSIONS

This research on the production and comprehension of the marginal island + resumptive structure reveals another important properties of both systems. First, it appears that the production system is only moderately incremental, and the amount of look-ahead that the system needs is determined in part by the speaker's strategy for managing the communicative situation. Second, the more marginal structure takes more processing resources to produce, but nevertheless it is a form the production system chooses; it is not the result of poor planning. This finding leads to our third conclusion, which is that the production system has a modular architecture, because the message level system does not consider grammatical constraints when it creates a message level representation for the grammatical encoder. Fourth, the language production system appears to be somewhat egocentric; it considers mainly its needs when it creates utterances, and it does not try to avoid producing a form that the comprehension system will dislike (as revealed by our grammaticality judgment data).

What are some of the more general implications? We have seen that the research strongly suggests non-parity between the production and comprehension systems (contrary to what Pickering & Garrod, 2004, advocate). The two systems do not consult the exact same database of grammatical rules, as indicated by the finding that the production system allows the island + resumptive structure to leak through, but the comprehension system tends to reject them. Assuming that the two systems are distinguishable, we can ask which one seems to have priority? Given that the production system seems to force the comprehension system to handle a structure the latter does not like, it can be argued that it is the production system that has priority. At the same time, clearly the two systems interact; if they did not, conversations would be impossible. Moreover, there are theoretical approaches to both domains which assume a certain amount of architectural integration: Models of language production use the comprehension system to filter out bad utterances (Levelt, 1989), and there are models of language comprehension which use analysis by synthesis (comprehension system tries to generate the input utterance) to accommodate semantic effects on parsing and other syntactic decisions (Townsend & Bever, 2001).

What all of this means is that although the production and comprehension systems can certainly be studied independently, real progress in understanding the architecture used for language processing will take place when we compare the two and determine the way they work together. This approach will allow us to learn more about humans' remarkable ability to communicate efficiently. And, of course, these investigations will inform us about the nature of the mind, which is the central question in cognitive science.

REFERENCES

Bailey, K. G. D., & Ferreira, F. (2003). Disfluencies influence syntactic parsing. *Journal of Memory and Language, 49*, 183-200.

Bailey, K. G. D., & Ferreira, F. (2005). The disfluent hairy dog: Can syntactic parsing be affected by non-word disfluencies? In J. Trueswell & M. K. Tanenhaus (Eds.), *Approaches to studying world-situated language use: Bridging the language-as-product and language-as-action traditions* (pp. 303-316). Cambridge, MA: MIT Press.

Bock, J. K. (1986). Syntactic persistence in language production. *Cognitive Psychology, 18*, 355-387.

Bock, K., & Miller, C. A. (1991). Broken agreement. *Cognitive Psychology, 23*, 45-93.

Bock, K., & Cutting, J. C. (1992). Regulating mental energy: Performance units in language production. *Journal of Memory and Language, 31*, 99-127.

Clark, H. H. (1996). *Using language*. Cambridge University Press.

Creswell, C. (2002). Resumptive pronouns, wh-island violations, and sentence production. *Proceedings of the Sixth International Workshop on Tree Adjoining Grammar and Related Frameworks (TAG+6)*, 101-109. Universita di Venezia.

Ferreira, F. (2000). Syntax in language production: An approach using tree-adjoining grammars. In L. Wheeldon (Ed.), *Aspects of language production* (pp. 291-330). Philadelphia, PA: Psychology Press.

Ferreira, F., & Bailey, K. G. D. (2004). Disfluencies and human language comprehension. *Trends in Cognitive Science, 8*, 231-237.

Ferreira, F., & Swets, B. (2002). How incremental is language production? Evidence from the production of utterances requiring the computation of arithmetic sums. *Journal of Memory and Language, 46*, 57-84.

Ford, M., & Holmes, V. M. (1978). Planning units in sentence production. *Cognition, 6*, 35-53.

Garrett, M. F. (1988). Processes in language production. In F. J. Newmeyer (Ed.), *Language: Psychological and biological aspects* (pp. 69-96). New York: Cambridge University Press.

Griffin, Z., & Bock, K. (2000). What the eyes say about speaking. *Psychological Science, 11*, 274-279.

Just, M. A., & Carpenter, P. A. (1993). The intensity of thought: Pupillometric indices of sentence processing. *Canadian Journal of Experimental Psychology, 47*, 310-339.

Levelt, W. J. M. (1989). *Speaking: From intention to articulation*. Cambridge, MA: MIT Press.

Levelt, W. J. M., Richardson, G., & La Heij, W. (1985). Pointing and voicing in deictic expressions. *Journal of Memory and Language, 24*, 133-164.

Pickering, M. J., & Branigan, H. P. (1998). The representation of verbs: Evidence from syntactic priming in language production. *Journal of Memory and Language, 39*, 633-651.

Pickering, M. J., & Garrod, S. (2004). Toward a mechanistic psychology of dialogue. *Behavioral and Brain Sciences, 27*, 169-190.

Prince, E. (1990). Syntax and discourse: A look at resumptive pronouns. *Proceedings of the Berkeley Linguistics Society, 16*, 482-497.

Ross, J. (1967). Constraints on variables in syntax. Unpublished doctoral dissertation, MIT.

Smith, M., & Wheeldon, L. (2001). Syntactic priming in spoken sentence production—an online study. *Cognition, 78*, 123-164.

Townsend, D. J., & Bever, T. G. (2001). *Sentence comprehension: The integration of habits and rules.* Cambridge, MA: MIT Press.

Trueswell, J., & Tanenhaus, M. K. (Eds.). (2005). *Approaches to studying world-situated language use: Bridging the language-as-product and language-as-action traditions.* Cambridge, MA: MIT Press.

17 On the Relationship Between Perception and Production in L2 Categories

Núria Sebastián-Gallés and Cristina Baus
Parc Científic de Barcelona-Hospital Sant Joan de Déu, Barcelona, Spain

One common assumption in the second language (L2) acquisition literature is that there must be a direct relationship between individuals' capacity to perceive and produce foreign sounds. The rationale underlying
this assumption is the following: It is difficult to see how a particular
sound could be properly produced if it is not properly perceived. Different theoretical backgrounds have been put forward to account for the
relationship between these two modalities. Some authors argue for a
common representation for both perception and production, usually of
an articulatory nature (See e.g., Pisoni, 1995; or Goldstein & Fowler, 2003),
while others assume separate representations, with complex links
mapping one onto the other (e.g., Flege, 1995, 2003, among others).

Although from a theoretical perspective there is a lot of agreement
concerning the relationship between perception and production, when
data from individual experiments are reviewed, the correlation between
them is not as robust as one might expect. Interestingly, not many studies
have directly compared perception and production in L2 category learning. One of the few studies that has is that of Flege, MacKay, and Meador
(1999). These authors studied the perception and production of English
vowels by Italian natives with different degrees of L2 proficiency. The
correct perception and production of ten English vowels and seven
Italian vowels was assessed. A correlation analysis was performed between correct perception and production scores. The correlation was sig-

nificant for non-natives (r = .64, p < .001), indicating that, as a group, L2 learners who accurately perceive foreign sounds are also better at producing them, whereas poor perceivers are frequently poor producers, as well. In that study, data about difficult L2 sounds were analyzed separately. In particular, the performance of English-natives and Good- and Poor-L2 native-Italian speakers were compared for the /ʌ/ vs. /æ/ and /ʌ/ vs. /ɒ/ contrasts. In this case, Good and Poor L2 producers did not show differences on the perceptual task. However, good producers performed better than poor producers on the /ʌ/ vs. /a/ contrast (/a/ being the Italian vowel to which Italian natives most likely assimilate English /ʌ/). Ceiling effects could not explain the lack of differences in the first two comparisons, since both native Italian groups performed significantly worse than Native English speakers.

In all theoretical accounts of the relationship between perception and production, the notion of "representation" or "category" of foreign sounds plays a central role. As mentioned above, some proposals assume the existence of a common representation both for perception and production, while others assume the existence of separate representations, distinct for each modality. However, sound categories have complex internal structures, with different types of knowledge, even within modality. It is common that language "units" are composed of multidimensional representations. For instance, let us consider the representation of words (as lexical labels) in the mental lexicon. In the well-known "tip of the tongue effect", speakers may not be able to retrieve the full segmental content of a string, but they can retrieve information about the first phoneme (Caramazza & Miozzo, 1997; Miozzo & Caramazza, 1997); this can be interpreted as indicating that the sound pattern of a particular word is composed of several stored representations. This same rationale can be applied to the way sound categories are represented: They must cover information about their acoustic/articulatory properties,[1] allophonic variation, frequency of occurrence, and so on.

It is not easy to observe the complex structure of the representation of sound categories in ordinary L1 speech processing. Natives, in general, show consistent degrees of performance across tasks; that is, across many different tasks they produce optimal scores (except when distorted or modified speech is used). In contrast, non-natives are usually highly sensitive to contextual effects or task properties, even in optimal perceptual

---

[1]No theoretical claim is made about the existence of unitary or separate representations for perception and production.

(and production) circumstances. For instance, Lively, Pisoni, Yamada, Tohkura, and Yamada (1994) studied the identification of English /ɹ/ and /l/ by Japanese monolinguals. This contrast is usually very difficult to perceive for these listeners (and indeed, the overall performance in that experiment was around 65% in a two-alternative choice). Still, when particular phonetic environments were inspected, important differences as a function of those environments were observed. When the /ɹ-l/ contrast appeared intervocalically (as in the minimal pair "belly-berry"), participants were at chance level (around 55%). However, when the contrast appeared in final word position (like in the minimal pair "peer-peel"), participants perceived the contrast quite well (the percentage of correct responses rose to above 80%). This context-dependent performance is not observed in natives. In the Flege et al. (1999) study just reviewed, English natives never performed below A' scores[2] of .90 for the different English contrasts; in particular, for the /ʊ-u/, /i-ɪ/ and /ʌ-ɒ/ contrasts the A' values were practically identical (above .95). However, for all Italian natives, independently of their competence level in English, there were significant differences in performance across the contrast pairs. This is most remarkable for the case of early and highly skilled native Italians. These participants obtained very high A' scores (all of them above .90) with the /ʊ-u/, /i-ɪ/ and /ʌ-ɒ/ contrasts. Together, these results indicate that natives have robust and highly structured representations of phonetic information that allow them to optimally process the speech signal in a wide variety of situations. On the contrary, non-natives may possess less robust knowledge, with less well-integrated representations that lead to context-dependent variation.

The aim of the present work is to add evidence regarding the coherence and systematicity of phonetic representations in natives, and the lack of robustness of these representations in non-natives. To achieve this goal, two groups of participants were compared across different perceptual (and one production) tasks. The bilinguals were highly experienced and skilled Catalan-Spanish bilinguals. One group used Catalan as their maternal language (Catalan natives) and the other group used Spanish as their L1 (Spanish-Catalan bilinguals). To our knowledge, this is the first time that L2 learners have been systematically compared across a variety of perceptual tasks.

---

[2]A' is a non-parametric version of the d' statistic.

Results from previous studies: Spanish-Catalan bilinguals

Previous research has shown that many highly skilled Spanish-Catalan bilinguals have problems perceiving some Catalan-specific contrasts. These bilinguals acquired only Spanish in the first years of their lives, but from the age of 3-4 years were continuously exposed to Catalan. They received a bilingual education and at the time of testing were using both languages in their ordinary lives. Spanish and Catalan are Romance languages with differences at the phonological level; Spanish has five vowels (/a/-/e/-/i/-/o/-/u/) and no vowel reduction, while Catalan has eight vowels and allows vowel reduction (/a/-/ɛ/-/e/-/i/-/u/-/o/-/ɔ/-/ə/). Interestingly, the Spanish mid-front vowel /e/ is produced with intermediate values to the two mid-front Catalan vowels. In a prototype rating study, Bosch, Costa, and Sebastián-Gallés (2000) obtained the following values for these three mid-front vowels: Spanish /e/ had values of F1 of 474 Hz and F2 of 2054; Catalan /e/ yielded values of 405 Hz and 2054 Hz for F1 and F2 respectively; and the Catalan /ɛ/ prototype corresponded to a vowel of F1 = 641 Hz and F2 = 1948 Hz. It has to be noted, though, that Spanish /e/ is closer to Catalan /e/ than to Catalan /ɛ/.[3] This particular distribution can be considered an instantiation of the "single category assimilation" (Best, 1995), which according to models of L2 acquisition should lead to perception and production difficulties (see also Flege, 1995).

Given that our purpose is to assess the performance of L2 listeners and speakers across different tasks, it was decided to choose tasks in which different types of phonetic-phonological representations would presumably be involved. Natives and non-natives were tested in the perception of the Catalan-specific vowel contrast /e-ɛ/ in three tasks: a categorical perception (categorization) task, a gating task, and a lexical decision task. Also, participants were tested in a production task (picture naming). In the following, the main results of our previous studies using these tasks are briefly reviewed.

Pallier, Bosch, and Sebastián (1997) presented Spanish-dominant (L1 Spanish) and Catalan-dominant (L1 Catalan) Spanish-Catalan bilinguals

---

[3]In fact, in an unpublished study we observed that some instances of Catalan /ɛ/ are identified as exemplars of the category /a/ and some exemplars of Catalan /e/ are identified as exemplars of the category /i/ by Spanish natives (Sebastián-Gallés & Bosch, 1999).

with a continuum of seven synthesized stimuli ranging from /e/ to /ɛ/. The results showed that Catalan-dominant participants clearly classified stimuli 1 to 3 as members of the category /e/ and stimuli 5 to 7 as members of the category /ɛ/ (stimulus 4 was ambiguous for this population). In contrast, Spanish-dominant bilinguals performed randomly: The average percentage of categorizations as a member of one of the two categories did not differ from chance for all seven stimuli. This result revealed that these bilinguals were unable to properly categorize the stimuli according to Catalan categories. However, it would be misleading to assume that all Spanish-dominant bilinguals performed at chance. In fact there were three different patterns. Some of the participants behaved like the Catalan-dominant listeners, others systematically inverted the categories and, finally, others were actually random in their responses. This variability in the pattern of responses was not observed in the Catalan-dominant group, where almost all participants correctly identified the stimuli.

Sebastián-Gallés and Soto-Faraco (1999) compared Catalan-dominant bilinguals to a subset of the Spanish-dominant bilinguals using a modification of the gating task. Importantly, in this study, only Spanish-dominant participants who did not differ from the Catalan-dominant group in their performance in the last gate were studied. That is, only Spanish-dominant participants who successfully perceived the contrast were included. The gating task was modified such that from the first gate, participants were presented with two alternatives from which they had to choose. The results showed that, as a group, even Spanish-dominant bilinguals who were able to select the correct alternative at the last gate were not as efficient as Catalan-dominant ones in the gating task. Indeed, they needed more gates (more information) to correctly pick the right alternative. Nonetheless, some Spanish-dominant bilinguals matched the performance of the Catalan-dominant group.

Sebastián-Gallés and Bosch (2003) and Sebastián-Gallés, Echeverría, and Bosch (submitted) asked participants to perform a lexical decision task in Catalan. In this study non-words were constructed by changing a single vowel of a real word. In the experimental stimuli, the change was the replacement of the vowel /e/ by the vowel /ɛ/, and vice-versa. In these stimuli, but not in the control stimuli, where the change involved a vowel replacement that corresponded to a categorical change in Spanish, Spanish-dominant bilinguals performed significantly worse than Catalan-dominant bilinguals. Indeed, only about 10% of the Spanish-dominant bilinguals performed within the range of the Catalan-dominant bilinguals for the experimental stimuli.

Although the performance of the Spanish-dominant bilinguals was not equivalent in all three tasks, it is worth mentioning that in all of the above revised studies there was a wide range of individual variation: Some participants performed indistinguishably from Catalan natives, while others were totally "deaf" to the contrast, with most of the individuals falling in between. In fact, in the categorical task, about one third of the participants performed like natives and another third produced a mirror-image pattern. As for the gating task, if only the performance in the final gate is considered, and all the participants—both selected and non-selected in the final sample—are analyzed, less than 20% of the Spanish-dominant bilinguals performed as Catalan natives. Finally, the lexical decision task was the most restrictive, since only about 10% of the participants performed like natives. But, would the same Spanish-dominant bilinguals who succeeded in one of the tasks succeed in the others? In the previous experiments, different participants were tested and it is impossible to assess whether there is any systematic pattern of responses of L2 learners. Thus, in the present research, the very same participants were tested across the three tasks just mentioned and compared with a group of Catalan-Spanish bilinguals (L1 Catalan).

Population under study

The population under study consisted of undergraduate students attending the University of Barcelona. All of them were born in Catalonia,[4] and most of them were born in Barcelona or its metropolitan area. Eighty participants were born in Spanish monolingual families, and up to the age of 3 to 4 years at the latest, their contact with Catalan was only occasional. Twenty participants, in contrast, had Catalan as the only family language. All of them had received a bilingual education and declared themselves to be highly fluent in both languages.

---

[4]There are important differences in the vowel system across different Catalan dialects. In order to avoid potential problems, participants were carefully screened so that bilinguals from dialects showing relevant discrepancies from the Barcelona dialect were not included in the study. Also, because some dialects of Spanish make the /e-ɛ/ contrast (in particular those from the eastern provinces of Andalusia), individuals with one or more parents from these provinces were not included in the sample.

Categorical perception (categorization task)

The same method, procedure and stimuli as those used in the Pallier et al. (1997) study were used here. Participants were presented with a continuum of seven synthesized stimuli ranging from the vowel /e/ to the vowel /ɛ/. They were asked to determine if stimuli sounded more like the first vowel of the Catalan word "Pere" (which was /e/, "Pere" meaning "Peter") or "pera" (which was /ɛ/, "pera" meaning "pear"). The average percentage of /e/ categorizations for stimuli 1 and 2 and for stimuli 6 and 7 were computed for each subject. The averages for the Spanish-dominant participants were 80.55% and 27.68%, while for the Catalan-dominant ones were 95.86 % and 5.55%, respectively. A categorization score was computed by subtracting both percentages. Scores closer to 100 reflected that participants had considered stimuli 1 and 2 as members of the /e/ category and stimuli 6 and 7 as members of the /ɛ/ category. Negative scores indicated that participants' responses showed a reverse pattern. Scores close to zero reflected that participants did not respond differentially to stimuli 1 and 2 than to stimuli 6 and 7. Individual categorization scores are plotted in Figure 17.1. No Catalan-dominant bilingual gave either random or reverse responses, while a significant percentage of the Spanish-dominant bilinguals did. However, most of these bilinguals performed similar to the Catalan-dominant group.

Even though no Catalan-dominant bilingual showed a reverse pattern in the present study, since some of them did in the study by Pallier et al. (1997), discrimination scores were transformed into their absolute values. To determine the pattern of performance of natives, categorization score means and standard deviations for the Catalan-dominant bilinguals were scored. A cut-off point of minus three standard deviations was calculated,[5] yielding a value of 60.59. Only one Catalan-dominant bilingual scored below this value (3.33%). Nineteen Spanish-dominant bilinguals scored (absolute value) below this cut point (31.67%), meaning that they had a rather flat response profile (only four Spanish-dominant bilinguals scored with a "correct" mirror pattern above 60.59, but with a negative value, 6.67%).

---

[5]This procedure has been used in the past to determine the "nativelike" performance of non-natives (see e.g., Munro, Flege, & MacKay, 1996, who, however, used two standard deviations rather than three as a cut-off point).

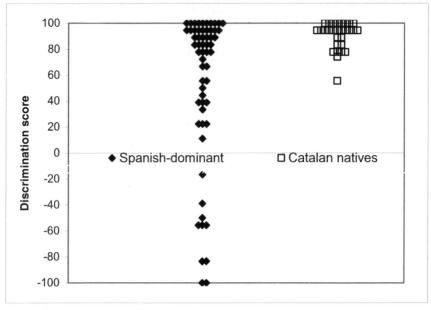

FIG. 17.1. Categorization task: Individual discrimination scores for each group of participants.

Gating task

The second task participants were tested with was the gating task. The method and procedure was exactly the same as in Sebastián-Gallés and Soto-Faraco (1999). However, in this case, stimuli were real Catalan words, instead of non-words. Four minimal-pair words with the Catalan-contrast /e-ɛ/ were selected. Each minimal pair was presented four times, and each member of the pair twice, leading to sixteen experimental trials. Participants were presented with successive gates of the target stimuli and, from the first presentation, they were given two alternatives that were visually displayed on the screen. The following table shows the percentage of each bilingual type as a function of the number of erroneous choices in the last gate.

TABLE 17.1.

Percentage of erroneous choices at the last gate								
	0%	6.25%	12.5%	18.75%	25%	31.25%	37.5%	43.75%	50% >
S L1	13.33	5	3.33	5	20	11.67	16.67	16.67	8.33
C L1	53.33	23.33	16.67	0	3.33	3.33	0	0	0

Almost all Catalan-dominant participants made two or fewer erroneous selections at the last gate, while slightly more than 20% of the Spanish-dominant participants responded within this range.

Again, the mean and standard deviation for the Catalan-dominant bilinguals were calculated and a cut-off point (three standard deviations above the mean) was calculated to establish the boundary of the native-Catalan population. In this case, the value was 4.6. Only one Catalan-dominant bilingual scored above this value (3.33%), while 32 Spanish-dominant bilinguals exceeded the criteria (53.33% of this population).

Lexical decision task

The same materials and procedure as those of Sebastián-Gallés and Bosch (2003) and Sebastián-Gallés et al. (submitted) were used. Participants were aurally presented with three stimuli types: (1) Catalan words containing the vowel /ɛ/, like /gəʎɛðə/ (meaning "bucket") and the corresponding non-word, made by changing the vowel /ɛ/ into /e/ ("ɛ-stimuli"); (2) Catalan words containing the vowel /e/, like /finestrə/ (meaning "window") and the corresponding non-word, made by changing the vowel /e/ into /ɛ/ ("e-stimuli"); and (3) control words, containing any vowel other than /e-ɛ/, such as /ʎənsɔl/ (meaning "bed sheet") and the corresponding non-word made by replacing the full (stressed) vowel by any vowel other than /e-ɛ/ (and not making any real Catalan word). Participants were asked to perform an auditory lexical decision task. They were specifically warned that the non-words were made by changing only one vowel and that in most of the cases the replacement would be an exchange of the vowel /e-ɛ/. Because there was a bias in the Spanish-dominant participants to consider e-stimuli and ɛ-stimuli non-words as real words, A' statistics were used. A' was thus considered an index of discrimination between words and non-words, and therefore an indication of the participants' ability to form a "correct" lexical representation according to Catalan phonology. As in the Sebastián-Gallés and Bosch (2003) and Sebastián-Gallés et al. (submitted) studies, Spanish-dominant bilinguals performed very well on the Control stimuli; the average A' was .94 (Catalan natives scored .97). However, for the e-stimuli and ɛ-stimuli, the performance of the Spanish-dominant bilinguals was clearly worse, though above chance; the average A' scores were .69 and .71, respectively. As in the previous tasks, the averages and standard deviations of the e-stimuli and ɛ-stimuli were computed, and a cut-off point of three standard deviations below the means was established. For the e-stimuli, the average was .929 and the standard deviation.055; for the ɛ-stimuli they were .902 and .054, respectively. As a

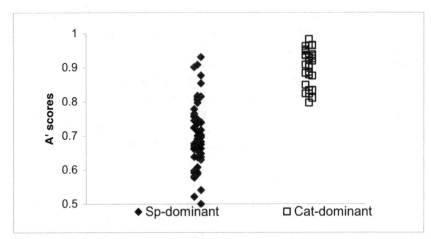

FIG. 17.2. Lexical decision task: Individual scores as a function of participants' group. Results for the e-closed stimuli.

result, the cutpoint for the e-stimuli was .766, and .739 for the ε-stimuli. No Catalan-native scored below these values, but only eleven Spanish-dominant bilinguals scored above both of these values, which meant that only 18.3% of them performed like Catalan natives. For both the e-stimuli and ε-stimuli, Spanish-dominant bilinguals ranged from random performance (A' of .5) to near perfect discrimination (A' of .96). Figure 17.2 shows the individual scores.

Comparison of tasks

As expected, Catalan natives performed optimally in all tasks (the participant who failed to pass the criteria at the categorization task was not the same as the one who failed in the gating task). The interesting results are those of the Spanish-dominant bilinguals, whose percentage of successful performance varied greatly across tasks.

The crucial analysis was the comparison of participants' performance across the three tasks. The following table shows the percentage of Spanish-dominant participants that successfully completed each task.

TABLE 17.2.

Categorization	Gating	Lexical Decision	% of participants
✗	✗	✗	23%
✓	✗	✗	27%
✓	✓	✗	28%
✓	✓	✓	12%

These four combinations included 90% of the Spanish-dominant participants; the remaining 10% was evenly distributed in the remaining combinations.

As the pooled results and the following table show, the three tasks were increasingly difficulty for Spanish-dominant participants to perform. In most of the cases, successful performance in the lexical decision task, also implied a successful performance in the other two tasks.

TABLE 17.3.

Percentage of Spanish-dominant bilinguals that scored within the range of Catalan-natives for each perception task		
Categorization	Gating	Lexical Decision
68.3%	46.6%	18.3%

Perception vs. Production

Participants were also asked to perform a picture naming task on sixty pictures. The names of some of the pictures included the vowels /e/ and /ɛ/. In a preliminary analysis, we compared a subset of Catalan-dominant participants (n = 10), a subset of those Spanish-dominant participants who did not pass the criteria for any of the three tasks (Bad Spanish-dominant producers, n = 10) and all of the participants who passed the criteria of the three tasks (Good Spanish-dominant producers, n = 7). Five naïve Catalan natives, without any training in Phonetics, scored on a two-point scale the correct pronunciation of each word. A score of zero meant a perfect Catalan pronunciation (native) and a score of 1 meant a Spanish accent. In this way, an overall pronunciation score was obtained. Scores ranged from 300 (all words being pronounced with a strong Spanish accent) to zero, perfect Catalan native pronunciation, for all stimuli. The average production score for the Catalan natives was 57 (ranging from 10 to 94). For the good Spanish-dominant perceivers, the pronunciation score was 64 (ranging from 10 to 123). Finally, for the bad Spanish-dominant perceivers, the average pronunciation score was 139 (ranging from 94 to 186).

Although the sample is too small to perform reliable correlations and to draw definitive conclusions, it seems that when very restrictive criteria for perception tasks are applied, a clear relationship between perception and production can be established. However, it has to be acknowledged that these are just initial results, and that to more precise analyses comparing individuals' performance in each task will be required to fully achieve the goals of the present research.

CONCLUSION

A great deal of research has been devoted to analyzing the perception and production abilities of second language learners. This chapter presented preliminary evidence for an approach that compares individuals' performance across different tasks as an attempt to better understand what it means to acquire a new L2 category.

A group of L1 Catalan, Catalan-Spanish bilinguals and another group of L1 Spanish, Spanish-Catalan bilinguals were tested in three perceptual tasks and in a production task. The three perceptual tasks were selected so as to cover a wide spectrum of phono-lexical representations: A categorization task with isolated and synthesized stimuli, a gating task, and a lexical decision task. The results showed that participants' success in each task varied greatly. The categorization task was the easiest one, probably because stimuli were presented in isolation, without any coarticulation or masking from surrounding sounds, so that participants could rely on their acoustic information to perform the task. However, note that slightly more than 30% of the Spanish-dominant participants failed to pass this task.

The gating task showed an intermediate level of difficulty. In this case, stimuli were words that, by virtue of being naturally produced were also coarticulated. The very nature of the gating task, in which the speech signal is presented in fragments, can, at least in some gates, eliminate some of the potential coarticulation and backwards masking (induced by the following phonemes) and thus facilitate the task. Recall that the Japanese natives tested by Lively et al. (1994) performed quite well in perceiving the /ɹ-l/ contrast when it appeared in word-final position. It could be argued that the gating task transformed some of the crucial phonemes into "final position" phonemes. Another factor that may have facilitated performance was that before every trial, the two alternatives participants had to choose from were presented auditorily. Thus, although by the time of the identification point participants had already listened to at least 2 to 3 gates, they might still have had some residual memory traces to rely upon when performing the task.

Such information was not available in the lexical decision task. In that task, not only were stimuli naturally produced and thus, highly coarticulated, but participants could only rely on their long-term memory store (the mental lexicon) to correctly perform the task. This proved to be the most difficult task for the Spanish-dominant bilinguals. Most participants who had been able to correctly perform the categorization and gating tasks could not reach the same performance level that Catalan-natives did for the lexical decision task.

The production task was, as far as the preliminary data can show, also very demanding. Contrary to other production studies, in which the target stimuli are aurally presented in advance (see e.g., Flege et al., 1999), participants in our study were given no previous information as to how to pronounce the pictures' names. The data we have presented only refer to the most extreme cases of our population: those L2 learners who fail in all perceptual tasks, and those who succeed in all of them. These data, although interesting, just confirm the correlation between perception and production observed in other studies (such as Flege et al., 1999). New analyses comparing the performance in each task, and also exploring the performance of L2 learners who partially succeed in the perceptual tasks, are currently under way.

The relationship between perception and production is a complex one. If we are to better understand it, more precise definitions of concepts such as "acquiring a new L2 category" are needed. The research presented here is intended as a step in this direction.

ACKNOWLEDGMENTS

This research was supported by the McDonnell Foundation (JSMF20002079 MBM-Research Grant), the Human Frontier Science Program (RGP 68/2002), and the Spanish Ministerio de Ciencia y Tecnología (BSO2001-3492-C04-01). The authors thank Begoña Díaz and Xavier Mayoral for their help testing subjects and technical support. The authors also thank Albert Costa and Bratt Mahon for their helpful comments on earlier versions of this chapter.

REFERENCES

Best, C. T. (1995). A direct realist view of cross-language speech perception. In W. Strange (Ed.), *Speech perception and linguistic experience* (pp. 171-206). Baltimore, MD: York Press.

Bosch, L., Costa, A., & Sebastián-Gallés, N. (2000). First and second language vowel perception in early bilinguals. *European Journal of Cognitive Psychology, 12*, 189-222.

Caramazza, A., & Miozzo, M. (1997). The relationship between syntactic and phonological knowledge in lexical access: Evidence from the "tip-of-the-tongue" phenomenon. *Cognition, 64*, 309-343.

Flege, J. E. (1995). Second language speech learning: Theory, findings and problems. In W. Strange (Ed.), *Speech perception and linguistic experience* (pp. 233-272). Baltimore, MD: York Press.

Flege, J. E. (2003). Assessing constraints on second-language segmental production and perception. In N. Schiller & A. Meyer (Eds.), *Phonetics and phonology in language comprehension and production. Differences and similarities.* (Vol. 6, pp. 319-355). Berlin: Mouton de Gruyter.

Flege, J. E., MacKay, I. R. A., & Meador, D. (1999). Native Italian speakers' production and perception of English vowels. *Journal of the Acoustic Society of America, 106,* 2973-2987.

Goldstein, L., & Fowler, C. A. (2003). Articulatory phonology: A phonology for public language use. In N. O. Schiller & A. S. Meyer (Eds.), *Phonetics and phonology in language comprehension and production. Differences and similarities* (Vol. 6, pp. 159-207). Berlin: Mouton de Gruyter.

Lively, S. E., Pisoni, D. B., Yamada, R. A., Tohkura, Y., & Yamada, T. (1994). Training Japanese listeners to identify English /r/ and /l/ III. Long-term retention of new phonetic categories. *Journal of the Acoustic Society of America, 96,* 2076-2087.

Miozzo, M., & Caramazza, A. (1997). The retrieval of lexical-syntactic features in tip-of-the-tongue states. *Journal of Experimental Psychology: Learning, Memory and Cognition, 23,* 1410-1423.

Munro, M. J., Flege, J. E., & MacKay, I. R. A. (1996). The effects of age of second language learning on the production of English vowels. *Applied Psycholinguistics, 17,* 313-334.

Pallier, C., Bosch, L., & Sebastián, N. (1997). A limit on behavioral plasticity in vowel acquisition. *Cognition, 64,* B9-B17.

Pisoni, D. (1995). *Some thoughts on "normalization" in speech perception* (Research on Spoken Language Processing, Progress Report 20): Department of Psychology, Indiana University.

Sebastián-Gallés, N., & Bosch, L. (1999). *Estudios sobre los espacios vocálicos en bilingües catalán-español: Las fronteras entre categorías.* Paper presented at the IV Simposio de Psicolingüística, Madrid, Spain.

Sebastián-Gallés, N., & Bosch, L. (2003). *The representation of native and non-native lexical items in early bilinguals.* Paper presented at the 15th International Congress of Phonetic Sciences, Barcelona, Spain.

Sebastián-Gallés, N., Echeverría, S., & Bosch, L. (submitted). The influence of initial exposure in the representation of lexical items: Comparative data of early and simultaneous bilinguals. Manuscript submitted for publication.

Sebastián-Gallés, N., & Soto-Faraco, S. (1999). On-line processing of native and non-native phonemic contrasts in early bilinguals. *Cognition, 72,* 112-123.

18

Signing for Viewing: Some Relations between the Production and Comprehension of Sign Language

Karen Emmorey
The Salk Institute for Biological Studies, USA

In 1987, Anne Cutler wrote a chapter titled "Speaking for Listening" in which she discussed how speakers accommodate their output to suit their listeners' needs at all levels of the speech production process. In this chapter, we explore similar issues with respect to sign language. In this case, the interplay between language producers and language perceivers involves visual, rather than auditory perception, and manual, rather than vocal production. Our exploration focuses primarily on the level of form—how visual perception and manual production interact at the level of phonology. Speculations regarding the development of visual-motor integration for sign language, implications of the direct perception of the sign articulators, and some unique problems that sign language raises for the perceptual loop hypothesis of language monitoring are presented. Some of this discussion must of necessity be speculative because, unlike the army of psycholinguists studying spoken language processing, there are only a handful of sign language psycholinguists, and sign languages were only recognized as full-fledged human languages around the 1960s. Much research remains to be done, and understanding the nature of sign language production and perception (and the interplay between the two) will enhance our understanding of the nature of linguistic systems and how they are processed by the human brain.

THE SIGNER AS AN EMBODIED MIRROR NEURON: COUPLING VISUAL PERCEPTION AND MANUAL ARTICULATION

Recently, primate studies have identified "mirror" neurons within area F5 (inferior ventral premotor cortex) that respond both when a monkey manipulates an object and when the monkey observes another individual grasping or manipulating the object (e.g., Rizzolatti et al., 1996). Like mirror neurons, signers must associate an observed manual movement with a self-generated movement of the same form. Sign language comprehension and production requires a direct coupling between action observation and action execution. However, unlike mirror neurons recorded in monkey, signing is not tied to object manipulation. Mirror neurons fire only when an object is present or understood to be present and do not fire when just the grasping movement is presented (Gallese, Fadiga, Fogassi, & Rizzolatti, 1996). Furthermore, unlike grasping and reaching movements, sign articulations are structured within a phonological system of contrasts. The hand configuration for a sign is determined by a phonological specification stored in the lexicon, not by the properties of an object to be grasped. The existence of a stored representation of an action might alter the nature of mirror neurons, if they exist in the human brain. That is, rather than being object-oriented, human mirror neurons might code for action representations that are retrieved (or constructed) during language production and that are perceived as the same action produced by another individual.

Crucially, however, mirror neurons do not *explain* how language production and perception are linked (Goldstein & Fowler, 2003). It is not at all clear how a mirror neuron "recognizes" the correspondence between a visually-observed action and a self-executed action of the same form. In fact, understanding how signer-viewers (or speaker-listeners) map production to perception and vice versa may have implications for understanding how mirror neurons come to achieve their function. For example, the potential role of mirror neurons for language is clear: to make communication between individuals possible by establishing parity between self-produced forms and perceived forms. However, the role of mirror neurons in the context of behavior for non-human primates is currently unclear, particularly given that imitation is not a frequently observed behavior in the wild (Tomasello, Savage-Rumbaugh, & Kruger, 1993). Understanding how parity of linguistic form emerges during development might provide some insight into the possible function(s) of mirror neurons in non-human primates. For example, if early linguistic parity of form emerges in the absence of referential meaning, it would suggest that recognizing purpose or meaning in an observed action is not a necessary function of mirror neurons in non-human primates.

Visual-motor integration is a critical step in establishing relationships between visually perceived manual actions and self-produced actions. The development of visual-motor coupling appears to be under way soon after birth in humans. For example, the spontaneous arm-waving of newborns is not random. Van der Meer, van der Weel, and Lee (1995) showed that neonates move an arm that they can see much more than they move their unseen arm. Furthermore, neonates actively resist a force in order to keep their arm in view, and such resistance is not observed when the force is applied to the arm they can't see. Interestingly, the same result is found when neonates view their arm on a video-monitor, suggesting that there is a very early link between self-produced arm movements and identical distally perceived movements. Early visual-motor coupling allows infants to establish a frame of reference for visually guided action, which they will need for successful reaching at age four to five months. For infants exposed to sign language, establishing a relationship between hand/arm movements and visually perceived articulations is critical for establishing early linguistic parity between perception and production. In addition, these infants must also establish parity between their own hand/arm movements and the visually perceived movements observed in the ambient sign language.

Babies exposed to sign language produce manual babbling that is parallel to vocal babbling produced by hearing children exposed to speech (Petitto & Marentette, 1991; Petitto, Holowka, Sergio, Levy, & Ostry, 2004). Canonical manual babbling, like canonical vocal babbling, occurs between seven and ten months, is produced without referential meaning, and has a repeated cyclic structure. Manual babbling is also linked to first signs, indicating that babbling is an important linguistic stage, not just the product of stereotypic motor actions. For example, the most frequent locations and handshapes observed in a baby's babbling are also observed most frequently in that baby's first signs. Handshapes and locations favored during babbling also participate most often in sub-stitution errors found in early sign production (Cheek, Cormier, Repp, & Meier, 2001). Babbling may reflect the maturation of a mechanism that maps patterned perceptual input (either auditory or visual) to related motoric output (either vocal or manual). The development of this per-ceptual-motor connection allows human infants to discover the units that serve to express linguistic meaning, whether encoded in speech or in sign.

An interesting difference between the development of vocal and manual babbling is that auditory feedback is automatic for vocal babbling: hearing babies hear their own sounds. Although deaf babies sometimes produce vocal babbling, these vocalizations are produced relatively late with a low rate of cyclicity (Oller & Eilers, 1988). Lack of auditory feedback affects deaf infants' ability to produce reduplicated syllable-like babbling. In contrast, hearing babies who are exposed only to speech also produce a type of manual babbling, but with less cyclicity than sign-exposed babies (Meier & Willerman, 1995). Unlike deaf children producing vocal babbling, hearing children receive visual feedback from their own gestures and see nonlinguistic gestures produced by adults around them. However, visual feedback for manual babbling is not automatic. The baby must be looking at his or her hands. It is currently unknown whether sign-exposed babies look more at their hands during manual babbling. Visual feedback might be important in developing parity between linguistic units in perception and production, a critical achievement for sign-exposed infants. However, manual-gaze during babbling, if it exists, is likely to be short-lived because neither children nor adults track their hands while signing. Almost all visual feedback from one's own signing occurs in peripheral vision (see the section "Sign monitoring and the perceptual loop hypothesis").

The coupling between perception and production for sign language is parallel to that required for nonlinguistic motor actions. Both types of articulatory gestures are perceived directly by the visual system, and a line of sight is required for perception. In contrast, for spoken language, articulatory gestures are recovered primarily from an acoustic signal, and the vocal articulators are largely hidden from view. Although visual information is important (e.g., the McGurk effect), it is not essential (we can understand radio broadcasts). We next explore some of the ramifications of the direct perception of visual articulation for sign, and conversely, the consequences of the indirect perception of the speech articulators.

SOME IMPLICATIONS OF THE DIRECT PERCEPTION OF SIGN ARTICULATIONS

Just as speakers alter their speech according to the needs of their listener, signers alter their signing according to the needs of their viewer, and there are similar trade-offs between ease of perception and ease of articulation. For example, proximalization of movement is articulatorily more effortful, but visually more salient (Brentari, 1998). Proximalization of movement occurs when joints closer to the torso are moved during articulation, and it is often observed during "shouted sign" or when signing to a large audience. To illustrate, the citation form of the ASL sign

GIVE involves outward movement of the wrist and elbow; the perceptually enhanced form of this sign adds movement from the shoulder. In contrast, distilization of movement involves only joints distal to the torso and is articulatorily easy, but less salient perceptually. For example, the perceptually reduced form of GIVE involves articulation of the wrist only, with no movement of the elbow or shoulder. Distilization of movement often occurs during "quiet" or casual signing. These trade-offs suggest that specific joints may not be specified in the articulation of signs and that some abstract movement categories might be perceptually-based (Crasborn, 2001).

However, given the direct perception of the sign articulators, there might be no need for a distinction between the perceptual and articulatory features of signs. That is, perceptual targets may not exist. Only articulatory targets may be relevant. For speech, many sounds can be made in more than one way. For example, the same vowel can be produced with different jaw positions, and a change in pitch can be produced either by extra respiratory effort or by altering the tension of the vocal cords (Ladefoged, 2000). What is critical is the perceptual target, not the specific articulatory means of achieving it. Crasborn (2001) argues that, despite the direct perception of the sign articulators, perceptual targets exist for sign as well.

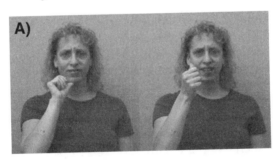

FIG. 18.1. Illustration of the ASL sign NOT produced (A) normally and (B) with distal articulation (perceptually reduced).

The argument is based on whispering data from Sign Language of the Netherlands, but examples can be found in American Sign Language as well. Specifically, when some signs are whispered, a change in location (path movement) is realized as a change in orientation. Figure 18.1 provides an example from ASL in which the citation form of the sign NOT is produced with outward movement from the chin, whereas the whispered form is produced with a change in hand orientation and no path movement. Crasborn (2001) argues that *change in location* and *change in orientation* are abstract perceptual categories that can be articulated either by proximal or distal joints. That is, there is an abstract perceptual target that does not refer to the articulatory means employed to make it visible. Thus, despite directly observable articulations, perceptual factors nonetheless may characterize aspects of phonological form.

In summary, languages universally exhibit an interplay between perception and production. For sign language, visibility can affect the form of articulation. Perceptually enhanced or reduced forms are produced depending in part upon the distance between the viewer(s) and signer. Lexical choice is also affected by visibility functions. For example, two-handed variants are more likely to be produced when visibility is decreased by distance or obstacles, whereas one-handed fingerspelled words are often substituted for lexical signs during whispered signing.[1] For both sign and speech, there is a trade-off between ease of articulation and ease of perception. In this sense, sign articulations are not like other types of manual activities, such as reaching or grasping that have no perceptual representation or component. There is no "grasping for viewing." It would be interesting to discover whether the gestures that accompany speech are similarly affected by visibility. For example, does shouting or whispering affect the form of manual gesticulation? Do speakers talking to a large crowd perceptually enhance their gestures, even when using a microphone? Since spontaneous gestures are not conventionalized (McNeill, 1992), there is no mentally represented perceptual target, and addressees have no gestural mental representations that are shared with speakers. An examination of the similarities and differences between the production of sign language and gestures that accompany speech may provide clues to the type of perceptual targets that exist and whether they are necessarily tied to phonological representations.

Finally, just as the hearing speakers become auditorily tuned to perceive the sound contrasts of their native language, ASL signers appear to

---

[1]Fingerspelled words consist of a sequence of handshapes that represent the letters of an English word.

be visually-tuned to perceive manual contrasts in American Sign Language. Emmorey, McCullough, and Brentari (2003) found evidence of categorical perception for phonologically distinctive hand configurations in ASL. Categorical perception (CP) refers to the finding that stimuli are perceived categorically rather than continually, despite continuous variation in form. Evidence for categorical perception is found when perceivers partition continuous stimuli into relatively discrete categories and when discrimination performance is better across a category boundary than within a category. In our experiments, we presented native deaf signers and hearing nonsigners with computer generated images of signs that varied continuously with respect to either hand configuration or place of articulation (see Figure 18.2). Subjects performed an "ABX" discrimination task in which they saw two images from a continuum and decided whether the third image was most similar to the first or second image. They also performed an identification task in which each image was categorized with respect to the endpoints of the continuum.

Deaf signers and hearing nonsigners demonstrated similar category boundaries for both hand configuration and place of articulation. This result is consistent with previous studies that found deaf and hearing

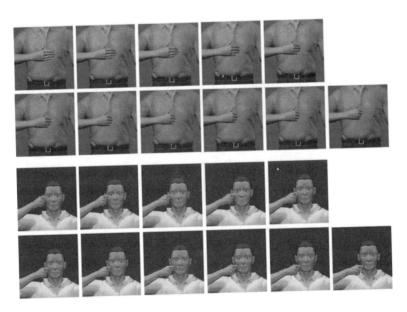

FIG. 18.2. Illustration of an ASL hand configuration continuum from a B hand configuration to an A hand configuration (top) and an ASL place of articulation continuum from the upper cheek to the lower chin (bottom).

subjects exhibit similar perceptual groupings and confusability patterns for hand configuration and for place of articulation (Lane, Boyes-Braem, & Bellugi, 1976; Poizner & Lane, 1978). Thus, these ASL categories may have a perceptual as well as a linguistic basis. However, only deaf signers exhibited evidence of categorical perception, and only for phonemic hand configurations. Only deaf signers were sensitive to category boundaries in the discrimination task, performing significantly better across category boundaries than within a hand configuration category.

Neither group exhibited categorical perception for place of articulation. Lack of a CP effect for place of articulation may be due to more variable category boundaries. In speech, CP effects are modulated by the nature of the articulation of speech sounds. For example, CP effects are often weak or not present for vowels, perhaps because of the more continuous nature of their articulation compared to stop consonants (Fry, Abramson, Eimas, & Liberman, 1962). The same may be true for place of articulation in sign language. For example, the location of signs can be displaced within a major body region in casual signing (Brentari, 1998) or completely displaced to the side during whispering. Category boundaries for place of articulation appear to be much less stable than for hand configuration. Categorical perception may only occur when articulations are relatively discrete for both sign and speech.

The fact that only deaf signers exhibited categorical perception for ASL hand configurations indicates that linguistic experience is what drives these effects. However, categorical perception effects are weaker for sign than for speech. Deaf signers' discrimination ability within hand configuration categories was better than the near-chance discrimination ability reported within stop consonant categories for speech (e.g., Liberman, Harris, Hoffman, & Griffith, 1957). However, the sign language results resemble discrimination functions observed for CP in other visual domains, such as faces or facial expressions (e.g., Beale & Keil, 1995; de Gelder, Teunisse, & Benson, 1997). Discrimination accuracy within visual categories tends to be relatively high; generally participants perform with about 70% to 85% mean accuracy rates within categories. The difference in categorical perception effects between speech and sign may arise from psychophysical differences between audition and vision.

In sum, deaf signers appear to develop special abilities for perceiving aspects of sign language that are similar to the abilities that speakers develop for perceiving speech. The fact that only deaf signers exhibited a categorical perception effect for hand configuration indicates that this effect arises from linguistic experience. These findings suggest that categorical perception emerges naturally as part of language processing, regardless of language modality. Thus, despite direct perception of the sign articulators, perceptually-based categories and features appear to exist within sign phonology. However, further research is needed to discover how variations in joint articulation or in place of articulation are understood as instances of the same sign form. Studies of sign language processing may turn out to inform theories of high-level vision that deal with similar issues (e.g., how is a jointed object recognized as "the same" from different angles or with different joint positions?).

SIGN MONITORING AND THE PERCEPTUAL LOOP HYPOTHESIS

Figure 18.3 presents the model of speech production proposed by Levelt, Roelofs, and Meyer (1999). It is unknown to what extent this model applies to signed languages. For example, although there is some evidence for the existence of syllables in signed languages (see Brentari, 1998), there is little evidence for syllabification processes, syllable internal structure (onsets, rhymes), or the existence of a syllabary. And of course, sign articulation does not result in a sound wave, and this raises the interesting question of self-monitoring by signers. For speakers, Levelt et al. (1999) propose an internal loop for prearticulatory monitoring of speech production and an external loop in which the sound wave resulting from articulated speech is processed by the speaker's normal speech comprehension mechanism. However, signers do not look at their own hands and cannot see their own faces (linguistic facial expressions are critical for both lexical and syntactic processing). Thus, the visual input they receive from their own sign output is quite distinct from the visual signal that the sign comprehension mechanism receives when processing the signing of another person.

Nonetheless, signers do indeed monitor their signed output and interrupt themselves when an error is detected, often producing an editing expression along with a repair. When an error is detected signers produce manual editing expressions such as WRONG or NO and also nonmanual expressions (e.g., a head shake) that are sometimes produced while the manual sign error is held in space (Emmorey, 2002). The ability to produce an editing expression while simultaneously articulating the error may be a modality unique aspect of monitoring and repair for signed languages. However, the exact timing properties of nonmanual editing expressions remains to be investigated.

The locus of repairs in sign language has recently been studied by Hohenberger, Happ, and Leuninger (2002). Hohenberger et al. (2002) found that sign errors were repaired much faster than speech errors. The locus of repairs for speakers is most often after the word (Levelt, 1983), but for

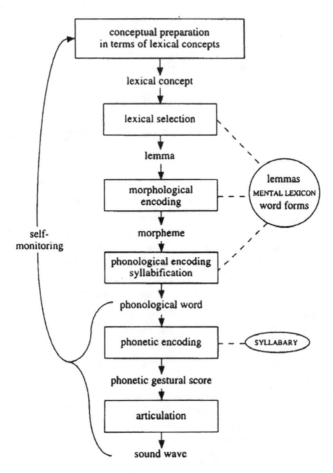

FIG. 18.3. The language production model proposed by Levelt, Roelofs, and Meyer (1999). Reproduced with permission from Cambridge University Press.

signers, errors were most often detected somewhere within the sign, that is, before the signer has finished articulating the sign containing the error. In fact, a small proportion of sign repairs (7%) occurred before the sign was articulated. For example, during transitional movement, a hand-shape error might be produced and repaired before articulation of the target sign began. Such early repairs might occur for spoken language but they may not create enough acoustic change to be audible. Manual articulators are larger and slower than the vocal articulators (the tongue, velum, vocal chords), and signs are roughly twice as long as words, on average (Bellugi & Fischer, 1972). Hohenberger et al. (2002) hypothesized that the longer articulation time for signs allows for earlier detection of sign errors compared to speech errors. Early repair of errors also can account for the relative rarity of whole sign exchange errors, such as "LIKE, MAYBE TASTE" for "TASTE, MAYBE LIKE" ("Taste it, maybe you'll like it"; Klima & Bellugi, 1979). If errors are detected early for sign languages, then the second exchanged sign may never be produced.

Data from sign errors, editing expressions, and repairs provide evidence for the external monitoring of sign output. Studies of sign-based working memory provide some evidence for an internal monitoring loop. Signers exhibit poorer memory for ASL signs when asked to simultaneously produce manual movements during encoding (articulatory suppression), providing evidence for a manual motoric encoding of ASL signs (Wilson & Emmorey, 1997). In addition, signers exhibit a sign-length effect, with poorer memory for lists of long signs than lists of short signs, and this effect disappears with articulatory suppression (Wilson & Emmorey, 1998). This pattern of effects indicates that working memory for sign language involves a "submanual" articulatory rehearsal mechanism. The existence of such an articulatory loop within sign-based working memory invites the possibility of a similar prearticulatory monitoring loop during sign production. However, whether prearticulatory monitoring in sign language involves a phonological or phonetic level of encoding is unknown.

With respect to the perceptual loop hypothesis and external sign monitoring, an important question is whether signers *visually* monitor their own output. Speakers parse the acoustic signal of their own incoming speech and that of others. Is there any evidence that signers visually parse their own output? First, it is clear that signers do not look at their hands while signing, and they also do not track the hands of their interlocutor. During sign perception, addressees primarily fixate on the signer's face and rarely look at the signer's hands (Siple, 1978). During sign production, the default location of gaze is at the addressee, but signers change their eye gaze to convey several different types of information. We have recently found that signers shift their eye gaze toward locations in signing space in order to mark verbal arguments (Thompson, Emmorey, & Kluender, 2004). A change in eye gaze by a signer is also used as a discourse perspective marker and can serve social regulatory functions such as maintaining the floor. Suffice it to say that during sign production, unlike sign perception, eye gaze is not static and serves many linguistic functions. It would appear that visual feedback during sign production is peripheral in both a figurative and literal sense.

Some tentative evidence for visual monitoring of sign output comes from signers with Usher's syndrome, a form of *retinitis pigmentosa* involving loss of peripheral vision. Individuals with Usher's syndrome are generally born deaf and begin to lose their peripheral vision in their late 20's or early 30's. They develop tunnel vision that gradually narrows until they become completely blind. It has been anecdotally reported that signers with Usher's syndrome have a smaller signing space; that is, they sign in a more constrained space. An example is shown in Figure 18.4a (from a commercially available videotape). The signer with Usher's syndrome produces the sign INTRODUCE high in signing space, close to his face. The sign is normally produced near the waist, as shown in Figure 18.4b. If visual monitoring is important to sign production, this would explain why signers with Usher's syndrome have such a constrained signing space—they need to visually perceive their own output. It has also been observed (again anecdotally) that when signers with Usher's syndrome become completely blind, their signing space increases. It is possible that these signers have been "released" from visual monitoring because they can no longer see their own output. However, systematic studies of deaf-blind signers and signers with Usher's syndrome need to be conducted to determine whether the restricted and raised signing space of signers with Usher's syndrome is due to the importance of visual monitoring. Another possibility is that the restricted signing space is actually a signal to the sighted addressee to produce signs in a restricted space so that the individual with Usher's syndrome can see their signing. That is, the person with Usher's syndrome is indicating "sign like me so I can see you." Completely blind signers use tactile signing, and thus, such a communicative signal is not necessary. Another

FIG. 18.4. The sign INTRODUCE produced by a signer with Usher's syndrome and a normally sighted signer. The image of the signer with Usher's syndrome is reproduced with permission from the video *DEAF-BLIND Getting Involved: A conversation*, produced by Sign Media, Inc. Copyright 1992 Theresa Smith.

open question is whether signers with Usher's syndrome are actually *parsing* the visual signal from their signing or whether they are simply keeping track of the general location of their hands.

An interesting question related to visual feedback during sign production is whether stuttering occurs in sign language. Stuttering in speech is hypothesized to involve perceptual distortions of auditory feedback. Delayed auditory feedback can improve fluency for stutterers but impairs fluency for normal speakers (Bloodstein, 1995). To my knowledge, there have been no published case reports or descriptions of stuttering in sign.

Although an early survey of teachers of the deaf by Silverman and Silverman (1971) suggested that "stutter-like" behavior might occur during signing, no clear description of such behavior was provided. Morgan (personal communication) reports a potential case of a seven-year-old deaf child with a familial history of stuttering (his hearing parents stutter). The child scored above age-level on tests of British Sign Language comprehension, but during his spontaneous signing, he often repeated signs or parts of signs. However, he also has other non-linguistic motor impairments and thus may suffer from a more general apraxia, rather than from a specific stuttering disorder (see Morgan, this volume, for a discussion of developmental sign language disorders). There have also been anecdotal reports of ASL-English bilinguals who stutter when speaking, but not when signing. In fact, one individual indicated to me that he learned ASL as a way to avoid stuttering in English.

Neuroimaging studies of self-monitoring of spoken language indicate that monitoring of self-generated speech involves the superior temporal cortex bilaterally, in regions associated with the processing speech that has been generated externally (McGuire, Silbersweig, & Frith, 1996). Furthermore, in a PET study of stutterers, Braun et al. (1997) found these same regions did NOT activate during dysfluencies. Braun et al. (1997) hypothesize that auditory cortices within superior temporal cortex fail to provide integrated sensory feedback to anterior motor regions. To the extent that stuttering is caused or exacerbated by impairments in auditory feedback, stuttering may be rare in sign language because the nature of visual feedback is distinct from auditory feedback for speech. That is, visual input from self-generated signing may not be as integrated with motoric output as auditory input from self-generated speech.

In sum, signers monitor their output such that when they detect an error or an ill-chosen sign, they interrupt themselves and repair the utterance. Data from error repairs and working memory studies suggest the existence of an internal monitoring process in which errors are intercepted before they are overtly produced. However, future studies must determine what level of representation is internally monitored during sign production. Finally, visual feedback may be important for external sign monitoring, but it cannot be processed by the signer's "normal comprehension mechanisms" as is claimed for external self-monitoring of spoken language (Levelt et al., 1999). No visual information regarding linguistic facial expressions (critical to both lexical and syntactic parsing) is available for self-generated signing, and the visual signal from self-generated signing is a distorted version of externally-generated signing, for example, the view of the hands is from behind, the signal is in the far periphery of vision, some signs are not visible at all, and movement is in the opposite direction of externally observed movement.

WHAT DOES SIGN LANGUAGE TELL US ABOUT RELATIONS BETWEEN PERCEPTION AND PRODUCTION?

Evidence from signed languages indicates that input and output systems are mutually constraining for all human languages. For both sign and speech, there is an interplay between production and perception requirements. For signed languages, the interplay is between the visual system and the motor system controlling manual articulation. Ease of articulation and ease of perception are balanced and modulated by the properties of these two systems, but the nature of the trade-offs is parallel to speech. In addition, language processing appears to involve perceptual tuning, even when the articulators are directly perceived. Categorical perception of linguistic categories may arise when category boundaries are relatively stable and when the articulation of category members is relatively discrete, rather than continuous.

Evidence from signed languages also suggests that language output may not be universally parsed by the same mechanisms that parse language input. Signers may not rely much on visual parsing of their output because they must move their eye gaze during sign production and the visual input signal from their own signing is incomplete and visually quite distinct from externally-generated signing. This leads one to speculate on the relative importance of the external perceptual loop versus the internal loop for spoken language monitoring. Perhaps speakers monitor their internal representations even after overt articulation, relying more on the internal than the external monitor.

Finally, investigations of the link between perception and production for sign language may provide unique insight into the link between action observation and action execution in non-linguistic domains and in non-human primates. Some investigators have hypothesized that action perception may automatically and unconsciously engender an internal simulation of that action (a forward model) which can serve to anticipate observed actions (e.g., Blakemore & Decety, 2001). Sign language provides an outstanding tool for addressing questions about how the human action system might contribute to action perception. Like mirror neurons, signers must associate the visually perceived manual actions of another signer with self-generated actions of the same form. Sign perception might be accompanied by an unconscious internal simulation of sign production (the motor theory of sign perception). The distinct biological basis of sign language results in a unique interface between vision and language and between action systems and language production. Investigation of this interface will not only inform us about relations between linguistic perception and production, but it will provide insight into broader issues within cognitive neuroscience.

ACKNOWLEDGMENT

This work was supported by a grant from the National Institutes of Health (R01 HD13249).

REFERENCES

Beale, J. M., & Keil, F. C. (1995). Categorical effects in the perception of faces. *Cognition, 57,* 217-239.

Bellugi, U., & Fischer, S. (1972). A comparison of sign language and spoken language. *Cognition, 1,* 173-200.

Blakemore, S.-J., & Decety, J. (2001). From the perception of action to the understanding of intention. *Nature Reviews, 2,* 561-567.

Bloodstein, O. (1995). *A handbook on stuttering* (5th ed.). Chicago: National Easter Seal Society.

Braun, A. R., Varga, M., Stager, S., Schulz, G., Selbie, S., Maisog, J. M., Carson, R. E., & Ludlow, C. L. (1997). Altered patterns of cerebral activity during speech and language production in developmental stuttering. An H 2 (15)O positron emission tomography study. *Brain, 120,* 761-784.

Brentari, D. (1998). *A prosodic model of sign language phonology.* Cambridge, MA: MIT Press.

Cheek, A., Cormier, K., Repp, A., & Meier, R. P. (2001). Prelinguistic gesture predicts mastery and error in the production of early signs. *Language, 77,* 292-323.

Crasborn, O. (2001). *Phonetic implementation of phonological categories in Sign Language of the Netherlands.* LOT: The Netherlands.

Cutler, A. (1987). Speaking for listening. In A. Allport & D. MacKay (Eds.), *Language perception and production: Relationship between listening, speaking, reading, and writing* (pp. 23-40). San Diego, CA: Academic Press.

de Gelder, B., Teunisse, J-P., & Benson, P. J. (1997). Categorical perception of facial expressions: Categories and their internal structure. *Cognition & Emotion, 11,* 1-22.

Emmorey, K. (2002). *Language, cognition, and the brain: Insights from sign language research.* Mahwah, NJ: Lawrence Erlbaum Associates.

Emmorey, K., McCullough, S., & Brentari, D. (2003). Categorical perception in American Sign Language. *Language and Cognitive Processes, 18,* 21-45.

Fry, D. B., Abramson, A. S., Eimas, P. D., & Liberman, A. M. (1962). The identification and discrimination of synthetic vowels. *Language and Speech, 5,* 171 – 189.

Gallese, V., Fadiga, L., Fogassi, L., & Rizzolatti, G. (1996). Action recognition in the premotor cortex. *Brain, 119,* 593-609.

Goldstein, L., & Fowler, C. (2003). Articulatory phonology: A phonology for public use. In N. O. Schiller & A. S. Meyer (Eds.), *Phonetics and phonology in language comprehension and production: Differences and similarities* (pp. 159-208). Berlin: Mouton de Gruyter.

Hohenberger, A., Happ, D., & Leuninger, H. (2002). Modality-dependent aspects of sign language production: Evidence from slips of the hands and their repairs in German Sign Language. In R. Meier, K. Cormier, & D. Quinto-Pozos (Eds.), *Modality and structure in signed and spoken languages* (pp. 112-142). Cambridge, UK: Cambridge University Press.

Klima, E., & Bellugi, U. (1979). *The signs of language.* Cambridge, MA: Harvard University Press.

Ladefoged, P. (2000) *A course in phonetics.* Oxford: Blackwell.

Lane, H., Boyes-Braem, P., & Bellugi, U. (1976). Preliminaries to a distinctive feature analysis of American Sign Language. *Cognitive Psychology, 8,* 263-289.

Levelt, W. J. M. (1983). Monitoring and self-repair in speech. *Cognition, 14,* 41- 104.

Levelt, W. J. M., Roelofs, A., & Meyer, A. S. (1999). A theory of lexical access in speech production. *Behavioral and Brain Sciences, 22,* 1-75.

Liberman, A. M., Harris, K. S., Hoffman, H. S., & Griffith, B. C. (1957). The discrimination of speech sounds within and across phoneme boundaries. *Journal of Experimental Psychology, 54,* 358-368.

McGuire, P. K., Silbersweig, D. A., & Frith, C. D. (1996). Functional neuroanatomy of verbal self-monitoring. *Brain, 119,* 907-917.

McNeill, D. (1992). *Hand and mind: What gestures reveal about thought.* Chicago: University of Chicago Press.

Meier, R. P., & Willerman, R. (1995). Prelinguistic gesture in deaf and hearing infants. In K. Emmorey & J. Reilly (Eds.), *Language, gesture, and space* (pp. 391-409). Hillsdale, NJ: Lawrence Erlbaum Associates.

Oller, K., & Eilers, R. E. (1988). The role of audition in infant babbling. *Child Development, 59,* 441-466.

Petitto, L. A., & Marentette, P. F. (1991). Babbling in the manual mode: Evidence for the ontogeny of language. *Science, 251,* 1493-1496.

Petitto, L., Holowka, S., Sergio, L., Levy, B., & Ostry, D. (2004). Baby hands that move to the rhythm of language: Hearing babies acquiring sign languages babble silently on the hands. *Cognition, 93,* 43-73.

Petitto, L., Poizner, H., & Lane, H. (1978). Discrimination of location in American Sign Language. In P. Siple (Ed.), *Understanding language through sign language research* (pp. 271-287). New York: Academic Press.

Poizner, H., & Lane, H. (1978). Discrimination of location in American Sign Language. In P. Siple (Ed.), *Understanding language through sign language research* (pp. 271-287). New York: Academic Press.

Rizzolatti, G., Fadiga, L., Matelli, M., Bettinardi, V., Perani, D., & Fazio, F. (1996). Premotor cortex and the recognition of motor actions. *Cognitive Brain Research, 71*, 491-507.

Silverman, F. H., & Silverman, E. M. (1971). Stutter-like behavior in manual communication of the deaf. *Perceptual & Motor Skills, 33*, 45-46.

Siple, P. (1978). Visual constraints for sign language communication. *Sign Language Studies, 19*, 97-112.

Thompson, R., Emmorey, K., & Kluender, R. (2004). The relationship between eye gaze and agreement in American Sign Language: An eye-tracking study. Manuscript under review.

Tomasello, M., Savage-Rumbaugh, S., & Kruger, A. C. (1993). Imitative learning of actions on objects by children, chimpanzees, and enculturated chimpanzees. *Child Development, 64*, 1688-1705.

Van der Meer, A. L., van der Weel, F. R., & Lee, D. N. (1995). The functional significance of arm movements in neonates. *Science, 267*, 693-695.

Wilson, M., & Emmorey, K. (1997). A visual-spatial "phonological loop" in working memory: Evidence from American Sign Language. *Memory and Cognition, 25*, 313-320.

Wilson, M., & Emmorey, K. (1998). A "word length effect" for sign language: Further evidence on the role of language in structuring working memory. *Memory and Cognition, 26*, 584-590.

Section 4

Model
and
Experiment

19 From Popper to Lakatos: A Case for Cumulative Computational Modeling

Ardi Roelofs
Max Planck Institute for Psycholinguistics and
F.C. Donders Centre for Cognitive Neuroimaging,
Nijmegen, The Netherlands

An important problem with several modeling enterprises in psycholinguistics is that they are not cumulative, unlike successful experimental research. For example, in the field of language production, quite a few models focus on a few findings only instead of trying to account simultaneously for a wide range of data. Even worse, some investigators treat their models like their toothbrushes by using them only for their own data. There is no guarantee that these micromodels can be integrated into a single comprehensive macromodel, because micromodels are often mutually incompatible. Moreover, experimental tests of models developed by others are often conducted in the world of a misinterpreted Popper, where testing models is like skeet shooting.[1] The aim is to shoot

---

[1] Lakatos (1970) distinguished three Poppers: Popper$_0$, Popper$_1$, and Popper$_2$. "Popper$_0$ is the dogmatic falsificationist who never published a word: He was invented — and 'criticized' — first by Ayer and then by many others. Popper$_1$ is the naive falsificationist, Popper$_2$ the sophisticated falsificationist. The *real* Popper developed from dogmatic to a naive version of methodological falsificationism in the twenties; he arrived at the *'acceptance rules' of sophisticated falsificationism* in the fifties. Thus the real Popper consists of Popper$_1$ together with some elements of Popper$_2$" (p. 181). Skeet shooting is often defended by referring to the mythical Popper$_0$.

down models with falsification bullets. Alternatively, Lakatos proposed to treat models like graduate students. Once admitted, one tries hard to avoid flunking them out (of course, not at all costs) and one spends much time and effort on their development so that they may become long-term contributors to science (cf. Newell, 1990).

In this chapter, I make a case for Lakatos-style or cumulative computational modeling and model testing. This involves working with a single model that accounts for a wide range of existing data and that is incrementally extended and tested on new data sets. First, I contrast cumulativeness in relation to modeling with the noncumulative toothbrush and skeet shooting approaches. Next, I describe the cumulative modeling approach in which models are treated like graduate students. Finally, I demonstrate the cumulative modeling approach by describing the scientific career of one of my own model graduate students, namely the WEAVER++ model of spoken word production.

TOOTHBRUSHES, SKEET SHOOTING, AND GRADUATE STUDENTS

Cumulativeness in relation to modeling means that in developing models one builds on earlier modeling results, just as one does in cumulative experimental research. Cumulativeness in relation to modeling is not always seen as a virtue. For example, a goldfield for modeling in psychology is the literature on the color-word Stroop task (Stroop, 1935), one of the most widely used tasks in academic and applied psychology (between 1965 and 2003, some 2000 articles appeared on the task, partly reviewed by MacLeod, 1991). The task requires naming the ink color of written color words or reading the words aloud. The basic finding is that participants are much slower and make more errors in naming the ink color of an incongruent color word (e.g., saying "red" to the written word BLUE in red ink) than the ink color of a congruent word (the word RED in red ink). When the task is to read aloud the words and to ignore the ink colors, there is no congruity effect. Despite the extensive accumulating literature on this phenomenon, Stroop modeling has not been cumulative.

Since the early 1990s, the literature on Stroop has been dominated by the model of Cohen, Dunbar, and McClelland (1990). This feedforward model was discarded by its main designer, Cohen, in the mid-1990s (Cohen & Huston, 1994) in favor of a similar interactive model. However, the new model was not tested against all the data that motivated the construction of the old model. Moreover, no experiments were run that tested the new against the old model. Rather, it seems that the old feedforward model was dismissed only because interactiveness had become part of the Zeitgeist. So, it is unclear whether the new interactive model represented any improvement over the old feedforward model.

Although Cohen et al. (1990) did not conduct any new experiment to empirically test their Stroop model against extant models in the literature, there was at least an attempt to provide an account of a wide range of existing data. Unfortunately, this is not even attempted in two popular approaches to modeling and testing models in psycholinguistics, namely the toothbrush and the skeet shooting approaches.

The toothbrush approach involves constructing a model for your own data only. Success for the model is claimed by pointing to the fit of the model to the data it was designed to explain. For example, Cutting and Ferreira (1999) and Starreveld and La Heij (1996) reported new data on word production together with new models that were designed to account for these data. The toothbrush approach is popular with several journals, because it leads to self-contained publications. The article reports new data and a model that accounts for the new data. The model is often very simple, because the only thing it has to do is to account for the reported data and nothing else. Regularly, the approach is defended as an application of Ockham's razor: Accept the simplest model that works for the reported data. It is thereby forgotten that Ockham's rule does not apply to both model and data. Ockham understood his principle as recommending models that make no more assumptions than is necessary to account for the phenomena. But he did not advocate to keep the number of phenomena to a minimum. Ockham's rule is an important guiding principle in model construction (do not introduce any needless assumptions in your model) and a last resort in testing between models. It applies when two models make identical predictions or when there are no more phenomena to use as a test between models. But the latter is almost never the case in psycholinguistics.

The biggest problem with the toothbrush approach is that it cuts on both the number of theoretical assumptions and the number of phenomena. Moreover, there is no attempt at snowballing, that is, to build on earlier empirical and modeling results. Ultimately, however, we want to have unified theories explaining how language works (i.e., how language is acquired and used in production and comprehension). The toothbrush approach commonly leads to several micromodels each capturing a different aspect of reality but together not giving a consistent picture.

For example, motivated by empirical phenomena suggesting interaction, but perhaps also partly inspired by the Zeitgeist, most existing computationally implemented models of spoken word production are interactive (e.g., Cutting & Ferreira, 1999; Dell, Schwartz, Martin, Saffran,

& Gagnon, 1997; Starreveld & La Heij, 1996). However, the design characteristics of these models differ greatly. For example, the model of Cutting and Ferreira (1999) assumes inhibitory interactions, whereas the models of Dell et al. (1997) and Starreveld and La Heij (1996) do not. Also, the empirical domains of the models differ. For example, the model of Dell et al. (1997) was designed to explain speech errors, whereas the model of Starreveld and La Heij (1996) was designed to explain production latencies. Because the design characteristics and domains of the models differ, collectively they do not make up a single interactive model. Therefore, what counts as empirical success for one interactive model does not automatically count as success for all the other models. For example, Dell et al. (1997) addressed interactive effects on segmental speech errors and Starreveld and La Heij (1996) addressed interactive effects in the picture-word interference task. However, the model of Starreveld and La Heij cannot account for the interactive effects on segmental speech errors, simply because it has no segmental level of representation. Moreover, the model of Dell et al. cannot account for the interactive effects in the picture-word interference task, simply because it cannot account for latencies at all. Thus, it makes little sense to point to the success of the interactive approach by referring to the success of the various interactive models. Instead, to make a convincing case for an interactive account, a unified interactive model is required that can account for a wide range of findings both on production errors and latencies.

In the skeet shooting approach, the aim of the experimenter is to collect data that blast models. If the collected data disagree with one or more models, the mission is accomplished and the data are published with the recommendation that a completely new model is developed. For example, Caramazza and Costa (2000) reported a series of experiments that tested the response set assumption made by the WEAVER++ model of spoken word production (Levelt, Roelofs, & Meyer, 1999; Roelofs, 1992). According to Caramazza and Costa (2000), the outcomes of their experiments were problematic for WEAVER++ and they demanded a fundamental modification of the model: "It is not obvious that minor changes to the model—that is, changes that do not alter the fundamental architecture of the model—would be successful in this regard" (p. B61). Therefore, Caramazza and Costa (2000) took it that their study "undermines the model as a whole" (p. B61). They concluded that "if one were willing to drop the response set principle used in WEAVER++, the *new* model would have to be able to account for the data reported here and the various other data that were previously used to support the old WEAVER++ model" (p. B61). Although the response set assumption was assumed to be refuted by Caramazza and Costa (2000), an alternative was not considered.

The skeet shooting approach is also popular with journals, because it gives the impression that we are making scientific progress. After all, we have eliminated a model or a class of models. But usually, no answer is given to the critical question: What next? The problem is that models may be wrong for various reasons. For example, models may be incomplete. In the latter case we only need to extend the model rather than construct a completely new one. Alternatively, only a small change to an existing model may be required to remedy the problem. For example, in response to Caramazza and Costa (2000), I argued that there is no need for a fundamental change of the WEAVER++ model (Roelofs, 2002). Instead, the supposedly problematic findings of Caramazza and Costa (2000), and all previous findings that support the model, could be explained by assuming that a response set is only marked in memory when the number of responses is small and can be kept in short-term memory. Thus, a small change in an assumption of the model could do the job. There is a motto in politics saying that you cannot beat something with nothing. You cannot beat a candidate simply by pointing to inadequacies, but you must offer an alternative. The same applies to testing and modeling. But the skeet shooting approach fails to point to new directions.

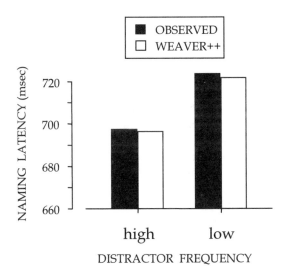

FIG. 19.1. The effect of high- versus low-frequency distractors in picture naming: Observed data (Miozzo & Caramazza, 2003) and WEAVER++ simulation results.

Moreover, when proposing an alternative, it is important to make sure that the alternative is really warranted. When a model is rejected and a new assumption is considered as the starting point of a new model, it should be excluded that the rejected model with the new assumption would fit the data equally well. For example, Miozzo and Caramazza (2003) observed that high-frequency distractor words yielded less interference than low-frequency distractor words in picture naming and they argued that "it is clear that the distractor frequency interference effect seriously challenges a popular model of lexical access", namely WEAVER++ (p. 249). To account for their novel finding, Miozzo and Caramazza (2003) proposed a new frequency-sensitive mechanism by which distractors are actively blocked. But Roelofs (2003) and Roelofs and Hagoort (2002) proposed exactly such a blocking mechanism, namely production rules blocking out distractors, although they did not *explicitly* assume that the blocking rules are frequency sensitive. However, given that *all* production rules in WEAVER++ are frequency sensitive (as acknowledged by Miozzo & Caramazza, 2003), frequency-sensitive blocking of distractors is entailed. Figure 19.1 shows that when the frequency of the blocking rules is manipulated, WEAVER++ fits the data of Miozzo and Caramazza (2003) without difficulty. To conclude, in rejecting a model and proposing a new assumption as the starting point of a new model, one should not be blind to the possibility that making the new assumption for the rejected model would fit the data equally well. If the latter is the case, the data require a model patch rather than a construction from scratch.

As an alternative to the toothbrush and skeet shooting approaches, I propose to treat models like graduate students. Once admitted, you spend time and effort on their development in the hope that they become long-term contributors to psycholinguistics. You extend their theoretical content and empirical coverage by confronting them with new data sets. Of course, they are flunked out when they fail too many tests or when they are not productive for a long period of time.

Treating models like graduate students represents a more conservative approach to model testing than skeet shooting. The conservative protectiveness is not unreasonable. In an empirical science like psycholinguistics, we try hard to achieve approximate truths. It would be a mistake to believe that we can find a single simple model that captures the whole truth and nothing else. Instead, we hope to see the light by a strategy of continual approximations. It is said that Thomas Edison ran more than two thousand experiments before he got an adequately working light bulb. When asked how he felt about having failed so many times, Edison replied "I never failed once. It just happened to be a 2000 step process". Moreover, we try to avoid the mistake of Jorge Luis Borges' (1985) cartographers, who constructed a map that was as big and detailed as the country itself—capturing most of reality but being completely useless. In order to be useful, models have to simplify reality. When we find discrepancies between model and data, it is therefore reasonable to first try to patch rather than to rebuild from scratch. As with training real graduate students, constructing a new model is a costly project, taking much time and effort. Moreover, when discrepancies between model and data appear, it is often not immediately obvious where the difficulty lies. It may be located in a fundamental assumption of the model, but it may as well be merely a defect in one of the simplifying assumptions, auxiliary hypotheses, or measurement assumptions that had to be made in order to connect the model with data. Increasing complexity or revising the auxiliary hypotheses or measurement assumptions may be sufficient to save the model.

The critical importance of localizing the fault rather than just noting that there exists a discrepancy was pointed out by Popper and Lakatos. Whereas nineteenth century philosophers of science tended to stress the importance of justifying a model, Popper stressed the importance of finding and understanding discrepancies. Discrepancies can only arise when models stick out their neck by excluding certain data patterns ("No guts, no story"). Models should be falsifiable. According to Popper, we can only make scientific progress when there are discrepancies between model and data. A discrepancy is not necessarily a falsification. As indicated, the trouble may be located in a fundamental assumption of the model, but it may as well be merely a shortcoming of an auxiliary hypothesis or a measurement assumption. A discrepancy only leads to scientific progress if it shows the way to a new theoretical claim, either in terms of a revision of theory or model, a revised auxiliary hypothesis, a revised measurement assumption, or a new theory or model.

For Popper, falsification concerned a relation between model and data, although "in most cases we have, before falsifying a hypothesis, another one up our sleeves" (Popper, 1959: 87). For Lakatos, there *must* be an alternative, that is, a presumed new insight: "There is no falsification before the emergence of a better theory. ... Refutation without an alternative shows nothing but the poverty of our imagination in providing a rescue hypothesis" (Lakatos, 1970: 119-120). In cumulative computational modeling, there is, by definition, always an alternative.

CUMULATIVE COMPUTATIONAL MODELING

A computational model is a formalization of a theory in terms of a computer program (unfortunately, in practice, computational models are frequently constructed without a theory, which holds especially for many connectionist models, see Norris, this volume). Computational models have many advantages over verbal models. Computational models guarantee the sufficiency and internal consistency of a theory. By running computational models as computer simulations, one can assess whether the theoretical assumptions are sufficient to explain the data. Moreover, computer simulations reveal whether the theoretical assumptions are mutually consistent, because inconsistencies will stop a simulation. Another advantage of computational models over verbal models is that they generate precise predictions.

A disadvantage of computational models compared to verbal models is that in order to make the model run as a computer simulation, sometimes assumptions have to be made that were not part of the theory. Thus, a computational model may be more specific than its theory. This complicates the testing of model and theory. When we find discrepancies between model and data, the trouble may lie in the specific assumptions of the model or in the assumptions of the theory that it implements. When the problem lies in the model-specific assumptions, revision of these assumptions may be sufficient to save both theory and model. Of course, when the trouble lies in the assumptions of the theory that the model implements, revision or rejection of the theoretical assumptions is necessary to save theory and model. Figure 19.2 illustrates the empirical cycles.

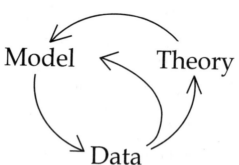

FIG. 19.2. The two main empirical cycles involved in constructing and testing a model for a theory.

Given that the ultimate goal of psycholinguistic research is to obtain comprehensive theories of how language works, it makes little sense to develop models that focus on a few findings only instead of trying to account concurrently for a wide range of data. Moreover, it makes no sense to construct models for your own data only. There is no warranty that these micromodels can be integrated into a single comprehensive macromodel, because micromodels are often irreconcilable. Moreover, it makes little sense to test models with the only aim to obtain a mismatch between model and data. A discrepancy should be a new beginning of theorizing. Thereby, theorizing and modeling should be cumulative, just like successful experimental psycholinguistic research.

Cumulativeness in relation to modeling can take a number of forms. The best known form is probably *nested modeling* (e.g., Coltheart, Rastle, Perry, Langdon, & Ziegler, 2001; Jacobs & Grainger, 1994). In nested modeling, a more extensive version of a model is tested against a more restricted version of the same model to see which model version gives a better fit to a particular set of data. A pitfall is overfitting. The more complex model may provide a better fit only because it has more parameters and therefore can fit not only the main trend but also some of the noise (random error) in the data. The remedy is to test for generalizability, that is, to test the simple and complex versions on other relevant sets of data (e.g., Pitt & Navarro, this volume). For example, overfitting of a model of spoken word recognition may be prevented by testing it not only on data obtained by lexical decision, but also on data from phoneme monitoring, word spotting, eye tracking, and so forth. If the more complex model did better than the simple model on the lexical decision data because it fitted some of the noise in the data, it most likely does worse on the wider range of data sets.

Nested modeling by itself does not lead to comprehensive models of how language works. A model of word recognition tested on data from lexical decision and phoneme monitoring remains a model of word recognition regardless of whether it is also tested on word spotting and eye-tracking data. In order to attain comprehensive models of how language works, one needs to extend models beyond the empirical domain for which they were originally developed. For example, to attain a model of spoken word recognition *and* word production, one needs to extend the model of spoken word recognition by including assumptions about word production, or vice versa, and test the extended model on relevant data. The incremental extension of a model to a new empirical domain outside its current scope is *incremental modeling*. Note that an incremental extension of a model also implies an incremental extension of the corresponding theory. Extending a model of spoken word recognition by including assumptions about word production implies making theoretical assumptions about word production. Every extension should rule out certain data patterns.

Unfortunately, compared to nested modeling, incremental modeling further complicates the testing of model and theory, which is the price paid for achieving comprehensive coverage. When we find discrepancies between the extended model and data, the trouble may lie in the assumptions of the extension or in assumptions of the original model and theory. Given that there are more possible loci of trouble, cumulative modeling and testing might seem to be a hopelessly complicated endeavor. However, in practice, this is not the case, especially not if one extends a model in a modular fashion by adding theoretical assumptions without changing existing ones. This guarantees that the fits of the original model are preserved.

A SKETCH OF THE SCIENTIFIC CAREER OF WEAVER++

In this section, I demonstrate the incremental approach by describing the scientific career of one of my own models, namely WEAVER++. I describe some of the major steps in developing WEAVER++. The steps range from WEAVER++'s origin as a model designed to explain chronometric findings on lemma retrieval from picture-word interference experiments to its current state as a comprehensive model of the various processes underlying word production, including its relation with spoken and visual word recognition, their attentional control, the self-monitoring for speech errors, and the relation between self-monitoring and speech comprehension. Whereas the original model was designed to explain chronometric data, recently WEAVER++ has been extended to eye-tracking, electrophysiological, and neuroimaging data. Stroop-like tasks have run as a continuous thread trough WEAVER++'s career and they are therefore used for illustrative purposes.

Figure 19.3 gives an overview of all the processing components assumed by the current version of WEAVER++. The architecture of the model is derived from Levelt's (1989) blueprint of the speaker. The blueprint embeds the architecture in the general context of sentence and discourse production. The architecture distinguishes between conceptual preparation, lemma retrieval, and word-form encoding, with the encoding of forms further divided into morphological, phonological, and phonetic encoding. Information is retrieved from a lexical network by spreading activation. During conceptual preparation, concepts are flagged as goal concepts. In lemma retrieval, a goal concept is used to retrieve a lemma from memory, which is a representation of the syntactic properties of a word, crucial for its use in sentences. For example, the lemma of the word *red* says that it can be used as an adjective. Lemma retrieval makes these properties available for syntactic encoding processes. In word-form encoding, the lemma is used to retrieve the morphophonological properties of the word from memory in order to construct an appropriate articulatory program. For example, for *red* the morpheme <red> and the speech segments (e.g., /r/) are retrieved and a phonetic plan is generated. Finally, articulation processes execute the motor program, which yields overt speech.

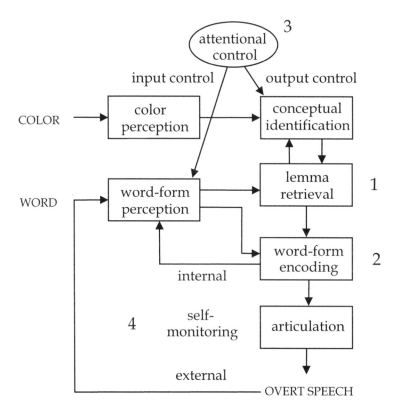

FIG. 19.3. The architecture of WEAVER++. The numbers indicate major steps in the incremental development of the model: (1) lemma retrieval, (2) word-form encoding, (3) attentional control, and (4) self-monitoring and its relation with speech comprehension.

Assume a speaker wants to refer to the ink color of the word BLUE in red ink. This involves the conceptual identification of the color based on the perceptual input and its designation as goal concept (i.e., RED(X)), the retrieval of the lemma of the corresponding word (i.e., *red*), and the encoding of the form of the word. The final result is a motor program for the word "red", which can be articulated. In performing the color-word Stroop task, aspects of word planning are under attentional control. The system has to achieve color naming rather than word reading ("output control") and the irrelevant input (the word in color naming) has to be suppressed ("input control"). Moreover, speakers monitor their performance. In Stroop's (1935) original experiments, participants had to repair their errors, and this still holds for most psychometric applications of the task.

WEAVER++'s career started about a decade ago as an anonymous computational model of lemma retrieval (Roelofs, 1992). Although the model was developed within the theoretical framework of Levelt's blueprint of the speaker, it did not simply implement the theoretical assumption about lemma retrieval in the blueprint. Instead, the model instantiated a new set of assumptions. To highlight that computational models implement a theory, the first publication on the model was called "A spreading-activation *theory* of lemma retrieval in speaking" (Roelofs, 1992).

As a next step, a computational model of word-form encoding was developed. The editor of the journal of the first publication on the word-form encoding model, David Balota, suggested that I choose a name for it (Roelofs, 1996). I decided for the name WEAVER, which is an acronym of Word-form Encoding by Activation and VERification. The acronym intended to capture the fact that words are encoded in the model by activating, selecting, and connecting types of verbal information. Unlike the lemma retrieval model, WEAVER largely followed the theoretical assumptions of the blueprint. A full description and motivation of WEAVER was published under the title "The WEAVER model of word-form encoding in speech production" (Roelofs, 1997).

The lemma retrieval model and the WEAVER model of word-form encoding were subsequently combined into a single model of word planning. This model was published as an implementation of a general theory of lexical access (Levelt et al., 1999). To highlight the incremental nature of the modeling, the combination of models was called WEAVER++. The ++ refers to the ++-operator in the C programming language, meaning "incremental extension". Thus, WEAVER++ means "incremental extension of WEAVER". Moreover, WEAVER++ plans words incrementally. Lemmas are selected for lexical concepts, morphemes for lemmas, segments for morphemes, and syllable programs for syllabified segments. Also, syllabification of segments proceeds incrementally from the beginning of the word to its end.

A combination of models may be more than the sum of the component models, because the combination may include claims about the relation between the components. Roelofs (1992) proposed an interactive model for lemma retrieval and Roelofs (1997) proposed a feedforward model for word-form encoding. In these articles, no claim was made concerning the relation between lemma retrieval and word-form encoding. Levelt et al. (1999) made the claim that only selected lemmas activate their speech segments and this was implemented by WEAVER++.

In recent years, WEAVER++ has been further extended to other domains. In addition to language, numerals constitute the second most important symbolic system employed by humans. A WEAVER++ implementation has been made for naming dice, digits, and number words. Moreover, the model has been used to address the issue of how two languages are represented and controlled in bilingual individuals. Simulations have been run for English-Spanish Stroop task performance (Roelofs, 2003). Moreover, to examine the issue of similarities and differences in word-form encoding between languages, a WEAVER++ implementation has been made (by Train-Min Chen) for a language that is very different from Dutch and English, namely Mandarin Chinese, the language with the largest number of native speakers in the world.

A further extension of WEAVER++ concerned making assumptions about the relationship between spoken word production and word recognition, assumptions about self-monitoring for speech errors, and assumptions about the relation between self-monitoring and speech comprehension (Roelofs, 2004). Moreover, WEAVER++ has been extended to the domain of attentional control. In their classic paper "Attention to action: Willed and automatic control of behavior", Norman and Shallice (1986) made a distinction between "horizontal threads" and "vertical threads" in the control of behavior. Horizontal threads are strands of processing that map perceptions onto actions and vertical threads are attentional influences on these mappings. Behavior arises from interactions between horizontal and vertical threads. WEAVER++ implements specific claims about how the horizontal and vertical threads are woven together in planning spoken words. A central claim embodied by WEAVER++ is that the control of word perception and production is achieved symbolically rather than purely associatively. WEAVER++'s lexical network is accessed by spreading activation while condition-action rules determine what is done with the activated lexical information depending on the task. When a goal symbol is placed in working memory, the attention of the system is focused on those rules that include the goal among their conditions (e.g., those for color naming rather than reading in the Stroop color naming task).

The fruitfulness of the incremental modeling approach was recently demonstrated by WEAVER++'s successful simulation of 16 classic data sets on Stroop-like performance, mostly taken from the review by MacLeod (1991), including incongruency, congruency, reverse Stroop, response set, semantic gradient, time course, stimulus, spatial, multiple task, manual, bilingual, training, age, and pathological effects (Roelofs, 2003). With only 3 free parameters taking 2 values each to accommodate task differences (color naming, picture naming, word reading, manual responding), the model accounts for 96% of the variance of the 16 studies. In addition, new empirical work refuted a rescue hypothesis for the model of Cohen et al. (1990), supported an assumption of WEAVER++, and confirmed a critical prediction of the model.

The functional architecture of WEAVER++ has also successfully been used in analyses of data on word production from neuroimaging and electrophysiological studies. For example, Indefrey and Levelt (2000) used the functional architecture in a meta-analysis of 58 brain imaging studies on word production in the literature. The studies included picture naming, verb generation (generating a use for a noun, e.g., saying "hit" to HAMMER), word reading, and pseudoword reading. The lower panel of Figure 19.4 relates the word planning stages to areas of the human brain. Moreover, WEAVER++ successfully simulated data from functional magnetic resonance imaging (fMRI) studies, in particular, the fMRI BOLD (Blood Oxygen Level Dependent) response in different subregions within Wernicke's area during speech production and comprehension tasks. Whereas left perisylvian areas, including the areas of Broca and Wernicke, map colors and words onto the corresponding articulatory programs, the anterior cingulate cortex (on the medial surface of the human brain) and the dorsolateral prefrontal cortex subserve attentional control. The upper panel of Figure 19.4 relates attentional control processes to areas of the human brain. Evidence suggests that the dorso-lateral prefrontal cortex serves to maintain the goals in working memory. WEAVER++ instantiates the view that the anterior cingulate achieves input- and output control. WEAVER++ successfully simulated the fMRI BOLD response in the anterior cingulate during Stroop task performance (Roelofs & Hagoort, 2002).

How does WEAVER++ simulate data? In all simulations, WEAVER++ ran through time in discrete steps, each of which was assumed to correspond to 25 milliseconds in real time. On every time step, activation spread from node to node in the network and the rules tested their con-

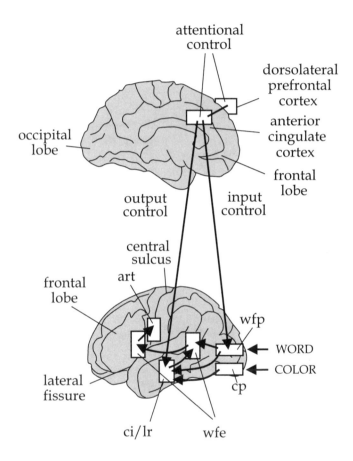

FIG. 19.4. The neural correlates of word planning and attentional control in the Stroop task. Medial view (upper panel) and lateral view (lower panel) of the left hemisphere of the human brain. The word planning system achieves color naming through color perception (cp), conceptual identification (ci), lemma retrieval (lr), word-form encoding (wfe), and articulatory processing (art); word-form perception (wfp) activates lemmas and word forms in parallel. Word reading minimally involves word-form perception (wfp), word-form encoding (wfe), and articulatory processing (art). The attentional control system achieves output and input control.

ditions or they performed an action. I go through a simulated color-word Stroop trial to illustrate this. Assume that the color has to be named of a red color patch on which the word BLUE is superimposed, whereby the word is presented 100 milliseconds before the color patch (the stimulus onset asynchrony or SOA is –100 milliseconds). The simulation starts with the lemma node of *blue* receiving external activation. Activation then spreads through the network, with the lemma node of *blue* sending a proportion of its activation to the concept node BLUE(X). This node in its turn sends activation to other concept nodes. After the number of time steps that is the equivalent of 100 milliseconds (the SOA), the concept node RED(X) receives external input from the color patch. On the next time step, the production rule for the selection of RED(X) fires and RED(X) becomes flagged as goal concept. Simultaneously, activation spreads from RED(X) to *red*. After the selection threshold of the lemma of *red* is exceeded (i.e., *red* should be more active than *blue* by a certain amount), the production rule for the selection of *red* fires. Although the selection threshold has been reached for the lemma of *blue* earlier because of the preexposure of the word BLUE, the production rule for *blue* did not fire because BLUE(X) was not flagged as the goal concept.

By following this simulation procedure, lemma retrieval times for different experimental conditions may be obtained. Assume it takes 7 time steps in the model (which would map onto 175 milliseconds real time) to retrieve the lemma of *red* in naming a red patch with BLUE superimposed. This retrieval time may then be compared with the time it takes to retrieve lemmas for other stimuli, such as a red patch without a word superimposed. Assume it takes 5 time steps (i.e., 125 milliseconds) to retrieve the lemma *red* for this stimulus. The simulated Stroop interference effect would then be 2 time steps or 50 milliseconds. By comparing simulated and observed effects, the fit between model and data may be determined. Glaser and Glaser (1982) observed 45 milliseconds Stroop interference for this particular situation, so the simulated effect would be in close agreement with the real observation.

SUMMARY AND CONCLUSIONS

I made a case for cumulative computational modeling and testing. This involves working with a single model that accounts for a wide range of existing data and that is extended and tested on new data sets. I first pitted cumulative modeling against two popular methods in psycholinguistics that are not cumulative, namely the toothbrush and skeet shooting approaches. Next, I described the cumulative approach in which models are treated like graduate students. Finally, I demonstrated the productivity of the cumulative approach by describing the scientific career of my own model graduate student WEAVER++. Cumulative modeling does not guarantee success, but it is also not a blind alley, unlike the other approaches. The basic problem with the other approaches is that they do not commit themselves to a strategy of continual approximation. Once started, they do not take any further steps. However, if it took Edison more than two thousand cumulative steps to see the light, we cannot expect to arrive any quicker at a comprehensive understanding of how language works.

REFERENCES

Borges, J. L. (1985). On rigor in science. In J. L. Borges (Ed.), *Dreamtigers* (p. 90). Austin, Texas: University of Texas Press.

Caramazza, A., & Costa, A. (2000). The semantic interference effect in the picture-word interference paradigm: Does the response set matter? *Cognition, 75*, B51-B64.

Cohen, J., Dunbar, K., & McClelland, J. (1990). On the control of automatic processes: A parallel distributed processing account of the Stroop effect. *Psychological Review, 97*, 332-361.

Cohen, J. D., & Huston, T. A. (1994). Progress in the use of interactive models for understanding attention and performance. In C. Umiltà & M. Moscovitch (Eds.), *Conscious and nonconscious information processing: Attention and Performance XV* (pp. 453-476). Cambridge, MA: MIT Press.

Coltheart, M., Rastle, K., Perry, C., Langdon, R., & Ziegler, J. (2001). DRC: A dual route cascaded model of visual word recognition and reading aloud. *Psychological Review, 108*, 204-256.

Cutting, J. C., & Ferreira, V. S. (1999). Semantic and phonological information flow in the production lexicon. *Journal of Experimental Psychology: Learning, Memory, and Cognition, 25*, 318-344.

Dell, G. S., Schwartz, M. F., Martin, N., Saffran, E. M., & Gagnon, D. A. (1997). Lexical access in aphasic and nonaphasic speakers. *Psychological Review, 104*, 801-838.

Glaser, M. O., & Glaser, W. R. (1982). Time course analysis of the Stroop phenomenon. *Journal of Experimental Psychology: Human Perception and Performance, 8*, 875-894.

Indefrey, P., & Levelt, W. J. M. (2000). The neural correlates of language production. In M. Gazzaniga (Ed.), *The new cognitive neurosciences* (pp. 845-865). Cambridge, MA: MIT Press.

Jacobs, A. M., & Grainger, J. (1994). Models of visual word recognition: Sampling the state of the art. *Journal of Experimental Psychology: Human Perception and Performance, 20*, 1311-1334.

Lakatos, I. (1970). Falsification and the methodology of scientific research programmes. In I. Lakatos & A. Musgrave (Eds.), *Criticism and the growth of knowledge* (pp. 91-196). Cambridge, UK: Cambridge University Press.

Levelt, W. J. M. (1989). *Speaking: From intention to articulation*. Cambridge, MA: MIT Press.

Levelt, W. J. M., Roelofs, A., & Meyer, A. S. (1999). A theory of lexical access in speech production. *Behavioral and Brain Sciences, 22*, 1-38.

MacLeod, C. M. (1991). Half a century of research on the Stroop effect: An integrative review. *Psychological Bulletin, 109*, 163-203.

Miozzo, M., & Caramazza, A. (2003). When more is less: A counterintuitive effect of distractor frequency in the picture-word interference paradigm. *Journal of Experimental Psychology: General, 132*, 228-252.

Newell, A. (1990). *Unified theories of cognition*. Cambridge, MA: Harvard University Press.

Norman, D. A., & Shallice, T. (1986). Attention to action: Willed and automatic control of behavior. In R. J. Davidson, G. E. Schwarts & D. Shapiro (Eds.), *Consciousness and self-regulation. Advances in research and theory* (Vol. 4, pp. 1-18). New York: Plenum Press.

Popper, K. (1959). *The logic of scientific discovery*. New York, NY: Basic Books.

Roelofs, A. (1992). A spreading-activation theory of lemma retrieval in speaking. *Cognition, 42*, 107-142.

Roelofs, A. (1996). Serial order in planning the production of successive morphemes of a word. *Journal of Memory and Language, 35*, 854-876.

Roelofs, A. (1997). The WEAVER model of word-form encoding in speech production. *Cognition, 64*, 249-284.

Roelofs, A. (2002). Set size and repetition matter: Comment on Caramazza and Costa (2000). *Cognition, 80*, 283-290.

Roelofs, A. (2003). Goal-referenced selection of verbal action: Modeling attentional control in the Stroop task. *Psychological Review, 110*, 88-125.

Roelofs, A. (2004). Error biases in spoken word planning and monitoring by aphasic and nonaphasic speakers: Comment on Rapp and Goldrick (2000). *Psychological Review, 111*, 561-572.

Roelofs, A., & Hagoort, P. (2002). Control of language use: Cognitive modeling of the hemodynamics of Stroop task performance. *Cognitive Brain Research, 15*, 85-97.

Starreveld, P. A., & La Heij, W. (1996). Time-course analysis of semantic and orthographic context effects in picture naming. *Journal of Experimental Psychology: Learning, Memory, and Cognition, 22*, 896-918.

Stroop, J. R. (1935). Studies of interference in serial verbal reactions. *Journal of Experimental Psychology, 18*, 643-662.

20 How do Computational Models Help us Develop Better Theories?

Dennis Norris
MRC Cognition and Brain Sciences Unit, Cambridge, UK

What's a theory?

Computational models are a good thing, or so most of us believe. But, what are they actually good for, and how do they help us develop better theories? Here I assume that even if there is somebody out there who doesn't think that models are a good thing, we all think that theories are fundamental to any scientific enterprise. Although consideration of the nature of scientific theories is a big enough topic to occupy the entire academic career of a sizeable proportion of the planet's philosophers, I will focus on what I consider to be the central component of a scientific theory: To provide an explanation of some phenomena, observation, or set of data. That is, to explain how and why something happens.

Is a computational model a theory?

It is easy to fall into the trap of thinking that computational models are just theories. But computational models don't necessarily provide the essential ingredient of a theory: They don't necessarily explain things. For example, a mathematical model or computer simulation might not explain anything, even if it does a great job at simulating the data. Ken Forster has illustrated this by asking us to imagine that his next door neighbor can make the correct prediction about the outcome of any experiment on word recognition (Forster, 1994). Does that make Ken's next door neighbor a good theory of word recognition? Clearly not. The existence of Ken's neighbor doesn't explain how or why human word

331

recognition works the way it does. On the other hand, I'd love to have access to the proclamations of Ken's imaginary neighbor. It would save the tedious task of running experiments. The important message of Forster's illustration is that a model needs to amount to something more than replacing one thing we don't understand with something else we don't understand. A computational model is of no value unless we can understand what it does. This issue was a real concern in the early days of connectionist modeling (cf. McCloskey, 1991). Some might argue that it continues to be a problem with much current connectionist modeling. If a connectionist network is trained to perform some task, such as reading aloud (e.g., Seidenberg & McClelland, 1989) and, after training, produces human-like behavior, how much does this actually explain? The fact that a model can simulate the data doesn't tell us anything other than that a model of this sort can perform the task. Until we understand how it works, such a model provides no more explanation than Ken's neighbor. But, at least Ken's neighbor can predict the outcome of experiments! The real insights from connectionist models generally come from examining the networks to discover how they manage to perform the task, and by comparing the performance of networks with different architectures or representations. In themselves, computational models are no substitute for good theories.

On the other hand, we shouldn't dismiss models entirely just because we don't understand how they work. Models are often valuable because they can provide proof that systems embodying particular computational principles or mechanisms really are capable of simulating the data. That is, they provide proof of principle. If someone claims that the data is inconsistent with models with property X, and it is then shown that a model with property X can simulate the data, then the simulation makes an important theoretical contribution, even if no one is quite sure how it works.

Some people hold that computational models are just formalizations of theories. This is slightly different from the view that models are the same as theories, because it implies that you are starting from something that offers some kind of explanation. For example, Herb Simon (2002) writes that "The term 'computational model' is used for a theory that is stated definitively enough that precise reasoning ... can be performed on it to infer the course of system behavior." While this might occasionally be the case for some theories, and perhaps is often the case for mathematical models in disciplines such as physics, it is rarely true of computational models in psychology. That is, there is rarely a straightforward one-to-one mapping between model and theory. As I illustrate later, when one tries to construct a computational model of a psychological theory, the model often contains assumptions not in the theory. For example, a theory might be neutral with respect to how some particular process is implemented. But some decisions or assumptions need to be made to make the simulation work. Also, for good reasons, models often omit important parts of the theory. For example, some parts of a theory might be just too hard to simulate, but one wouldn't want that to rule out any computational simulations of the theory. Parts of the model might be simplified, or fed with hand crafted input, so that other parts of the theory can be tested. For example, models of written or spoken word recognition rarely concern themselves with the early stages of visual or auditory perception. These processes are generally outside the scope of the models, but the models clearly need to be supplied with some input. Maybe such models just wouldn't qualify as 'computational models' according to Herb Simon, but they can be very useful.

WHY BUILD COMPUTATIONAL MODELS?

If computational models aren't really theories, then why build them? Well, computational models might not be isomorphic with theories, but they can be used to formalize the process of generating predictions from theoretical assumptions. That is, they provide a crucial link between theory and data. The psychological literature is full of debates that read like pantomime dialogue: "My theory predicts that", "Oh no it doesn't", "Oh yes it does". A properly formulated computational model can help resolve these debates by providing a formal demonstration that, when implemented as a computer program, the theory really does (or doesn't) make the predictions claimed of it. Even setting aside the technical difficulty of constructing simulations, this isn't a trivial task. As we will see later, one must be absolutely certain that the final behavior of the model is driven solely by the critical theoretical assumptions under investigation, and not by things that are either added to, or left out, of the simulation.

Models of word recognition provide a good example of how theoretical progress is critically dependent on the development of properly formulated computational models. In research on word recognition, models don't just resolve debates over what theories predict, they are often the only way that even the theorists themselves can be sure what their theories predict. It is no surprise that almost all influential models of spoken or written word recognition are computational. The behavior of these models is always dependent on the actual set of words that are in the model's lexicon, and how the representations of these words relate to each other (e.g., effects of neighborhood density or competition). That is, the behavior of the models doesn't follow directly or predictably from the mechanisms and processes in the model. The behavior is determined by the interaction between those mechanisms and the words in the lexicon. Different words will be processed differently depending on which other words are in the lexicon. Trying to work out in your head how thousands of words interact is an impossible task for mere mortals. Simulations are essential. For example, in some of our own work on the Shortlist model, it has proved difficult to even hazard a guess as to how certain changes will alter the model's performance.

Another area where the behavior of models is hard to predict is the case of stochastic models. Many models (e.g., Page & Norris, 1998; Ratcliff, 1978) assume that some components of psychological processes are prone to noise—that is, the outcome of the processes is not always the same. Frequently there is no simple analytical procedure (i.e., no mathematical formula) that can predict the average outcome of these processes, and the only option is to run the model many thousands of times. The models produce noisy data, just like real human subjects do, and the outcome is impossible to predict with any precision. The frustrating thing here is that even the behavior of very simple models with very few parameters becomes hard to predict once noise is added.

This is why computational models have become indispensable in many areas of cognitive psychology—we just couldn't make the link between theory and data without them.

Why you should build a model even if you don't think you need one

Building models is a valuable theoretical exercise—even if they don't work. Building models makes you think. When you sit down and try to cast your theory as a computer program, sometimes that bright idea you had turns out not to be so clever after all. Modeling makes you think about the problem at a level of detail well beyond what most of us apply to our verbal theories. With verbal theories, it is very easy to skate over hidden assumptions and convince yourself that your wonderful new creation really does explain the data. When you try to formulate your ideas as computer code, you frequently realize that there is something missing from your theory, or that a particular mechanism you propose just won't behave the way you thought it would. So, it's back to the drawing board to see if you can rescue your precious theory, or maybe you even have to concede that it's never going to work at all. You can make all of this valuable progress before you've even written a line of code.

It is sometimes said that the hallmark of a mature science is cumulative progress. A science comes of age when there is a sound theoretical bedrock on which we can build ever more detailed and refined theories. As theories become more complex, the formal discipline of modeling is almost the only way to achieve that cumulative progress. Much verbal theorizing is fragmented. Each report of new data is accompanied by a new theory that sometimes doesn't apply to much other than the new data. If a verbal theory is extended, there is always a worry that the new parts of the theory might have implications for the way the theory accounts for existing data. When you extend a computational model to explain new phenomena, or to accommodate new data, it's relatively easy to check that nothing you've added to the old model has changed it's predictions. In other words, you are forced to develop an integrated theory that explains new phenomena by extending the scope of the previous theory. This is sometimes referred to as "nested theory development". I say little about this here because it is the focus of the chapter by Ardi Roelofs.

A DOUBLE DISSOCIATION BETWEEN MODELS AND THEORIES

I've made the case that models and theories aren't the same thing. I'll illustrate this by the classic neuropsychological technique of demonstrating a double dissociation between the two. There are theories that don't have models, and models that don't have theories. Both theories with no models, and models with no theories, fall into the "Oh yes it does", "Oh no it doesn't" category. That is, it is hard to say that these theories and models are right or wrong. But that is exactly what is wrong with them. I'll illustrate this dissociation with a couple of my least favorite examples. The choice of examples is driven entirely by personal prejudice.

Short-term memory is simply activation of long-term memory

Some memory researchers have suggested that there is no independent *short-term memory* (STM). STM is nothing more than the temporary activation of corresponding representations in long-term memory (LTM) (e.g., Ruchkin, Grafman, Cameron, & Berndt, 2003). This suggestion might seem attractive because of its parsimony. Why postulate two stores if you can do it all with one? The usual counter-argument to this view is to cite neuropsychological evidence for a dissociation between LTM and

STM (e.g., Vallar & Baddeley, 1984). But this argument doesn't seem to carry much weight with STM-as-LTM theorists. It is worth noting that while there are several computational models of STM (Brown, Preece, & Hulme, 2000; Burgess & Hitch, 1992, 1999; Henson, 1998; Page & Norris, 1998), there are no models that treat STM as activation of LTM. Maybe there is a good reason for this. One of the fundamental problems that face any model of STM is how to remember lists like "1,1,2,1,1" in the correct order. That's certainly not difficult for people. But, it requires representing that the same digit, which we would expect to have a single long-term representation, is repeated 4 times. This is sometimes referred to as a *binding* problem. If you have a STM that can contain representations that are copies of LTM representations, or are bound to LTM representations (e.g., with the equivalent of pointers from STM objects to LTM) it isn't difficult to store such sequences. If the only mechanism you have is LTM activation, then this sequence is likely to be remembered as simply "1,2". That is, the LTM representation for "1" will be strongly activated, and the representation for "2" will be weakly activated. The LTM representations won't code the number of digits, or the relative position of the "1"s relative to "2". It is simple to say that STM is activated LTM, but not so simple to produce a computational model demonstrating how this might work. It is probably even harder to show that this could be done without introducing some specialized mechanism that was responsible solely for the storage of short-term information that is, a STM. So, here is a theory with no model. In fact, because there is not even a hint of how it might work in practice, it probably isn't a theory at all. That's the moral of this short story: If you have no idea how your theory might be translated into a model, it probably isn't a very good theory in the first place. I can't resist adding another example here. Along with James McQueen and Anne Cutler, I have argued that there is no benefit to be had during word recognition in having information from the lexicon feed back to influence the identification of pre-lexical units such as phonemes (Norris, McQueen, & Cutler, 2000a). As the commentaries on Norris et al. (2000a) reveal, not everybody is convinced by our argument. But we are still waiting for those who believe that feedback is beneficial, to produce a model to support their claim. More importantly, we're still waiting for them to produce a theory.

Models without theories

The idea that you could develop a model with no theory might seem rather strange. If you have a model, then surely you must have had a theory? Surprisingly enough, there are some models that simulate data very precisely, but fail to explain how human behavior produces the data simulated by the model. An extreme case might be a model that could be tweaked to simulate any conceivable pattern of data. Such a model wouldn't tell us anything worthwhile at all (cf. Roberts & Pashler, 2000, 2002). The theory would be "Anything can happen". Many early connectionist networks were also 'models with no theories', because the theory was often little more than "Things are done with distributed representations" (cf. Forster, 1994, for a critique of such models). However, in some cases, it is less immediately obvious that the model doesn't really offer an explanation. The simulations look good, and the model does incorporate some sensible theoretical principles.

Two example of models without a proper theory are the perturbation model of memory (Lee & Estes, 1977, 1981) and simulations of eye-movements during spoken word recognition presented by Allopenna, Magnuson, and Tanenhaus (1998). The perturbation model simulates serial position curves, mainly in immediate serial recall experiments. In these experiments subjects are presented with a sequence of items (frequently digits or letters) and are required to recall the items in the correct order. The perturbation theory is a statistical model that generates predictions of the probability that each item in a list is recalled at each output position. For example, it simulates the fact that items at either end of a list are more likely to be recalled in their correct position than are items in the middle of a list. The problem is that the model doesn't explain how any particular list is actually recalled. In effect, the model describes the data, but doesn't describe the behavior or mechanism that produces the data.

Allopenna et al. present simulations using TRACE (McClelland & Elman, 1986) that suffer from exactly the same problem. They simulated data from an experiment tracking listeners' eye movements to pictures of objects as subjects listened to sentences. The sentences could contain either the names of those objects, or the names of phonologically similar objects. For example, the sentence might be *Pick up the beaker, now put it in front of the diamond* and there might be pictures of a beaker, a beetle, a speaker and a control such as a carriage. Activation of the spoken words was simulated in TRACE. TRACE can simulate the probability of recognizing each word at each moment in time. Plots of these probabilities show an excellent fit to the eye movement data (i.e., the probability of fixating on the different pictures). The fit is so good, that surely it must be a good model (see Roberts & Pashler, 2000, 2002, for further discussion of the relation between good fits and the quality of models). But, consider what subjects must be doing whenever the model predicts that they are equally likely to fixate either of two pictures. Clearly subjects can only be fixating one of the two pictures at any point, but the model doesn't say which one. In fact, the model doesn't say how long each picture will be fixated for either. Predictions at one point in time are completely independent of the following point in time. The model therefore predicts that, from moment to moment, the subjects' eyes flicker randomly from picture to picture. Although the model does a very good job at simulating behavior averaged over trials, it doesn't give a plausible explanation for what subjects do on an individual trial. To use terminology that Tanenhaus and Magnuson use elsewhere, the model doesn't have a linking hypothesis (Tanenhaus, Magnuson, McMurray, & Aslin, 2000).

SHORTLIST: A CASE STUDY OF THE RELATION BETWEEN MODEL AND THEORY

Shortlist (Norris, 1994) is a model of how we recognize the words in continuous speech. The overall structure of the computational model is shown in Figure 20.1. The input to the model is a sequence of phonemes. A lexical lookup process then identifies all of the words that corresponds to sequences of phonemes in the input. So, for example, the input *catalog* would match the words *cat, cattle, a, log,* and *catalog.* These words are then entered into an interactive activation network where words that overlap in the input (e.g., 'cattle' and 'log') are connected together by inhibitory links. Words in the network receive input proportional to the number of phonemes they contain. Because words that overlap in the input inhibit each other, they are unlikely to be activated together. The network therefore settles on a set of activated words that don't overlap each other, and this almost always corresponds to the sequence of words intended by the speaker.

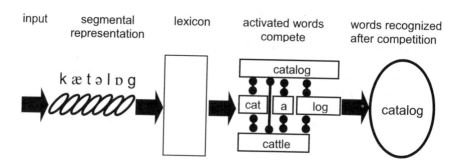

FIG. 20.1. Shortlist.

Fundamentally, the model is very similar to TRACE (McClelland & Elman, 1986). The major difference is that whereas TRACE has feedback from lexical to pre-lexical representations, Shortlist has a completely feedforward architecture. Furthermore, TRACE has a multiply duplicated lexicon so that there is a node corresponding to every word in the lexicon starting at every possible phoneme position in the input. In Shortlist there is a single lexicon and words are only considered in the interactive activation process once they have bottom-up support from the input.

The central theoretical assumptions behind the original Shortlist model are listed below:

T1 The flow of information from pre-lexical to lexical levels is bottom-up only. This was the central motivation for the original Shortlist model.
T2 Bottom-up selection of multiple lexical candidates is based on both matching and mismatching information (i.e., a claim about the procedure for computing a match between input and lexical entries).
T3 Matching lexical candidates (and only those candidates) enter into a competition process that optimizes the parsing of the input into words.
T4 There is no need for explicit lexical segmentation (i.e., the model doesn't need to be told where words begin and end in the input).

Now the assumptions in the computational implementation of Shortlist:

M1 The input to the model is a string of phonemes
M2 The input contains no phoneme deletions, insertions or substitutions (i.e., there are no errors in the perceptual analysis).
M3 The dictionary contains a single canonical representation of each word (i.e., no account of pronunciation variation).
M4 Lexical lookup is by means of a serial search through a dictionary.
M5 The match between the input and lexical entries is computed by counting +1 for each matching phoneme in the correct position, -3 for each mismatching phoneme.
M6 Matches between input phonemes and the corresponding phonemes in a lexical entry are all-or-none (i.e., there is no account of phoneme similarity).
M7 The candidates are entered into the network just by wiring them in as required.
M8 Overlapping candidates are connected by inhibitory links.
M9 Competition is performed by an interactive-activation network.
M10 The model output is a pattern of lexical activations over time.

None of these assumptions is an assumption of the underlying theory. To make the model work, I had to make at least ten extra assumptions that aren't stated in the theory. Some of these assumptions concern issues where there seem to be no overwhelming theoretical reasons to constrain the way the model works. For example, the model uses a string of pho-nemes as input, but the model would work just as well with a string of phonetic features. Discovering the exact form of pre-lexical representa-tions is the "big" question in speech recognition. It would be crazy to decide that we shouldn't build models of word recognition until we have first solved this problem.

The other main class of assumptions are those where simplifications have been made to make the model work. For example, we could extend the model to deal with cases where the input might be misanalysed so that the phonemes presented as input to the model might have some phonemes added, or some deleted. But this didn't seem worth doing, as it wouldn't help in simulating any of the data sets that Shortlist has been applied to.

In Norris (1994) it was very much left as an exercise for the reader to work out which assumptions were part of the "core theory" and which were just pragmatic moves to implement the model. This has led to some confusion as to what the underlying theory really is. The decision to per-form lexical competition with an interactive-activation network with in-hibitory links between competing words has sometimes been taken to be a core theoretical claim. However, hiding away in the original paper is a note that the same function could have been performed by the kind of dynamic programming techniques used in automatic speech recognition. It isn't necessary to understand how dynamic programming works. The important message here is that it is very different from an interactive-ac-tivation network, but it should be possible to make a dynamic program-ming algorithm behave just like the network—and it is (Scharenborg, Norris, ten Bosch, & McQueen, submitted). This illustrates that we often know that there are alternative ways in which a model might compute some function, but we have no data, or a priori reason, to choose one of these ways rather than another. In effect, we are saying that the theory is neutral as to the exact implementational details. However, the theory does need to be implemented, so we have to make a choice. But we need to remember that this is a modeling assumption, and not a core part of the theory. Of course, that doesn't mean we aren't interested in how competition really happens. It means we haven't got a clue how it really works, and we are hoping that the pragmatic solution we have adopted behaves much like the real thing. If later on we find that competition is computed in a completely different way, and that it actually behaves differently, then we could be in trouble.

One way of understanding competition in Shortlist is in terms of Marr's (1982) distinction between computational, algorithmic, and implementational levels of description. The whole idea of competition is part of a computational analysis of the problem. If there are no reliable cues in the signal to indicate where words begin and end, there just has to be a mechanism like competition. This is true irrespective of whether we are talking about human speech recognition, or automatic speech recognition systems. The need for competition follows from an analysis of the task of recognizing connected speech—it is the only way to do it. But Shortlist is neutral with respect to the choice of algorithm or implementation. How competition is performed involves a claim about algorithms. One might want to claim that competition really does involve inhibition of the sort that is embodied in an interactive activation network, and not some form of dynamic programming. These are two alternative algorithms that achieve the same computational result. Currently there seems to be no principle or data that would allow us to choose one algorithm over another. Of course, eventually one would hope that it would be possible to make informed claims about how algorithms are actually implemented in the brain, but that is something we are unlikely to be able to do in the near future for higher level cognitive processes.

One further part of the model that warrants comment is the process of incorporating candidate words in the shortlist into the competition process. This is another example of the binding problem mentioned in the discussion of STM. There I drew attention to the problem of memorizing a string containing more than one token of a particular digit. Intuitively at least, it seem implausible that there are multiple identical lexical representations of digits, or any other words. If that is the case, how do we construct a representation that might need to contain several tokens of the same word? We (Norris, McQueen, & Cutler, 2000b) titled one of our papers "Feedback on feedback on feedback: It's feedforward". Maybe this is hard to understand out of context, but it would be even harder to understand if you could only represent one token of the word "feedback". Representing multiple tokens isn't too difficult in the STM case, because the representations of items in a list can be separate. But, in speech, potential candidates can overlap in the input. Whether a word is recognized or not depends on how it overlaps with other words. It isn't too difficult to write a computer program to do this, but it isn't at all clear how the brain might perform such a task. Working out how the brain solves the binding problem is another one of those "big" questions.

What did we gain from building the Shortlist model?

First, it helped make the case that the lexical-feedback used in TRACE, wasn't actually necessary. Autonomous feed-forward models work fine. Second, TRACE effectively treats the entire lexicon as candidates. Shortlist demonstrated that you need very few candidates in the candidate set. Both of these can be considered to be "proof of principle" demonstrations. The model shows that particular computational principles can perform particular functions. In other words, the mechanisms proposed by the theory really will do what they are supposed to do. Having established that the underlying principles were sound, we were then able to try to make the critical "cumulative progress". We performed experiments to show that there really was a competition process as proposed in the model (McQueen, Norris, & Cutler, 1994; Norris, McQueen, & Cutler, 1995), which enabled us to reject the early version of the Cohort model (Marslen-Wilson, 1987; Marslen-Wilson & Welsh, 1978).

Second, having established the viability of a bottom-up model we could build on that and try to develop the model further. The model has undergone three significant revisions (Norris et al., 1995, 1997, 2000a). Interestingly, the most substantial revision was motivated by the discovery that the model did something that human listeners never did. In both McQueen et al. (1994) and Norris et al. (1995) we asked listeners to press a button when they heard a real word embedded at the start of a nonsense word. One of the filler stimuli was the nonsense word *jumpəv*. Shortlist identified *jumper*, which was never noticed by the listeners, nor indeed, by the experimenters who designed the materials (in British English, the final /r/ in *jumper* is not pronounced).

Did this departure from human performance reflect a flaw in the theory? Well, it certainly was a deficiency in the theory, but it was a huge plus for the model. The model had drawn our attention to something we had never even thought about. It seems that people find it very hard to spot words in this task when this would leave a single consonant or consonant cluster remaining. In English, content words always contain vowels. Listeners behave as though they are trying to parse the nonsense words into a sequence of "possible words". The phoneme [v] has no vowel and is not a possible word, and this makes listeners less likely to accept the segmentation *jumper* plus *v*, than *jump* plus *əv*.

After confirming this informal observation experimentally, we went on to extend the model to develop what we referred to as the Possible Word Constraint (Norris, McQueen, Cutler, & Butterfield, 1997). An added bonus of this modification of the model was that it provided a better and simpler account of earlier data on speech segmentation that we had simulated in the model (Norris et al., 1995). A failure of the model had led us to develop a simpler model that accounted for more data. A rare occurrence indeed, but one that would never have happened without a computational model.

WHAT DOES IT ALL MEAN?

Let's suppose that you have developed a model, it simulates the data, and you know how the model works. This is the point where most modelers just bathe in that warm glow of self-satisfaction. Make the most of it, it only lasts until the reviews of your paper come back telling you that you should add a few extra simulations of the reviewers favorite bits of data. But is that the end of the story? No. Now comes the bit that most modelers don't even bother with. Getting a model to work is only one step toward answering the "how" and "why" questions that lead to a real explanation. For any set of data, there is a potentially infinite set of theories (almost all of them wholly implausible) that would be consistent with the data. The same is true of models. So, what is it about your model that makes it able to simulate the data?

I've already touched on this issue when I tried to separate out the model-specific assumptions from the theoretical assumptions in Shortlist. What I tried to do was to abstract away from the implementation, and concentrate on the set of theoretical principles that were really explaining why the model works. In Shortlist, lexical competition is important, but the way it is implemented probably isn't. The explanation lies in the competition, not in the fact that it uses inhibitory connections between words. The model works because it has particular properties, and one of them is competition. One could build other models that might appear very different but, if they had the same properties, they could still simulate the data. What we need to know about models is not just that they work, or even how they work, but why they work.

This is clearly expressed in the following quotation from Grossberg (1987: 23-24):

> "As each research group injects a stream of new models into this sprawling literature, it becomes ever more essential to penetrate behind the many ephemeral differences between models to the deeper architectural level on which a formal model lives. What are the key issues, principles, mechanisms, and data that may be used to distinguish one model from another? How may we decide whether two seemingly

> different models are really formally equivalent, or are prob-
> ing profoundly different aspects of cognitive processing."

This is an issue that is especially important for understanding connectionist learning models. One thing connectionist learning models are
good at is extracting statistical regularities in their inputs. Indeed, it is
sometimes tempting to say that connectionism in psychology is statistics
for the non-statistician. As I mentioned earlier, it is often hard to work
out how such models work, but it is every bit as important to discover
why they work. For example, if they work because they compute statistics (e.g., the statistics relating spelling to pronunciation, or semantic
features to words), then unless one wishes to argue that the particular
connectionist algorithm like back-propagation (Rumelhart, Hinton, &
Williams, 1986) is a true reflection of the way computation of these statistics is implemented in the brain, the underlying explanation is really
that behavior is driven by some process that computes the relevant statistics. This is by no means a trivial claim. If some particular behavior
would emerge from almost any system that computed the right statistics,
this tells us something very important. It tells us how much specialist
pre-wired knowledge and architecture we need to build into the system.

CONCLUSIONS

A good model must be judged in terms of what it contributes to the explanation of the phenomena under investigation. Modeling really is a
good thing, but not an end in itself. The first benefit of modeling is that it
may focus your attention on details of the theory that you wouldn't
otherwise have thought about. To produce a working computer program
you may have to revise your theory, or even abandon it altogether. If I
had to rank order the benefits of computational modeling, "Modeling
makes you think" would be at the top of the list. But, even if you manage
to produce a model that can simulate the data, that isn't the end of the
story. Just having a model won't automatically explain how things work
or, more importantly, why things work the way they do. As Roberts and
Pashler note, a theory that could explain almost any pattern of data
wouldn't be very illuminating. If you are successful at building a model,
and that model was designed as a straightforward computational implementation of a carefully formulated theory, you need to make sure you
understand exactly how the model relates to the theory. Does the model
work solely because it instantiates the assumptions in the theory, or does
it work because of something that was added to implement the model?
Next comes the really important bit. Once you have established that the

model does the right thing, for the right reasons, then you need to ask what it is about the model that enables it to simulate the data. Why does this model work? Is there something special about exact computations your model performs? Perhaps there is nothing much about the specifics of your model that makes it work. Maybe the model just happens to incorporate the right set of principles, and any model that incorporated those principles would do the job. Discovering that yours isn't the one true model might not sound too satisfying, but it is likely to mean that you are on the way to having an explanation. You will have begun to explain how and why things work. Simulations from the model will convince you (and maybe even your critics) that the theory makes the right predictions, but it is only by thinking about the model that you will be able to explain why things work the way they do.

REFERENCES

Allopenna, P. D., Magnuson, J. S., & Tanenhaus, M. K. (1998). Tracking the time course of spoken word recognition using eye movements: Evidence for continuous mapping models. *Journal of Memory and Language, 38*, 419-439.

Brown, G. D., Preece, T., & Hulme, C. (2000). Oscillator-based memory for serial order. *Psychological Review, 107*, 127-181.

Burgess, N., & Hitch, G. J. (1992). Toward a Network Model of the Articulatory Loop. *Journal of Memory and Language, 31*, 429-460.

Burgess, N., & Hitch, G. J. (1999). Memory for serial order: A network model of the phonological loop and its timing. *Psychological Review, 106*, 551-581.

Forster, K. I. (1994). Computational modeling and elementary process analysis in visual word recognition. *Journal of Experimental Psychology: Human Perception and Performance, 20*, 1292-1310.

Grossberg, S. (1987). Competitive learning: From interactive activation to adaptive resonance. *Cognitive Science, 11*, 23-63.

Henson, R. N. A. (1998). Short-term memory for serial order: The start-end model. *Cognitive Psychology, 36*, 73-137.

Lee, C. L., & Estes, W. K. (1977). Order and position in primary memory for letter strings. *Journal of Verbal Learning and Verbal Behaviour, 6*, 395-418.

Lee, C. L., & Estes, W. K. (1981). Item and order information in short-term memory: Evidence for multilevel perturbation processes. *Journal of Experimental Psychology: Human Learning and Memory, 7*, 149-169.

Marr, D. (1982). *Vision: A computational investigation into the human representation and processing of visual information.* San Francisco: Freeman & Co.

Marslen-Wilson, W. D. (1987). Functional parallelism in spoken word-recognition. *Cognition, 25*, 71-102.

Marslen-Wilson, W. D., & Welsh, A. (1978). Processing interactions and lexical access during word-recognition in continuous speech. *Cognitive Psychology, 10*, 29-63.

McClelland, J. L., & Elman, J. L. (1986). The TRACE model of speech perception. *Cognitive Psychology, 18*, 1-86.

McCloskey, M. (1991). Networks and theories: The place of connectionism in cognitive science. *Psychological Science, 2,* 387-395.

McQueen, J. M., Norris, D., & Cutler, A. (1994). Competition in spoken word recognition: Spotting words in other words. *Journal of Experimental Psychology: Learning, Memory, and Cognition, 20,* 621-638.

Norris, D. (1994). Shortlist: A connectionist model of continuous speech recognition. *Cognition, 52,* 189-234.

Norris, D., McQueen, J. M., & Cutler, A. (1995). Competition and segmentation in spoken-word recognition. *Journal of Experimental Psychology: Learning, Memory, and Cognition, 21,* 1209-1228.

Norris, D., McQueen, J. M., Cutler, A., & Butterfield, S. (1997). The possible-word constraint in the segmentation of continuous speech. *Cognitive Psychology, 34,* 191-243.

Norris, D., McQueen, J. M., & Cutler, A. (2000a). Merging information in speech recognition: Feedback is never necessary. *Behavioral and Brain Sciences, 23,* 299-370.

Norris, D., McQueen, J. M., & Cutler, A. (2000b). Feedback on feedback on feedback: It's feedforward — Authors' response. *Behavioral and Brain Sciences, 23,* 352-370.

Page, M. P. A., & Norris, D. (1998). The primacy model: A new model of immediate serial recall. *Psychological Review, 105,* 761-781.

Ratcliff, R. (1978). A theory of memory retrieval. *Psychological Review, 85,* 59-109.

Roberts, S., & Pashler, H. (2000). How persuasive is a good fit? A comment on theory testing. *Psychological Review, 107,* 358-367.

Roberts, S., & Pashler, H. (2002). Theory development should begin (but not end) with good empirical fits: A comment on Roberts and Pashler (2000) — Reply to Rodgers and Rowe (2002). *Psychological Review, 109,* 605-607.

Ruchkin, D. S., Grafman, J., Cameron, K., & Berndt, R. S. (2003). Working memory retention systems: A state of activated long-term memory. *Brain and Behavioral Sciences, 26,* 709-777.

Rumelhart, D. E., Hinton, G. E., & Williams, R. J. (1986). Learning internal representations by error propagation. In D. E. Rumelhart & J. L. McClelland (Eds.), *Parallel distributed processing: Explorations in the microstructure of cognition,* Vol. 1 (pp. 318-362). Cambridge, MA: MIT Press.

Tanenhaus, M. K., Magnuson, J. S., McMurray, B., & Aslin, R. N. (2000). No compelling evidence against feedback in spoken word recognition. *Behavioral and Brain Sciences, 23,* 348-349.

Scharenborg, O., Norris, D., ten Bosch, L., & McQueen, J. M. (submitted). How should a speech recognizer work? Manuscript submitted for publication.

Seidenberg, M. S., & McClelland, J. L. (1989). A distributed, developmental model of word recognition and naming. *Psychological Review, 96,* 523-568.

Simon, H. A. (2002). Computational Models: Why build them? In L. Nadel (Ed.), *Encyclopaedia of Cognitive Science* (pp. 616-624). London: McMillan.

Vallar, G., & Baddeley, A. D. (1984). Fractionation of working memory: Neuropsychological evidence for a phonological short-term store. *Journal of Verbal Learning and Verbal Behavior, 23,* 151-161.

21 Tools for Learning About Computational Models

Mark A. Pitt and Daniel J. Navarro
Ohio State University, Columbus, Ohio, USA

In the broad field of psycholinguistics, the modeling of language processing has evolved over the last couple of decades into a prominent subfield
that now exerts substantial influence on the direction of the discipline
(Christiansen & Chater, 2001). It has sparked new ways of thinking about
how language is produced and perceived, most notably in the context of
localist connectionist models. With these positive developments have
come new challenges, such as devising tests to distinguish among competing models.

The experimental method has proven to be well-suited for testing
theoretical assumptions from which computational models are built. Differences between models can lead to contrasting qualitative predictions
across experimental conditions, such as two main effects for one model
and an interaction for its competitor. When successful, this method of
model testing can yield evidence that convincingly discriminates between models.

Because such definitive tests are not always possible, researchers
must explore the intricacies and nuances of the models in order to identify
conditions in which the models could be empirically distinguished from
one another. This can be very much a hit-and-miss undertaking because
language processing models are often so complex that it is difficult to
understand, let alone anticipate their full range of behaviors. Two consequences of this are evident in the literature. One is the discovery of an
emergent property of a model, whereby it exhibits a behavior that was
not purposefully or knowingly built into it. The model always possessed
the behavior, but the difficulty in understanding the full consequences of

our design choices when building the model can leave us unaware of some of its capabilities. A related problem, which shows up too often in the broader cognitive science literature, is making what seems like a reasonable qualitative prediction about model performance that turns out to be wrong. For example, a researcher may collect what appear to be compelling data against a model (e.g., double dissociation), only to be shown afterwards through simulations or data fitting that the model in question can indeed produce the observed pattern of results. Because it is difficult to discern the full capabilities of one model, let alone assess the similarities and differences of two, experiments that clearly discriminate between two models are not as common as one would like.

An additional challenge has to do with the incremental approach to model development. Results that once discriminated between two models will no longer do so after the less successful model is modified to accommodate new data. Although this process should result in the models converging on the design of the language system, the similarity is functional, not necessarily structural. That is, the models will perform similarly across many testing situations (i.e., fit data or simulate phenomena), but be architecturally different. Performance differences to distinguish such models can be difficult to find.

In this chapter, we introduce two methods for comparing quantitative models that can assist in tackling the aforementioned problems. The first focuses on inspecting the properties of the model itself to learn about its built-in power to simulate results. The second is a method for identifying an experimental design that has the potential to distinguish between pairs of models.

MINIMUM DESCRIPTION LENGTH: A METHOD FOR CHOOSING BETWEEN TWO MODELS

The primary criterion used to choose among a set of models is the ability to simulate an experimental result. Most often this is quantified as a model's goodness of fit (GOF) to data collected in an experiment. This is a necessary condition that all models must satisfy to be considered a possible description of the language process under study. The ability of a model to fit the data is determined not only by whether the model is a good approximation to the language process, but also by two properties of the model itself, collectively referred to as its *complexity* (Myung, 2000). The property most readers will be familiar with is the number of parameters a model possesses. The more parameters there are in a model, the better it will fit the data. Essentially, each parameter adds an ad-

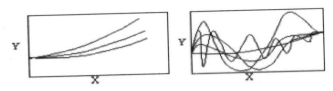

FIG. 21.1. Simple models (left panel) produce only a few patterns, whereas complex models (right panel) can produce a diverse range of patterns.

ditional degree of freedom to the model that allows it to absorb more variance in the data, thus improving fit.

Another dimension of a model that affects its ability to fit data is its functional form, which refers to the way in which the parameters, and possibly input, are combined in the model's equation. For example, Oden and Massaro's (1978) Fuzzy Logical Model of Perception has two parameters on a given trial. Anderson's (1981) Linear Integration Model also has two. As can be seem in the equations below, the parameters are combined differently. They are multiplied in FLMP, but added in LIM. It turns out that FLMP's multiplicative functional form makes it much more flexible in fitting data than LIM (Pitt, Kim, & Myung, 2003).

$$\text{FLMP: } p_{ij} = \frac{\theta_i \lambda_j}{\theta_i \lambda_j + (1 - \theta_i)(1 - \lambda_j)}$$

$$\text{LIM: } p_{ij} = \frac{\theta_i + \lambda_j}{2}$$

A model's complexity is directly related to its flexibility in fitting diverse data patterns. With its many parameters and powerful functional form, a complex model can produce many different data patterns, as depicted in the right-hand graph of Figure 21.1. A simpler model will have fewer parameters and a less powerful functional form. As shown in the left graph, it generates only one pattern, which changes little as the parameters of the model are varied across their ranges.

The increase in flexibility that comes with additional complexity means that GOF will also increase positively with complexity. This relationship is depicted schematically in the top graph of Figure 21.2, with complexity on the x axis and a measure of fit, such as percent variance accounted for (r^2) on the y axis. By virtue of its complexity alone, not its close approximation to the language process, a model can provide

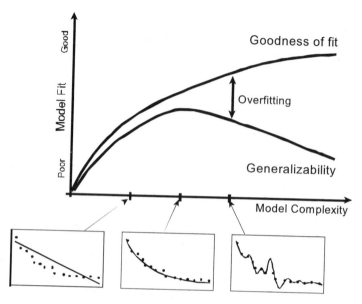

FIG. 21.2. The relation between goodness of fit, generalizability and model complexity.

the best fit to the data. It is this problem that makes GOF a poor model selection criterion (Roberts & Pashler, 2000).

If GOF should be avoided, what should replace it? This question has been studied intensively in allied fields (Linhart & Zucchini, 1986). The consensus is that GOF should be replaced by *generalizability*, which seeks to choose the model whose performance (i.e., fit) generalizes best to data sets from replications of that same experiment (or is *expected* to do so, according to some suitable measure: see below). That is, do not choose the model that fits a single sample of data well. Rather, choose the model that fits all samples (i.e., replications) well. By doing so, the problem that befalls GOF is avoided—an inability to distinguish variation due to random error across samples from variation due to the language process itself.

The problem with GOF, and how generalizability overcomes it, is illustrated in Figure 21.2. The data points in the three bottom graphs are the same. The models (lines) increase in complexity from left to right. As they do, GOF increases as well. If GOF were the selection criterion, the model in the right-most graph would be chosen, since it fits the data perfectly. The model in the middle graph fits the data less well, but notice that it captures the main downward trend and not the minor deviations of each point from this trend, which the right-hand model picks up.

Which of these models best describes the data? Advocates of generalizability would pick the middle model because it captures the main trend well and is not side-tracked by the noise in the data (i.e., random error present in each data point). The sensitivity of the right-most model to the random noise is what makes it overly complex. Model A, in contrast, is overly simple. The straight line does not capture the decelerating trend in the data.

The lower line in the top graph depicts how fit and complexity are related when generalizability is used as a model selection criterion. It is an inverted U-shaped function that can be thought of as having two halves. In the first half, the complexity of the model must match the complexity of the pattern in the data. This is why generalizability increases as fit improves. If model complexity exceeds the peak of the function, generalizability will start to drop because the model will begin to fit random error, not just the regularity we attribute to the language process under study. Another way to think about generalizability is that it tries to strike a balance between the complexity of the model and the complexity needed to describe the regularity in the data.

Although the concept of generalizability is easy to describe, quantifying it has been a nontrivial undertaking. Short summaries of various approaches can be found in Pitt, Myung, and Zhang (2002). They derive a theoretical estimate of generalizability using only a *single* sample. The state of the art method today is the Minimum Description Length (MDL; Rissanen, 1996, 2001). It is elegant and conceptually quite simple to understand, although sometimes computationally challenging to implement. Given a set of data and two models, imagine that you varied the parameters of each model across their ranges and for each combination of parameter values fit the models to the data. You would end up with a very long list of fits, some being much better fits than others (MDL uses a lack-of-fit measure so smaller values are best). After summing these best fits, you would end up with a measure of each models' flexibility. The smaller the value, the greater the model's flexibility.

The flexibility of a complex model will allow it to produce a few exceptionally good fits to the data, but this very same flexibility, which is due to excessive parameterization and its functional form, will cause it to generate a majority of fits that are poor, making the MDL value large. In essence, overly complex models are penalized for having more complexity than is needed to capture the regularity in the data. For a simpler model, the situation is very different. Although no one fit may be as good as the complex model, the reduced flexibility of the simpler model will mean that there will be fewer fits overall, the fits will not differ greatly from one another, and quite possibly all of the fits might not be too poor (compare the graphs in Figure 21.1). The MDL value of this simpler model could well be smaller. In short, a simpler model is penalized less severely because of its reduced flexibility, whatever the reason, be it fewer parameters or a simpler functional form.

Although this discussion has centered on model complexity, it is important to note that MDL does not favor the simpler of two models just because of the model's simplicity. Rather, a model's fit to the data is evaluated relative to its complexity to make the best inference as to which model most likely generated the data. MDL is a statistical inference tool that, at its most basic level, is not unlike statistical inference used in hypothesis testing. Given a small sample of data, we decide which conclusion to draw given its probability of being sampled by chance from the population. Similarly, MDL extracts as much information from the data sample *and the models* to make the best inference as to which model generated the data. We have found that it works quite well in choosing models in multiple areas of cognitive psychology (information integration, categorization, psychophysics; Pitt et al., 2002).

This short discussion of model complexity is meant to raise awareness of the difficulties of model selection. Although a model's good fit to data can, on the surface, seem like convincing evidence in support of a model, caution should be exercised in interpreting the fit until the reason for the good fit is known. Is it because the model is a good approximation of the language process being studied, or is it due to the model's complexity? Sensitivity to this issue will ensure a good fit is not misinterpreted.

LANDSCAPING: INVESTIGATING THE RELATION BETWEEN MODELS AND DATA

Although neutralizing the effects of complexity is important, to avoid selecting the wrong model, MDL only scratches the surface in informing us about model behavior. In addition to knowing that model A is more complex than model B, we would like to know where this extra complexity comes from, and how and when it affects model performance. In short, we would like insight into the inner workings of the models, their similarities and differences, so that informative tests to distinguish them can be designed and carried out.

We have begun to develop tools for gaining this insight. *Landscaping* is the first of these. It has been successfully applied to statistical models (Navarro, Pitt, & Myung, 2004; see also Pitt et al., 2003), and as of this writing it is being adapted to localist connectionist models (Pitt, Navarro, Kim, & Myung, 2004). The approach is the same in both modeling contexts. What differs is how it is implemented. We describe and demonstrate it in the context of statistical models because its application has been worked out more fully.

Two computational models that are functionally quite similar can be difficult to distinguish because, as mentioned in the introduction, an experimental setup that will lead to differing predictions can be elusive. One reason for this is that the experimental method is a rather course procedure for testing quantitative models. The choice of experimental design and the exact levels of the independent variables are decisions most often made from a consideration of the verbal model and intuitions about how best to manipulate the variables. The most well-thought-out experiment can yield data that are minimally informative because both models end up fitting the data well enough that neither can be rejected with confidence. This outcome could be avoided if, before conducting the experiment, we knew how the models would behave relative to one another. Landscaping provides this information. It does so by taking advantage of the precision of computational models to identify the circumstances in which model performance differs.

Landscaping relies on GOF to compare models, but does so in a way that is consistent with the spirit of generalizability. Instead of comparing models on their ability to fit a single data set, we compare their fits to a

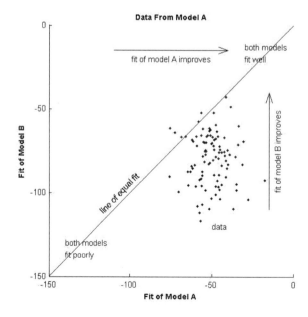

FIG. 21.3. Schematic diagram of a landscape.

large number of data sets. When graphed, they yield a landscape of fits that inform us about model distinguishability. This is illustrated in Figure 21.3. *Maximum Likelihood* (ML) is used as the measure of fit. When the log ML value is taken, a negative value is obtained, with values closer to zero indicating a better fit.

Landscape creation begins by generating 1000 data sets from model A, and these data are fit by both models. The x axis in the figure denotes model A's fit, and the y axis denotes model B's fit. Each of the dots represents one data set. By drawing a diagonal line across the middle of the plot (at $x = y$), we observe that points above the line correspond to data sets that model B fits better than model A, whereas the opposite is true of points below the line. This line is referred to as a *criterion line*, or *decision threshold*. Data that both models fit very well will fall in the top right corner, whereas data that both models fit poorly will fall in the bottom left corner. By plotting the relative fits to the data, we obtain a landscape that enable us literally to see how closely model B can mimic model A. It would be nice if model A always provided better fits to its own data, but in practice this is not always true.

Construction of a landscape requires that data be generated from one of the models. In order to produce a data set, parameter values are needed. In the real world, it is rarely if ever known in advance which parameters values are most likely to be good ones (i.e., ones that yield model behavior that is similar to human performance). This is, after all, the very reason for the existence of free parameters. When comparing two models it is crucial to acknowledge this uncertainty. One way to do this is to specify a probability distribution over parameter values, and then sample the parameter values from this distribution. While we have used Jeffreys' distribution (e.g., Robert, 2001), a range of distributions might be used for this purpose.

ILLUSTRATIVE APPLICATIONS

In this section, we present three concrete examples of how landscaping can be fruitfully employed to learn about model distinguishability. In the first example, we show how landscaping (and MDL) can be used to help design more discriminating experiments. In the second, we demonstrate how it can be used to assess the informativeness of past data in discriminating between models. In the final example, we briefly show how landscaping can be used to highlight the complex ways in which models can interact with one another, and the implications this has for model selection. More details on these examples can be found in Navarro, Myung, Pitt, and Kim (2003) and Navarro et al. (2004).

Experimental Design

The first example we consider uses the information integration models LIM and FLMP presented earlier. Suppose that we want to discriminate between them using a two-choice phoneme categorization task (e.g., choose /ba/ or /da/) with a two by eight design, and 24 participants. This design involves two different levels of one information source (e.g., visual) and eight different levels of the other (e.g., auditory). Thus there are a total of 16 stimuli that may be produced by combining the two evidence sources. This is not an uncommon experimental setup, yet the landscaping plots shown in Figure 21.4 reveal that model distinguishability is asymmetric across data sets. When data are generated by FLMP (left graph), the FLMP model provides a superior fit to virtually all data sets. The long tail of the distribution indicates a sizeable majority of these are quite decisive. When LIM generated the data (right graph), the two models fit the data about equally well, as indicated by the tightly packed distribution that hugs the criterion line.

What are the implications of this outcome? If the language process is truly FLMP-like, then there will be no problem validating this with the 2x8 design because FLMP will provide the best fit to the data. If the process is actually LIM-like, then it will be much more difficult, if not impossible, to distinguish between them. It would be preferable to conduct an experiment whose design does not suffer from this limitation

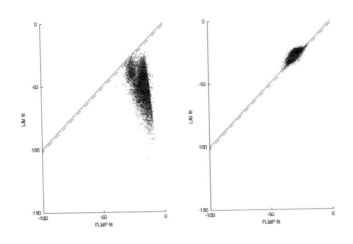

FIG. 21.4. Landscapes for FLMP (left panel) and LIM (right panel), assuming a two by eight design without unimodal conditions.

so the models could be distinguished regardless of the form of the language process. Landscaping can assist in identifying such a design.

It turns out that a minor alteration remedies the asymmetry. The preceding design does not ask how participants would respond when only one source of evidence is provided, even though the models make different predictions in these circumstances. LIM predicts $p_i = \theta_i$ whereas FLMP predicts that $p_i = \theta_i / (1 - \theta_i)$. By adding the 10 extra "unimodal" stimuli (two visual alone and eight auditory alone) to the design and then repeating the analysis, we obtain the landscapes in Figure 21.5. Clearly, the new design is far better able to discriminate between FLMP and LIM. Most notably, the data generated by LIM yield a distribution of relative fits that has now moved away from the criterion line.

The effects of differences in model complexity can also be evaluated in a landscape plot. Because complexity differences between models are constant within an experimental design, the criterion line will shift toward the more complex model by the amount the two models differ in complexity. The dashed lines in Figures 21.4 and 21.5 incorporate this adjustment, and represent the MDL criterion (actually an approximation; see Rissanen, 2001) instead of the ML criterion. Notice that in Figure 21.5 the relative-fit distributions are so far from both lines that it really does not matter which model selection criterion one uses to compare the

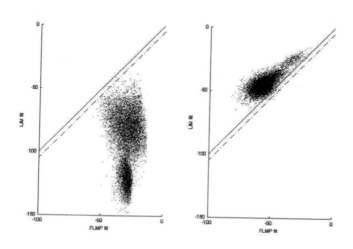

FIG. 21.5. Landscapes for FLMP (left panel) and LIM (right panel), assuming a two by eight design with unimodal conditions added. The solid line is the ML threshold and the dashed line is the MDL one.

models. Both would perform about equally well. The right panel in Figure 21.4, in contrast, is an example of a case where good statistics can sometimes make up for the flaws in a design. With the ML criterion, 31% of the LIM distribution falls on the wrong (FLMP) side of the (solid) decision line. Although the (dashed) MDL criterion is very close to the ML criterion, it makes an enormous difference in model selection accuracy. Only 3.6% of the LIM data sets are now misclassified (on the wrong side of the criterion line).

In summary, the second design is far more likely to distinguish the models and has the attractive property of being able to collect data that clearly favor one model or the other because both relative-fit regions are distinct. Furthermore, it is much less sensitive to the choice of model-selection statistic.

Informativeness of Empirical Data

In addition to assisting with the design of future experiments, landscaping can be used to shed light on the informativeness of data collected in past experiments. A content area in which it has been fruitfully applied in this manner is in comparing forgetting (retention) functions. The basic problem in modeling retention is to express the probability y of remembering a previously observed stimulus, after some amount of time t has passed since it was seen. A typical retention experiment consists of several time intervals, and measurements of y at each interval. The application of landscaping in this context is particularly useful because retention models tend to mimic each other quite well. Furthermore, since commonly used MDL approximations such as the one discussed by Pitt et al. (2002) tend to behave poorly in these cases (see Navarro, 2004), it is all the more important to have a quantitative methodology to guide model comparison.

Consider the functions $y = a \exp(-bt^c)$ and $y = a_1 \exp(-b_1 t) + a_2 \exp(-b_2 t) + a_3$. The first "power-exponent" (PE) function is from Wickelgren's (1972) strength-resistance theory of retention, while the second "sum of exponentials" (SE) function was suggested by Rubin, Hinton, and Wenzel (1999). Both functions produce the decreasing, negatively accelerated curves that are highly typical of retention data, and provide good fits to the large number of data sets available (e.g., Rubin & Wenzel, 1996). Moreover, both satisfy Jost's law: If two traces have equal strength at time t, but are of different ages, then the older one should decay less rapidly from that point on.

Nevertheless, the two models represent different theoretical ideas: The PE function is based on the notion of a single memory trace whose decay is subject to two different factors. It is the action of these factors

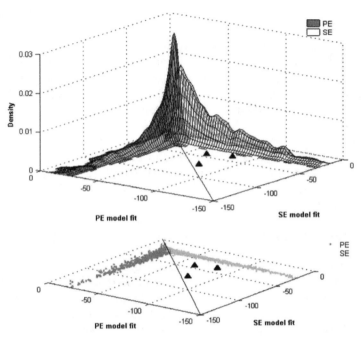

FIG. 21.6. Landscapes for the retention functions. The lower panel shows raw landscapes, while the upper panel shows estimated densities. The locations of empirical data are shown by triangles.

that produces Jost's law. However, in the SE function, there are three different memory stores, each decaying with a constant deceleration. In this function, Jost's law is produced by the multiplicity of stores.

The experimental design that was used to generate the data comes from a recognition memory experiment of Rubin et al. (1999), chosen because the design was large (in number of retention intervals and participants) and because it was replicated three times. Landscapes for the two models are shown in the lower panel of Figure 21.6, which is simply a graph like that in Figure 21.5, but laid flat and rotated 45 degrees instead of standing upright. The same data are shown in the upper graph, which also includes a third (vertical) dimension that represents the estimated probability with which a generated data set falls in a particular location in the landscape (for additional examples, see Navarro et al., 2004). The lightly shaded data sets were generated by the SE model, while the darker ones came from the PE model.

Note that the highest density regions are concentrated near the criterion line. The models also have quite pronounced tails, indicating that they can be distinguished. Furthermore, when we overplot the fits of the models to the empirical data from the three recognition experiments of Rubin et al. (the triangles), clear evidence for SE over PE is visible. Two of the three points are not just below the criterion line, but quite close to the SE distribution, and just as importantly, far from the PE distribution.

With hindsight, this outcome makes a good deal of sense. The experimental designs used in the Rubin et al. paper did not employ a distractor task, so the empirical data may represent a mixture of traces from short-term and long-term stores (John Wixted, personal communication). Since the PE function incorporates only a single trace and is not designed to accommodate short-term memory, these findings are highly interpretable.

Note that the landscapes make such a conclusion much easier to support. Imagine, for instance, that we had presented Figure 21.6 with only the triangles (which is equivalent to a Table of ML fits). It would seem a little rash to draw such strong conclusions, particularly since SE has more parameters than PE, so its superior fit is a little suspect. However, the landscapes provide information about the representativeness of a relative fit, which assists in interpreting the empirical data. The landscapes allow us to conclude with more confidence that SE really does perform better on these data, but there are also some aspects of the data that it clearly does not capture.

Model Selection

In this final example, we demonstrate how landscaping can reveal some of the quirks of model selection. We consider Nosofsky's (1986) Generalized Context Model (GCM), and an extension of this model, GCM-γ (Shin & Nosofsky, 1992). Both models aim to account for the way in which people assign stimuli to categories. Thus, data sets for these models consist of probabilities of category membership for all stimuli. In the GCM, the probability that an observed stimulus is judged to belong to a particular category is proportional to that stimulus' similarity to a set of stored exemplars (previously learned stimuli) from that category. In the GCM-γ model, the probability of category membership is assumed to be proportional to some power γ of this similarity. Obviously, the GCM is a special case of the GCM-γ when $\gamma = 1$.

Shin & Nosofsky (1992) had participants first learn dot patterns that varied along dimensions identified in a previous multidimensional scaling experiment. Transfer of training was measured in a subsequent classification test. When the models are landscaped using this experimental setup, the results are somewhat surprising given the presumed similarity of the models. As is evident in Figure 21.7, the landscapes are remarkably different from each other. This is true despite the fact that

GCM is a special case of GCM-γ. This outcome arises because the γ parameter enables GCM-γ to generate a large set of new data patterns that GCM cannot. This set is so large that GCM-like patterns are in the minority, being very atypical of GCM-γ.

Comparison of the solid decision threshold (ML) to the broken one (MDL) reveals that the latter is far superior. Since the models are nested, ML classifies all patterns as belonging to the more complex model, GCM-γ. To compensate for complexity differences between the models, as measured using the MDL criterion, the criterion line should be shifted downward by 5.2 units in both landscapes (units refer to log-odds increments). Although this minimally affects model selection when fitting GCM-γ data (misclassification errors are still close to 0), selection improves for the GCM data, but errors are still quite high at 67%.

Why was the complexity adjustment not better? Comparison of the landscapes reveals that complexity only partly accounts for the differences between the models. Complexity measures like MDL consider the relation between a model and data, but do not consider the interrelation between models as well. This limitation of scope results in a complexity measure that can suggest only a constant correction to the ML criterion. In the Shin and Nosofsky experiment, however, GCM and GCM-γ have a complicated relationship with each other as well as with the data.

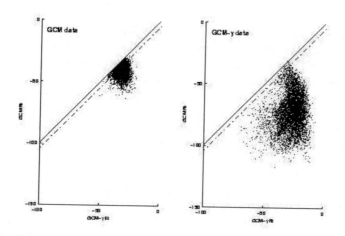

FIG. 21.7. Landscapes for GCM (left panel) and GCM-? (right panel). The solid line denotes the ML decision criterion, while the broken line is the MDL criterion.

Because the GCM landscape is so sharply defined, almost any pattern inside that region (which is basically a semi-circular area) is more representative of GCM. Anything outside of this area is more representative of GCM-γ. Therefore, the best way to discriminate between these models would be to define a nonlinear decision threshold along the borders of this semi-circular region. At present, measures of model complexity like those provided by MDL cannot achieve this.

CONCLUSION

Computational modeling has advanced the field of psycholinguistics by sharpening our understanding of theoretical ideas and their potential. To build a model, assumptions about process and representation must be formulated, which adds precision to one's description of the language system.

The very success of modeling raises new and difficult issues. One of these is how to compare and select between competing models. The consequences of the design choices made in model construction must be understood to succeed in either. Otherwise one runs the risk of being misled in the same way a garden-path sentence misleads a reader. The two quantitative tools introduced in this chapter are intended to assist in this enterprise. Landscaping is a simple yet powerful tool for assessing model distinguishability. MDL is useful for selecting among quantitative models, where the goal is to maximize generalizability, not goodness of fit. The three examples presented here (assessing the distinguishability of models within an experimental design, evaluating the informative of data in distinguishing models, and discovering complex relationships between models and data) are meant to demonstrate the usefulness and versatility of these complementary tools. We hope they are of practical use.

ACKNOWLEDGMENTS

The authors were supported by NIH grant R01-MH57472. The second author was also supported by a grant from the Office of Research at OSU.

REFERENCES

Anderson, N. H. (1981). *Foundations of information integration theory*. New York: Academic Press.
Christiansen, M. H., & Chater, N. (2001). *Connectionist psycholinguistics*. Westport, CT: Ablex.
Linhart, H., & Zucchini, W. (1986). *Model selection*. New York: Wiley.

Myung, I. J. (2000). The importance of complexity in model selection. *Journal of Mathematical Psychology, 44*, 190-204.

Navarro, D. J. (2004). A note on the applied use of MDL approximations. *Neural Computation, 16*, 1763-1768.

Navarro, D. J., Myung, I. J., Pitt, M. A., & Kim, W. (2003). Global model analysis by landscaping. In R. Alterman & D. Kirsh (Eds.), *Proceedings of the 25th Annual Conference of the Cognitive Science Society*. Boston, MA [CD-ROM].

Navarro, D. J., Pitt, M. A., & Myung, I. J. (2004). Assessing the distinguishability of models and the informativeness of data. *Cognitive Psychology, 49*, 47-84.

Nosofsky, R. M. (1986). Attention, similarity, and the identification-categorization relationship. *Journal of Experimental Psychology: General, 115*, 39-57.

Oden, G. C., & Massaro, D. W. (1978). Integration of featural information in speech perception. *Psychological Review, 85*, 172-191.

Pitt, M. A., Myung, I. J., & Zhang, S. (2002). Toward a method of selecting among computational models of cognition. *Psychological Review, 109*, 472-491.

Pitt, M. A., Kim, W., & Myung, I. J. (2003). Flexibility versus generalizability in model selection. *Psychonomic Bulletin & Review, 10*, 29-44.

Pitt, M. A., Navarro, D. J., Kim, W., & Myung, J. I. (2004). Global model analysis by parameter space partitioning. Manuscript submitted for publication.

Rissanen, J. (1996). Fisher information and stochastic complexity. *IEEE Transaction on Information Theory, 42*, 40-47.

Rissanen, J. (2001). Strong optimality of the normalized ML models as universal codes and information in data. *IEEE Transactions on Information Theory, 47*, 1712-1717.

Robert, C. P. (2001). *The Bayesian choice* (2nd ed.). New York: Springer.

Roberts, S., & Pashler, H. (2000). How persuasive is a good fit? A comment on theory testing. *Psychological Review, 107*, 358-367.

Rubin, D. C., Hinton, S., & Wenzel, A. (1999). The precise time course of retention. *Journal of Experimental Psychology: Learning, Memory & Cognition, 25*, 1161-1176.

Rubin, D. C., & Wenzel, A. (1996). One hundred years of forgetting: A quantitative description of retention. *Psychological Review, 103*, 734-760.

Shin, H. J., & Nosofsky, R. M. (1992). Similarity-scaling studies of dot-pattern classification and recognition. *Journal of Experimental Psychology: General, 121*, 278-304.

Wickelgren, W. A. (1972). Trace resistance and decay of long-term memory. *Journal of Mathematical Psychology, 9*, 418-455.

22 Rational Models of Comprehension: Addressing the Performance Paradox

Matthew W. Crocker
Saarland University, Germany

A fundamental goal of psycholinguistic research is to understand the architectures and mechanisms that underlie language comprehension. Such an account entails an understanding of the representation and organization of linguistic knowledge in the mind and a theory of how that knowledge is used dynamically to recover the interpretation of the utterances we encounter. While research in theoretical and computational linguistics has demonstrated the tremendous complexities of language understanding, our intuitive experience of language is rather different. For the most part people understand the utterances they encounter effortlessly and accurately. In constructing models of how people comprehend language, we are thus presented with what we dub the *performance paradox*: How is it that people understand language so effectively given such complexity and ambiguity?

In our pursuit and evaluation of new theories, we typically consider how well a particular model is able to *account* for observed results from the relevant range of controlled psycholinguistic experiments (empirical adequacy), and also the ability of the model to *explain* why the language comprehension system has the form and function it does (explanatory adequacy). Interestingly, research since the late-1970s has led to tremendous variety in proposals for parsing, disambiguation, and reanalysis mechanisms, many of which have been realized as computational models. However, while it is possible to classify models—for example, according to whether they are modular, interactive, serial, parallel, or probabilistic—consensus at any concrete level has been largely elusive.

We argue here for an alternative approach to developing and assessing theories and models of sentence comprehension, which offers the possibility of improving both empirical and explanatory adequacy, while also characterizing *kinds of models* at a more relevant and informative level than the architectural scheme noted above. In the following subsections, we emphasize the important fact that a model's coverage and behavior should not be limited to a few "interesting" construction types, but must also extend to realistically large and complex language fragments, and must account for why most processing is typically rapid and accurate, in addition to modeling pathological behaviors. We then argue that while the *algorithmic* description of a theory is essential to adequately assess its behavior and predictions, the theory of processing must also be stated at a more abstract level, for example, Marr's *computational* level (Marr, 1982). In addressing these issues, we suggest that many of the ideas from *rational analysis* (Anderson, 1991) provide important insights and methods for the development, evaluation, and comparison of our models. In the subsequent section, we then discuss a number of existing models that can be viewed within a rational framework in order to more concretely exemplify our proposals.

Garden Paths versus Garden Variety

One great puzzle of human language comprehension, which we have termed the performance paradox, is how easily people understand language despite its complexity and ambiguity. More puzzling is the fact that research in human sentence processing pays relatively little attention to this most fundamental and self-evident claim. In contrast, sentence processing research has focused largely on *pathological* phenomena: a relatively small proportion of ambiguities causing difficulty to the comprehension system. Examples include garden-path sentences, such as the well-known main verb/reduced-relative clause ambiguity initially noted by Bever (1970):

(1) The horse raced past the barn fell.

In such sentences the verb *raced* is initially interpreted as the main verb, and only when the true main verb *fell* is reached can the reader determine that *raced past the barn* should actually have been interpreted as a reduced relative clause (cf., *The horse which was raced past the barn fell*). In this relatively extreme example, readers may not be able to recover the correct meaning at all, while other constructions may be interpretable but result in some conscious or experimentally measurable difficulty.

The idea behind such research is to use information about parsing and interpretation preferences, combined with the factors that modulate them—such as frequency, context, and plausibility—to gain insight into the underlying comprehension system (see Crocker, 1999, for an overview). While this empirical research strategy might be seen as tacitly assuming rapid and accurate performance in general—relying on pathologies only as a means for revealing where the "seams" are in the architecture of the language comprehension system—existing models of processing typically focus on accounting *only* for these pathologies. Furthermore, with few exceptions, existing models can be considered toy implementations at best, with lexical and syntactic coverage limited to what is necessary to model some subset of experimental data. Thus while such models may provide interesting and sophisticated accounts of familiar experimental findings, they provide no account of more general performance. Many theories have not been implemented at all, making it even more problematic to assess their general coverage and behavior.

Models à la Carte

Within the general area of computational psycholinguistics, a striking picture emerges when one compares the state of affairs in lexical processing with that in sentence processing. While there are relatively few models of lexical processing which are actively under consideration (see Norris, 1999), there exist numerous theories of sentence processing with relatively little consensus for any one in particular (Crocker, 1999; Townsend & Bever, 2001, chap. 4). The diverse range of models stems primarily from the compositional and recursive nature of sentence structure, combined with ambiguity at the lexical, syntactic and semantic levels of representation. The result is numerous dimensions of variation along which algorithms for parsing and interpretation might differ, including:

- *Linguistic knowledge:* What underlying linguistic representations, levels, interfaces, and structure-licensing principles are assumed? How is lexical knowledge organized and accessed?
- *Architectures:* To what extent is the comprehension system organized into modules? What are the temporal dynamics of information flow in modular and non-modular architectures?
- *Mechanisms:* What mechanisms are used to arrive at the interpretation of an utterance? Are representations constructed serially, in parallel, or via competition? How does reanalysis take place?

However, while the formal and computational properties of language logically entail that a large number of processing models is possible, the space of models should be constrained by available empirical processing evidence. To some extent this has been achieved. Virtually all models, for example, share the property of strict incrementality. That is, the parsing mechanism integrates each word of an utterance into a connected, inter-pretable representation as the words are encountered (Frazier, 1979; Crocker, 1996). Beyond this, however, there is little agreement about even the most basic mechanisms of the language comprehension system.

Sentence processing research has long been preoccupied, for example, by the issue of whether the human language processor is fundamentally a restricted or unrestricted system, with various intermediate positions being proposed. Broadly, the restricted view holds that processing is served by informationally encapsulated modules, which construct only one interpretation (e.g., Frazier, 1979; Crocker, 1996). Unrestricted, or constraint-based, models on the other hand, assume that possible inter-pretations are considered in parallel, with all relevant information poten-tially being drawn upon to select among them (MacDonald, Pearlmutter, & Seidenberg, 1994; McRae, Spivey-Knowlton, & Tanenhaus, 1998).

However, while there exists a compelling body of empirical evidence demonstrating the rapid influence of plausibility (Pickering & Traxler, 1998) and visual information (Tanenhaus, Spivey-Knowlton, Eberhard, & Sedivy, 1995; Knoeferle, Crocker, Scheepers, & Pickering, in press) during comprehension, falsification of restricted processing architectures has not been possible. Furthermore, there is no direct empirical evidence sup-porting parallelism, i.e., that people simultaneously consider multiple interpretations for a temporarily ambiguous utterance as it unfolds.

Another area where mechanisms have proven difficult to distinguish empirically is reanalysis: When does the parser decide to abandon a par-ticular analysis, and how does it proceed in finding an alternative? Con-sider the following example:

(2) The Australian woman saw the famous doctor had been drinking.

There is strong evidence that, for constructions such as this, people initially interpret the noun phrase *the famous doctor* as the direct object of *saw* (e.g., Pickering, Traxler, & Crocker, 2000), raising the question of how people recover the ultimately correct structure, in which that noun phrase becomes the subject of the complement clause. Sturt, Pickering, and Crocker (1999) defend a representation preserving repair model for recovering from misanalysis (Sturt & Crocker, 1996), while Grodner, Gibson, Argaman, and Babyonyshev (2003) argue the same data can be accounted for using a destructive, re-parsing mechanism. Again, two apparently opposing models appear consistent with the same empirical findings.

Challenges

In summarizing the discussion above, we identify four key limitations, some or all of which affect most existing accounts of human sentence processing. We suggest these have contributed to both the lack of generality and comparability of our models, which has in turn stymied convergence within the field:

Limited scope: Models traditionally focus on some particular aspect of processing, emphasizing, for example, lexical ambiguity, structural attachment preferences, word order ambiguity, or reanalysis. Few proposals exist for a unified, implementable model of, for example, lexical *and* structural processing *and* reanalysis. To the extent that such proposals do exist (e.g., Jurafsky, 1996; Vosse & Kempen, 2000), they are still typically so narrow in coverage that assessing general performance is difficult.

Model equivalence: Some models, while different in implementational detail, are virtually equivalent in terms of their behavior. For example, the symbolic model proposed by Sturt and Crocker (1996) overlaps substantially with Stevenson's (1994) hybrid connectionist model with regard to what structures are recovered during initial structure building and reanalysis. Indeed, even the Grodner et al. (2003) account might be considered as *functionally equivalent*: Even though the precise reanalysis mechanism is fundamentally different from that of Sturt and Crocker (1996) and Stevenson (1994), the "state" of the models is fundamentally identical as each word is processed.

Measure specificity: Models often vary with respect to the kind of experimental paradigms and observed measures they seek to account for. Models of processing load have relied primarily on self-paced reading data (Gibson, 1998; Hale, 2003), while theories of parsing rely on a variety of measures (e.g., first pass, regression path duration, and total time) from eye-tracking during reading (e.g., Crocker, 1996; Frazier & Clifton, 1996). Some recent accounts are built upon the visual world paradigm, which monitors eye-movements in visual scenes during spoken comprehension (e.g., Tanenhaus et al., 1995; Knoeferle et al., in press), thus measuring attention, not processing complexity. Even more extremely, some models are based almost exclusively on neuroscientific measures, such as event-related potentials (Friederici, 2002; Schlesewsky &

Bornkessel, in press), placing little emphasis on accounting for existing behavioral data.

Weak linking hypotheses: Establishing the relationship between a model and empirical data demands a *linking hypothesis*, which maps the model's behavior to empirically observed measures. In explaining reading time data, for example, various models have assumed processing time is due to structural complexity (Frazier, 1985), backtracking (Abney, 1989; Crocker, 1996), non-determinism (Marcus, 1980), non-monotonicity (Sturt & Crocker, 1996), re-ranking of parallel alternatives (Jurafsky, 1996; Crocker & Brants, 2000), storage and integration cost (Gibson, 1998), the reduction of uncertainty (Hale, 2003), or competition (McRae et al., 1998). In addition, most models make only qualitative predictions as to the relative degree of difficulty. Those models which attempt more quantitative links with reading time data (McRae et al., 1998) fail to account for how structures are actually built (unlike the models outlined above), and are also highly fit to individual syntactic constructions.

TOWARD RATIONAL MODELS

On the basis of discussion thus far, it should not be concluded that theories of sentence understanding posit particular processing architectures and implementations arbitrarily. In addition to linguistic assumptions, models are often heavily motivated and shaped by assumptions concerning cognitive limitations. Marcus (1980), Abney (1989), and Sturt and Crocker (1996) propose parsing architectures designed to minimize the computational complexity of backtracking. Some models argue that the sentence processor prefers less complex representations (Frazier, 1979), or assume other restrictions on working memory complexity. Other models restrict themselves by adopting a particular implementational platform, such as connectionist networks and stochastic architectures, as a way of incorporating cognitively-motivated mechanisms (e.g., Stevenson, 1994; Vosse & Kempen, 2000; Christiansen & Chater, 1999; Sturt, Costa, Lombardo, & Frasconi, 2003).

Indeed it seems uncontroversial that human linguistic performance is to some extent shaped by such specific architectural properties and cognitive limitations. It is also true, however, that relatively little is known about the extent to which this is the case, let alone the precise manner in which such limitations affect human language understanding. We therefore suggest that by focusing on specific processing architectures and mechanisms and cognitive limitation, theories of sentence processing are forced into making stipulations without concrete empirical justification, but which nonetheless impact on the overall behavior of models.

An alternative approach to developing a theory of sentence processing is to shift our emphasis away from particular mechanisms, and towards the nature of the sentence processing *task*:

> *An algorithm is likely understood more readily by understanding the nature of the problem being solved than by examining the mechanism (and the hardware) in which it is solved.* (Marr, 1982: 27)

The critical insight here is that it can be helpful to have a clear statement of what the goal of a particular system is—and the function it seeks to compute—in addition to a model of how that goal is achieved, or how that function is actually implemented. For example, a systematic preference for argument attachment over modifier attachment, as argued for extensively by Pritchett (1992), can be viewed as providing an overarching explanation for a number of different preference strategies in the literature. Indeed, Crocker (1996) argues that Pritchett's theory, which seeks to maximize satisfaction of syntactic and semantic constraints, can be viewed as realizing an even more general goal of human language processing:

> *Principle of Incremental Comprehension* (PIC): The sentence processor operates in such a way as to maximize comprehension of the sentence at each stage of processing. (Crocker, 1996: 106)

Such a statement in itself says little about the specific mechanisms involved and is indeed consistent with a range of proposals in the literature. It is, rather, intended as a claim about what kinds of models can be considered, and a general explanation for why they are as they are (namely, because they satisfy the PIC). This claim goes beyond saying that comprehension is incremental, something that is true of virtually all current models, and predicts that at points of ambiguity, the preferred structure should be the one that is maximally interpretable: For example, it establishes the most dependencies, or maximizes role assignment and reception.

Focusing on the nature of the problem thus shifts our attention to the goals of the system under investigation, and the relevant properties of the environment. Anderson (1991) notes that there is a long tradition of attempting to understand cognition as *rational*: Not because it follows some set of normative rules, but because it is optimally adapted to its task and environment. On the assumption that the comprehension system is rational, we can derive the optimal function for that system from a specification of the goals and the environment. The *Principle of*

Incremental Comprehension does this rather implicitly: It assumes the goal is to correctly understand the utterance, and the environment is one in which language is both ambiguous and encountered incrementally.

In order to determine more precisely the function that comprehension seeks to optimize, we need also consider computational constraints in order to avoid deriving a function that is cognitively implausible in some respects (e.g., construction and evaluation of all—possibly infinite—interpretations, seems relatively implausible). However, an important aim of this kind of analysis is to see how much can be explained by avoiding appeal to such constraints except when they are extremely well motivated.

It should be clear that in adopting a Marrian/Andersonian approach, we address several of the potential pitfalls that have plagued model builders to date: emphasis on what function is computed (Marr's computational level), rather than specific algorithms and implementations should lead to better consensus, and more straightforward identification of models which are equivalent (in that they implement the same function). Furthermore, the approach emphasizes general behavior and performance, rather than the construction of models that are over-fitted to a few phenomena.

Inspired by Anderson's rational analysis, Chater, Crocker, and Pickering (1998) motivate the use of probabilistic frameworks for characterizing and deriving mathematical models of human parsing and re-analysis. Probabilistic models of language processing typically optimize for the likelihood of ultimately obtaining the correct analysis for an utterance (Manning & Schütze, 1999).[1]

This goal of adopting the most likely analysis, or interpretation, of an utterance seems plausible as a first hypothesis for a *rational* comprehension system. That is, in selecting among possible interpretations for an utterance, adopting the most likely one would be an optimally adaptive solution. Given our overriding assumption of incremental processing, this selection can also be applied at each point in processing: prefer the (partial) interpretation that is most likely, given the words of the sentence that have been encountered thus far.

---

[1] We can formally express the *Principle of Likelihood* (PL) using notation standardly used in statistical language processing (Manning & Schütze, 1999):

(eq 2) $\hat{t} = \underset{t \in T : yield(t)=s}{\arg\max} \ P(t \mid s, K)$

The expression simply states that, from the set of all interpretations T which have as their yield the sentence s, we select the interpretation t which has the greatest probability of being correct given the s, and our knowledge K.

There are some very important and subtle issues concerning our use of probabilities here. Firstly, using a probabilistic framework to reason about, or characterize, the behavior of a system does not explicitly entail that people actually use probabilistic mechanisms (e.g., frequencies) but rather that such a framework can provide a good characterization of the system's behavior. That is, non-probabilistic systems could exhibit the behavior characterized by the probabilistic theory. Of course, (some) statistical mechanisms will also be consistent with the behavior dictated by the probabilistic meta-theory, but these will require independent empirical justification.

Furthermore, probabilities may be used as an abstraction. For example, if a sentence s is globally ambiguous, having two possible structures, we might suggest that the probabilities, $P(t_1 | s,K)$ and $P(t_2 | s,K)$, for the two structures provide a good *estimate* or characterization of which is "more likely". This is a perfectly coherent statement, even though the real reason one structure is preferred is presumably due to a complex array of lexical and syntactic biases, semantics and plausibility, pragmatics and context (some or all of which may in turn be probabilistic). That is, we are simply using probabilities as a short-hand representation, or an abstraction, of more complex preferences, which allows us to reason about the behavior of the language processing system (see Chater et al., 1998, for detailed discussion).

It is in general not possible to determine probabilities precisely, rather we typically attempt to *estimate* probabilities using frequency counts from large corpora or norming studies (McRae et al., 1998; Pickering et al., 2000). Indeed, the usefulness of likelihood models in computational linguistics has led to a tremendous amount of research into how probabilistic language models can be developed on the basis of data-intensive, corpus techniques (see Manning & Schütze, 1999, for both an introduction and survey of recent models).

In the following two sections we outline several examples of how the *Principle of Likelihood* has been applied to the development of particular models of language processing. Such models can be considered theories at Marr's algorithmic level, in that they provide a characterization of *how* the language processor implements the maximum likelihood function.

Lexical Ambiguity Resolution

Corley and Crocker (2000) present a broad-coverage model of lexical category disambiguation based on the *Principle of Likelihood*. Specifically, they suggest that for a sentence consisting of words $w_0 \ldots w_n$, the sentence processor adopts the most likely part-of-speech sequence $t_0 \ldots t_n$. More specifically, their model exploits two simple probabilities: *(i)* the conditional probability of word w_i given a particular part of speech t_i, and (ii) the probability of t_i given the previous part of speech t_{i-1}.[2] As each word of the sentence is encountered, the system assigns it that part-of-speech t_i which maximizes the product of these two probabilities. This model capitalizes on the insight that many syntactic ambiguities have a lexical basis (MacDonald et al., 1994), as in (3):

(3) The warehouse prices/makes are cheaper than the rest.

These sentences are temporarily ambiguous between a reading in which *prices* or *makes* is the main verb or part of a compound noun. After being trained on a large corpus, the model predicts the most likely part of speech for *prices*, correctly accounting for the fact that people understand *prices* as a noun, but *makes* as a verb (see Crocker & Corley, 2002, and references cited therein). Not only does the model account for a range of disambiguation preferences rooted in lexical category ambiguity, it also explains why, in general, people are highly accurate in resolving such ambiguities.

Corley and Crocker's model provides a clear example of how we can use probabilistic frameworks to characterize both the function to be computed according to the rational analysis, and also to derive a practical, cognitively plausible *approximation* of this function which serves as the actual model (refer to (eq 2) and (eq 3) in footnote 2). Of course, subsequent empirical research might suggest the bi-gram model is inadequate and should be replaced by, for example, a tri-gram model. Any such evidence, however, would only involve revision at the *algorithm level*, not of the overarching *rational analysis*, or *computational level*, since the tri-

---

[2]Formally, we can write this as a function which selects that part-of-speech sequence which results in the highest probability:

$$\text{(eq 2)} \quad \hat{t}_0...\hat{t}_n = \underset{t_0...t_n}{\arg\max}\, P(t_0...t_n, w_0...w_n)$$

Directly implementing such a model presents cognitive and computational challenges. On the one hand, the above equation fails to take into account the incremental nature of processing (i.e., it assumes all words are available simultaneously), while on the other hand, the accurate estimation of such probabilities is computationally intractable due to data sparseness. Their approach, therefore, is to approximate this function using a bi-gram model, which incrementally computes the probability for a string of words as follows:

$$\text{(eq 3)} \quad P(t_0...t_n, w_0...w_n) \cong \prod_{i=1}^{n} P(w_i \mid t_i) P(t_i \mid t_{i-1})$$

gram model still approximates the maximum likelihood function posited by the *Principle of Likelihood.*

Syntactic Processing

While it provides a simple example of rational analysis, Corley and Crocker's model cannot be considered a model of sentence processing, as it only deals with lexical category disambiguation. As noted above, directly estimating the desired probability of syntactic trees is problematic, since many have never occurred before. Thus, rather than trying to associate probabilities with entire trees, statistical models of syntactic processing typically associate a symbolic component that generates linguistic structures with a probabilistic component that assigns probabilities to these structures. A probabilistic context free grammars (PCFG), for example, associates probabilities with each rule in the grammar, and computes the probability of a particular tree by simply multiplying the probabilities of the rules used in its derivation (Manning & Schütze, 1999, chap. 11).

In developing a model of human lexical and syntactic processing, Jurafsky (1996) further suggests using Bayes' Rule to combine structural probabilities generated by a probabilistic context free grammar with other probabilistic information, such as subcategorization preferences for individual verbs. The model therefore integrates multiple sources of experience into a single, mathematically well-founded framework. In addition, the model uses a beam search to limit the amount of parallelism required.

Jurafsky's model is able to account for a range of parsing preferences reported in the psycholinguistic literature. However, it might be criticized for its limited coverage, that is, for the fact that it uses only a small lexicon and grammar, manually designed to account for a handful of example sentences. In the computational linguistic literature, on the other hand, broad coverage probabilistic parsers are available that compute a syntactic structure for arbitrary corpus sentences with generally high accuracy. This suggests there is hope for constructing psycholinguistic models with similar coverage, potentially explaining more general human linguistic performance. Indeed, more recent work on human syntactic processing has investigated the use of PCFGs in wide coverage models of incremental sentence processing (Crocker & Brants, 2000). Their research demonstrates that even when such models are trained on large corpora, they are indeed still able to account not only for a range of human disambiguation behavior, but also exhibit good performance on natural text. Related work also demonstrates that such broad coverage probabilistic models maintain high overall accuracy even under the strict memory and incremental processing restrictions (Brants & Crocker, 2000) that seem necessary for cognitive plausibility. Finally, Hale (2003) extends the use statistical parsing models to providing a possible explanation of processing load, rather than ambiguity resolution.

The Informativity Model

The models just outlined all begin with the assumption that the *Principle of Likelihood* best characterizes the function of the sentence comprehension system. It is important to note, however, that alternative rational analyses may emerge, depending on the precise definition of the problem. Chater et al. (1998) argue that a more plausible rational analysis of human sentence processing must take into account a number of important cognitive factors before an appropriate optimal function can be derived. In particular, they consider the following:

- Linguistic input contains substantial local ambiguity, which is resolved incrementally.
- People consciously consider only one preferred, or *foregrounded*, interpretation of an utterance at any given time during parsing.
- Immediate reanalysis is typically much easier than delayed reanalysis, and therefore is a lower cost operation.

In deriving a rational analysis of interpretation, Chater et al. argue that the human parser is optimized so as to incrementally resolve each local ambiguity as it is encountered (Church & Patil, 1982). The result of the analysis is a function which includes not only likelihood, but also another measure, *specificity*, which determines the extent to which a particular analysis is "testable". That is, specificity measures the extent to which subsequent input will assist in either confirming or rejecting the foregrounded structure. On this account, the initially favored analysis is the one that is both "fairly likely" and "fairly testable". The measure, which they term *informativity* (I), balances *likelihood* (P) and *specificity* (S), such that the interpretation which maximizes the product of these two is foregrounded at each point in processing.[3]

---

[3]Again, we can formalize this straightforwardly as follows:

(eq 5) $\hat{t} = \underset{t \in T : yield(t)=s}{\arg\max} \ I(t) = P(t) \bullet S(t)$

This model contrasts with pure likelihood accounts in predicting that the sentence processor will prefer the construction of testable analyses over non-testable ones, except where the testable analysis is highly unlikely. The result will be a greater number of easy misanalyses (induced by less probable but more testable analyses), and a smaller number of difficult misanalyses (induced by more probable but less testable analyses). This in turn means that the ultimately correct analysis will usually be obtained quickly, either initially or after rapid reanalysis.

The most compelling empirical support for the *Principle of Informativity* stems from experiments by Pickering et al. (2000), in which the plausibility of a low frequency structural alternative (the NP-complement subcategorization frame for a verb like *realized*) was manipulated, as in *The athlete realized his {goals* vs. *shoes} ... were out of reach.* Assuming a likelihood-based model, which would foreground an S-complement, there should be no effect of plausibility given that the low probability NP-complement option would no be considered during initial analysis.[4] Reading time experiments demonstrated, however, a striking asymmetry between frequency bias and actual processing performance, indicating that the low frequency alternative was immediately considered during on-line sentence comprehension. Pickering et al. argued that the low frequency NP-complement analysis is locally more 'specific', and hence can be evaluated earlier than the high frequency S-complement alternative. For a system with limited processing resources, such a strategy is advantageous, as it minimizes the cost of reanalysis.

Pickering et al. (2000) define the specificity of an analysis as a measure of how strongly that analysis constrains the sentence's continuation. A highly specific analysis entails that the parser has strong expectations about the subsequent input. If these expectations are fulfilled, then this is taken as further support for the analysis, and parsing continues. If expectations are not fulfilled, the parser knows to immediately pursue an alternative analysis. Thus, Informativity predicts that the parser may prefer an analysis that is less probable than another, if it is more specific. While this leads to more misanalyses than a pure likelihood model, they are precisely those misanalyses from which the parser can recover quickly: An analysis that is potentially incorrect (i.e., improbable) would only be adopted if highly specific, hence the parser will be able to recognize and correct the error quickly.

---

[4]Though see Crocker & Brants (2000) for an explanation of why their model does in fact account for this data.

As noted by Pickering et al. (2000), the *Principle of Informativity* differs crucially from the *Principle of Likelihood* in that it favors the construction of interpretable dependencies, thus providing an overarching rational analysis explanation for previously proposed strategies in the literature, such as Minimal Attachment (Frazier, 1979), theta-attachment (Pritchett, 1992), and the Principle of Incremental Comprehension (Crocker, 1996) among others.

The main point here, however, is not to argue whether the *Principles of Likelihood* or *Informativity* provide a better characterization of the function computed, but rather to highlight how different rational analyses can be developed, and their predictions, tested. Settling on a theory or analysis at Marr's computational level enables us to constrain and compare the models which approximate such a theory. Furthermore, it allows us to distinguish data which falsifies a particular model from data which falsifies the more general theory. This is crucial, since models will typically be an imperfect approximation of the theory (taking into account, e.g., cognitive limitations on memory or processing, or simple practical/implementational constraints), and hence a particular model may well make slightly differing predictions from the computational theory.

CONCLUSIONS

This chapter has argued for a shift in how we go about developing models of human language comprehension. We suggest that by adopting insights from rational analysis, we will not only make more progress in developing our *theories*, but also in building, evaluating, and comparing our *models*.

1. Rational theories include a high-level characterization of the function computed by the comprehension system, independent of specific architectural and mechanistic assumptions or stipulations. As such, a rational analysis provides both a predictive and explanatory basis for the mechanisms that implement it.
2. The existence of a rational theory can help in identifying models that are functionally similar, differing primarily in implementation, and hopefully assist in identifying points of convergence among theories.
3. Rational analyses derive from the primary observation that the comprehension is optimally adapted to the task of understanding. This places increased emphasis on explaining general performance, rather than modeling a handful of ambiguous constructions.

We have briefly summarized a collection of models that can be straightforwardly viewed as rational. Many probabilistic models of comprehension can be seen as deriving from the more general *Principle of Likelihood* (see also Jurafsky, 2003, for an overview). We have shown, however, that differing assumptions concerning the nature of the comprehension task can result in optimal functions other than likelihood, as in the case of the *Principle of Informativity*, and also observed that such an analysis provides greater compatibility with existing, non-probabilistic, proposals in the literature. Indeed, it is important not to conflate, *a priori*, probabilistic models with frequency-based models. While many researchers do assume that the probabilities in their models are derived from frequency of occurrence, we may also use it simply as short-hand for likelihoods which are derived from other sources (e.g., plausibility, rather then probability).

There are at least two weaknesses of the rational analysis approach. First, the relatively abstract nature of a computational theory results in a relatively weak linking hypothesis. Typically, the theory will provide only qualitative predictions about processing, for example, which interpretation should be preferred. This is simply due to the fact that more precise accounting of observed measures, such as reading times, will be dominated by the specific mechanisms that implement the theory, and those of the other perceptual systems involved. For example, most of the variance in reading times is accounted for by factors such as word length and frequency (Keller, 2003). This "weakness" can actually be viewed positively, in that it allows us to distinguish the qualitative predictions of the theory from the more quantitative predictions of specific models which we may be considering as implementations of the theory.

Secondly, the approach is most appropriate in theorizing about cognitive systems that can be viewed as optimally adapted to their task and environment. If the function of the system is shaped primarily by cognitive limitations or specific properties of the neural hardware, then such an analysis is seriously compromised. This contrasts starkly with the many models of sentence processing that are motivated precisely on the basis of cognitive limitations (working memory, parsing complexity) or specific processing architectures (e.g., connectionist networks, or modular information processing).

We argue here, however, that there is sufficient evidence for the adaptive nature of human comprehension—including the rapid use of frequency information, visual and linguistic context, plausibility and world knowledge, as well as more general evidence for the speed, accuracy, and robustness of the comprehension system—to warrant the pursuit of rational accounts.

ACKNOWLEDGMENTS

The author would like to acknowledge the financial support of the DFG funded project ALPHA, (SFB-378: "Resource Adaptive Cognitive Processes"). This chapter has also benefited substantially from the comments and discussion received from participants of the MPI Four Corners Workshop series in Nijmegen, notably Harald Baayen, as well as the ongoing intellectual contributions from Nick Chater and Martin Pickering concerning many of the ideas presented here. Finally, I would also like to thank my colleagues Pia Knoeferle and Marshall Mayberry for comments on a previous draft.

REFERENCES

Abney, S. (1989). A computational model of human parsing. *Journal of Psycholinguistic Research, 18*, 129-144.

Anderson, J. R. (1991). Is human cognition adaptive? *Behavioral and Brain Sciences, 14*, 471-517.

Bever, T. (1970). The cognitive basis for linguistic structures. In J. Hayes (Ed.), *Cognition and the development of language* (pp. 279-362). New York: Wiley.

Brants, T., & Crocker, M. W. (2000). Probabilistic parsing and psychological plausibility, In *Proceeding of the International Conference on Computational Linguistics (COLING 2000)*, Saarbrücken, Germany, 111-117.

Chater, N., Crocker, M. W., & Pickering, M. (1998). The rational analysis of inquiry: The case for parsing. In N. Chater & M. Oaksford (Eds.), *Rational analysis of cognition* (pp. 441-468). Oxford, UK: Oxford University Press.

Christiansen, M. H., & Chater, N. (1999). Toward a connectionist model of recursion in human linguistic performance. *Cognitive Science, 23*, 157-205.

Church, K., & Patil, R. (1982). Coping with syntactic ambiguity or how to put the block in the box on the table. *American Journal of Computational Linguistics, 8*, 139-149.

Corley, S., & Crocker, M. (2000). The modular statistical hypothesis: Exploring lexical category ambiguity. In M. Crocker, M. Pickering & C. Clifton, Jr. (Eds.), *Architectures and mechanisms for language processing* (pp. 135-160). Cambridge, UK: Cambridge University Press.

Crocker, M. (1999). Mechanisms for sentence processing. In S. Garrod & M. Pickering (Eds.), *Language processing* (pp. 191-232). London: Psychology Press.

Crocker, M. (1996). *Computational psycholinguistics: An interdisciplinary approach to the study of language*. Dordrecht, NL: Kluwer.

Crocker, M., & Brants, T. (2000). Wide coverage probabilistic sentence processing. *Journal of Psycholinguistic Research, 29*, 647-669.

Crocker, M., & Corley, S. (2002). Modular architectures and statistical mechanisms: The case from lexical category disambiguation. In P. Merlo & S. Stevenson (Eds.), *The lexical basis of sentence processing* (pp. 157-180). Amsterdam: John Benjamins.

Frazier, L. (1979). *On comprehending sentences: Syntactic parsing strategies.* PhD thesis, University of Connecticut, CT.

Frazier, L. (1985). Syntactic complexity. In D. Dowty, L. Kartunnen, & A. Zwicky (Eds.), *Natural language parsing* (pp. 129-189). Cambridge UK: Cambridge University Press.

Frazier, L., & Clifton, C., Jr. (1996). *Construal.* Cambridge, MA: MIT Press.

Friederici, A. (2002). Towards a neural basis of auditory sentence processing. *Trends in Cognitive Sciences, 6,* 78-84.

Gibson, E. A. F. (1998). Linguistic complexity: Locality of syntactic dependencies. *Cognition, 68,* 1-76.

Grodner, D., Gibson, E., Argaman, V., & Babyonyshev, M. (2003). Against repair-based reanalysis in sentence comprehension. *Journal of Psycholinguistic Research, 32,* 141-166.

Hale, J. (2003). The information conveyed by words in sentences. *Journal of Psycholinguistic Research, 32,* 101-124.

Jurafsky, D. A (1996). Probabilistic model of lexical and syntactic access and disambiguation. *Cognitive Science, 20,* 137-194.

Jurafsky, D. A. (2003). Probabilistic modeling in psycholinguistics: Linguistic comprehension and production. In R. Bod, J. Hay & S. Jannedy (Eds.), *Probabilistic linguistics.* Cambridge, MA: MIT Press.

Keller, F. (2003). A probabilistic parser as a model of global processing difficulty. In *Proceedings of the 25th Annual Conference of the Cognitive Science Society* (pp. 646-651). Mahawah, NJ: Lawrence Erlbaum Associates.

Knoeferle, P., Crocker, M., Scheepers, C., & Pickering, M. (in press). The influence of the immediate visual context on incremental thematic role-assignment: Evidence from eye-movements in depicted events. *Cognition.*

MacDonald, M. C., Pearlmutter, N. J., & Seidenberg, M. S. (1994). The lexical nature of syntactic ambiguity resolution. *Psychological Review, 101,* 676-703.

McRae, K., Spivey-Knowlton, M. J., & Tanenhaus, M. K. (1998). Modelling the influence of thematic fit (and other constraints) in on-line sentence comprehension. *Journal of Memory and Language, 38,* 283-312.

Manning, C., & Schütze, H. (1999). *Foundations of statistical natural language processing.* Cambridge, MA: MIT Press.

Marr, D. (1982). *Vision: A computational investigation into the human representation and processing of visual information.* San Francisco: Freeman.

Marcus, M. P. (1980). *A theory of syntactic recognition for natural language.* Cambridge, MA: MIT Press.

Norris, D. (1999). Computational psycholinguistics. In R. A. Wilson & F. C. Keil (Eds.), *The MIT Encyclopedia of Cognitive Science.* Cambridge, MA: MIT Press.

Pickering, M., & Traxler, M. (1998). Plausibility and recovery from garden paths: An eye-tracking study. *Journal of Experimental Psychology: Learning, Memory and Cognition, 24,* 940-961.

Pickering, M., Traxler, M., & Crocker, M. W. (2000). Ambiguity resolution in sentence processing: Evidence against likelihood. *Journal of Memory and Language, 43,* 447-475.

Pritchett, B. (1992). *Grammatical competence and parsing performance*. Chicago: University of Chicago Press.

Schlesewsky, M., & Bornkessel, I. (in press). On incremental interpretation: Degrees of meaning accessed during language comprehension. *Lingua*.

Stevenson, S. (1994). Competition and recency in a hybrid network model of syntactic disambiguation. *Journal of Psycholinguistic Research, 23,* 295-322.

Sturt, P., & Crocker, M. (1996). Monotonic syntactic processing: A cross-linguistic study of attachment and reanalysis. *Language and Cognitive Processes, 11,* 449-494.

Sturt, P., Pickering, M., & Crocker, M. W. (1999). Structural change and reanalysis difficulty in language comprehension. *Journal of Memory and Language, 40,* 136-150.

Sturt, P., Costa, F., Lombardo, V., & Frasconi, P. (2003). Learning first-pass structural attachment preferences with dynamic grammars and recursive neural networks. *Cognition, 88,* 133-169.

Tanenhaus, M. K., Spivey-Knowlton, M. J., Eberhard, K. M. & Sedivy, J. E. (1995). Integration of visual and linguistic information in spoken language comprehension. *Science, 268,* 632-634.

Townsend, D. J., & Bever, T. G. (2001). *Sentence comprehension: The integration of habits and rules*. Cambridge, MA: MIT Press.

Vosse, T., & Kempen, G. (2000). Syntactic structure assembly in human parsing: A computational model based on competitive inhibition and a lexicalist grammar. *Cognition, 75,* 105-143.

23

Computation and Cognition: Four Distinctions and their Implications

W. Tecumseh Fitch
University of St. Andrews, Scotland

INTRODUCTION

In this chapter, I discuss four computational distinctions at the heart of natural computation, and thus relevant to the central and most interesting question of cognitive science: "How the brain computes the mind". I assume that we can think of cognition as a form of computation, implemented by the tissues of the nervous system, and that the unification of high-level computational theories of cognitive function with detailed, local-level understanding of synapses and neurons is the core goal of cognitive (neuro)science. Thus I am concerned her e with how the brain *computes* the mind, following Alan Turing's seminal gambit (Turing, 1950), and much of subsequent cognitive science, in thinking that intelligence is a kind of computation performed by the brain. By thus asserting that the brain is a kind of computer, I must immediately clarify that the natural computations performed by the brain differ dramatically from those implemented by modern digital computers (Richards, 1988). Computation (the acquisition, processing, and transformation of information) is a more general process than the serial, binary computation performed by common digital computers. From this viewpoint, the assertion that the brain is a kind of computer is a mild one. It amounts to nothing but the everyday assumption that the brain is an organ responsible for acquiring, remembering, processing and evaluating sensory stimuli, and using the knowledge thus acquired to plan and generate appropriate action.

Maintaining this more abstract concept of computation is critical, because an overly literal application of the concepts of contemporary serial computer technology, such as the hardware/software distinction, can be deeply misleading. In the brain, memories and plans are stored by modifying its physical form and connections ("hardware") continually. The crucial distinction is between a neuron's morphology, through which it stores relevant aspects of past experience, and its current activation, through which it participates in the myriad natural computations the brain is performing at any moment in time. Nor can neural computation be adequately captured by current connectionist simulations. Despite the value of each of these as metaphors, neither is adequate as a model of the vertebrate brain. One goal of this chapter is to make clear why. The other goal is more prospective and thus inevitably more speculative. I introduce four well-established distinctions in computation, and then explore their implications for some critical unsolved problems in cognitive science (neural coding, consciousness, meaning and language evolution), hoping to point the way toward some promising paths to solving them, and thus the central question of cognitive science.

I will discuss "the" brain, but little of my discussion will be limited to the human brain. The vertebrate nervous system is a conservative structure (relative to the respiratory system, for example). Indeed, most basic aspects of cellular neurophysiology and neuronal morphology are common to all animals from worms to mammals. Among vertebrates, the basic groundplan of the brain is common to all vertebrates, from fish to birds and primates, including myriad specific details such as the nuclei and paths of the cranial nerves, or the connectivity and function of pain, thirst or pleasure pathways. There are no neurotransmitters found in humans that are not also found in fish, and no novel neuronal or tissue types in humans not also found in a cat. The key innovations of mammals—an expanded olfactory system and a layered neocortex—are also found in a dog, mouse or any other mammal (Krubitzer, 1995). Furthermore, from a cognitive perspective, all of the basic components of the mind, such as those underlying the senses, motor control and memory, and cognitive states such as sleep, attention, pain, pleasure, fear or anticipation, are shared with other vertebrates.

Thus, when I refer to "the brain" I mean the vertebrate brain in general. Nonetheless, the human mind clearly differs, in qualitative ways, from that of other animals, and a satisfactory neural theory of the mind must explain why. No "magic bullet" (novel neurotransmitter, neuronal morphology, or tissue type) appears to account for these differences. Brain size alone is inadequate to explain them: An elephant, dolphin, or whale brain is larger than a human's, but these animals do not have language, complex technology, or elaborate cultural and ethical systems like ours. The safest assumption at present is that some relatively subtle aspects of the larger-scale organization of the human brain differ from other vertebrates, probably in a way influenced by but not reducible to brain size or brain/body ratio, and that these organizational novelties underlie the qualitative computational novelties of our species (Deacon, 1997). Understanding these differences is another core problem of cognitive neuroscience.

FOUR KEY COMPUTATIONAL DISTINCTIONS

Analog versus Digital

Perhaps the most fundamental distinction in computation is the analog/digital distinction, because it maps onto the fundamental distinction in mathematics between the discrete integers and the continuous real numbers. Although virtually every device termed a "computer" in contemporary parlance is a digital computer, many simple control systems surrounding us are actually analog computers: thermostats, lightbulb dimmers, spark plug distributors or other engine control systems, and many others. These systems have in common their simplicity (the dimmer switch is equivalent to a single "multiply" operation) and their specialization: Each is devoted to performing a single restricted type of function. In contrast, the general-purpose digital computer instantiated by the central processing unit (CPU) of a computer is extremely complex (with millions of transistor switches) and indeed general: It is equally well-suited for spell-checking, filtering sounds, adjusting the contrast of a photo, or editing video images. It achieves this flexibility by having a small set of abstract, powerful operations (add, multiply, AND, OR, branch operations and the like) which can be combined into more complex programs to perform virtually any computation conceivable (given a clever enough programmer). The price paid for this flexibility is that the digital computer must always work with discrete values: It must subdivide the continuous world (where any value is possible) into a series of integers where only a finite number of pre-chosen values can be represented. However, though a digital system can only represent a limited number of values, with adequate memory we can chose an arbitrarily large number of these to suit our needs.

In the early days of computing, both analog and digital computers were common, and some fairly sophisticated analog computers were widely used (e.g., analog computers that could solve arbitrary second order differential equations). In those days, memory was very limited and expensive, and the virtues of analog computers were widely recognized. Certain difficulties raised by digital computing were problematic, but the invention of the von Neumann architecture (where data and program are both stored in digital memory to allow virtually any calculation to be performed by a single machine), combined with ever larger and cheaper memory, made the eventual triumph of general purpose digital computing inevitable. An excellent description of the virtues and failings of both styles of computing is von Neumann (1958).

How does the analog/digital distinction apply to the brain? A neuron either fires an action potential, or doesn't, and all its action potentials are essentially equivalent. Thus the output of the neuron can be represented by a single bit, which at any moment in time is either zero or one. The brain can (apparently) represent the world and solve all the problems it does with this digital *lingua franca*. However, this is not the whole story. Although the *output* of a neuron is digital, its *inputs* come in the form of analog graded potentials, and the computations a neuron performs by integrating all of these thousands of inputs are also, for the most part, analog. John von Neumann was aware of this, and his idealization of the brain as a digital computer was thus an educated gambit: How far can we get if we abstract away from the analog aspects of neuronal computation? The answer, if the ever-increasing power of modern, general purpose digital computers is any guide, is "very far indeed". Nonetheless, despite its practical success, it seems clear today that von Neumann's gambit was ultimately unsuccessful as a model of the brain. Problems that are trivially easy for even a simple computer (e.g., dividing two 16-digit numbers) are very difficult for an unaided human. But contemporary von Neumann computers fail at the very tasks the brain excels at: Problems easily solved by an infant or a fish (e.g., distinguishing figure from ground) are very difficult for computers. And problems solved by every normal child before the age of five, like deriving the meaning of sentences, still seem hopelessly difficult computationally, despite a half-century of programming effort.

A promising attempt to resuscitate the analog component of neural computation, which I will call the connectionist gambit, has as one core insight the fact that over a longer time scale, the output of a neuron can be seen as continuous, in the sense that the number of spikes per second (the neuron's *activation level*) approximates a continuous value (e.g., between 0 and 1.0). Despite some significant advantages (especially in the realms of nicely handling noisy, distorted or incomplete input) neural nets however turn out to be limited in some critical ways, and have not fulfilled their initial apparent promise (Marcus, 2001). It now seems clear, after five hard-working, well-funded decades of AI and two of connectionism, that neither of these approaches alone is adequate to solve the key problems of neural computation and cognition. Perception and motor control at the level of a fish is still well beyond state-of-the-art robots, and performing vision or language at human levels is a programmer's dream far beyond the reach of existing architectures.

Recent discoveries in neurophysiology suggest a reason for these practical failures. Both gambits agreed on taking the neuron as the key unit of computation. While one approach idealized the neuron as digital and the other as analog, both represented it by a single number (either integer or real). In fact, each individual neuron is a hybrid analog/digital computing machine. Its myriad analog inputs, coming from the synapses that join it to hundreds or thousands of other neurons, are combined and transformed into an all-or-none digital action potential, and apparently both sides of this hybrid computational system are important (Häusser & Mel, 2003; Debanne, 2004). Exciting recent discoveries in cellular neurophysiology indicate that the voltage-gated channels that trigger action potentials exist in the dendritic trees of some neurons, and play a critical role in the computation that the neuron performs (Wei et al., 2001). Thus, representing a neuron as a simple blob, with multiple synapses attached to it and gated by some threshold function, is inadequate. A typical neuron, with its tree-like form, instantiates a minicomputer irreducible to a single number, whether real or discrete. The future of computational neuroscience lies in systems which have as their core computational primitives less-idealized neurons: hybrid analog-digital devices that transform their data in complex ways.

Serial versus Parallel

Perhaps the most striking distinction that arises when comparing modern digital computers with the brain is between serial and parallel processing. A kitchen analogy (Churchland, 1995) makes the difference clear. When trimming carrots, you can either trim each one individually (serial operation) or can line them up on the cutting board, and with one knife stroke trim them all at once (parallel operation). The brain is a massively parallel processing system: Millions of computations are occurring simultaneously across the cortical surface at any given time. Although a typical laptop has some degree of such independence (e.g., the VLSI chip dedicated to displaying graphics is largely independent of the CPU), the CPU itself is a serial machine: It does one thing at a time. The reason it can do so much is because each operation is executed very rapidly: The 1 Gigahertz machine I'm typing on can perform one billion (10^9) serial mathematical operations per second.

Historically, mathematics has developed along serial lines. The operations and algorithms used in human calculation or theorem proving are virtually always implemented one step at a time. Thus, it was natural when designing and programming early computers to use serial algorithms. However, it was already clear to von Neumann that this is not the way the brain does things. Neurons are sloppy, unreliable, and slow compared to transistors. An average "clock speed" in the cortex is 100 Hz or 100 operations per second (this is both roughly the transit time between cortical layers and a high-end firing rate for typical cells; the auditory system runs faster, e.g., 1000 Hz). A brain process that had to undergo 1000 serial operations with neurons would take 10 seconds, and accumulate so much error that the end result might well be useless. Instead, even very complex neural operations like recognizing a face happen in around a quarter of a second. The brain accomplishes this by performing the millions of operations involved in parallel, with only a few serial steps (say five from ganglion cells in the retina to the fusiform gyrus of cortex). Von Neumann termed this dimension "logical depth": A serial digital computer is suited by its speed and accuracy to deep algorithms involving many steps, while the brain is limited by its biological components to a shallow few.

Why don't digital computers do their operations in parallel, achieving even greater speed? Some do: Parallel processing machines (e.g., the Connection Machine) exist but have never fared well, due to the difficulty of programming such machines. The speed attainable in theory is rarely attained in practice because of various annoying practical issues (e.g., many of the parallel processors end up idly waiting for some other computation to finish). Newer parallel systems (e.g., Beowulf) are just getting started and their promise is hard to evaluate at present. Thus, except for a few specialized problems, serial computers rule the silicon world, while in the biological world, parallel systems are king.

The virtues of parallel processing are well known, and already thoroughly catalogued by connectionists (an enthusiastic and accessible introduction (Churchland, 1995). Parallel processing algorithms tend to be robust in the face of noisy input, have an ability to generalize over multiple exemplars, can complete basic patterns and are resistant to losses of computational units (real neurons die unpredictably). All of these are brain-like skills that serial algorithms fare poorly on, and were the primary reason for the enthusiasm in cognitive science in the 1990s for connectionist approaches. Unfortunately, the parallel architectures currently available have important limitations, also well-catalogued: They are slow to learn and their ability to induce general rules or abstract away from known contexts is limited (Marcus, 2001). However, these cannot be limitations of parallel systems in principle (the brain *is* a parallel system, and avoids these problems), but of currently available algorithms and architectures. There is good reason to hope that computer scientists can improve upon the current situation. A new wave of more brainlike parallel processing is beginning, in which hundreds or even thousands of individual microcomputers are networked together via fast intranet, and the promise of this approach is only beginning to be explored.

As this new wave of parallel architectures progresses, it will be important to recognize two distinct levels of parallel processing in the brain. First, at the level of an individual neuron, is the integration of information over synapses. A typical pyramidal cell in cortex has around 1000 separate inputs onto its dendritic arbor and cell body, and the cell's activity at any moment is a complex transformation of these inputs (Häusser & Mel, 2003). Each synapse is individually and locally updated, so the cell is a true parallel distributed processor. Furthermore, there is a cell-level economy (based on how often it fires, its uptake of neurotrophins, and myriad other factors) that influences all of its synapses. The limit is in programmed cell death (apoptosis) which plays a critical role in the developing nervous system: when a single cell dies, all of its synapses die with it. However, as far as other cells are concerned, a neuron has a single discrete output: its "decision" to fire (or not), which is distributed via its axonal arbor to all of the cells downstream of it. Thus, there is already massive parallel processing and then compression of information at the single cell level. Furthermore, these two processes interact: the cell-level decisions to fire often propagate back to its synapses, and playing a role in parallel synaptic modification.

The second, global level of parallel processing is at the level of large assemblages of neurons (e.g., all the pyramidal cells in a single region of cortex like V1 or A1). This level, typically highlighted in connectionist discussions of the brain, has thousands of inputs *and* outputs. The end product of a computation at this level is not typically compressed through a single output channel, and thus the effect of the transformation must be "read off" the activity of many neurons. This makes the neurophysiologist's job difficult, since the information present at this global level can only be discerned via multi-unit recordings. Fortunately techniques for acquiring and analyzing multi-unit recordings are advancing rapidly. It also complicates the computational theorist's job, since it is the complex, transformed output of the neuronal minicomputer that enters into the more global multicellular parallel processing algorithms. Only at the final output level of the whole nervous system is brain-level parallel processing finally compressed and channeled into the final decisions of motor control and action.

The traditional connectionist metaphor elides this local/global distinction: Although connectionist nets are loosely modeled on the higher level (nodes are often called "neurons") they actually better parallel the lower, single cell layer. The adjustable "multiply" units at the heart of a connectionist architecture are computationally equivalent to a single dendritic compartment. Thus a typical connectionist model (with perhaps 1000 such units) is more comparable to a single neuron, than a network of cells. However, because the output of such nets is not typically channeled through a single output, this aspect emulates the global parallel system. The next wave of neural modeling, already well under way and a major current focus of computational neuroscientists, involves more biologically accurate models of single neurons, connected into more realistic networks (increasingly, on parallel systems like Beowulf). Despite the challenges of its complexity, this approach seems to offer hope of solving some of the problems suffered by typical connectionist models.

Summarizing, it is a vast oversimplification to think of the brain simply as a parallel analog machine. Each individual neuron is a complex analog-to-digital converter, processing thousands of synapses of input in parallel and converting them to a single, digital output. The brain is composed of 100 billion such minicomputers, running in parallel, and includes a final output level (of attention, decision, and action) that is essentially serial. Progress in understanding the computational problems the brain solves may necessitate models of neural computation that respect this complexity, and are considerably more complicated than those cognitive scientists typically entertain. While this complexity may seem daunting, the apparent failures of both von Neumann's and the connectionist gambit, which have already explored the possibilities and revealed the limitations of the two simplest abstractions, leave us little option. The good news is that the rapidly-advancing field of computational neuroscience is hot on the trail of such models, and neuroscience is generating reams of data to test them empirically. The vast computing power available today with large networks of individual computers means we can implement and test models at this level of complexity without major technological difficulty.

Feedforward versus Feedback

The next distinction has long been recognized as central in engineering, and goes by several names. Two everyday examples may make this feedforward/feedback distinction intuitive. First, a visual analogy. An image reflected in a tinted mirror, or a rippled lake surface, is transformed: the reflected image is darker, or rippled. These are examples of a feedforward or "one-pass" transformation: the operation of reflection occurs just once. Feed-forward transformations can be quite simple (like the mirror image) or extremely complex (the time-varying reflections from a wind-rippled lake). If we now artfully arrange two mirrors, one tinted and the other normal, so that the image of one falls upon the other, we suddenly see an infinite receding set of images: mirrors within mirrors within mirrors. A single transformation of "tinting" is suddenly repeated uncountably many times by the simple expedient of having its output reflected back in as a new input. One mirror gives one application of the tinting operation, while two mirrors, when properly arranged, give infinite applications. This is a feed-back or "recurrent" system.

A second analogy is acoustic Facing a cliff in the middle of an open space, you clap your hands and hear a single echo. The sound from your hands travels to the wall, and is reflected back to your ears a bit later, in subtly changed form (usually with high frequencies removed). But if you are standing between two buildings (or in a canyon) and clap your hands, you hear an endless series of echoes, of gradually decreasing intensity ("reverberation"). Like the two mirrors, a reverberant space could theoretically "ring" forever, echoing till the end of time. Practically, of course, losses render the reverberant sound inaudible rather quickly (20 s or so), but we can easily build a system that adds a bit of energy with each pass, say with a microphone, amplifier and speaker. Point the microphone towards the speaker, snap your fingers, and the multiply-transformed sound will hold steady or (more likely) swell to an unpleasant screech. Such "feedback", familiar to any concert-goer, is usually an annoyance, but the same principle can be used to musical effect when properly controlled (e.g., by Jimi Hendrix).

While feed-forward systems have only a single shot at their input, feedback systems are contrived in such a way that their last output becomes their next input, and so have (in principle) infinite opportunities to apply whatever transformation they embody. Any feedback system thus has a feed-forward system at its heart, but differs by including some additional way to rechannel some output back into its input. Engineers characterize the transformation performed by a signal processing system as its "impulse response". Because of the theoretically infinite nature of feedback systems they are called "infinite impulse response", or IIR, systems. In contrast, the output of a feed-forward system, fed a finite signal, is itself finite. Such systems are termed FIR (finite impulse response). Because of the importance of this distinction in signal processing, especially filter design, engineers have fully explored, and mathematically formalized, the advantages and disadvantages of each class of system (e.g., Oppenheim & Schafer, 1989)

The fundamental advantage of feedforward systems is that they are fast, straightforward to understand, and can preserve timing details (they don't distort phase). The fundamental advantage of feedback systems is power: they can do a lot with a rather limited transformation. An engineer building a filter with five multiply operations can do some practically useful things in an IIR filter. In contrast, a five-multiply FIR filter will, because of its one-pass nature, have trivial power compared to its IIR equivalent. This power does not come without a price: Feedback systems fed a complex signal always distort phase, or disrupt timing, and furthermore are difficult to understand in all but the simplest cases. Worse, feedback systems can generate uncontrolled runaway behavior (like the annoying sound system feedback mentioned previously).

Flat versus Hierarchical Structure

The last distinction I will discuss is critical in modern linguistics, where it was first formalized, but perhaps less clearly recognized in other branches of cognitive science. This is the distinction between what I call *flat* and *hierarchical structure* (the linguist's version, following Chomsky, 1957), is between finite-state grammars and phrase structure grammars). In flat structures, all of the elements have equal status: A list of words ("juice coffee milk carrots") or numbers (6177769541) has no organization beyond the serial order of its elements. However, as soon the number list is rewritten as a US phone number, (617) 776-9541, a level of organization above this serial order is evident (the first three numbers are the area code for Boston, etc.) Alternatively, if the structure was +61 7 776 9541, the first two numbers could be the country code for Australia. The two strings, although sharing the same sequence of digits, have different hierarchical structures. Repeated application of branching algorithms quite naturally generates such tree-like structures, and computer science is full of tree-building and -parsing algorithms (decision trees, search trees, suffix trees, etc.; see Skiena, 1998). Such trees also appear in motor control and in phonology: A word is a higher-order structure made up of its phonemic and syllabic components.

"Chunking" into higher order, abstract components is pronounced in language: A sentence like "I'll trade you some juice and coffee for your milk and carrots" has a complex hierarchical grammatical structure beyond the order of the words. The appreciation of this structure was foundational for modern linguistics because it invalidated behaviorist approaches which sought to portray language as a serial sequencing operation. This point, made forcibly by Chomsky (1959) in his critique of Skinner, was foundational for modern linguistics and all of cognitive science (see Jackendoff, 2002) for a more detailed exposition). Phrase structure seems to be critical not just for human language but many other aspects of our cognition: Music, mathematics, and social reasoning all involve hierarchical structures. Humans both produce and process hierarchically-structured stimuli, and actively prefer such stimuli

(Morgan, Meier, & Newport, 1989). What makes this proclivity striking is the lack of evidence for such abilities in nonhuman primates. For example, monkeys appear to hear a melody as just a sequence of notes, rather than a coordinated, interrelated system of related pitches (D'Amato, 1988; Wright, Rivera, Hulse, Shyan, & Neiworth, 2000). Monkeys exposed to auditory output from a finite state grammar, with only flat structure, easily learn it, spontaneously generalizing to novel grammatical stimuli, but fail to do so when exposed to a carefully-matched phrase-structure grammar (Fitch & Hauser, 2004). Although too few species have been examined to reach any broad conclusions, and apes may have greater abilities to generate hierarchical structures in the motor domain (e.g., Greenfield, 1991; Byrne & Russon, 1998), hierarchical processing does not seem as widespread in animals as in humans. Thus, unlike the first three distinctions, which are equally relevant to neural computation in all vertebrates, the well-developed hierarchical abilities observable in humans may reflect a computational distinction implemented preferentially in the human brain.

Hierarchicality has several distinct meanings, and a key distinction in language is between recurrent and recursive systems. Any feedback system with loops in it (e.g., all of neocortex) is recurrent, even if only a small or very simple component of its output loops back into its output. Recursive systems, although similar, are more restricted and powerful: The entire complex last output can serve as the next input. This difference is moot for very simple multiply operations but quite relevant in language, where the output of a syntactic operation may be a complex phrase-structure tree. When this can feed back to the input, and thus serve as the starting point for a more elaborate tree, true recursion in the linguistic sense results. This naturally generates sentences such as "I know that you want me to think that you are happy" or "John thinks that Mary believes that Hans wants ..." and the like, with no obvious upper bound to the number of embedded clauses. Although phone numbers have some hierarchical structure, you cannot embed one phone number into a second and expect to produce another valid phone number, any more than you can embed one syllable into another to get a new valid syllable. Recursive hierarchicality probably does not apply to phonology.

Importantly, structure-preserving recursion allows the creation of long complex phrases from a few simple rules, exhibiting the power typical characteristic of any recurrent system at a more sophisticated level. A fully recursive tree building algorithm, that takes a structured output and passes that entire structure back in as input, is quite demanding computationally. The apparatus to support recursion in computer science (typically a "stack" which preserves intermediate function calls and their results) is complex, and is not implemented in all computer languages. There are only two aspects of language that appear to support fully recursive hierarchicality: syntax and semantics. This dual ability can be illustrated by a single example, in the sequence:

1. Bob likes Mary.
2. John suspects that Bob likes Mary.
3. Susan realizes that John suspects that Bob likes Mary. (etc...)

Each sentence is built, recursively, from its predecessor, by simply adding a new agent and mental action (semantically speaking) or subject and verb (syntactically speaking). The structure of "Bob likes Mary" is still contained in either of its more complex successors. This embedding process can go on indefinitely: There is no limit built in to the generative process (although there are clearly limits on memory and comprehension of the output sentence). The ability to "embed" mental states within other mental states, at the semantic level, and phrases within phrases, at the syntactic level, constitutes fully recursive hierarchicality. This difference, best exemplified by language, has important computational implications: Recursive algorithms require a structure-preserving feedback mechanism which ordinary recurrent algorithms do not.

IMPLICATIONS FOR COGNITION AND LANGUAGE

I next explore some broader implications of these distinctions, in no particular order, starting with an important implication of the feedforward/feedback distinction for the role of time in neural computation. In some feedforward systems (e.g., a delay line), time is spread out over space. A neural example is in the cochlea: because it takes time for an acoustic signal to travel up the basilar membrane, neurons at different locations correspond to different arrival times. By contrast, in a feedback system, that is, in auditory cortex, time is not "laid out" in space. A feedback-style IIR filter still processes information in the time domain, but does so by folding its output back into input. This fact makes IIR systems harder to understand, but as already pointed out, is a source of their power as well. Many computational neuroscientists and cognitive scientists believe that temporal processing (as opposed to spatial processing of the type familiar in the visual system) plays an important but still poorly understood role in neural computation. Thus there is an important distinction between feedforward systems like the cochlea and feedback systems like the cortex. Recurrent loops like those in A1 can do powerful temporal processing with no need for delay lines, and it would be premature to conclude that such temporal processing is insignificant in auditory computation (Shamma, 2001). On the contrary, given that all neocortical areas are rich in recurrent connections, it seems more likely that models of the visual system focusing solely on spatially-distributed processing are oversimplified. It would be odd if the computational power intrinsic to such feedback systems were not used in neural computation.

The Price of Feedback: A second implication of the feedforward/feedback distinction for natural computation is profound (Braitenberg, 1977). Given a single neuron performing some transformation, all we need is to place that neuron in a loop to raise its operation to the nth power. This is easily accomplished by looping part of its axonal arbor back into its dendritic arbor or having a downstream region project back to the upstream region feeding it. Such recurrent loops are a fundamental characteristic of mammalian neocortex. Despite the tendency to think of information flow in the brain as being one-way, all layers of cortex are heavily back-connected to the regions "before" them in this chain (including their thalamic inputs outside of cortex). Feedback in the brain, as in an amplifier, can get out of control: If inhibition fails to keep excited neurons from overexciting their neighbors in a feedback loop, the entire cortex can blow out of control, and an epileptic seizure is the result. This is an inevitable consequence of the recurrent nature of neocortex: a high price paid for the power of feedback. Interestingly, although the cerebral cortex is basically a feedback system, the cerebellum is almost entirely feedforward. The parallel fibers carrying information through the cerebellum synapse with a Purkinje cell only once, and there are no recurrent loops at all within cerebellar cortex. Because a feedforward system like the cerebellum does not distort phase, it is perfectly suited to computing timing details are crucial to coordinated cognition and action. A price is paid for phase accuracy as well, however: the cerebellum has as many or more cells then the cerebral cortex, and each Purkinje cell takes about 10,000 synapses (and up to 200,000 synapses, averaging ten times more synapses than an average pyramidal cell in cerebral cortex). These large numbers follow from the information-processing principle already mentioned: More processors must be dedicated to a feedforward system to achieve a desired effect.

Rhythmic Coding: A more speculative implication of the flat vs. hierarchical distinction for cognition concerns how the brain can use time to code information. Traditionally, neuroscientists assume that firing rate (a continuous number) codes neuronal activation, an assumption shared by most connectionist models. The long-recognized problem with this idea is that it takes too long to get an accurate reading (e.g., Stein, 1967). A neuron firing at 0.2 Hz (every 5 seconds) might take a minute of continuous reading before an accurate average value was obtained: far too long for most practically useful computations. Because action potentials are expensive, firing at 100 Hz burns a huge amount of energy and simply increasing the firing rate is of limited applicability (one reason the auditory system, with many fast-firing neurons, is one of the most metabolically expensive components of the brain). Thus, while firing rate is undoubtedly an important way the nervous system codes information, its inadequacies as the sole code have been clear for many years, leading theorists to suggest other temporal coding schemes. A different way to code information, one with great computational power and thus considerable theoretical appeal, would be to use hierarchical temporal structure, or rhythm, to code information. In musical parlance, periodicity or "tempo" is distinct from "rhythm". Any periodic event, recurring at a certain rate, has a tempo. A rhythm is more: a temporal structure *invariant* over changes in tempo. Many different rhythms exist which share the same tempo and the number of events. Thus, a significant amount of bandwidth is left over in a simple rate-coding system (where tempo alone conveys information): Specific inter-spike timing regularities could code additional information. We know that, depending on their precise timing, a volley of action potentials can either excite a downstream neuron or not (Rieke, Warland, de Ruyter van Steveninck, & Bialek, 1997). This means that neurons are clearly capable of "recognizing" rhythms (transforming their input differently depending on its temporal structure), suggesting that hierarchical structure in a spike train from a given neuron has a considerably greater potential to code information than if it were organized as simply flat structure, where each spike is equal. Although a search for such hierarchical structure will be complicated by the fact that "neuronal rhythms" might change as firing rate changes (unlike the musician's rhythm, which stays the same), the computational power added by such a coding scheme would render it quite appealing, because it allows more information to be encoded, quickly, with no additional and expensive action potentials.

Consciousness: The serial/parallel distinction has an interesting implication for the function(s) of consciousness. I assume that consciousness is a specific, concrete component of neural functioning, that (like most aspects of neural function such as perception or action) it has both subjective and objective sides. By definition, only the latter is available for scientific study in non-linguistic organisms. There is nothing specific to consciousness about this, nor does it pose a mysterious "hard problem" for neuroscience. For further discussion and defense of this position see Churchland (1995) and Dennett (1991). Although there is no doubt that the brain is a massively parallel machine, our mental experience is curiously serial. Although we often do several things at once, we typically attend to just one of them. As Dennett has aptly put it, consciousness is like a serial machine running on a parallel architecture. I hypothesize that this serial nature of consciousness is a computational necessity, one that solves an inevitable problem faced by parallel processing systems that can learn. Coherent updating in a parallel system demands a system for credit and blame allocation, so that each of the semi-independent processing units (neurons, or small assemblages thereof) be informed about the final "decision" of the system as a whole. To see why, imagine you are about to engage in some complex novel action (say crossing a dangerous ravine). In parallel, your brain computes, unconsciously and automatically, various possibilities for accomplishing this goal (Dennett & Kinsbourne, 1995). Each of these possibilities may be equipotent during the preparatory stage: indeed each might be perfectly good possible solutions to the problem. In the end, however, one must be chosen and implemented: The myriad possibilities must be winnowed down into a single decision. Now comes the problem: The crossing is made, either successfully or not, and the brain needs some way of distinguishing the myriad equiprobable possibilities it just considered, and rejected, from the one actually implemented. It must "brand" the motor program actually chosen to assign credit (or blame, in the case of failure) to the proper neurons, who can then update their synapses appropriately. I suggest that conscious awareness is simply the subjective counterpart of this necessarily serial neural function, a function that must be present if a massively parallel processing system is to learn from its experience.

Meaning: Meaning is a core unsolved problem of cognitive science. The difference between the semantics of music and language provides an interesting contrast for beginning an exploration of the computational structure of meaning. Spoken language and music are both complex, culturally-transmitted, hierarchical systems based on sound. To a first approximation, language is meaningful (in the sense of being capable of conveying an unlimited number of specific propositions), and music is not. However, music does convey *something*, as illustrated by the fact that we can reliably map a piece of music onto non-sonic domains (like dance or emotion). Both systems thus map sound onto something, which is propositional semantic content in the case of language, and something else for music. I suggest that this "something else" can be captured by the analog/digital distinction. In language, sound maps onto discrete, categorical conceptual dimensions, while in music, sound maps onto continuous, analog dimensions. The speed and intensity of notes in music will map onto the speed and intensity of a dancer's movements, but how fast or hard you say the "a" in "cat" has no influence on the categorical meaning of the word. Thus, the basic sound/meaning mapping in language is digital and categorical, while music maps on to the analog and continuous. This is why music is so well suited to linking with the motor movements of dance, or with emotions. Both dance and emotion have an essentially analog, continuous component. The conceptual mapping performed by music seems nicely captured by Manfred Bierwisch's term "gestural form" (Bierwisch, 1979).

However, this is oversimplified. Some marginal musical styles convey discrete concepts via musical forms (e.g., "tympani roll = thunder" and the like). More importantly, language has a musical, prosodic side. Spoken language manages to get the best of both worlds: using its discrete-to-discrete mapping capability to allow the specification of an unlimited set of specific meanings, but retaining a musical analog-to-analog capability to convey subtle emphasis and emotion via prosody. Nonetheless, analog vs. discrete mapping seems to capture a basic distinction between language and music. This mapping distinction has an interesting empirical implication. If we want to understand the difference between analog and digital interpretive mappings, an experimental comparison of musical and linguistic interpretation provides an excellent place to start. If there are distinctive cognitive and neural processes underlying this difference, a comparison of musical and linguistic processing should be a good way to discover them (e.g., Koelsch et al., 2004). Furthermore, the substantial variation among normal individuals in musical talent, which dwarfs the variation in linguistic ability among normal humans, provides a valuable empirical wedge into the question of the neural bases of these types of natural computation. Thus, the application of the analog/digital distinction to the problem of meaning raises some intriguing experimental possibilities.

Language Evolution: Finally, I explore some implications of the hierarchical vs. flat structure distinction for the evolution of language. Some degree of hierarchical structure, perhaps limited to motor control, may be part of the basic vertebrate cognitive toolkit. In communication systems, some form of phonological phrase structure appears to characterize bird and whale song, and human music. But fully recursive hierarchy, where phrases are embedded within phrases, appears to be unique to human language. Cognitive algorithms for recursively generating complex sentence structures must be implemented with the same neurons and neurotransmitters as any other operations. How could such a novel capacity evolve? Perhaps it represents a modification of some preexisting ability: Three possibilities are a preexisting primate communication system, motor control and Machiavellian social intelligence. While the vocal communication systems of our primate ancestors clearly provided the precursors of many aspects of speech, they seem to be lacking recursive phrase structure. And to the extent that nonhuman primates calls have hierarchical structure at all (e.g., in gibbon "song"), order is not freely permutable but seems fixed in its sequential structure. The interpretive abilities of primates in this domain seem to be much greater than their production capabilities (e.g., Cheney & Seyfarth, 1990; Zuberbühler, 2002). Thus, it is far from clear that the vocal communication system of our common ancestor with chimps had characteristics suitable to provide an evolutionary precursor for this key hierarchical aspect of language. Motor control seems a more promising precursor system for hierarchicality, as recognized by several theorists (e.g., Greenfield, 1991; Byrne & Russon, 1998). The kind of flexible hierarchical control implicit in the ability to catch prey while locomoting, or to grasp and manipulate tools, appears a promising precursor of hierarchical structure in the vocal realm. However, nothing in the domain of nonhuman motor control has the recursive, structure-preserving hierarchicality characteristic of language. Thus, while I think it is very plausible that motor hierarchicality is closely linked to phonological hierarchicality (not just in human speech but in music and probably in birdsong as well), it is ill-suited as a precursor to the syntactic and semantic level of hierarchicality in language.

A more plausible precursor ability for recursive self-embedding is provided by the cognitive operations concerned with social intelligence, particularly the Machiavellian intelligence so typical of primates (Byrne & Whiten, 1988). Recursive embedding seems obviously useful in social life, and particularly the ability to conceptualize the thoughts of others. While the concept "John intends to attack me" may be useful, the ability to entertain a higher-order concept that "My friend Joe sees that John intends to attack me" could provide a decisive advantage for coalition-forming primates like chimps or baboons. And once a single such level of mental embedding was widespread, it is easy to see how a further level would become selective: "John sees that my friend Joe will aid me if he attacks now, and will wait till I'm alone to attack". Recent evidence suggests that baboons can apply some degree of hierarchical cognition when interpreting the calls of others (Bergman, Beehner, Cheney, & Seyfarth,

2003). This and other data suggest that some recursive, hierarchical-structure-preserving embedding of "minds within minds" may already have been present in our shared ancestor with chimps. Such mind-reading recursion has the proper computational structure to provide a precursor ability for the recursive hierarchical signature of syntax and semantics. If true, this might explain why birds do not seem to have evolved anything like language, despite the presence of many of the requisite cognitive abilities. They may lack the conceptual abilities associated with Machiavellian "mind-reading", more typical of primates. However, a note of caution is warranted, since the communication systems of songbirds like crows and other corvids, which share the vocal abilities of other songbirds but live in large, complex social groups and thus might be good candidates for complex mind-reading abilities, are still very poorly understood.

Summarizing, I have discussed four distinctions at the heart of computation and explored some of their implications for contemporary cognitive science. I suggest that progress in understanding natural computation will require a more complex model of neural processing, that respects the complexity of the neuron and the complex ways in which the brain implements the analog/digital and serial/parallel distinctions. These distinctions will be especially important for understanding the role of temporal processing in natural computation. I suggested that the serial/parallel distinction has an important implication for the evolution of consciousness, which far from being epiphenomenal seems to be a core computational requirement for successful learning in a parallel architecture. With regard to language, I propose that the analog/digital distinction provides an interesting cut into the problem of meaning, with some testable empirical consequences. Finally, I suggested that the flat/hierarchical distinction so crucial for understanding the evolution of syntax and semantics in human language seems more likely to derive phylogenetically from the "mind-reading" conceptual capabilities of non-human primates than the phonological structure of animal communication systems.

ACKNOWLEDGMENTS

I thank M. Bierwisch, T. Deacon, D. Dennett, P. Földiak, M. Kinsbourne, D. Raubenheimer, S. Thompson-Schill, and an anonymous reviewer for helpful discussions and/or comments on the manuscript.

REFERENCES

Bergman, T. J., Beehner, J. C., Cheney, D. L., & Seyfarth, R. M. (2003). Hierarchical classification by rank and kinship in baboons. *Science, 302*, 1234-1236.

Bierwisch, M. (1979). Gestische Form als Bedeutung musikalischer Zeichen. *Jahrbuch Peters 1978*, 161-178.

Braitenberg, V. (1977). *On the texture of brains*. New York: Springer.

Byrne, R. W., & Whiten, A. (1988). *Machiavellian Intelligence: Social expertise and the evolution of intellect in monkeys, apes and humans*. Oxford: Clarendon Press.

Byrne, R. W., & Russon, A. E. (1998). Learning by imitation: A hierarchical approach. *Behavioral and Brain Sciences, 21*, 667-684.

Cheney, D. L., & Seyfarth, R. M. (1990). *How monkeys see the world: Inside the mind of another species*. Chicago: Chicago University Press.

Chomsky, N. (1957). *Syntactic structures*. The Hague: Mouton.

Chomsky, N. (1959). Review of "Verbal Behavior". *Language, 35*, 26-58.

Churchland, P. M. (1995). *The engine of reason, the seat of the soul*. Cambridge, MA: MIT Press.

D'Amato, M. R. (1988). A search for tonal pattern perception in cebus monkey: Why monkeys can't hum a tune. *Music Perception, 5*, 452-480.

Deacon, T. W. (1997). *The symbolic species: The co-evolution of language and the brain*. New York: Norton.

Debanne, D. (2004). Information processing in the axon. *Nature Reviews Neuroscience, 5*, 304-316.

Dennett, D. C. (1991). *Consciousness explained*. Boston: Little, Brown & Co.

Dennett, D. C., & Kinsbourne, M. (1995). Time and the observer: The where and when of consciousness in the brain. *Behavioral and Brain Sciences, 15*, 183-247.

Fitch, W. T., & Hauser, M. D. (2004). Computational constraints on syntactic processing in a nonhuman primate. *Science, 303*, 377-380.

Greenfield, P. M. (1991). Language, tools, and brain: The ontogeny and phylogeny of hierarchically organized sequential behavior. *Behavioral and Brain Sciences, 14*, 531-595.

Häusser, M., & Mel, B. (2003). Dendrites: Bug or feature? *Current Opinion in Neurobiology, 13*, 372-383.

Jackendoff, R. (2002). *Foundations of language*. New York: Oxford University Press.

Koelsch, S., Kasper, E., Sammler, D., Schulze, K., Gunter, T. C., & Friederici, A. D. (2004). Music, language, and meaning: Brain signatures of semantic processing. *Nature Neuroscience, 7*, 511-514.

Krubitzer, L. (1995). The organization of neocortex in mammals: are species differences really so different? *Trends in Neurosciences, 18*, 408-417.

Marcus, G. F. (2001). *The algebraic mind: Integrating connectionism and cognitive science*. Cambridge, MA: MIT Press.

Morgan, J. L., Meier, R. P., & Newport, E. L. (1989). Facilitating the acquisition of syntax with cross-sentential cues to phrase structure. *Journal of Memory and Language, 28*, 360-374.

Oppenheim, A. V., & Schafer, R. W. (1989). *Discrete-time signal processing*. Englewood Cliffs, NJ: Prentice-Hall.

Richards, W. (Ed.). (1988). *Natural computation*. Cambridge, MA: MIT Press.

Rieke, F., Warland, D., de Ruyter van Steveninck, R., & Bialek, W. (1997). *Spikes: Exploring the neural code*. Cambridge, MA: MIT Press/Bradford Books.

Shamma, S. (2001). On the role of space and time in auditory processing. *Trends in Cognitive Sciences, 5*, 340-348.

Skiena, S. S. (1998). *The algorithm design manual*. New York: Springer.

Stein, R. B. (1967). The information capacity of nerve cells using a frequency code. *Biophysical Journal, 7*, 797-826.

Turing, A. M. (1950). Computing machinery and intelligence. *Mind, 59*, 433-460.

von Neumann, J. (1958). *The computer and the brain*. New Haven, CT: Yale University Press.

Wei, D.-S., Mei, Y.-A., Bagal, A., Kao, J. P. Y., Thomspon, S. M., & Tang, C.-M. (2001). Compartmentalized and binary behavior of terminal dendrites in hippocampal pyramidal neurons. *Science, 293*, 2272-2275.

Wright, A. A., Rivera, J. J., Hulse, S., Shyan, M., & Neiworth, J. J. (2000). Music perception and octave generalization in rhesus monkeys. *Journal of Experimental Psychology: General, 129*, 291-307.

Zuberbühler, K. (2002). A syntactic rule in forest monkey communication. *Animal Behaviour, 63*, 293-299.

Author Index